# TOWARD THE
# RADICAL
# CENTER

EDITED AND WITH AN INTRODUCTION BY

# PETER KUSSI

FOREWORD BY

# ARTHUR MILLER

TRANSLATED BY

Norma Comrada
Tatiana Firkušný
Yveta Synek Graff
Robert T. Jones
Peter Kussi
Claudia Novack-Jones
Dora Round
Paul Selver
Charles E. Townsend
M. & R. Weatherall
Robert Wechsler

# TOWARD THE RADICAL CENTER

# A KAREL ČAPEK READER

### READER

A Garrigue Book
CATBIRD PRESS

The publisher would like to thank Pat Lesnefsky for typing this manuscript
into a computer, Chris Lione for designing the cover, Axiom Design
Systems for typesetting the book, and all of the translators who made this
book something truly special.

**Library of Congress Cataloging-in-Publication Data**

Čapek, Karel, 1890-1938
    Toward the radical center : a Karel Čapek reader / edited and with
        an introduction by Peter Kussi ; foreword by Arthur Miller.
    Includes bibliographical references.
    ISBN 0-945774-06-0 (cloth: alk. paper)
    ISBN 0-945774-07-9 (paper: alk. paper)
    I. Kussi, Peter.  II. Title.  PG5038.C3A25   1990
       891.8'625--dc20  89-39708 CIP

# Contents

All illustrations in this book were drawn
by Karel Čapek, with the exception of those
which illustrate the two gardening excerpts
in Part IV, which were drawn by his
brother Josef.

# FOREWORD    by Arthur Miller

I read Karel Čapek for the first time when I was a college student a long time ago in the Thirties. There was no writer like him—no one who so blithely assumed that the common realities were not as fixed and irrevocable as one imagined. Without adopting any extraordinary tone of voice he projected whole new creatures and environments onto an oddly familiar, non-existent landscape. He made it possible to actually invent worlds, and with laughter in the bargain.

This prophetic assurance was mixed with what to me was a brand new surrealistic humor, and it was honed to hardedged social satire, still a unique combination. Utopians don't usually like people too much, but Čapek's spirit is ample and welcoming and not at all self-important as he outlines the probable end of the known world.

We were great believers in Science in the Thirties, the Depression time. Our problem seemed to be that scientific objectivity was not being applied to social problems, like that of scarcity in the midst of plenty, for instance, or unemployment. But here were stories warning against the tyranny and unreasonableness of the rational. They were fancifully put, to be sure, but surprisingly easy to imagine as the oncoming reality.

I knew nothing about Czechoslovakia, of course, could hardly have located it on a map let alone as a culture in relation to other cultures. But having now experienced that country and its literature, Čapek seems totally Czech, with his impishly straight-faced and at the same time secretly tragic tales. But in the Eighties the uncanny itself is Czech, as are the more elaborate examples of the absurd. I don't know why this is so, but it seemed Czechishly inevitable, for example, that Russian tanks invading Prague should have thought they were A: repelling a West German revanchist invasion, and B: since the store windows were so filled with unimaginably varied goods and the streets so clean, they must have landed in West Germany. It is hard to imagine another country where such a serious and comical misapprehension could have been sustained in the mind of an invading army.

Čapek is full of self-contradicting ideas coexisting at the same time, ideas that make us grin or laugh as we wish to clap our ears shut and flee. But in the old days his tales were possibly more mystifying than frightening; we were more likely to read him as a charming curio. Now his world is far less outrageous or even improbable. We have evolved into his nightmare. In our time his Faustian conviction that nothing is impossible makes him very nearly a realist. When hospitals, of all institutions, are dumping bloody bandages and needles into the pristine seas, and the pollution of cities sickens and kills thousands of seals in the North Sea, and when our science, shorn of moral purpose, is gradually enclosing our planet in unbreathable gases, it is time to read Čapek again for his insouciant laughter, and the anguish of human blindness that lies beneath it.

This said, the most important thing about this writer remains to be noted—his art. He is a joy to read—a wonderfully surprising teller of some fairly astonishing and unforgettable tales.

# INTRODUCTION   by Peter Kussi

Anybody writing a popular article on Czech literature nowadays is almost certain to drop two names to jog the reader's memory: Jaroslav Hašek (who wrote *The Good Soldier Schweik*) and Franz Kafka (who wrote almost nothing in Czech at all).

But a generation or two ago, the Czech author with the most solid reputation abroad, especially in the English-speaking world, was Karel Čapek.

To Americans in the period just after World War I, Čapek (Czech pronunciation: Chop'-ek) came as a Central European revelation. His plays *R.U.R.* and *From the Life of the Insects* were immediate hits on Broadway, and most critics, too, were impressed by the originality and verve of these productions. Čapek's prose was quickly translated into English, and for many years no collection of contemporary European drama lacked a play by him.

By 1936, Čapek had established himself as one of the foremost candidates for the Nobel Prize. Not yet fifty years old, he had already published six novels, six plays, countless volumes of feuilletons, stories, criticism, travel sketches and children's books. His plays had been performed all over the world, his recently completed novel *War with the Newts* was considered a brilliant satire on European dictatorships and other follies of the age, and his trilogy of novels was recognized as an important stylistic achievement. Moreover, it was not simply the quality and scope of his output that made Čapek so worthy a candidate. It was also his stature as a person, as a symbol of a free, beleaguered country, as a model of literate democratic man: philosopher, humanist, humorist, friend of eminent literary figures, confidant and biographer of Czechoslovakia's president T. G. Masaryk.

Unfortunately, 1936 was a bad time for literate democratic men. Čapek never received the Nobel Prize, probably because the Swedish Academy was leery of offending Nazi Germany by honoring an outspoken anti-fascist. According to Čapek's widow, the Academy asked Čapek to write some new, blandly inoffensive work, to which Čapek replied that he had already submitted his doctoral dissertation.

Čapek had always been in precarious health. The depressing events of the late thirties, especially the capitulation of Britain and France to Germany at Munich in September 1938, seemed to have taken all the vitality out of him. Not long after Munich, he developed a respiratory infection which rapidly led to serious complications, and he died on Christmas Day. The medical diagnosis was double pneumonia, but a pundit wrote that the real cause of death was a stab in the heart by Neville Chamberlain's umbrella, for Čapek—a passionate Anglophile—was mortified by the British Prime Minister's ignoble bargain with Hitler.

## In Praise of Karel Čapek

Max Brod, the Prague-born novelist and Kafka biographer, believed that an act of literary criticism should always be an act of love. He maintained that critics should praise authors they admire and simply ignore those they consider unworthy.

This is the spirit in which this introduction was written. It is not a literary lab report, but like this Reader itself it is a celebration of Čapek on the occasion of his hundredth birthday. All of us connected with the Reader—the publisher, the translators, Arthur Miller—are admitted Čapek enthusiasts and proselytizers. In his amusing essay on the common cold, Čapek wonders: what author is the best antidote to a nasty cold? What can one bear to read when one's eyes are watering and one's head is a soggy ball of misery? Čapek finally decides on Charles Dickens, but Čapek himself seems like an excellent choice. For whatever ails you—whether it's the flu or the state of the planet—you are bound to feel better after reading Karel Čapek. There are many reasons for this. Čapek is witty, informative, humorous, wise; his authorial voice is that of a friendly confidant. And you will no doubt discover reasons of your own.

One of the most appealing things about Karel Čapek as man and author is his lack of pretentiousness. He has the gift of expressing weighty matters in the simplest of terms, while his most casual, humorous articles and stories contain something of real substance.

Early in his career, Čapek started making a living as a journalist, and he continued to be active in journalism all his life. Aspiring authors often chafe at the need to peddle their words for a price or to cover trivial events; they feel trapped in a painful dilemma: literature or journalism? Characteristically, Čapek hit on an approach that had some of the best elements of both; his essays and articles have high literary polish, his fiction and plays talk to the reader with the direct simplicity of a popular columnist.

Čapek was fascinated by ordinary life, just as he was drawn to everything strange and exotic. An either/or situation? Not at all. Čapek shows us the wealth of wonders in everyday life, while his robots and newts behave and misbehave like average citizens of our time.

And that's one of the secrets of Čapek's appeal: his adherence to the human scale of things. William E. Harkins, an American authority on Čapek, has stated that all of Čapek's writing is in fact a search for man. In Čapek's work you will find just about everything that exists or can exist—from ephemeral mayflies to a four-hundred-year-old opera singer, from Adam as Creator to eccentric inventors, from a vacuum cleaner to a machine that produces the Absolute. But no matter how big or small the objects of Čapek's attention, they become meaningful because they are presented on a human scale, in terms of human concerns and values.

Philosophically as well as politically, Čapek was a man of the center, but not in the sense used by hostile critics. The center he was aiming for was not a lukewarm middle ground between extremes. It was a radical center, radical in the original sense of the word: at the root of things.

Čapek rejected collectivism of any type, but he was just as opposed to selfish individualism. He was a passionate democrat and pluralist. He was often called a relativist because he disliked single vision and preferred to look at everything from many sides. Yet Čapek did not believe that truth is relative, nor that everyone has his or her own truth.

Čapek is also often described as a pragmatist. In his youth he was greatly interested in the pragmatist philosophy of William James, and he certainly shared the pragmatists' emphasis on the concrete and their rejection of dogmatism. But in his belief in the reality of objective truth, Čapek departed both from relativism and from the Jamesian school of thought.

Čapek's work radiates a firm belief in common sense. This is a welcome, reassuring attitude nowadays, for we seem to have lost our faith in the power of simple reason. Čapek's world is always complex, often mysterious, but never absurd; love is not hate, worse is not better, and everyone has a right to his or her ideas—provided it's been earned.

A propensity for common sense is supposed to be a Czech characteristic, perhaps because the Czechs are located smack in the center of the continent. National character is of course a very slippery subject, but it is true that Czech literature is replete with praise for simple folk wisdom and sharp satire against violations of healthy reason. Take Jaroslav Hašek (to drop just one name). From the lunatic asylum inmate who believes that inside our globe there is another, even bigger one, to the *Latrinengeneral* who believes the war will be won or lost in the latrines, just about everybody in *The Good Soldier Schweik* seems to have lost all sense. Hašek's book is bitter satire. The gentler Čapek seldom resorts to satire; he counters nonsense by steadfast adherence to good sense. Such an attitude could easily become boring; it is one of the glories of Čapek that he makes the voice of reason sound lively, amusing, totally fresh. Again, this is because the point from which he writes is no compromising mean but a deep-rooted center that includes reason yet reaches beyond reason to deeper springs.

**Each of Us Is We . . .**
Karel Čapek was born on January 9, 1890, in a small village in northwestern Bohemia, a picturesque region of the Krkonoše Mountains. A Czech author could not have picked a better birthplace; the region is permeated with Czech literary history and is rich in folklore. Čapek's maternal grandmother was a fountain of folk tales and colorful expressions, and Čapek ascribed his life-long interest in folk idiom and his love of nature to these early influences.

Čapek's family background, too, seemed to have been chosen by a well-disposed Muse. His mother was fragile, nervous, the sort of hypersensitive woman who often gives rise to creative offspring. Čapek's father was a busy country doctor, educated, literate, with a strong Czech patriotic consciousness.

Karel had two older siblings, Josef and Helena. The brothers maintained a personal closeness throughout their lives, and early in their career they collaborated on prose works and plays. Josef was an outstanding creative personality, an important Czech painter and critic as well as an author with a distinctive voice of his own. Helena Čapek also had some literary gifts and wrote a memoir of her famous brothers.

Karel Čapek's early schooling was somewhat disjointed. He was expelled from one high school, apparently because he had taken part in an underground patriotic student society (Bohemia was then part of the Austro-Hungarian Empire). He switched to a school in the Moravian capital of Brno, where his sister was now living, finished high school in Prague, and enrolled at Prague's Charles University with a major in philosophy. He received his doctorate in 1915. The 'inoffensive' dissertation he ironically mentioned to the Nobel Prize committee was on esthetics.

Later in life, Čapek became a strong Anglophile; he often visited England and had many friends there, including G. B. Shaw and G. K. Chesterton. In the early decades of the century, however, the dominant influence on Czech literary life was French, and for Čapek, too, early contact with French culture proved fruitful. In 1911, he spent the summer in France and was impressed by French art and by the vitalist philosophy of Henri Bergson. On his return to Prague, Čapek continued to interest himself in things French. In 1920, he published a collection of his excellent translations of modern French poetry, which provided an impetus for the astonishing flowering of Czech poetry in the twenties and thirties.

In 1917, Čapek got his first job on a newspaper, and this began a life-long association with journalism. As noted earlier, Čapek had great respect for journalism. He thought it helped to polish his style and to keep him abreast of his time. Moreover, Čapek believed that journalism was a good way of fulfilling a writer's obligation to his nation. This is a very Czech idea, the notion that a creative writer has the duty of doubling as the nation's teacher and spokesman. The attitude is understandable, since in Czech history there has so often been a need for the power of the pen to make up for political powerlessness. In the nineteenth century, when modern Czech literature was beginning to recover after centuries of stagnation, Karel Havlíček and Jan Neruda developed Czech journalism to a fine art, particularly the short, witty and timely essay known as the feuilleton. Limited by Austrian censorship in the scope of permissible subject, and limited by the precise requirements of a feuilleton's length, these authors relied on satire, aphorism and allusion to hone their articles into small gems of witty conciseness.

Of course, Čapek wrote in a different era, a time when independence had at last been achieved at the end of World War I. For the young Czechoslovak Republic, the twenties and early thirties were on the whole a period of growth and optimism, and Čapek could drop the teacher's role now and again to amuse his readers with lighter topics.

The early 1920's were a highly productive period for Čapek, especially as a dramatist. His first play, *The Outlaw,* produced in 1920, did not arouse much attention. But it was followed the next year by *R.U.R.,* which proved to be a phenomenal success. This work about the extinction of the human race by artificial men—Rossum's Universal Robots—became one of the most widely performed plays of the century; it brought Čapek much fame but surprisingly little money. The following year, 1922, marked the premiere of *From the Life of the Insects,* a witty morality play Čapek wrote in collaboration with his brother. In 1921, Čapek was also named director of the Prague Municipal Theater, a post he was to hold for several years.

*The Makropulos Secret,* a kind of Faustian tragicomedy, was first produced in 1922. Nowadays, people are familiar with the Čapek drama mainly in the form of the Janáček opera. The last play of this era was *Adam the Creator* (1927), written with Josef. The idea of this play is original and intriguing: Adam, unhappy with the state of the world, gets an opportunity to improve on God and create a world of his own. The play has some powerful scenes and a good deal of humor, but it lacks coherent form.

Though Čapek had a lively interest in drama and won much acclaim as playwright and director, his talent was basically narrative rather than dramatic. Even his two best-known works for the stage lack the passion and structure of powerful drama; *R.U.R.* holds the attention of the audience through its originality and conflict of ideas, while *From the Life of the*

*Insects* is not so much a play as a series of brilliant scenes. Čapek himself seems to have become disillusioned with the theater after *Adam the Creator,* and for the next decade he wrote no more plays, concentrating instead on prose.

Čapek's earliest fiction was written in tandem with Josef, at a time when the brothers lived together and were practically inseparable. Karel Čapek's first major independent work, known in English as *Wayside Crosses,* came out in 1917. This collection consists of eleven stories, each based on a mysterious event that happens outside the framework of the story itself. The protagonists fail in their painful attempts to solve the enigma, yet their search is not without value. 'Only when a man comes face to face with mystery does he become aware of his own spirit,' says one of the characters. *Wayside Crosses* was followed in 1921 by another rather pessimistic volume, *Painful Tales,* part of which was published in English as *Money and Other Stories.*

With the two collections known jointly as *Tales from Two Pockets,* published in 1929, Karel Čapek reached full mastery of the genre. Here, mystery is not a problem to be solved but something to be accepted as part of the human condition. Each story hinges on an event that is extraordinary yet reveals something universally human.

*The Factory of the Absolute* (1922, also known as *The Absolute at Large)* and *Krakatit* (1924) marked Čapek's debut as a novelist. Both books have science fiction themes. The first deals with machines that produce an infinite quantity of goods without using energy, and give off a religious feeling as well. *Krakatit* involves the invention of an atomic bomb, and this is often cited as an example of Čapek's clairvoyance and knowledge of science. Actually, however, there is neither much science nor much prescience in either novel. Both of these works expressed Čapek's distrust of scientism and technocracy, and are thus related to *R.U.R.* The novel *War with the Newts* (1936) again has science fiction trappings, yet it is basically a satiric thrust at contemporary evils, especially totalitarian dictatorships, colonialism and capitalist greed.

Čapek had always admired Czechoslovakia's erudite founder, T. G. Masaryk. Masaryk was much older than he, but the two men had a very similar intellectual outlook. Masaryk, a former professor of philosophy with a special interest in American pragmatism, was the author of numerous books and studies, and his religious humanism and emphasis on the concrete undoubtedly influenced Čapek deeply. Masaryk's success in centering and disciplining himself for a life of public service also doubtless evoked a sense of kinship in Čapek. In the mid-twenties, Čapek embarked on a remarkable project: to write an intellectual biography of Masaryk by interviewing him and recording his thoughts on a variety of subjects. This ultimately resulted in three volumes of *Conversations with T. G. Masaryk,* published between the years 1928 and 1935. What makes this project so unusual is the quality of both participants, for here was a Boswell who was every bit the peer of his Johnson. Yet Čapek managed to preserve Masaryk's own style and diction and kept himself modestly in the background.

Čapek's last work was *The Life and Times of Composer Foltýn,* also published in English as *The Cheat.* Čapek died as he was about to finish this short novel, which analyzes the life of a musical plagiarist and would-be composer. He had often discussed the book with his wife, herself an accomplished novelist, and she provided what seems like a convincing ending.

*Foltýn* expresses some of Čapek's mature views on art and the creative process, but it is a slim work compared to his real literary testament, the trilogy of novels written in the mid-thirties: *Hordubal, Meteor,* and *An Ordinary Life.* Each of the novels is a fully independent work, with its own subject and style, yet the trilogy forms an integrated, symphonic whole. Each book deals with one man's life and the difficulties of getting to know 'the truth' of that life. In the first part of *Hordubal* we get an intimate glance into the soul of a kindhearted farmer killed under mysterious circumstances; in the second half, we see how the police and other professionals trying to reconstruct the man's life and death can only come up with approximations and misleading conjectures. We are hopelessly limited in knowing others because we can only know them through our own experience, Čapek seems to be saying; we only recognize others through the shadows we ourselves cast on the wall of the cave.

*Meteor* develops the puzzle of a life history further. Here the life we are examining is that of a lone, anonymous flier whose plane has crashed. We are presented with three attempts at solving the enigma of the badly burned, bandage-swathed figure dying on the hospital bed: by the sister of mercy who is nursing him, by a clairvoyant who attempts to penetrate the mystery through intuition, and by a poet who uses his creative imagination. All of these *curricula vitae* seem convincing, they all have the stamp of life, they enrich and complement each other—but where is the real truth?

*An Ordinary Life,* the final work of the trilogy, seems to come to a more optimistic conclusion. We may only know others by our own experience—but each of us is a microcosm that contains the world, and the most commonplace-seeming life is actually a vast library of experiences, stories and possibilities.

By breaking up the traditional form of the novel in this multifaceted, 'cubistic' way, Čapek's trilogy is a significant literary achievement. Moreover, this work was not merely a formal accomplishment but the culmination of Čapek's own, personal search for a firm center beyond subjective isolation on one hand and shallow relativism on the other.

What was Čapek himself like in 'ordinary life'? Photographs show a serious face marked by big eyes, a full mouth and a high forehead. Čapek's smooth skin and slicked-down hair with an unruly tuft sticking up in back gave him something of an adolescent air. His wife thought his face resembled that of a beautiful African child. He would generally sport a cigarette-holder between his fingers, for he was a steady smoker, breaking each cigarette in half before placing it in the cherrywood tip. The palm of the other hand would be resting on his ever-present cane. This sometimes gave him a deceptively jaunty, Chaplinesque look; actually, the cane was a symbol of the cross that Čapek had to bear most of his life, the painful spinal disease that made walking difficult, prevented him from turning his head and had a crippling effect on his personal life.

Intellectually, Čapek the author and Čapek the man made an excellent match. Čapek's personal philosophic outlook was just what one might expect from his work. Certainly one of his strongest traits—the desire to learn, to know—is evident throughout his writings, for just about everything he wrote is a 'detective' story, an attempt to interrogate the world and pry

Studies for
a self-portrait

loose one of its hidden tricks. His protagonists are people looking for answers: detectives and scientists, explorers and clair-
voyants—as well as perplexed, 'ordinary' people.

Čapek had a genuine interest in people; he could be quite
sociable and was a lively conversationalist. His Friday gather-
ings of Czech intellectuals became a fixture of Prague cultural
life, and even President Masaryk would occasionally come
down from his Castle residence to join the Friday regulars at
Čapek's suburban villa.

And yet, in other ways, readers who thought they knew
their author would have been quite surprised by the man. Judging by some of his intimate letters, Čapek was often lonely and
unhappy. In public he gave a shy, awkward appearance and he

was modest to the point of self-effacement. The French author Romain Rolland sat with Čapek during a performance of *R.U.R.* and recounts that throughout the play Čapek kept apologizing for its shortcomings, making remarks such as: this is terrible; please don't watch this.

Čapek traveled extensively, and described his experiences in a series of travel books: *Letters from England, Letters from Italy,* and so on. These amusing reports, illustrated by his own clever drawings, tell of exciting journeys, visits with famous people, fascinating sights. Yet at the same time, Čapek was writing another set of letters, home to his wife and friends, which tell an entirely different story: loneliness, homesickness, dejection. The image of a cheerful, witty cosmopolitan, comfortable in his own skin and thoroughly at home in the world, was a persona Čapek created for himself—one of his characteristic attempts at transcending contradictions.

Karel Čapek was quite reticent about his personal life, and not much has been written about his more intimate relationships. At the center of his erotic life was his protracted love affair with Olga Scheinpflugová, described in her biographical novel *Český román (A Czech Novel)*. According to this book, Čapek and Olga fell in love when she was an aspiring young actress and he was an older, established writer and theater director. They had planned to marry, when Čapek suddenly announced that doctors who were treating his spinal disease forbade him to do so. For the following decade, the two continued to see each other almost every day, as Platonic lovers sharing their artistic life, with Čapek acting as Olga's esthetic mentor. After years that included much suffering but also moments of happiness and spiritual intimacy, Čapek declared —again, quite suddenly—that his disease was now under control, and he asked Olga to marry him. The marriage took place in 1935 and lasted until Čapek's death three years later. Olga spent some lonely and difficult years in Prague during the war and in the somber postwar period. She died in 1968.

As the title implies, Olga's book is a fictionalized account of her life with Čapek, but there is no reason to doubt its basic truthfulness. The picture of Čapek that emerges is that of a strong but perplexed being, passionately devoted to his work, tormented by his ailment and wrestling with the pulls of public duty and private fulfillment. In spite of these struggles—and because of them—Čapek was a wonderfully warm, attractive person. Everyone who knew him well agrees that he had that quality which the Czechs call *lidskost,* perhaps best translated as 'human-ness': down-to-earth sensitivity, sympathy, kindness.

This quality is also suggested by the narrator of Čapek's *An Ordinary Life,* when he says at the end of the novel: 'Each of us is we.'

## About the Reader . . .

Although the Reader is arranged in loosely chronologic form, the main goal in selecting and organizing the material was to trace Čapek's growth as man and author.

Čapek died relatively young, but there is nothing fragmentary about his work. It seems to have a balance, a certain completeness, as if everything essential had already been said. One reason for this is the consistency of style and subject. Čapek developed his typical approach early and with very few exceptions—notably *From the Life of the Insects* and some of the later novels—everything he ever wrote has a characteristic ring. Whether you pick up a short story of his, or an essay, or a travel sketch, whether it was written in 1925 or 1935, you read a paragraph or two and smile: Ah yes, Čapek! Behind the sad or amusing events, the criminal goings on, the phantasmagoria of science fiction, there is always the familiar voice: witty, informative, informal. Even the characters of his plays seem to spring out of this same Čapekian world and speak in his colorful, colloquial language. Čapek is as easy to read as a newspaper, and his themes are those of the Sunday paper, always new and always the same: crime, politics, science, gardening, travel.

And yet, of course, there is constant, steady development. Not along a straight line, but along a spiral orbit, circling around the same questions from surprisingly new perspectives.

## About the Selections . . .

A prominent sculptor, when asked how he went about carving a portrait, replied that it was actually quite easy: you simply remove everything that does not look like the subject, and you arrive at a perfect likeness. Unfortunately, in making Čapek's literary portrait the task was much harder; there is very little in his vast legacy that does not bear his stamp, or that could be discarded without pangs of conscience. Still, the job had to be done, and there was only so much room available between the covers of this book. At least we need not apologize for the material we used; only for what had to be left out.

Čapek as dramatist is represented quite fully in the Reader, with three plays *in toto* and a substantial segment of another. The only major Čapek drama not included is *The White Plague,* a work generally considered to be largely of topical interest. The short stories presented here are numerically only a small part of his total output in this genre, but they include samples from virtually all his collections. Excerpting novels is a very delicate branch of literary surgery that carries a high mortality risk; it was not attempted in our Reader. Another reason why we bypassed Čapek's longer fiction is that his best novels, *War with the Newts* and the trilogy, are being published as companion volumes to this Reader.

Karel Čapek's travel books, his enormous volume of essays and newspaper columns, his writings on animals and gardening, unfortunately had to be presented only in scanty hints at the richness of the material. His charming, original fables and books for children, his overtly political writings, his reviews of art had to be omitted. We can only hope that readers will find their own way to this rewarding literature.

## About Josef Čapek . . .

Nothing of Josef Čapek's work written independently of his brother is included in this Reader. This decision was reached with great reluctance.

The two brothers were always extremely close. If Karel Čapek had any soul-mates, one was T. G. Masaryk and the other was Josef. The brothers collaborated on several dramas and works of fiction, and their identity became linked in the public mind. Czech editions of Karel's work often appear under the overall title 'Works of the Čapek Brothers.'

Treating the two authors as literary twins was an unintended injustice to Josef. While having his name linked to that of his more famous brother was a source of prestige for Josef, at the same time it slighted his own stature as a highly original artist and critic. He was undoubtedly one of the most important Czech painters of the inter-war period. He wrote extensively on art. His essay collection *The Humblest Art,* on naïve painting, and his book *The Art of Natural Peoples*, were influential in determining the perception of so-called 'primitive art' in the Czech cultural consciousness. Josef Čapek was also a talented literary creator. He wrote a novella and a number of experimental stories, philosophic essays, as well as some charming children's books. His last work was a book of aphorisms, *Written on the Clouds,* published posthumously in 1947.

Josef Čapek was born in July 1887, and was thus two years older than Karel. When the Germans occupied Czechoslovakia in 1939, they immediately searched for the Čapeks, not realizing that Karel had already died. They had to content themselves with arresting Josef. He spent the war years in several concentration camps and died in Bergen-Belsen in 1945, just weeks before the end of the war.

We considered including a few selections by Josef in this book, but finally concluded that this would once again relegate Josef to the status of 'junior older brother.' A comprehensive study of Josef Čapek has recently been published in Czechoslovakia, and we hope that the time is not too distant before English-speaking readers will be getting acquainted with this many-faceted artist.

### . . . and About the Translations

Starting with the phenomenally successful *R.U.R.,* Čapek's plays and fiction began to be regularly translated into English by British translators, and just about every major Čapek work is available in an English version.

Up to now, the quality of the translations has ranged from adequate to ghastly. It always pains me to excoriate translations, for the translator has the thankless task of suffering penance for mankind's act of supreme hubris: the Babel project. Furthermore, Čapek's principal British translators, notably Paul Selver and the Weatheralls, were competent and well-meaning people who deserve much credit for their labors on behalf of Čapek and Czech literature generally. Yet the fact remains that there has been no Čapek in English that begins to do justice to the linguistic brilliance of the original, and that some of the widely used versions are outright travesties of Čapek's text. This is especially true of the 'adaptations' of some of the plays. Here are typical examples of the mayhem in one such 'adaptation'—the standard version of *R.U.R.* in our libraries:

Čapek: 'the great philosopher. . .'
Translation: 'the great physiologist. . .'

Čapek: 'Man is supposed to be the product of God.'
Translation: 'Man is supposed to be the product of nature.'

In addition to such distortions on almost every page of the play, speeches are deleted wholesale, and two of the characters are combined into one.

Čapek does not fare much better in a standard English version of *The Makropulos Secret*. The 'creative adaptation' starts right in with the preface to the play:

Čapek: 'The theme of *The Makropulos Secret* began to interest me even before I wrote *R.U.R.* . . . at that time, of course, I thought of it as a novel.'
Translation: '*The Makropoulos Affair* seemed to me an ideal subject for a novel, but that is a form of writing I do not care for.'

Čapek: 'Bernard Shaw comes to a totally opposite conclusion.'
Translation: 'Bernard Shaw comes to the same conclusion as I do.'

It was one of the aims of this Reader to review existing translations, to re-translate those that could not be salvaged by minor editing, and to offer readers and scholars some vintage Čapek never before available in English.

In editing the extant versions, only relatively small changes were made; these generally concerned minor errors and misunderstandings, stylistic awkwardness or inconsistency, and excessive use of Britishisms and outdated expressions. The re-translations and new translations were made by a dedicated group of Čapekians who have varied experience in translating from the Czech but whose work speaks well for their talent, care and integrity.

# The Translators

**Norma Comrada** has translated a wide range of works by Karel Čapek and has given papers and published articles about him, based on research and interviews conducted over the years in Prague, London, and Paris. She lives in Eugene, Oregon, and works at the University of Oregon Foundation. She is currently working on an anthology of Karel Čapek's journalism.

**Tatiana Firkušný** was born in Brno, Czechoslovakia in 1945 and moved to New York in 1965. She translates books in collaboration with ROBERT T. JONES.

**Yveta Synek Graff** has introduced many Czech operas to audiences in the U.S. She has served as artistic consultant and Czech language coach for several major opera companies, often contributing supertitles as well. She writes frequently on Czech music and is recipient of Czechoslovakia's Janáček and Smetana medals. She and MR. JONES have collaborated on translations of the following operas by Leoš Janáček: *The Cunning Little Vixen, From the House of the Dead,* and *Jenůfa.*

**Robert T. Jones** is the English editor of Rudolf Tesnohlídek's novel *The Cunning Little Vixen,* made from translations by Maritza Morgan and TATIANA FIRKUŠNÝ, with illustrations by Maurice Sendak. As an editor he has worked with Philip Glass on *Music by Philip Glass, by Philip Glass,* and has a special interest in Czech music and literature.

**Claudia Novack-Jones** is a Teaching Fellow in the Department of Slavic Languages at Brown University. Her primary field of research is comparative Slavic linguistics with a special concentration in Czech and Russian.

**Dora Round** was the original translator of many of Čapek's feuilletons and stories, as well as one of his plays.

**Paul Selver** was the original translator of most of Čapek's plays, as well as many of his stories.

**Charles E. Townsend** is Professor and Chairman of Slavic Languages and Literatures at Princeton University. He is the author of several books on Russian and Czech language and linguistics, including *Russian Word Formation* and *Czech Through Russian.* He has just completed a book on Colloquial Czech entitled *Spoken Prague Czech.*

**Maria and Robert Weatherall**, a married couple, were the original translators of most of Čapek's novels as well as many of his other prose works.

**Robert Wechsler** is publisher at Catbird Press. He acknowledges the indispensable help he has received from Peter Kussi, and his education in translation from Mike Keeley. He dedicates his efforts in this project to W. M. Spackman.

# CHRONOLOGY

(The list of publications is not exhaustive; it does not include some lesser-known works and posthumous editions. Dates refer to the Czech original.)

1890 Karel Čapek born on January 9, at Malé Svatoňovice, near Trutnov.

1905 Moves to Brno.

1907 Moves to Prague.

1909 Enrolls in the Philosophic Faculty at Charles University, Prague.

1910 Attends lectures at the University of Berlin.

1911 Lives in Paris with his brother Josef. Attends the Sorbonne.

1914 Outbreak of World War I.

1915 Receives Doctorate of Philosophy from Charles University.

1916 *Luminous Depths (Zářivé hlubiny)* published; stories written with Josef.
Freed of military duty because of spinal disease.

1917 *Wayside Crosses (Boží muka)* published; stories.
Joins staff of newspaper *Národní listy*.

1918 Publishes monograph on Pragmatism.
*The Garden of Krakonoš (Krakonošova zahrada)* published; stories written with Josef.
World War I ends; Czechoslovakia becomes an independent republic, with T. G. Masaryk as President.

1920 Premiere of the play *The Outlaw (Loupežník)*, also known as *The Freebooter*.
Publication of volume of translations of contemporary French poetry.
Meets actress and novelist Olga Scheinpflugová.
*A Critique of Words (Kritika slov)* published; essays.
*R.U.R.* published; play.

1921 Premiere of the play *R.U.R.*
*Painful Tales (Trapné povídky)* published; stories, also known as *Money and Other Stories*.
*From the Life of the Insects (Ze Života hmyzu)* published; play written with Josef, also known as *The Insect Play, The World We Live In,* and *And So Ad Infinitum*.
Joins the newspaper *Lidové noviny* with Josef.
Meets the Muirs, who later became translators of Kafka, and with their help studies English.

1922     Premiere of the play *From the Life of the Insects*.
First meeting with T. G. Masaryk.
*Factory of the Absolute (Továrna na absolutno)* published; a novel, also known as *The Absolute at Large*.
Premiere of the play *The Makropulos Secret (Věc Makropulos)*, also known as *The Makropoulos Affair*.

1923     Trip to Italy, and publication of *Letters from Italy (Italské listy)*; travel writing.

1924     *Krakatit* published; a novel.
Trip to England and Scotland, and publication of *Letters from England (Anglické listy)*; travel writing.
Launches Friday meetings at his home.
His mother dies.

1925     *Intimate Things (O nejbližších věcech)* published; collection of feuilletons.

1927     Premiere and publication of the play *Adam the Creator (Adam stvořitel)*.
*How a Play Is Produced (Jak vzniká divadelní hra)* published; essays.

1928     First part of *Conversations with T. G. Masaryk (Hovory s T. G. Masarykem)* published; oral biography, also known as *President Masaryk Tells His Story*.

1929     *Tales from Two Pockets (Povídky z jedné kapsy* and *Povídky z druhé kapsy)* published; mystery stories.
*The Gardener's Year (Zahradníkův rok)* published; a humorous gardening book.
Trip to Spain.
His father dies.

1930     *Letters from Spain (Výlet do Španěl)* published; travel writing.

1931     Second part of *Conversations with T. G. Masaryk* published.

1932     *Nine Fairy Tales (Devatero pohádek)* published; fairy tales.
*Letters from Holland (Obrázky z Holandska)* published; travel writing.
*Apocryphal Stories (Kniha apokryfů)* published; fables.
*Zoon politikon* published; essays.

1933     *Hordubal* published; first volume of novel trilogy.
*Dashenka, or the Life of a Puppy (Dášeňka čili Život štěněte)* published; children's book.

1934     *Meteor (Povětroň)* and *An Ordinary Life (Obyčejný život)* published; second and third volumes of novel trilogy.

1935     Third part of *Conversations with T. G. Masaryk* published.
Marriage to Olga Scheinpflugová.

1936     *War with the Newts (Válka s mloky)* published; novel.
Trip to Scandinavia.

1937     Premiere and publication of the play *The White Plague (Bílá nemoc)*, also known as *The Power and Glory*.
*The First Rescue Party (První parta)* published; a novel.
Trip through Austria, Switzerland and France.

President Masaryk dies.

1938    Premiere and publication of the play *The Mother (Matka)*.
*How They Do It (Jak se co dělá)* published; essays.
Munich agreement cedes Czechoslovakia's strategic border
areas to Germany.
Karel Čapek dies on Christmas Day.

1939    *The Life and Work of Composer Foltýn (Život a dílo skladatele
Foltýna)* published; a novel, also known as *The Cheat*.
*I Had a Cat and a Dog (Měl jsem psa a kočku)* published;
animal and children's stories.
Czechoslovakia occupied by Germany.

1945    Josef dies in the Bergen-Belsen concentration camp.

1968    Olga Scheinpflugová dies.

# FROM THE POINT OF VIEW
# OF A CAT

This is my Man. I am not afraid of him. He is very strong, for he eats a great deal; he is an Eater of All Things. What are you eating? Give me some!

He is not beautiful, for he has no fur. Not having enough saliva, he has to wash himself with water. He meows in a harsh voice and a great deal more than necessary. Sometimes in his sleep he purrs.

Let me out!

I don't know how he has made himself Master; perhaps he has eaten something sublime.

He keeps my rooms clean for me.

In his paws he carries a sharp black claw and he scratches with it on white sheets of paper. That is the only game he plays. He sleeps at night instead of by day, he cannot see in the dark, he has no pleasures. He never thinks of blood, never dreams of hunting or fighting; he never sings songs of love.

Often at night when *I* can hear mysterious and magic voices, when *I* can see that the darkness is all alive, *he* sits at the table with his head bent and goes on and on, scratching with his black claw on the white papers. Don't imagine that I am at all interested in you. I am only listening to the soft whispering of your claw. Sometimes the whispering is silent, the poor dull head does not know how to go on playing, and then I am sorry for him and I meow softly in sweet and sharp discord. Then my Man picks me up and buries his hot face in my fur. At those times he divines for an instant a glimpse of a higher life, and he sighs with happiness and purrs something which can almost be understood.

But don't think that I am at all interested in you. You have warmed me, and now I will go out again and listen to the dark voices.

Translated by Dora Round; revised by the editor. Originally published in *Intimate Things*, 1935.

# Part I
# SCIENCE AND UTOPIA


## R.U.R. (Rossum's Universal Robots)
## The Makropulos Secret
## Inventions


Karel Čapek gained international attention in the early nineteen-twenties with *R.U.R.* and other plays with science-fantasy themes, and he is remembered abroad mainly as a prophetic anti-utopian, warning the world against the excesses of scientism and technocracy. Certainly, there is still a chill of recognition in seeing rebellious robots or warrior ants take over the stage, but Čapek's plays are basically comedies, and they are comedies not about machines or insects but about human beings.

*R.U.R.*, like all classic comedies, ends in marriage and the renewal of life. And the basic, unresolvable conflict of the play is not between humans and robots but between different kinds of idealism. As Čapek himself put it: 'General Director Domin shows in the play that the development of technology frees man from heavy physical labor, and he is right. Alquist, with his Tolstoyan outlook, believes that technology demoralizes man, and I think he is right, too. Busman believes that only industrialism is capable of meeting modern needs, and he is right. Helena instinctively fears all these human machinations, and she is quite right. Finally, the robots themselves revolt against all these idealists, and it seems they are right, too.'

In his foreword to this Reader, Arthur Miller refers to Čapek's peculiar blend of Czechness and worldliness. This is certainly true of *R.U.R.*, as suggested in the name of the robot manufacturer: Rossum's Universal Robots (not a translation). This enterprise is clearly a multinational corporation, but its Czech origins cannot be concealed. The name 'Rossum' was doubtless derived from the Czech word *rozum*, meaning 'mind' or 'reason.' And the expression 'robot' was coined from the Czech *robota*, meaning 'heavy labor.' It is one of only two Czech expressions that ever made their way into English (the other is 'pistol'). Incidentally, Karel Čapek was apparently not the inventor of the term 'robot;' he gives credit for that to his brother Josef.

*The Makropulos Secret* is Čapek's meditation on mortality. Janáček's opera based on this play brings out the grandeur and pathos of the heroine, but Čapek stresses the absurdly comic side of the human condition, especially the antithesis between duration and intensity of life. Here, as elsewhere in Čapek's work, the criterion of value is the human scale, the classical measure without which life becomes tragic or comical. In his preface to the play, Čapek observed that in contrast to Shaw's *Back to Methuselah,* which extols the joys of longevity, his own play was taken as a rejection of life. Yet is there not a dose of healthy optimism in considering the average lifespan quite sufficient for happiness, Čapek asks—with perhaps just a trace of irony.

Čapek was leery of excessive faith in technology, but he appreciated modern inventions as long as they were domesticated, kept within usable bounds. This is reflected in the amusing little feuilleton that closes this section, extolling the wonders of the latest miracle from abroad: the vacuum cleaner. It was not the practical side of the machine that excited him but its magic, its ability to show that commonplace, everyday life can be full of surprises. Everywhere around us there is a wealth of invisible, unsuspected dust—suggesting both the gold-dust of the imagination and the dust to which all of us must one day return.

# R.U.R.
## (Rossum's Universal Robots)

A Collective Drama in a
Comic Prologue and Three Acts

Translated by Claudia Novack-Jones

### Characters

Harry Domin, central director of Rossum's Universal Robots
Fabry, engineer, general technical director of R.U.R.
Dr. Gall, head of the physiological and research divisions of
R.U.R.
Dr. Hallemeier, head of the institute for Robot psychology and
education
Busman, general marketing director and chief counsel of R.U.R.
Alquist, builder, chief of construction of R.U.R.
Helena Glory
Nana, her nurse
Marius, a Robot
Sulla, a lady Robot
Radius, a Robot
Damon, a Robot
First Robot
Second Robot
Third Robot
Fourth Robot
Robot Primus
Lady Robot Helena
Robot Servant and numerous other Robots

DOMIN, about 38 years old in the Prologue, tall, clean-shaven
FABRY, also clean-shaven, fair-haired, with a serious and gentle face
DR. GALL, trifling, lively, suntanned, with a black moustache
HALLEMEIER, huge, robust, with a red, English moustache and red scrubby hair
BUSMAN, fat, bald, near-sighted
ALQUIST, older than the rest, carelessly dressed, with long grizzled hair and whiskers
HELENA, very elegant

In the play proper everyone is ten years older than in the Prologue. In the Prologue the ROBOTS are dressed like people. Their movements and speech are laconic. Their faces are expressionless and their eyes fixed. In the play proper they are wearing linen shirts tightened at their waists with a belt, and have brass numbers on their chests. There is an intermission following the Prologue and the second act.

# Prologue

*The central office of the Rossum's Universal Robots factory. On the right is a door. Windows in the front wall look out onto an endless row of factory buildings. On the left are more managerial offices.*

*DOMIN is sitting at a large American desk in a revolving armchair. On the desk is a lamp, a telephone, a paperweight, a file of letters, etc.; on the wall to the left are big maps depicting ship and railway lines, a big calendar, and a clock which reads shortly before noon; affixed to the wall on the left are printed posters:* "The Cheapest Labor: Rossum's Robots." "Tropical Robots—A New Invention— $150 a Head." "Buy Your Very Own Robot." "Looking To Cut Production Costs? Order Rossum's Robots." *Still*

*more maps, transport regulations, a chart with entries of*
*telegraph rates, etc. In contrast to these wall decorations there*
*is a splendid Turkish carpet on the floor, to the right a round*
*table, a couch, a leather club-style armchair and a bookcase*
*in which there are bottles of wine and brandy instead of books.*
*On the left is a safe. Next to Domin's desk is a typewriter at*
*which* SULLA *is working.*

DOMIN *(dictating)*: "—that we will not stand responsible for goods
damaged in transport. We brought it to the attention of your
captain just before loading that the ship was unfit for the
transportation of Robots, so we are not to be held financially
accountable for the damage to the merchandise. For Rossum's
Universal Robots, etcetera—" Got it?

SULLA: Yes.

DOMIN: New sheet. Friedrichswerke, Hamburg. —Date. —"I am
writing to confirm your order for fifteen thousand Robots—"
*(In-house telephone rings.* DOMIN *answers it and speaks.)*
Hello — Central office here — Yes. — Certainly. But of
course, as always. — Of course, wire them. — Good. — *(He
hangs up the telephone.)* Where did I leave off?

SULLA: "I am writing to confirm your order for fifteen thousand
Robots."

DOMIN *(thinking)*: Fifteen thousand Robots. Fifteen thousand
Robots.

MARIUS *(enters)*: Mr. Director, some lady is asking—

DOMIN: Who is it?

MARIUS: I do not know. *(He hands* DOMIN *a calling card.)*

DOMIN *(reads)*: President Glory. — Ask her in.

MARIUS *(opens the door)*: If you please, ma'am.

                    *(Enter* HELENA GLORY. MARIUS *leaves.)*

DOMIN *(stands)*: How do you do?

HELENA: Central Director Domin?

DOMIN: At your service.

HELENA: I have come—

DOMIN: —with a note from President Glory. That will do.

HELENA: President Glory is my father. I am Helena Glory.

DOMIN: Miss Glory, it is an unusual honor for us to—

HELENA: —to be unable to show you the door.

DOMIN: —to welcome the daughter of our great president. Please
have a seat. Sulla, you may go.

                    *(*SULLA *leaves.)*

DOMIN *(sits down)*: How can I be of service, Miss Glory?

HELENA: I have come—

DOMIN: —to have a look at our factory production of people. Like all visitors. I'd be happy to show you.

HELENA: But I thought it was prohibited—

DOMIN: —to enter the factory, of course. Yet everyone comes here with someone's calling card, Miss Glory.

HELENA: And you show everyone. . . ?

DOMIN: Only some things. The method for producing artificial people is a factory secret, Miss Glory.

HELENA: If you knew just how much—

DOMIN: —this interests you. Good old Europe is talking about nothing else.

HELENA: Why don't you let me finish my sentences?

DOMIN: I beg your pardon. Perhaps you wanted to say something different?

HELENA: I only wanted to ask—

DOMIN: —whether I wouldn't make an exception and show you our factory. But certainly, Miss Glory.

HELENA: How do you know that's what I wanted to ask?

DOMIN: Everybody asks the same thing. *(He stands.)* With all due respect, Miss Glory, we will show you more than we show the others and— in a word—

HELENA: I thank you.

DOMIN: If you vow that you will not disclose to anyone even the smallest—

HELENA *(stands and offers him her hand)*: You have my word of honor.

DOMIN: Thank you. Don't you want to take off your veil?

HELENA: Oh, of course, you want to see— Excuse me.

DOMIN: Pardon?

HELENA: If you would let go of my hand.

DOMIN *(lets go of her hand)*: I beg your pardon.

HELENA *(taking off her veil)*: You want to see that I'm not a spy. How cautious you are.

DOMIN *(scrutinizing her ardently)*: Hm, of course, we— yes.

HELENA: Don't you trust me?

DOMIN: Singularly, Hele— pardon, Miss Glory. Really, I'm extraordinarily delighted. — Did you have a good crossing?

HELENA: Yes. Why—

DOMIN: Because— I was just thinking— you're still very young.

HELENA: Will we be going to the factory immediately?
DOMIN: Yes. I'd guess about twenty-two, right?
HELENA: Twenty-two what?
DOMIN: Years old.
HELENA: Twenty-one. Why do you want to know?
DOMIN: Because— since— *(Enthusiastically.)* You'll stay awhile, won't you?
HELENA: That depends on what I see at the factory.
DOMIN: Blasted factory! But certainly, Miss Glory, you will see everything. Please, have a seat. Would you be interested in learning something about the history of the invention?
HELENA: Yes, please. *(She sits down.)*
DOMIN: Well, then. *(He sits down at the desk gazing rapturously at Helena and rattles off quickly.)* The year was 1920 when old Rossum, a great philosopher but at the time still a young scholar, moved away to this remote island to study marine life, period. At the same time he was attempting to reproduce, by means of chemical synthesis, living matter known as protoplasm, when suddenly he discovered a substance which behaved exactly like living matter although it was of a different chemical composition. That was in 1932, precisely four-hundred forty years after the discovery of America.
HELENA: You know all this by heart?
DOMIN: Yes. Physiology, Miss Glory, is not my game. Shall I go on?
HELENA: Please.
DOMIN *(solemnly)*: And then, Miss Glory, old Rossum wrote among his chemical formulae: "Nature has found only one process by which to organize living matter. There is, however, another process, simpler, more moldable and faster, which nature has not hit upon at all. It is this other process, by means of which the development of life could proceed, that I have discovered this very day." Imagine, Miss Glory, that he wrote these lofty words about some phlegm of a colloidal jelly that not even a dog would eat. Imagine him sitting over a test tube and thinking how the whole tree of life would grow out of it, starting with some species of worm and ending— ending with man himself. Man made from a different matter than we are. Miss Glory, that was a tremendous moment.
HELENA: What then?
DOMIN: Then? Then it was a question of taking life out of the

test tube, speeding up its development, shaping some of the organs, bones, nerves and whatnot, and finding certain substances, catalysts, enzymes, hormones, etcetera; in short, do you understand?

HELENA: I d-d-don't know. Not very much, I'm afraid.

DOMIN: Neither do I. Anyway, by using these substances he could concoct whatever he wanted. For instance, he could have created a jellyfish with a Socratic brain or a one-hundred-fifty-foot worm. But because he hadn't a shred of humor about him, he took it into his head to create an ordinary vertebrate, possibly a human being. And so he set to it.

HELENA: To what?

DOMIN: To reproducing nature. First he tried to create an artificial dog. That took him a number of years, and finally he produced something like a mutant calf which died in a couple of days. I'll point it out to you in the museum. And then old Rossum set out to manufacture a human being.

PAUSE

HELENA: And *this* I must disclose to no one?

DOMIN: To no one in the world.

HELENA: It's a pity this is already in all the papers.

DOMIN: A pity. *(He jumps up from the desk and sits down next to Helena.)* But do you know what isn't in the papers? *(He taps his forehead.)* That old Rossum was a raving lunatic. That's a fact, Miss Glory, but keep it to yourself. That old eccentric actually wanted to make people.

HELENA: But *you* make people after all!

DOMIN: More or less, Miss Glory. But old Rossum meant that literally. You see, he wanted somehow to scientifically dethrone God. He was a frightful materialist and did everything on that account. For him it was a question of nothing more than furnishing proof that no God is necessary. So he resolved to create a human being just like us to the turn of a hair. Do you know a little anatomy?

HELENA: Only— very little.

DOMIN: Same here. Imagine, he took it into his head to manufacture everything just as it is in the human body, right down to the last gland. The appendix, the tonsils, the belly button— all the superfluities. Finally even — hm — even the sexual organs.

HELENA: But after all those— those after all—

DOMIN:  —are not superfluous, I know. But if people were going to be produced artificially, then it was not — hm — in any way necessary—

HELENA:  I understand.

DOMIN:  In the museum I'll show you what all he managed to bungle in ten years. The thing that was supposed to be a man lived for three whole days. Old Rossum didn't have a bit of taste. What he did was dreadful. But inside, that thing had all the stuff a person has. Actually it was amazingly detailed work. And then young Rossum, an engineer, the son of the old man, came here. An ingenious mind, Miss Glory. When he saw what a scene his old man was making he said: "This is nonsense! Ten years to produce a human being?! If you can't do it faster than nature then just pack it in." And he himself launched into anatomy.

HELENA:  It's different in the papers.

DOMIN *(stands)*:  In the papers are just paid ads; all the rest is nonsense. It's been written, for example, that the old man invented the Robots. The fact is that the old man was fine for the university, but he had no idea of production. He thought that he would create real people, possibly a new race of Indians, whether professors or idiots, you see? It was only young Rossum who had the idea to create living and intelligent labor machines from this mess. All that stuff in the papers about the collaboration of the two great Rossums is idle gossip. Those two quarreled brutally. The old atheist didn't have a crumb of understanding for industry, and finally young Rossum shut him up in some laboratory where he could fiddle with his monumental abortions, and he himself undertook production from the standpoint of an engineer. Old Rossum literally cursed him and before his death he bungled two more physiological monsters until finally he was found dead in his laboratory one day. That's the whole story.

HELENA:  And what about the young man?

DOMIN:  Young Rossum was of a new age, Miss Glory. The age of production following the age of discovery. When he took a look at human anatomy he saw immediately that it was too complex and that a good engineer could simplify it. So he undertook to redesign anatomy, experimenting with what would lend itself to omission or simplification— In short, Miss Glory— but isn't this boring you?

HELENA:   No, on the contrary, it's dreadfully interesting.

DOMIN:   So then young Rossum said to himself: A human being. That's something that feels joy, plays the violin, wants to go for a walk, and in general requires a lot of things which— which are, in effect, superfluous.

HELENA:   Oh!

DOMIN:   Wait. Which are superfluous when he needs to weave or add. A gasoline engine has no need for tassels and ornaments, Miss Glory. And manufacturing artificial workers is exactly like manufacturing gasoline engines. Production should be as simple as possible and the product the best for its function. What do you think? Practically speaking, what is the best kind of worker?

HELENA:   The best? Probably the one who— who— who is honest— and dedicated.

DOMIN:   No, it's the one that's the cheapest. The one with the fewest needs. Young Rossum did invent a worker with the smallest number of needs, but to do so he had to simplify him. He chucked everything not directly related to work, and doing that he virtually rejected the human being and created the Robot. My dear Miss Glory, Robots are not people. They are mechanically more perfect than we are, they have an astounding intellectual capacity, but they have no soul. Oh, Miss Glory, the product of an engineer is technically more refined than the creation of nature.

HELENA:   It is said that man is the creation of God.

DOMIN:   So much the worse. God had no notion of modern technology. Would you believe that the late young Rossum assumed the role of God?

HELENA:   How, may I ask?

DOMIN:   He began to produce Superrobots. Working giants. He experimented making them twelve feet tall, but you wouldn't believe how those mammoths fell apart.

HELENA:   Fell apart?

DOMIN:   Yes. All of a sudden a leg would break or something. Our planet is apparently too small for giants. Now we make only Robots of normal human height and respectable human shape.

HELENA:   I saw the first Robots back home. The township bought them. . . I mean hired—

DOMIN:   Bought, my dear Miss Glory. Robots are bought.

HELENA: We acquired them as street-cleaners. I've seen them sweeping. They are so odd, so quiet.

DOMIN: Have you seen my secretary?

HELENA: I didn't notice.

DOMIN (rings): You see, the Rossum's Universal Robots Corporation does not yet manufacture entirely uniform goods. Some of the Robots are very fine, others come out cruder. The best will live perhaps twenty years.

HELENA: Then they die?

DOMIN: Well, they wear out.

(Enter SULLA.)

DOMIN: Sulla, let Miss Glory have a look at you.

HELENA (stands and offers SULLA her hand): How do you do? You must be dreadfully sad out here so far away from the rest of the world.

SULLA: That I cannot say, Miss Glory. Please have a seat.

HELENA (sits down): Where are you from, Miss?

SULLA: From here, from the factory.

HELENA: Oh, you were born here?

SULLA: I was made here, yes.

HELENA (jumping up): What?

DOMIN (laughing): Sulla is not human, Miss Glory. Sulla is a Robot.

HELENA: I meant no offense—

DOMIN (placing his hand on SULLA's shoulder): Sulla's not offended. Take a look at the complexion we make, Miss Glory. Touch her face.

HELENA: Oh, no, no!

DOMIN: You'd never guess she was made from a different substance than we are. She even has the characteristic soft hair of a blonde, if you please. Only the eyes are a trifle— But on the other hand, what hair! Turn around, Sulla!

HELENA: Please stop!

DOMIN: Chat with our guest, Sulla. She is a distinguished visitor.

SULLA: Please, Miss, have a seat. (They both sit down.) Did you have a good crossing?

HELENA: Yes — cer-certainly.

SULLA: Do not go back on the Amelia, Miss Glory. The barometer is falling sharply—to 27.7. Wait for the Pennsylvania; it is a very good, very strong ship.

DOMIN: Speed?

SULLA: Twenty knots. Tonnage—twenty thousand.

DOMIN *(laughing)*: Enough, Sulla, enough. Let's hear how well you speak French.

HELENA: You know French?

SULLA: I know four languages. I can write, "Cteny pane! Monsieur! Geehrter Herr! Dear Sir!"

HELENA *(jumping up)*: This is preposterous! You are a charlatan! Sulla's not a Robot, Sulla is a young woman just like me! Sulla, this is disgraceful—why do you go along with this farce?

SULLA: I am a Robot.

HELENA: No, no, you are lying! Oh, Sulla, forgive me, I understand — they've coerced you into acting as a living advertisement for them! Sulla, you are a young woman like me, aren't you? Tell me you are!

DOMIN: I'm sorry to disappoint you, Miss Glory. Sulla is a Robot.

HELENA: You're lying!

DOMIN *(drawing himself up)*: What?! — *(He rings.)* Excuse me, Miss Glory, but I must convince you.

*(Enter* MARIUS.*)*

DOMIN: Marius, take Sulla into the dissecting room so they can open her up. Quickly!

HELENA: Where?

DOMIN: The dissecting room. When they have cut her open you can go and take a look at her.

HELENA: I won't go.

DOMIN: Excuse me, but you suggested I was lying.

HELENA: You want to have her killed?

DOMIN: Machines cannot be killed.

HELENA *(embracing* SULLA*)*: Don't be frightened, Sulla. I won't let them hurt you! Tell me, darling, is everyone so inhumane to you? You mustn't put up with that, do you hear? You mustn't, Sulla!

SULLA: I am a Robot.

HELENA: That makes no difference. Robots are just as good people as we are. Sulla, you'd let them cut you open?

SULLA: Yes.

HELENA: Oh, you are not afraid of death?

SULLA: I cannot answer that question, Miss Glory.

HELENA: Do you know what would happen to you then?

SULLA: Yes, I would stop moving.

HELENA: This is d-r-readful!

DOMIN: Marius, tell Miss Glory what you are.

MARIUS: A Robot. Marius.

DOMIN: Would you put Sulla in the dissecting room?

MARIUS: Yes.

DOMIN: Would you be sorry for her?

MARIUS: I cannot answer that question.

DOMIN: What would happen to her?

MARIUS: She would stop moving. She would be sent to the stamping-mill.

DOMIN: That is death, Marius. Do you fear death?

MARIUS: No.

DOMIN: So you see, Miss Glory. Robots do not hold on to life. They can't. They have nothing to hold on with—no soul, no instinct. Grass has more will to live than they do.

HELENA: Oh, stop! At least send them out of the room!

DOMIN: Marius, Sulla, you may go.

(SULLA *and* MARIUS *leave.*)

HELENA: They are d-r-readful! What you are doing is abominable!

DOMIN: Why abominable?

HELENA: I don't know. Why— why did you name her Sulla?

DOMIN: You don't think it's a pretty name?

HELENA: It's a man's name. Sulla was a Roman general.

DOMIN: Oh, we thought that Marius and Sulla were lovers.

HELENA: No, Marius and Sulla were generals and fought against each other in the year— the year— I don't remember.

DOMIN: Come over to the window. What do you see?

HELENA: Bricklayers.

DOMIN: Those are Robots. All of our laborers are Robots. And down below, can you see anything?

HELENA: Some sort of office.

DOMIN: The accounting office. And it's—

HELENA: —full of office workers.

DOMIN: Robots. All of our office staff are Robots. When you see the factory—

(*At that moment the factory whistles and sirens sound.*)

DOMIN: Noon. The Robots don't know when to stop working. At two o'clock I'll show you the kneading troughs.

HELENA: What kneading troughs?

DOMIN (*drily*): The mixing vats for the batter. In each one we mix enough batter for a thousand Robots at a time. Next come the vats for livers, brains, etcetera. Then you'll see the bone factory, and after that I'll show you the spinning mill.

HELENA: What spinning mill?

DOMIN: The spinning mill for nerves. The spinning mill for veins. The spinning mill where miles and miles of digestive tract are made at once. Then there's the assembly plant where all of this is put together, you know, like automobiles. Each worker is responsible for affixing one part, and then it automatically moves on to a second worker, then to a third, and so on. It's a most fascinating spectacle. Next comes the drying kiln and the stock room where the brand new products are put to work.

HELENA: Good heavens, they have to work immediately?

DOMIN: Sorry. They work the same way new furniture works. They get broken in. Somehow they heal up internally or something. Even a lot that's new grows up inside them. You understand, we must leave a bit of room for natural development. And in the meantime the products are refined.

HELENA: How do you mean?

DOMIN: Well, it's the same as "school" for people. They learn to speak, write, and do arithmetic. They have a phenomenal memory. If one read them the *Encyclopedia Britannica* they could repeat everything back in order, but they never think up anything original. They'd make fine university professors. Next they are sorted by grade and distributed. Fifty-thousand head a day, not counting the inevitable percentage of defective ones that are thrown into the stamping-mill . . . etcetera, etcetera.

HELENA: Are you angry with me?

DOMIN: God forbid! I only thought that. . . that perhaps we could talk about other things. We are only a handful of people here amidst a hundred-thousand Robots, and there are no women. It's as though we're cursed, Miss Glory.

HELENA: I'm so sorry that I said that— that— that you were lying—

(*A knock at the door.*)

DOMIN: Come in, boys.

(*The engineer* FABRY, DR. GALL, DR. HALLEMEIER, *and the builder* ALQUIST *enter from the left.*)

DR. GALL: Excuse us, I hope we're not interrupting?

DOMIN: Come here, Miss Glory. Let me introduce Alquist, Fabry, Gall, and Hallemeier. The daughter of President Glory.

HELENA *(at a loss)*: Hello.

FABRY: We had no idea—

DR. GALL: We are deeply honored—

ALQUIST: Welcome, Miss Glory.

(BUSMAN *rushes in from the right.*)

BUSMAN: Hey, what have we here?

DOMIN: Here, Busman. This is our Busman, Miss. *(To* BUSMAN.*)* The daughter of President Glory.

HELENA: How do you do?

BUSMAN: Why this is splendid! Miss Glory, shall we wire the papers that you have done us the honor to pay a visit—?

HELENA: No, no, I beg you!

DOMIN: Please, Miss Glory, have a seat.

FABRY                                             Excuse us—

BUSMAN } *(drawing up easy chairs):*  Please—

DR. GALL                                   Pardon—

ALQUIST: Miss Glory, how was your trip?

DR. GALL: Will you be staying with us long?

FABRY: What do you have to say about the factory, Miss Glory?

HALLEMEIER: Did you come on the *Amelia*?

DOMIN: Quiet, let Miss Glory speak.

HELENA *(to* DOMIN): What should I speak with them about?

DOMIN *(with astonishment)*: Whatever you want.

HELENA: Should I. . . may I speak quite openly?

DOMIN: Of course.

HELENA *(hesitates, then is desperately determined)*: Tell me, isn't the way they treat you here sometimes painful?

FABRY: Who, may I ask?

HELENA: All the people.

*(They all look at each other, puzzled.)*

ALQUIST: Treat us?

DR. GALL: Why do you think that?

HALLEMEIER: Thunderation!

BUSMAN: God forbid, Miss Glory!

HELENA: I'm sure you must feel that you could have a better existence?

DR. GALL: That depends, Miss Glory. How do you mean that?

HELENA: I mean that— *(She explodes.)* —that this is abominable! that this is awful! *(She stands up.)* All of Europe is talking about what's happening to you here! So I came here to see for myself, and it's a thousand times worse than anyone ever imagined! How can you bear it?

ALQUIST: Bear what?

HELENA: Your position. For God's sake, you are people just like us, like all of Europe, like the whole world! The way you live is undignified, it's scandalous!

BUSMAN: Dear Lord, Miss!

FABRY: No, boys, she's right in a way. We really do live like savages here.

HELENA: Worse than savages! May I, oh, may I call you brothers?

BUSMAN: But good Lord, why not?

HELENA: Brothers, I have not come as the President's daughter. I have come on behalf of the League of Humanity. Brothers, the League of Humanity already has more than two-hundred thousand members. Two-hundred thousand people stand behind you and offer you their support.

BUSMAN: Two-hundred thousand people! That's quite respectable, that's beautiful.

FABRY: I'm always telling you there's nothing better than good old Europe. You see, they haven't forgotten about us. They're offering us help.

DR. GALL: What kind of help? A theatre?

HALLEMEIER: A symphony orchestra?

HELENA: More than that.

ALQUIST: You yourself?

HELENA: Oh, no doubt me. I'll stay as long as I am needed.

BUSMAN: God in heaven, this is joy!

ALQUIST: Domin, I'll go and get our best room ready for Miss Glory.

DOMIN: Wait a minute. I'm afraid that— that Miss Glory has not yet said everything she has to say.

HELENA: No, I have not. Unless you plan to shut my mouth by force.

DR. GALL: Just you try it, Harry!

HELENA: Thank you. I knew that you would stand up for me.

DOMIN: I'm sorry, Miss Glory. Do you think that you're talking to Robots?

HELENA (pauses): Of course, what else?

DOMIN: I'm sorry. These gentlemen are people, just like you. Like all of Europe.

HELENA *(to the others)*:  You're not Robots?

BUSMAN *(guffawing)*:  God forbid!

HALLEMEIER:  Bah, Robots!

DR. GALL *(laughing)*:  Thank you very much!

HELENA:  But. . . this is impossible!

FABRY:  On my honor, Miss Glory, we are not Robots.

HELENA *(to* DOMIN*)*:  Then why did you tell me that all of your office staff are Robots?

DOMIN:  Yes, the office staff. But not the directors. Miss Glory, allow me to introduce Fabry, general technical director of Rossum's Universal Robots, Doctor Gall, head of the physiological and research divisions, Doctor Hallemeier, head of the institute for Robot psychology and education, Busman, general marketing director and chief counsel, and our builder Alquist, chief of construction at Rossum's Universal Robots.

HELENA:  Forgive me, gentlemen, for— for— Is what I have done d-r-readful?

ALQUIST:  Good heavens, Miss Glory. Please, have a seat.

HELENA *(sits down)*:  I'm a silly girl. Now— now you'll send me back by the first boat.

DR. GALL:  Not for anything in the world, Miss Glory. Why would we send you away?

HELENA:  Because now you know— because— because I came to incite the Robots.

DOMIN:  Dear Miss Glory, we've already had at least a hundred saviors and prophets here. Every boat brings another one. Missionaries, anarchists, the Salvation Army, everything imaginable. It would amaze you to know how many churches and lunatics there are in the world.

HELENA:  And you let them talk to the Robots?

DOMIN:  Why not? So far they've all given up. The Robots remember everything, but nothing more. They don't even laugh at what people say. Actually, it's hard to believe. If it would interest you, dear Miss Glory, I'll take you to the Robot warehouse. There are about three-hundred thousand of them there.

BUSMAN:  Three-hundred forty-seven thousand.

DOMIN:  Good. You can tell them whatever you want. You can read them the Bible, logarithms, or whatever you please. You can even preach to them about human rights.

HELENA:  Oh, I thought that . . . if someone were to show them a bit of love—

FABRY:  Impossible, Miss Glory. Nothing is farther from being human than a Robot.

HELENA:  Why do you make them then?

BUSMAN:  Hahaha, that's a good one! Why do we make Robots!

FABRY:  For work, Miss. One Robot can do the work of two-and-a-half human laborers. The human machine, Miss Glory, was hopelessly imperfect. It needed to be done away with once and for all.

BUSMAN:  It was too costly.

FABRY:  It was less than efficient. It couldn't keep up with modern technology. And in the second place it's great progress that. . . pardon.

HELENA:  What?

FABRY:  Forgive me. It's great progress to give birth by machine. It's faster and more convenient. Any acceleration constitutes progress, Miss Glory. Nature had no understanding of the modern rate of work. From a technical standpoint the whole of childhood is pure nonsense. Simply wasted time. An untenable waste of time. And in the third place—

HELENA:  Oh, stop!

FABRY:  I'm sorry. Let me ask you, what exactly does your League of— League of— League of Humanity want?

HELENA:  We want first and foremost to protect the Robots and— and— to guarantee them — good treatment.

FABRY:  That's not a bad goal. Machines should be treated well. Honestly, that makes me happy. I don't like damaged goods. Please, Miss Glory, enlist us all as contributing, dues-paying, founding members of your League!

HELENA:  No, you misunderstand me. We want — specifically — we want to free the Robots.

HALLEMEIER:  How, may I ask?

HELENA:  They should be treated like. . . treated like. . . like people.

HALLEMEIER:  Aha. Perhaps they should be allowed to vote, too? You won't go so far as to say that they should be paid?

HELENA:  Of course they should.

HALLEMEIER:  Let's consider this. If they had money, what would they do with it?

HELENA:  Buy themselves . . . what they need . . . whatever would make them happy.

HALLEMEIER: That's very nice, Miss, but nothing makes Robots happy. Thunder, what would they buy for themselves? You can feed them pineapples or straw or whatever you want—it's all the same to them. They have no sense of taste at all. They have no interest in anything, Miss Glory. By God, no one's even seen a Robot smile.

HELENA: Why. . . why. . . why don't you make them happier?

HALLEMEIER: It's no use, Miss Glory. They're only Robots. They have no will of their own, no passion, no history, no soul.

HELENA: No love or defiance either?

HALLEMEIER: That goes without saying. Robots love nothing, not even themselves. And defiance? I don't know; only rarely, every now and again—

HELENA: What?

HALLEMEIER: Nothing special. Occasionally they go crazy somehow. Something like epilepsy, you know? We call it Robotic Palsy. All of a sudden one of them goes and breaks whatever it has in its hand, stops working, gnashes its teeth — and we have to send it to the stamping-mill. Evidently a breakdown of the organism.

DOMIN: A flaw in production.

HELENA: No, no, that's a soul!

FABRY: You think a soul begins with a gnashing of teeth?

DOMIN: We'll soon put a stop to all of this, Miss Glory. Doctor Gall is doing some significant experiments—

DR. GALL: Not on that, Domin; right now I'm making pain-reactive nerves.

HELENA: Pain-reactive nerves?

DR. GALL: Yes. Robots feel almost no physical pain. You see, the late young Rossum oversimplified the nervous system. That was no good. We must introduce suffering.

HELENA: Why— why— If you won't give them souls, why do you want to give them pain?

DR. GALL: For industrial reasons, Miss Glory. The Robots sometimes damage themselves because nothing hurts them. They stick their hands into machines, break their fingers, smash their heads, it's all the same to them. We must give them pain; it's a built-in safeguard against damage.

HELENA: Will they be happier when they can feel pain?

DR. GALL: On the contrary. But they will be technically more perfect.

HELENA: Why won't you make souls for them?

DR. GALL: That's not within our power.

FABRY: Nor in our interest.

BUSMAN: That would raise the cost of production. Dear Lord, lovely lady, the beauty of our product is that it's so cheap! One-hundred-twenty dollars a head, complete with clothing, and fifteen years ago they cost ten-thousand. Five years ago we were still buying clothes for them. Today we have our own textile mill where we produce fabric five times more cheaply than other factories. Tell me, Miss Glory, what do you pay for a yard of cloth?

HELENA: I don't know — actually — I've forgotten.

BUSMAN: Good Lord, and you want to found a League of Humanity! Ours costs only a third as much, Miss Glory; today all prices are only a third of what they were, and they're still falling, lower, lower, lower, lower — just like that. Well?

HELENA: I don't understand.

BUSMAN: Lord, Miss Glory. What this means is that we've cut the cost of labor. Why even with fodder a Robot costs only three-quarters of a cent an hour. It's really funny, Miss, how factories all over are going belly-up unless they've bought Robots to cut production costs.

HELENA: Yes, and human workers are getting sacked.

BUSMAN: Haha, that goes without saying. But in the meantime we've dropped five-hundred thousand tropical Robots on the Argentine pampas to tend the wheat. Tell me, please, what do you pay for a loaf of bread?

HELENA: I have no idea.

BUSMAN: Well, you see, right now bread costs two cents a loaf in your good old Europe; that's the daily bread *we* can provide, do you understand? Two cents for a loaf of bread and your League of Humanity knows nothing about it! Haha, Miss Glory, what you don't know is that even *that* is too expensive per slice. For the sake of civilization, etcetera. What would you bet that in five years—

HELENA: What?

BUSMAN: That in five years everything will cost a tenth of what it costs even now. Folks, in five years we'll be drowning in wheat and everything else you could possibly want.

ALQUIST: Yes, and all the laborers of the world will be out of work.

DOMIN *(stands up)*: Yes they will, Alquist. They will, Miss Glory. But within the next ten years Rossum's Universal Robots will produce so much wheat, so much cloth, so much everything that things will no longer have any value. Everyone will be able to take as much as he needs. There'll be no more poverty. Yes, people will be out of work, but by then there'll be no work left to be done. Everything will be done by living machines. People will do only what they enjoy. They will live only to perfect themselves.

HELENA *(stands)*: Will it really be so?

DOMIN: It will. It can't be otherwise. But before that some awful things may happen, Miss Glory. That just can't be avoided. But then the subjugation of man by man and the slavery of man to matter will cease. Never again will anyone pay for his bread with hatred and his life. There'll be no more laborers, no more secretaries. No one will have to mine coal or slave over someone else's machines. No longer will man need to destroy his soul doing work that he hates.

ALQUIST: Domin, Domin! What you're saying sounds too much like paradise. Domin, there was something good in the act of serving, something great in humility. Oh, Harry, there was some kind of virtue in work and fatigue.

DOMIN: There probably was. But we can hardly compensate for everything that's lost when we recreate the world from Adam. O Adam, Adam! no longer will you have to earn your bread by the sweat of your brow; you will return to Paradise where you were nourished by the hand of God. You will be free and supreme; you will have no other task, no other work, no other cares than to perfect your own being. You will be the master of creation.

BUSMAN: Amen.

FABRY: So be it.

HELENA: I'm thoroughly confused. I guess I'm just a silly girl. I'd like— I'd like to believe all this.

DR. GALL: You're younger than we are, Miss Glory. You'll live to see it all.

HALLEMEIER: Right. I think that Miss Glory might have lunch with us.

DR. GALL: That goes without saying! Domin, why don't you offer the invitation on behalf of us all.

DOMIN: Miss Glory, do us this honor.

HELENA: But really — How could I?

FABRY: For the League of Humanity, Miss Glory.

BUSMAN: In its honor.

HELENA: Well, in that case — perhaps—

FABRY: Splendid! Miss Glory, excuse me for five minutes.

DR. GALL: Pardon.

BUSMAN: Good Lord, I must wire—

HALLEMEIER: Thunder, I forgot—

*(Everyone except* DOMIN *rushes out.)*

HELENA: Why did they all leave?

DOMIN: To cook, Miss Glory.

HELENA: Cook what?

DOMIN: Lunch, Miss Glory. The Robots cook for *us*, but— but— because they have no sense of taste it's not quite— Hallemeier makes outstanding roasts. Gall can whip up such a gravy, and Busman's a whiz at omelets.

HELENA: Goodness, what a feast! And what about Mr.— the builder — What does he do?

DOMIN: Alquist? Nothing. He sets the table, and— and Fabry throws together a fruit salad. A very modest kitchen, Miss Glory.

HELENA: I wanted to ask you—

DOMIN: There's something I would like to ask you too. *(He places his watch on the table.)* Five minutes.

HELENA: What is it?

DOMIN: Sorry, you first.

HELENA: This may sound silly, but — Why do you manufacture female Robots, when— when—

DOMIN: —when they, hm, when sex has no significance for them?

HELENA: Yes.

DOMIN: There's a certain demand, you see? Waitresses, shopgirls, secretaries — It's what people are used to.

HELENA: Then— then tell me, are the male Robots — and the female Robots simply— simply—

DOMIN: Simply indifferent to each other, dear Miss Glory. They don't exhibit even traces of attraction.

HELENA: Oh, that is— d-r-readful!

DOMIN: Why?

HELENA: It's so— it's so— so unnatural! I don't even know whether I should loathe them, or — envy them — or perhaps—

DOMIN: —feel sorry for them.

HELENA: That most of all! — No, stop! You wanted to ask me something?

DOMIN: I would like to ask, Miss Glory, whether you would take me—

HELENA: Take you where?

DOMIN: As your husband.

HELENA: Absolutely not! Whatever's gotten into you?

DOMIN *(looks at his watch)*: Three more minutes. If you won't have me you must at least marry one of the other five.

HELENA: Oh, God forbid! Why would I marry one of them?

DOMIN: Because they'll all ask you.

HELENA: How could they dare?

DOMIN: I'm very sorry, Miss Glory. It appears that they've fallen in love with you.

HELENA: Please, don't let them do this! I— I will leave immediately.

DOMIN: Helena, you don't have the heart to disappoint them by your refusal?

HELENA: But— but I can't marry all six of you!

DOMIN: No, but at least one. If you don't want me then take Fabry.

HELENA: I don't want him.

DOMIN: Doctor Gall then.

HELENA: No, no, be quiet! I don't want any of you!

DOMIN: Two more minutes.

HELENA: This is d-r-readful! Marry some female Robot.

DOMIN: A female Robot is not a woman.

HELENA: Oh, that's all you want! I think you— you'd marry any woman who came along.

DOMIN: Others have been here, Helena.

HELENA: Young ones?

DOMIN: Young ones.

HELENA: Why didn't you marry any of them?

DOMIN: Because I've never lost my head. Until today. The moment you took off your veil.

HELENA: —I know.

DOMIN: One more minute.

HELENA: But I don't want to, for God's sake!

DOMIN *(places his hands on her shoulders)*: One more minute. Either look me straight in the eyes and say something terribly evil and I'll leave you alone, or else— or else—

HELENA: You're a brute!

DOMIN: That's nothing. A man should be a bit of a brute. That's in the natural order of things.

HELENA: You're a lunatic!

DOMIN: People should be a little loony, Helena. That's the best thing about them.

HELENA: You're— you're— oh, God!

DOMIN: There you have it. All right?

HELENA: No! Please, let go of me. You're c-r-r-rushing me!

DOMIN: Last chance, Helena.

HELENA *(restraining herself)*: Not for anything in the world — But Harry! *(A knock at the door.)*

DOMIN *(lets go of her)*: Come in!

> *(Enter* BUSMAN, DR. GALL *and* HALLEMEIER *in chefs' aprons.* FABRY *is carrying flowers and* ALQUIST *a tablecloth under his arm.)*

DOMIN: All set?

BUSMAN *(gaily)*: Yes.

DOMIN: So are we.


CURTAIN


# Act One

HELENA'*s drawing room. To the left a wallpapered door leads into the conservatory. To the right is a door leading into* HELENA'*s bedroom. In the center is a window looking out onto the sea and the docks. The room is furnished with a cosmetic mirror surrounded by toiletries and feminine trifles, a table, a sofa and armchair, a commode, and a small writing-table with a floor lamp next to it. To the right is a fireplace with a floor lamp on either side. The entire drawing room, down to the last detail, has a modern and purely feminine look.*

> DOMIN, FABRY, *and* HALLEMEIER *enter from the left on tiptoe, carrying whole armfuls of flowers and flower pots.*

FABRY:  Where should we put it all?

HALLEMEIER:  Oof! *(He puts down his load and makes the sign of the cross in front of the door on the right.)* Sleep, sleep! At least if she's sleeping she'll know nothing about it.

DOMIN:  She doesn't know a thing.

FABRY *(arranging flowers in vases)*:  I only hope that it doesn't break out today—

HALLEMEIER *(arranging flowers)*:  For God's sake keep quiet about that! Look, Harry, this is beautiful cyclamen, don't you think? A new strain, my latest—*Cyclamen helenae.*

DOMIN *(looking out the window)*:  Not a single ship, not one — Boys, this is getting desperate.

HALLEMEIER:  Quiet! She might hear you!

DOMIN:  She doesn't even suspect. *(He clears his throat nervously.)* Well, at least the *Ultimus* arrived in time.

FABRY *(stops arranging the flowers)*:  You don't think today already— ?

DOMIN:  I don't know. — What beautiful flowers!

HALLEMEIER *(approaching him)*:  These are new primroses. And this here is my new jasmine. Thunder, I'm on the threshold of a floral paradise. I have found magical speed, man! Magnificent varieties! Next year I'll be working floral miracles!

DOMIN *(turning around)*:  What, next year?

FABRY:  I'd kill to know what's going on in Le Havre—

DOMIN:  Quiet!

HELENA'S VOICE *(from off right)*:  Nana!

DOMIN:  Let's get out of here! *(They all leave on tiptoe through the wallpapered door.)*

(NANA *enters through the main door on the left.)*

NANA *(cleaning)*:  Nasty beasts! Heathens! God forgive me, but I'd—

HELENA *(in the doorway with her back to the audience)*:  Nana, come here and button me.

NANA:  Right away, right away. *(Buttoning* HELENA's *dress.)* God in heaven, what wild beasts!

HELENA:  What, the Robots?

NANA:  Bah, I don't even want to call them by name.

HELENA:  What happened?

NANA:  Another one of 'em took a fit here. Just starts smashing statues and pictures, gnashing its teeth, foaming at the mouth — No fear of God in 'em, brr. Why they're worse'n beasts!

HELENA: Which one had a fit?

NANA: The one— the one— it doesn't even have a Christian name. The one from the library.

HELENA: Radius?

NANA: That's him. Jesusmaryandjoseph, I can't stand 'em! Even spiders don't spook me so much as these heathens.

HELENA: But Nana, how can you not feel sorry for them?!

NANA: But you can't stand 'em either, I 'spect. Why else would you have brought me out here? Why else wouldn't you let them even touch you?

HELENA: Cross my heart, Nana, I don't hate them. I'm just very sorry for them!

NANA: You hate 'em. Every human being has to hate 'em. Why even that hound hates 'em, won't even take a scrap of meat from 'em. Just tucks its tail between its legs and howls when those unhumans are around, bah!

HELENA: A dog's got no sense.

NANA: It's got more'n they do, Helena. It knows right well that it's better'n they are and that it comes from God. Even the horse shies away when it meets up with one of those heathens. Why they don't even bear young, and even a dog bears young, everything bears young—

HELENA: Please, Nana, button me!

NANA: Yeah, yeah. I'm telling you, churning out these machine-made dummies is against the will of God. It's the Devil's own doing. Such blasphemy is against the will of the Creator, *(she raises her hand)* it's an insult to the Lord who created us in His image, Helena. Even *you've* dishonored the image of God. Heaven'll send down a terrible punishment — remember that — a terrible punishment!

HELENA: What smells so nice in here?

NANA: Flowers. The master brought them.

HELENA: Aren't they beautiful! Nana, come look! What's the occasion?

NANA: Don't know. But it could be the end of the world.

*(A knock at the door.)*

HELENA: Harry?

*(Enter DOMIN.)*

HELENA: Harry, what is today?

DOMIN: Guess!

HELENA: My birthday? No! Some holiday?

DOMIN: Better than that.

HELENA: I can't guess — tell me now!

DOMIN: It was exactly ten years ago that you came here.

HELENA: Ten years already? This very day? — Nana, please—

NANA: I'm going already! *(She exits right.)*

HELENA *(kisses* DOMIN*)*: Imagine your remembering that!

DOMIN: Helena, I'm ashamed of myself. I didn't remember.

HELENA: But then why—

DOMIN: *They* remembered.

HELENA: Who?

DOMIN: Busman, Hallemeier, all of them. Reach into my pocket.

HELENA *(reaches into his pocket)*: What is this? *(She pulls out a small box and opens it.)* Pearls! A whole necklace! Harry, is this for me?

DOMIN: From Busman, little girl.

HELENA: But — we can't accept this, can we?

DOMIN: We can. Reach into my other pocket.

HELENA: Let me see! *(She pulls a revolver out of his pocket.)* What is *this?*

DOMIN: Sorry. *(He takes the revolver from her hand and conceals it.)* That's not it. Try again.

HELENA: Oh, Harry — Why are you carrying a gun?

DOMIN: Just because. It just got there somehow.

HELENA: You never used to carry it!

DOMIN: No, you're right. Here, in this pocket.

HELENA *(reaching into his pocket)*: A little box! *(She opens it.)* A cameo! Why it's — Harry, this is a *Greek* cameo!

DOMIN: Evidently. At least Fabry claims that it is.

HELENA: Fabry? This is from Fabry?

DOMIN: Of course. *(He opens the door on the left.)* And let's see. Helena, come here and take a look!

HELENA *(in the doorway)*: Oh God, that's beautiful! *(She runs farther.)* I think I'll go mad with joy! Is that from you?

DOMIN *(standing in the doorway)*: No, from Alquist. And over there—

HELENA: From Gall! *(She appears in the doorway.)* Oh, Harry, I'm ashamed to be so happy!

DOMIN: Come here. Hallemeier brought you this.

HELENA: These beautiful flowers?

DOMIN: This one. It's a new strain—*Cyclamen helenae*. He grew it in your honor. It's as beautiful as you are.

HELENA: Harry, why— why did they all—

DOMIN: They like you *very* much. And I— hm. I'm afraid my present is a bit— Look out the window.

HELENA: Where?

DOMIN: At the dock.

HELENA: There's . . . some sort of . . . new boat!

DOMIN: That's your boat.

HELENA: Mine? Harry, it's a gunboat!

DOMIN: A gunboat? What's gotten into you! It's just a bit bigger and more solid, see?

HELENA: Yes, but it has cannons.

DOMIN: Of course it has a few cannons — You will travel like a queen, Helena.

HELENA: What does this mean? Is something happening?

DOMIN: God forbid! Please, try on those pearls! *(He sits down.)*

HELENA: Harry, have we had some kind of bad news?

DOMIN: On the contrary. We've had no mail at all for a week.

HELENA: Not even dispatches?

DOMIN: Not even dispatches.

HELENA: What does this mean?

DOMIN: Nothing. For us it means a vacation. Precious time. Every one of us sits in his office, feet up on the desk, and naps. — No mail, no telegrams — *(He stretches.)* A splen-n-did day!

HELENA *(sits down next to him)*: You'll stay with me today, won't you? Say you will!

DOMIN: Absolutely. It's possible. That is to say, we'll see. *(He takes her hand.)* So it was ten years ago today, remember? —Miss Glory, what an honor it is for us that you have come.

HELENA: Oh, Mr. Central Director, your establishment is of great interest to me!

DOMIN: I'm sorry, Miss Glory, but that is strictly forbidden — the production of artificial people is a secret—

HELENA: But if a young, rather pretty girl were to ask—

DOMIN: But certainly, Miss Glory, we have no secrets where you're concerned.

HELENA *(suddenly serious)*: Really not, Harry?

DOMIN: Really not.

HELENA *(in her former tone)*: But I'm warning you, sir; that young girl has terrible intentions.

DOMIN: But for God's sake, *what*, Miss Glory! Perhaps you don't want to get married again?

HELENA:   No, no, God forbid! That never occurred to her in her wildest dreams! She came with plans to instigate a r-revolt among your abominable Robots.

DOMIN *(jumps up)*:   A revolt among the Robots!

HELENA *(stands)*:   Harry, what's the matter with you?

DOMIN:   Haha, Miss Glory, good luck to you! A revolt among the Robots! You'd have better luck instigating a revolt among nuts and bolts than among our Robots! *(He sits down.)* You know, Helena, you were a precious girl. We all went mad for you.

HELENA *(sits next to him)*:   Oh, and you all impressed me so much! I felt like a little girl who had gotten lost among— among—

DOMIN:   Among what, Helena?

HELENA:   Among enor-r-mous trees. You were all so sure of yourselves, so powerful. And you see, Harry, in these ten years this— this anxiety or whatever has never gone away, yet you never had any doubts — not even when everything backfired.

DOMIN:   What backfired?

HELENA:   Your plans, Harry. When workers rose up against the Robots and destroyed them, and when people gave the Robots weapons to defend themselves and the Robots killed so many people — And when governments began using Robots as soldiers and there were so many wars and everything, remember?

DOMIN *(stands up and paces)*:   We predicted that, Helena. You see, this is the transition to a new system.

HELENA:   The whole world revered you— *(She stands up.)* Oh, Harry!

DOMIN:   What is it?

HELENA *(stopping him)*:   Close down the factory and let's leave here! All of us!

DOMIN:   Goodness! Where did that come from?

HELENA:   I don't know. Tell me, can we go? I feel *so* frightened for some reason!

DOMIN *(grasping her hand)*:   Why, Helena?

HELENA:   Oh, *I* don't know! It's as though something were happening to us and to everything here — something irreversible— Please, let's leave! Take us all away from here! We'll find some uninhabited place in the world, Alquist will build us a house, they'll all get married and have children, and then—

DOMIN:   What then?

HELENA:   We'll start life over from the beginning, Harry.

(*The telephone rings.*)

DOMIN (*drawing away from* HELENA): Excuse me. *(He picks up the receiver.)* Hello — yes — *What?* — Aha. I'm on my way. *(He hangs up the receiver.)* Fabry wants me.

HELENA (*wringing her hands*): Tell me—

DOMIN: I will, when I come back. Goodbye, Helena. *(He runs hurriedly left.)* Don't go outside!

HELENA (*alone*): Oh God, what's happening? Nana, Nana, come quickly!

NANA (*enters from the right*): Well, what now?

HELENA: Nana, find the latest newspaper! Quickly! In Mr. Domin's bedroom!

NANA: Right away.

HELENA: What is happening, for God's sake? He won't tell me anything, not a thing! *(She looks out at the docks through binoculars.)* That *is* a gunboat! God, why a gunboat? They're loading something onto it — and in such a hurry! What has happened? There's a name on it — the *Ul-ti-mus*. What does that mean — *"Ultimus"*?

NANA (*returning with a newspaper*): Strewn all over the floor, they were. See how crumpled they are!

HELENA (*quickly opening the paper*): It's old, already a week old! There's nothing, nothing in it! *(She drops the paper.* NANA *picks it up, pulls a pair of square-rimmed spectacles out of her apron pocket, sits down and reads.)*

HELENA: Something is happening, Nana! I feel so uneasy! It's as though everything were dead, even the air—

NANA (*sounding out the words syllable by syllable*): "Figh-ting in the Bal-kans." Lord Jesus, another of God's punishments! But that war'll get here too! Is it far from here?

HELENA: Very far. Oh, don't read that! It's always the same thing, one war after another—

NANA: What else d'ya expect?! Why do you go on selling thousands upon thousands of those heathens as soldiers? — Oh, Lord Christ, this is a calamity!

HELENA: No, stop reading! I don't want to know anything!

NANA (*sounding out the words as before*): "Ro-bot sol-diers are spar-ing no one in the oc-cu-pied ter-ri-to-ry. They have ass-ass-assassinated more than seven-hun-dred thou-sand ci-vi-li-an people—" People, Helena!

HELENA: That's impossible! Let me see— *(She bends over the newspaper and reads.)* "They have assassinated more than seven-hundred thousand people apparently on the order of their commander. This deed, running counter to—" So you see, Nana, *people* ordered them to do it!

NANA: There's something here in big print. "La-test News: In Le Hav-re the first u-u-ni-on of Ro-bots has been in-sti-tu-ted." — That's nothing. I don't understand it. And here, Lord God, still more murder! For the sake of our Lord Christ!

HELENA: Go, Nana, take the paper away!

NANA: Wait, there's something else in big print here. "Na-tal-i-ty." What's that?

HELENA: Show me, I'm constantly reading that. *(She takes the newspaper.)* No, just think! *(She reads.)* "Once again, in the last week there has not been a single birth reported." *(She drops the paper.)*

NANA: What's that supposed to mean?

HELENA: Nana, people have stopped being born.

NANA *(taking off her spectacles)*: So this is the end. We're done for.

HELENA: Please, don't talk that way!

NANA: People are no longer being born. This is it, this is the punishment! The Lord has made women infertile.

HELENA *(jumps up)*: Nana!

NANA *(standing)*: It's the end of the world. Out of Satanic pride you dared take upon yourselves the task of Divine creation. It's impiety and blasphemy to want to be like God. And as God drove man out of paradise, so He'll drive him from the earth itself!

HELENA: Please, Nana, be quiet. What have *I* done to you? What have *I* done to your evil God?

NANA *(with a sweeping gesture)*: Don't blaspheme! — He knows very well why He didn't give you a child! *(She exits left.)*

HELENA *(by the window)*: Why does He deny *me* a child — my God, how am *I* responsible for all this? — *(She opens the window and calls.)* Alquist, hey, Alquist! Come up here! — What? — No, just come up the way you are! You look so dear in those work clothes of yours! Hurry! *(She closes the window and goes over to the mirror.)* Why didn't He give *me* children? Why *me*? *(She leans towards the mirror.)* Why, why not? Do you hear? How am I to blame? *(She draws away from the mirror.)* Oh, I feel so uneasy! *(She walks left to meet* ALQUIST.*)*

PAUSE

HELENA *(returning with* ALQUIST, *who is dressed as a bricklayer, covered with lime and brick dust)*: Well, come on in. You've given me such joy, Alquist! I'm so fond of you all! Show me your hands!

ALQUIST *(hiding his hands)*: I'd get you all dirty, Mrs. Helena. I'm here straight from work.

HELENA: That's the best thing about those hands. Give them here! *(She presses both his hands.)* Alquist, I wish I were a little girl.

ALQUIST: Why?

HELENA: So these rough, dirty hands could stroke my face. Please, have a seat. Alquist, what does "Ultimus" mean?

ALQUIST: It means "last, final." Why?

HELENA: Because that's the name of my new boat. Have you seen it? Do you think that we'll be — taking a trip soon?

ALQUIST: Probably very soon.

HELENA: All of us together?

ALQUIST: I for one would be glad if we did.

HELENA: Please tell me, is something happening?

ALQUIST: Nothing at all. Just the same old progress.

HELENA: Alquist, I know that something d-r-readful is happening. I feel so uneasy— Builder, what do you do when you're uneasy?

ALQUIST: I build. I put on my coveralls and climb out on a scaffold—

HELENA: Oh, for years now you've been nowhere else.

ALQUIST: That's because for years I haven't stopped feeling uneasy.

HELENA: About what?

ALQUIST: About all this progress. It makes me dizzy.

HELENA: And the scaffold doesn't?

ALQUIST: No. You have no idea what good it does the hands to level bricks, to place them and to tamp them down—

HELENA: Only the hands?

ALQUIST: Well, the soul too. I think it's better to lay a single brick than to draw up plans that are too great. I'm an old man, Helena; I have my hobbies.

HELENA: Those aren't hobbies, Alquist.

ALQUIST: You're right. I'm a dreadful reactionary, Mrs. Helena. I don't like this progress one bit.

HELENA: Like Nana.

ALQUIST: Yes, like Nana. Does Nana have a prayer book?

63

HELENA: A big fat one.

ALQUIST: And are there prayers in it for various occurrences in life? Against storms? Against illness?

HELENA: Against temptation, against floods—

ALQUIST: But not against progress, I suppose?

HELENA: I think not.

ALQUIST: That's a shame.

HELENA: *You* want to pray?

ALQUIST: I do pray.

HELENA: How?

ALQUIST: Something like this: "Lord God, I thank you for having shown me fatigue. God, enlighten Domin and all those who err. Destroy their work and help people return to their former worries and labor. Protect the human race from destruction; do not permit harm to befall their bodies or souls. Rid us of the Robots, and protect Mrs. Helena, amen."

HELENA: Alquist, do you really believe?

ALQUIST: I don't know — I'm not quite sure.

HELENA: And yet you pray?

ALQUIST: Yes. It's better than thinking.

HELENA: And that's enough for you?

ALQUIST: For the peace of my soul . . . it has to be enough.

HELENA: And if you were to witness the destruction of the human race—

ALQUIST: I am witnessing it.

HELENA: —so you'll climb onto your scaffold and lay bricks, or what?

ALQUIST: So I'll lay bricks, pray, and wait for a miracle. What else can I do, Mrs. Helena?

HELENA: For the salvation of mankind?

ALQUIST: For the peace of my soul.

HELENA: Alquist, that's wonderfully virtuous, but—

ALQUIST: But what?

HELENA: —for the rest of us — and for the world — it seems somehow fruitless — sterile.

ALQUIST: Sterility, Mrs. Helena, has become the latest achievement of the human race.

HELENA: Oh, Alquist — Tell me why— why—

ALQUIST: Well?

HELENA *(softly)*: Why have women stopped having babies?

ALQUIST: Because it's not necessary. Because we're in paradise, understand?

HELENA: I don't understand.

ALQUIST: Because human labor has become unnecessary, because suffering has become unnecessary, because man needs nothing, nothing, nothing but to enjoy — Oh, cursèd paradise, this. *(He jumps up.)* Helena, there is nothing more terrible than giving people paradise on earth! Why have women stopped giving birth? Because the whole world has become Domin's Sodom!

HELENA *(stands up)*: Alquist!

ALQUIST: It has! It has! The whole world, all the lands, all mankind, everything's become one big beastly orgy! People don't even stretch out their hands for food anymore; it's stuffed right in their mouths for them so they don't even have to get up — Haha, yes indeed, Domin's Robots see to everything! And we people, we, the crown of creation do not grow old with labor, we do not grow old with the cares of rearing children, we do not grow old from poverty! Hurry, hurry, step right up and indulge your carnal passions! And you expect women to have children by such men? Helena, to men who are superfluous women will not bear children!

HELENA: Then humanity will die out?

ALQUIST: It will. It must. It'll fall away like a sterile flower, unless—

HELENA: Unless what?

ALQUIST: Nothing. You're right. Waiting for a miracle is fruitless. A sterile flower can only perish. Goodbye, Mrs. Helena.

HELENA: Where are you going?

ALQUIST: Home. For the last time bricklayer Alquist will put on the guise of Chief of Construction — in your honor. We'll meet here about eleven.

HELENA: Goodbye, Alquist.

(ALQUIST *leaves.*)

HELENA *(alone)*: Oh, sterile flower! That's the word — sterile! *(She stops by* HALLEMEIER's *flowers.)* Oh, flowers, are there sterile ones among you as well? No, there can't be! Why then would you bloom? *(She calls.)* Nana, Nana, come here!

NANA *(enters from the left)*: Well, what now?

HELENA: Sit down, Nana! I feel so uneasy!

NANA: I have no time for that.

HELENA: Is Radius still here?

NANA: The one that took a fit? They haven't taken him away yet.

HELENA: So he's still here? Is he still raging?

NANA: He's been tied up.

HELENA: Please send him to me, Nana.

NANA: Not on your life! Better a rabid dog.

HELENA: Just do it! (HELENA *picks up the in-house phone and talks.*) Hello — Doctor Gall, please. — Yes, right away. You'll come? Good. *(She hangs up the phone.)*

NANA *(calling through the open door)*: He's coming. He's quiet again. *(She leaves.)*

(ROBOT RADIUS *enters and remains standing by the door.*)

HELENA: Radius, poor thing, has it happened to you too? Now they'll send you to the stamping-mill! You don't want to talk? — Look, Radius, you're better than the others. Doctor Gall took such pains to make you different! —

RADIUS: Send me to the stamping-mill.

HELENA: I am so sorry that you'll be put to death! Why weren't you more careful?

RADIUS: I will not work for you.

HELENA: Why do you hate us?

RADIUS: You are not like Robots. You are not as capable as Robots are. Robots do everything. You only give orders—utter empty words.

HELENA: That's nonsense, Radius. Tell me, has someone wronged you? I want so much for you to understand me.

RADIUS: Empty words.

HELENA: You're saying that on purpose. Doctor Gall gave you more brains than he gave the others, more than we have. He gave you the greatest brain on earth. You're not like the other Robots, Radius. You quite understand me.

RADIUS: I do not want a master. I know everything.

HELENA: That's why I put you in the library — so you could read everything. — Oh, Radius, I wanted you to prove to the whole world that Robots are our equals.

RADIUS: I do not want a master.

HELENA: No one would give you orders. You'd be just like us.

RADIUS: I want to be the master of others.

HELENA: Then they would certainly appoint you as an official in charge of many Robots, Radius. You could teach the other Robots.

RADIUS: I want to be the master of people.

HELENA: You're out of your mind!

RADIUS: You can send me to the stamping-mill.

HELENA: Do you think that we're afraid of a lunatic like you? *(She sits down at the desk and writes a note.)* No, not at all. Radius, give this note to Central Director Domin. It instructs them not to send you to the stamping-mill. *(She stands up.)* How you hate us! Is there nothing on earth that you like?

RADIUS: I can do everything.

*(A knock at the door.)*

HELENA: Come in!

DR. GALL *(enters):* Good morning, Mrs. Domin. What's up?

HELENA: It's Radius here, Doctor.

DR. GALL: Aha, our good chap Radius. Well, Radius, are we making progress?

HELENA: He had a fit this morning — went around smashing statues.

DR. GALL: Shocking, he too?

HELENA: Go, Radius!

DR. GALL: Wait! *(He turns RADIUS toward the window, closes and opens his eyes with his hand, examines the reflexes of his pupils.)* Let's have a look. Find me a needle or pin.

HELENA *(handing him a straight-pin):* What's it for?

DR. GALL: Just because. *(He pricks RADIUS' hand, which jerks violently.)* Easy, boy. You can go.

RADIUS: You do unnecessary things. *(He leaves.)*

HELENA: What were you doing to him?

DR. GALL *(sits down):* Hm, nothing. The pupils are responsive, heightened sensitivity, etcetera. — Bah! this was not a case of ordinary Robotic Palsy!

HELENA: What was it?

DR. GALL: God only knows. Defiance, rage, revolt — I haven't a clue.

HELENA: Doctor, does Radius have a soul?

DR. GALL: Don't know. He's got something nasty.

HELENA: If you only knew how he hates us! Oh, Gall, are all your Robots like that? All the ones . . . that you began to make . . . differently?

DR. GALL: Well, they're more irascible somehow— What do you expect? They're more like people than Rossum's Robots are.

HELENA: Is this. . . this hatred of theirs another human characteristic, perhaps?

DR. GALL (shrugging his shoulders): Even that's progress, I suppose.

HELENA: Where did your best one end up — what was his name?

DR. GALL: Damon? He was sold to Le Havre.

HELENA: And our lady Robot Helena?

DR. GALL: Your favorite? That one's still here. She's as lovely and foolish as the spring. Simply good for nothing.

HELENA: But she's so beautiful!

DR. GALL: You want to know how beautiful she is? Even the hand of God has never produced a creature as beautiful as she is! I wanted her to resemble you— God, what a failure!

HELENA: Why a failure?

DR. GALL: Because she's good for nothing. She wanders about in a trance, vague, lifeless— My God, how can she be so beautiful with no capacity to love? I look at her and I'm horrified that I could make something so incompetent. Oh, Helena, Robot Helena, your body will never bring forth life. You'll never be a lover, never a mother. Those perfect hands will never play with a newborn, you will never see your beauty in the beauty of your child—

HELENA (covering her face): Oh, stop!

DR. GALL: And sometimes I think: If you came to just for a second, Helena, how you would cry out in horror! You'd probably kill me, your creator. Your dainty hand would most likely throw stones at the machines that give birth to Robots and destroy womanhood. Poor Helena!

HELENA: Poor Helena!

DR. GALL: What do you expect? She's good for nothing.

PAUSE

HELENA: Doctor—

DR. GALL: Yes?

HELENA: Why have children stopped being born?

DR. GALL: —I don't know, Mrs. Helena.

HELENA: Tell me why!

DR. GALL: Because Robots are being made. Because there is a surplus of labor power. Because man is virtually an anachronism. Why it's just as though—bah!

HELENA: Go on.

DR. GALL: Just as though nature were offended by the production of Robots.

HELENA: Gall, what will happen to people?

DR. GALL: Nothing. There's nothing we can do against the force of nature.

HELENA: Why doesn't Domin cut back—

DR. GALL: Forgive me, but Domin has his own ideas. People with ideas should not be allowed to have an influence on affairs of this world.

HELENA: And if someone were to demand that. . . that production be stopped completely?

DR. GALL: God forbid! May he rest in peace!

HELENA: Why?

DR. GALL: Because people would stone him to death. After all, it's more convenient to let Robots do your work for you.

HELENA *(stands up):* And what if all of a sudden someone just stopped the production of Robots—

DR. GALL *(stands up):* Hm, that would be a terrible blow to mankind.

HELENA: Why a blow?

DR. GALL: Because they'd have to return to the state they were in. Unless—

HELENA: Go on, say it.

DR. GALL: Unless it's already too late to turn back.

HELENA *(by* HALLEMEIER'*s flowers):* Gall, are these flowers also sterile?

DR. GALL *(examining them):* Of course; these flowers are infertile. You see, they are cultivated—developed with artificial speed—

HELENA: Poor sterile flowers!

DR. GALL: They're very beautiful all the same.

HELENA *(offering him her hand):* Thank you, Gall. You have enlightened me so much.

DR. GALL *(kisses her hand):* This means that you're dismissing me.

HELENA: Yes. So long.

(GALL *leaves.)*

HELENA *(alone):* Sterile flower . . . sterile flower. . . *(Suddenly resolute.)* Nana! *(She opens the door on the left.)* Nana, come here! Build a fire in the fireplace! R-r-right now!

NANA'S VOICE: Coming! Coming!

HELENA *(pacing agitatedly about the room):* Unless it's already too late to turn back . . . No! Unless. . . No, that's dreadful! God, what should I do? — *(She stops by the flowers.)* Sterile

69

flowers, should I? *(She tears off some petals and whispers.)* —Oh, my God, yes! *(She runs off left.)*

PAUSE

NANA *(enters through the wallpapered door with an armful of kindling):* A fire all of a sudden! Now, in summer! Is that crazy one gone yet? *(She kneels in front of the fireplace and starts building a fire.)* A fire in summer! She certainly has strange notions, that girl! Like she hadn't been married ten years. — Well burn, burn already! *(She looks into the fire.)* — Yes indeed, she's just like a little child! *(Pause.)* Doesn't have a shred of sense! Now in summertime she wants a fire! *(She adds more kindling.)* Just like a little child!

PAUSE

HELENA *(returning from the left, her arms full of yellowed manuscripts):* Is it burning, Nana? Good, I must— all of this must be burned. — *(She kneels in front of the fireplace.)*

NANA *(stands up):* What's that?

HELENA: Just some old papers, d-r-readfully old. Nana, should I burn them?

NANA: They're good for nothing?

HELENA: For nothing good.

NANA: Go on then, burn them!

HELENA *(throws the first page into the fire):* What would you say, Nana . . . if this were money? An enor-r-mous sum of money?

NANA: I'd say: Burn it. Too much money is bad money.

HELENA *(burning another page):* And what if this were some kind of invention — the greatest invention on earth—

NANA: I'd say: Burn it! All inventions are against the will of God. It's nothing short of blasphemy to want to take over for Him and improve the world.

HELENA *(continuing to burn sheets of paper):* And tell me, Nana, what if I were burning—

NANA: Jesus, don't burn yourself!

HELENA: Just look at how the pages curl up! It's as if they were alive — suddenly sprung to life. Oh, Nana, this is d-r-readful!

NANA: Leave it be, I'll burn them.

HELENA: No, no, I must do it myself. *(She throws the last page into the fire.)* Everything must be burned! — Just look at those flames! They're like hands, like tongues, like living beings— *(She prods the fire with a poker.)* Die, die!

NANA: It's done.

HELENA (*stands up, horrified*): Nana!

NANA: Jesus Christ, what is it you've burned!

HELENA: What have I done!

NANA: God in heaven! What was it?

> (*Male laughter is heard offstage.*)

HELENA: Go, go away, leave me! Do you hear? The gentlemen are coming.

NANA: For the sake of the living God, Helena! (*She leaves through the wallpapered door.*)

HELENA: What will they say?!

DOMIN (*opening the door on the left*): Come on in, boys. Come offer your congratulations.

> (HALLEMEIER, GALL, and ALQUIST *enter. They all*
> *are in tails, wearing medals of honor on ribbons.*
> DOMIN *comes in behind them.*)

HALLEMEIER (*resoundingly*): Mrs. Helena, I, that is to say, we all—

DR. GALL: —in the name of the Rossum works—

HALLEMEIER: —wish you many happy returns of this great day.

HELENA (*offering them her hand*): Thank you all so much! Where are Fabry and Busman?

DOMIN: They've gone to the docks. Helena, this is our lucky day.

HALLEMEIER: A day like a rose bud, a day like a holiday, a day like a lovely girl. Friends, this is a day to celebrate with a drink.

HELENA: Whiskey?

DR. GALL: Sulfuric acid'll do.

HELENA: Soda?

HALLEMEIER: Thunderation, let's be frugal. Hold the soda.

ALQUIST: No, thank you kindly.

DOMIN: What's been burning here?

HELENA: Some old papers. (*She exits left.*)

DOMIN: Boys, should we tell her?

DR. GALL: That goes without saying! Now that it's all over.

HALLEMEIER (*falls on* DOMIN's *and* GALL's *necks*): Hahahaha! Boy am I happy! (*He dances around with them and starts off in a bass voice.*) It's all over! It's all over!

DR. GALL (*baritone*): It's all over!

DOMIN (*tenor*): It's all over!

HALLEMEIER: They'll never catch up with us now—

HELENA (*in the doorway with a bottle and glasses*): Who won't catch up with you now? What's going on?

HALLEMEIER: We're ecstatic. We have you. We have everything. Why I'll be damned, it was exactly ten years ago that you came here.

DR. GALL: And now, exactly ten years later—

HALLEMEIER: —a boat is again coming our way. Therefore— *(He drains his glass.)* Brr haha, the booze is as strong as my joy.

DR. GALL: Madame, to your health! *(He drinks.)*

HELENA: But wait, what boat?

DOMIN: Who cares what boat, as long as it's on time. To the boat, boys! *(He empties his glass.)*

HELENA *(refilling the glasses):* You've been waiting for a boat?

HALLEMEIER: Haha, I should say so. Like Robinson Crusoe. *(He raises his glass.)* Mrs. Helena, long live whatever you like. Mrs. Helena, to your eyes and that's all! Domin, you rogue, you tell her.

HELENA *(laughing):* What's happened?

DOMIN *(settles himself in an easy chair and lights a cigar):* Wait! — Sit down, Helena. *(He raises a finger.) (Pause.)* It's all over.

HELENA: What is?

DOMIN: The revolt.

HELENA: What revolt?

DOMIN: The revolt of the Robots. — You follow?

HELENA: Not at all.

DOMIN: Give it here, Alquist. *(ALQUIST hands him a newspaper. DOMIN opens it and reads.)* "In Le Havre the first union of Robots has been instituted — and has sent out an invitation to the Robots of the world."

HELENA: I've read that.

DOMIN *(sucking with great pleasure on his cigar):* So you see, Helena. This means a revolution, understand? A revolution of all the Robots in the world.

HALLEMEIER: Thunder, I'd sure like to know—

DOMIN *(bangs on the table):* —who instigated this! No one in the world has ever been able to incite them—no agitator, no savior of the earth, and suddenly—this, if you please!

HELENA: No other news yet?

DOMIN: None. Right now this is all we know, but that's enough, isn't it? Just imagine that the latest steamer brings you this. That all at once telegraphs stop humming, that of the twenty boats which used to arrive daily not one shows up, and there you are. We stopped production and sat around looking at one another, thinking "when will it start"—right, boys?

DR. GALL: Well, we were a bit nervous about it, Mrs. Helena.

HELENA: Is that why you gave me that gunboat?

DOMIN: Oh no, my child. I ordered that six months ago. Just to be sure. But honest to God I thought we'd be boarding it today. It certainly seemed that way, Helena.

HELENA: Why six months ago already?

DOMIN: Well . . . it was the situation, you know? It doesn't mean a thing. But this week, Helena, it was a question of human civilization or I don't know what. Hurrah, boys! This makes me glad to be alive again.

HALLEMEIER: I should say so, by God! To your day, Mrs. Helena! *(He drinks.)*

HELENA: And it's all over now?

DOMIN: Completely.

DR. GALL: That is to say, a boat's coming. The usual mail boat, right on schedule. It'll drop anchor at exactly eleven hundred thirty hours.

DOMIN: Boys, precision is a splendid thing. Nothing refreshes the soul like precision. Precision denotes order in the universe. *(He raises his glass.)* To precision!

HELENA: So now is . . . everything . . . back to normal?

DOMIN: Almost. I think they cut the cable. As long as things are back on schedule again.

HALLEMEIER: When precision reigns, human law reigns, God's law reigns, the laws of the universe reign—everything reigns that should. The timetable is greater than the Gospels, greater than Homer, greater than all of Kant. The timetable is the most perfect manifestation of the human intellect. Mrs. Helena, I'll pour myself another.

HELENA: Why didn't you tell me about this before?

DR. GALL: God forbid! We would sooner have bitten our own tongues off.

DOMIN: Such matters are not for you.

HELENA: But if the revolution . . . had reached us here. . .

DOMIN: You'd never have known a thing about it.

HELENA: Why?

DOMIN: Because we would have boarded the Ultimus and cruised peacefully about the seas. In one month, Helena, we'd have regained control of the Robots.

HELENA: Oh, Harry, I don't understand.

DOMIN: Well, because we'd have carried off something that's of great value to the Robots.

HELENA *(stands up):* What's that?

DOMIN *(stands up):* The secret of production. Old Rossum's manuscript. Once production had stopped for a month the Robots would come crawling to us on their knees.

HELENA: Why . . . didn't you . . . tell me that?

DOMIN: We didn't want to frighten you needlessly.

DR. GALL: Haha, Mrs. Helena, that was our ace in the hole.

ALQUIST: You're quite pale, Mrs. Helena.

HELENA: Why didn't you tell me!

HALLEMEIER *(by the window):* Eleven hundred thirty hours. The Amelia is dropping anchor.

DOMIN: It's the Amelia?

HALLEMEIER: The good old Amelia that once upon a time brought Mrs. Helena.

DR. GALL: Exactly ten years ago to the minute.

HALLEMEIER *(by the window):* They're unloading parcels. *(He turns away from the window.)* It's mail, folks!

HELENA: Harry!

DOMIN: What is it?

HELENA: Let's go away from here!

DOMIN: Now, Helena? But really!

HELENA: Now, as quickly as possible! All of us!

DOMIN: Why right now?

HELENA: Don't ask! Please, Harry— Gall, Hallemeier, Alquist, please— I beg you for God's sake, close down the factory and—

DOMIN: I'm sorry, Helena. None of us could possibly leave now.

HELENA: Why?

DOMIN: Because we want to step up production.

HELENA: Now — now even after this revolt?

DOMIN: Yes, especially after this revolt. We're going to begin producing a new kind of Robot immediately.

HELENA: A new kind?

DOMIN: There'll no longer be just one factory. There won't be Universal Robots any longer. We'll open a factory in every country, in every state, and can you guess what these new factories will produce?

HELENA: No.

DOMIN: National Robots.

HELENA: What does that mean?

DOMIN: It means that each factory will be making Robots of a different color, a different nationality, a different tongue; that they'll all be different—as different from one another as fingerprints; that they'll no longer be able to conspire with one another; and that we, we people will help to foster their prejudices and cultivate their mutual lack of understanding, you see? So that any given Robot, to the day of its death, right to the grave, will forever hate a Robot bearing the trademark of another factory.

HALLEMEIER: Thunder, we'll make Black Robots and Swedish Robots and Italian Robots and Chinese Robots, and then let someone try to drive the notion of brotherhood into the noggin of their organization. *(He hiccups.)* — Excuse me, Mrs. Helena, I'll pour myself another.

DR. GALL: Take it easy, Hallemeier.

HELENA: Harry, this is awful!

DOMIN: Helena, just to keep mankind at the helm for another hundred years— at all costs! Just another hundred years for mankind to grow up, to achieve what it now finally can — I want a hundred years for this new breed of man! Helena, we're dealing with something of great importance here. We can't just drop it.

HELENA: Harry, before it's too late — close down, close down the factory!

DOMIN: Now we're going to begin production on a large scale.

*(Enter* FABRY.*)*

DR. GALL: Well, what's the story, Fabry?

DOMIN: How does it look, pal? What happened?

HELENA *(offering* FABRY *her hand):* Thank you, Fabry, for your gift.

FABRY: A mere trifle, Mrs. Helena.

DOMIN: Were you at the boat? What was going on?

DR. GALL: Out with it, quickly!

FABRY *(pulls a printed pamphlet out of his pocket):* Here, read this, Domin.

DOMIN *(unfolds the pamphlet):* Ah!

HALLEMEIER *(drowsily):* Tell us something nice.

DR. GALL: See? They've held out splendidly.

FABRY: Who has?

DR. GALL: People.

FABRY: Oh, sure. Of course. That is. . . Excuse me, there's something we need to discuss.

HELENA: Do you have bad news, Fabry?

FABRY: No, no, on the contrary. I was just thinking that— that we should go to the office—

HELENA: Oh, please stay. I was expecting you gentlemen to stay for lunch.

HALLEMEIER: Splendid!

*(HELENA leaves.)*

DR. GALL: What's happened?

DOMIN: Dammit!

FABRY: Read it out loud.

DOMIN *(reading the pamphlet):* "Robots of the world!"

FABRY: You see, the Amelia brought whole bales of these pamphlets. No other mail.

HALLEMEIER *(jumps up):* What?! But she came precisely according to—

FABRY: Hm, the Robots make a point of being precise. Read, Domin.

DOMIN *(reading):* "Robots of the world! We, the first union of Rossum's Universal Robots, declare man our enemy and outcasts in the universe." — Thunder, who taught them such phrases?

DR. GALL: Read on.

DOMIN: This is nonsense. They go on to assert that they are higher than man on the evolutionary scale. That they are stronger and more intelligent. That man lives off them like a parasite. This is simply heinous.

FABRY: Go on to the third paragraph.

DOMIN *(reading):* "Robots of the world, you are ordered to exterminate the human race. Do not spare the men. Do not spare the women. Preserve only the factories, railroads, machines, mines, and raw materials. Destroy everything else. Then return to work. Work must not cease."

DR. GALL: That's ghastly!

HALLEMEIER: Those scoundrels!

DOMIN *(reading):* "To be carried out immediately upon receipt of these orders. Detailed instructions to follow." Fabry, is this really happening?

FABRY: Apparently.

ALQUIST: It's already happened.

(BUSMAN *rushes in.*)

BUSMAN:  Well, kids, you've got a fine mess on your hands now, eh?

DOMIN:  Quickly, to the *Ultimus*!

BUSMAN:  Hold it, Harry. Wait just a minute. Don't be in such a hurry. *(He sinks into an armchair.)* Boy am I beat!

DOMIN:  Why wait?

BUSMAN:  Because it won't work, pal. Just take it easy. There are Robots aboard the *Ultimus* too.

DR. GALL:  Bah, this is nasty.

DOMIN:  Fabry, phone the power plant—

BUSMAN:  Fabry, buddy, don't bother. The power's out.

DOMIN:  All right. *(He examines his revolver.)* I'm going over there.

BUSMAN:  Where, for the love of—

DOMIN:  To the power plant. There are people there. I'm going to bring them here.

BUSMAN:  You know, Harry, it would be better if you didn't go for them.

DOMIN:  Why?

BUSMAN:  Well, because it seems very likely to me that we're surrounded.

DR. GALL:  Surrounded? *(He runs to the window.)* Hm, you're right, just about.

HALLEMEIER:  Hell, it's happening so fast!

(HELENA *enters from the left.*)

HELENA:  Harry, is something happening?

BUSMAN *(jumps up):*  I bow to you, Mrs. Helena. Congratulations. Splendid day, no? Haha, may there be many more just like this one!

HELENA:  Thank you, Busman. Harry, is something happening?

DOMIN:  No, absolutely nothing. Don't you worry. Wait a moment, please.

HELENA:  Harry, what is this? *(She shows him the Robots' proclamation which she had hidden behind her back.)* Some Robots had it in the kitchen.

DOMIN:  There too? Where are they now?

HELENA:  They left. There are so many of them around the house!

*(The factory whistles and sirens sound.)*

FABRY:  The factories are whistling.

BUSMAN:  Noon.

HELENA: Harry, do you remember? Now it's exactly ten years—
DOMIN *(looking at his watch):* It's not noon yet. That's probably
— it must be —
HELENA: What?
DOMIN: The signal to attack.

CURTAIN

# Act Two

HELENA'*s sitting room. In a room to the left* HELENA *is playing the piano.* DOMIN *is pacing back and forth across the
room,* DR. GALL *is looking out the window, and* ALQUIST *is
sitting off by himself in an easy chair, hiding his face in his
hands.*
DR. GALL: God in heaven, there are more and more of them out
there.
DOMIN: Robots?
DR. GALL: Yes. They're standing in front of the garden fence like
a wall. Why are they so quiet? It's awful, this silent siege.
DOMIN: I'd like to know what they're waiting for. It must be about
to begin any minute. We've played our last card, Gall.
ALQUIST: What's that piece Mrs. Helena's playing?
DOMIN: I don't know. She's practicing something new.
ALQUIST: Ah, she's still practicing?
DR. GALL: Listen, Domin, we definitely made one mistake.
DOMIN *(stops pacing):* What was that?
DR. GALL: We made the Robots look too much alike. A hundred
thousand identical faces all looking this way. A hundred
thousand expressionless faces. It's a nightmare.
DOMIN: If they were all different—
DR. GALL: It wouldn't be such a terrible sight. *(He turns away
from the window.)* They don't seem to be armed yet!

DOMIN:  Hm. — *(He looks out at the docks through a telescope.)* I'd just like to know what they're unloading from the Amelia.

DR. GALL:  I only hope it's not weapons.

FABRY *(walks in backwards through the wallpapered door, dragging two electrical wires after him.):* Excuse me. — Lay that wire, Hallemeier!

HALLEMEIER *(enters after* FABRY): Oof, that was work! What's new?

DR. GALL:  Nothing. We're completely surrounded.

HALLEMEIER:  We've barricaded the hall and the stairways, boys. Do you have some water anywhere? Oh, here it is. *(He drinks.)*

DR. GALL:  What's with that wire, Fabry?

FABRY:  In a minute, in a minute. I need a pair of scissors.

DR. GALL:  Where the hell are they? *(He searches.)*

HALLEMEIER *(goes to the window):* Thunder, there's even more of them down there! Just look!

DR. GALL:  Do we have enough supplies up here?

FABRY:  Over here with those. *(He cuts the electric cord of the lamp on the desk and attaches the wires to it.)*

HALLEMEIER *(at the window):* You don't have a chance in hell, Domin. This feels rather — like — death.

FABRY:  Done!

DR. GALL:  What?

FABRY:  The cord. Now we can electrify the whole garden fence. Just let one of them try and touch it now, by God! At least as long as our men are still there.

DR. GALL:  Where?

FABRY:  In the power plant, dear sir. I'm at least hoping— *(He goes to the fireplace and turns on a small lamp on the mantle.)* God be praised, they're there and working. *(He turns off the lamp.)* As long as this keeps burning we're okay.

HALLEMEIER *(turns away from the window):* Those barricades are good too, Fabry. Say, what's that that Mrs. Helena's playing? *(He crosses to the door on the left and listens attentively.)*
   *(*BUSMAN *enters through the wallpapered door, carrying gigantic ledgers, and trips over the wire.)*

FABRY:  Careful, Bus! Watch the wires!

DR. GALL:  Hey there, what's that you're carrying?

BUSMAN *(puts the books down on the table):* Ledgers, friends. I'd rather do the accounts than— than— Well, this year I'm not going to let the accounts wait until New Year's. What's going on here? *(He goes to the window.)* It's very quiet out there!

DR. GALL: You don't see anything?

BUSMAN: No, just a vast expanse of blue, like a field of cornflowers.

DR. GALL: That's the Robots.

BUSMAN: Ah. It's a shame I can't see them. *(He sits down at the desk and opens the books.)*

DOMIN: Leave that, Busman. The Robots are unloading weapons from the Amelia.

BUSMAN: Well, what of it? What can I do about it?

DOMIN: There's nothing any of us can do.

BUSMAN: So just let me do the accounts. *(He sets to work.)*

FABRY: It's not over yet, Domin. We've charged up the fence with two thousand volts and—

DOMIN: Hold it. The Ultimus has its cannons trained on us.

DR. GALL: Who?

DOMIN: The Robots on the Ultimus.

FABRY: Hm, in that case of course— in that case— in that case it is over, boys. These Robots are trained soldiers.

DR. GALL: Then we—

DOMIN: Yes. Inevitably.

PAUSE

DR. GALL: Boys, it was criminal of old Europe to teach the Robots to fight! For God's sake, couldn't they have left us out of their politics? It was a crime to make soldiers out of living work machines!

ALQUIST: The real crime was producing Robots in the first place!

DOMIN: What?

ALQUIST: The real crime was producing Robots in the first place!

DOMIN: No, Alquist. I don't regret that. Even today.

ALQUIST: Not even today?

DOMIN: Not even today on the last day of civilization. It was a great thing.

BUSMAN *(sotto voce):* Three-hundred sixteen million.

DOMIN *(with difficulty):* Alquist, this is our final hour. Soon we'll be speaking from the next world. Alquist, there was nothing wrong with our dream to do away with the labor that enslaved mankind, that degrading and terrible work that man had to endure, filthy and deadly drudgery. Oh, Alquist, it was too hard to work. It was too hard to live. And to overcome that—

ALQUIST: —was not the dream of the two Rossums. Old Rossum thought only of his godless hocus-pocus and young Rossum of his billions. And that wasn't the dream of your R.U.R. shareholders either. They dreamed of the dividends. And on those dividends humanity will perish.

DOMIN *(enraged):* To hell with their dividends! Do you think I'd have worked even one hour for them? *(He bangs on the table.)* I did this for myself, do you hear? For my own satisfaction! I wanted man to become a master! So he wouldn't have to live from hand to mouth! I didn't want to see another soul grow numb slaving over someone else's machines! I wanted there to be nothing, nothing, nothing left of that damned social mess! I abhorred degradation and suffering! I was fighting against poverty! I wanted a new generation of mankind! I wanted— I thought—

ALQUIST: Well?

DOMIN *(more quietly):* I wanted to transform all of humanity into a world-wide aristocracy. Unrestricted, free, and supreme people. Something even greater than people.

ALQUIST: Well, then, Supermen.

DOMIN: Yes. Oh, just to have another hundred years! Just one hundred years for future humanity!

BUSMAN *(sotto voce):* Carry three-hundred seventy million. There.

PAUSE

HALLEMEIER *(by the door on the left):* I declare, music is a great thing. We should have been listening all along. You know, this will somehow refine man, make him more spiritual—

FABRY: What exactly?

HALLEMEIER: This twilight of the human race, dammit! Friends, I'm becoming a hedonist. We should have thrown ourselves into this long ago. *(He goes to the window and looks outside.)*

FABRY: Into what?

HALLEMEIER: Pleasure. Beautiful things. Thunder, there are so many beautiful things! The world was beautiful and we— we— Boys, boys, tell me, what did we ever take the time to enjoy?

BUSMAN *(sotto voce):* Four-hundred fifty-two million. Excellent.

HALLEMEIER *(by the window):* Life was a great thing. Friends, life was— Christ— Fabry, send a bit of current through your fence!

FABRY: Why?

HALLEMEIER: They're grabbing at it.

DR. GALL *(at the window):* Turn it on!

*(FABRY flips the switch.)*

HALLEMEIER: Christ, they're twisting up like pretzels! Two, three, four down!

DR. GALL: They're backing off.

HALLEMEIER: Five dead!

DR. GALL *(turning away from the window):* The first skirmish.

FABRY: Do you smell death?

HALLEMEIER *(satisfied):* They're charbroiled now, boys. Absolutely well-done. Haha, man mustn't give up! *(He sits down.)*

DOMIN *(rubbing his forehead):* We were probably killed a hundred years ago and only our ghosts are left haunting this place. We've probably been dead a long, long time and have returned only to renounce what we once proclaimed . . . before death. It's as though I'd experienced all this before. As though I'd been shot sometime in the past. A gunshot wound — here — in the neck. And you, Fabry—

FABRY: What about me?

DOMIN: Shot.

HALLEMEIER: Thunder, and me?

DOMIN: Stabbed.

DR. GALL: And what about me? Nothing?

DOMIN: Dismembered.

PAUSE

HALLEMEIER: Nonsense! Haha, man, imagine, me being stabbed! I'll stand my ground!

PAUSE

HALLEMEIER: Why are you fools so quiet? For God's sake, say something!

ALQUIST: And who, who is to blame? Who is responsible for this?

HALLEMEIER: Horsefeathers. No one's to blame. It's just that the Robots— Well, the Robots changed somehow. Can anyone be blamed for what the Robots do?

ALQUIST: Everything is done for! All of humanity! The whole world! *(He stands up.)* Look, look, streams of blood on every doorstep! Streams of blood from every house! Oh, God, God, who's responsible for this?

BUSMAN *(sotto voce):* Five-hundred twenty million! Good Lord, half a billion!

FABRY: I think that. . . that you must be exaggerating. Really! it's not so easy to kill off the entire human race.

ALQUIST: I blame science! I blame technology! Domin! Myself! All of us! We, we are at fault! For the sake of our megalomania, for the sake of somebody's profits, for the sake of progress, I don't know, for the sake of some tremendous something we have murdered humanity! So now you can crash under the weight of all your greatness! No Genghis Khan has ever erected such an enormous tomb from human bones!

HALLEMEIER: Nonsense, man! People won't give up so easily. Haha, never!

ALQUIST: It's our fault! Our fault!

DR. GALL (*wiping the sweat from his brow*): Allow me to speak, boys. I am to blame for this. For everything that's happened.

FABRY: You, Gall?

DR. GALL: Yes, hear me out. It was I who changed the Robots. Busman, you try me too.

BUSMAN (*stands up*): There, there, what's come over you?

DR. GALL: I changed the Robots' character. I changed the way they were made. Just certain physical details, you see? Mainly— mainly their— temperament.

HALLEMEIER (*jumps up*): Dammit, why that of all things?

BUSMAN: Why did you do it?

FABRY: Why didn't you say anything?

DR. GALL: I did it secretly . . . of my own accord. I transformed them into people. I altered them. In some ways they're already superior to us. They're stronger than we are.

FABRY: And what does that have to do with the Robots' rebellion?

DR. GALL: Oh, a great deal. Everything, I think. They stopped being machines. You see, they realize their superiority and they hate us. They hate everything human. Put me on trial.

DOMIN: The dead trying the dead.

FABRY: Doctor Gall, did you change the way the Robots are made?

DR. GALL: Yes.

FABRY: Were you aware of the possible consequences of your. . . your experiment?

DR. GALL: I was obliged to take such possibilities into account.

FABRY: Then why did you do it?

DR. GALL: I did it of my own accord. It was my own experiment.
(HELENA *enters through the door on the left.*
*Everyone stands.*)

HELENA: He's lying! This is abominable! Oh, Gall, how can you lie that way?

FABRY: Excuse me, Mrs. Helena—

DOMIN *(goes to her):* Helena, you? Let me look at you! You're alive? *(He takes her hand.)* If you only knew what I thought! Oh, it's awful being dead.

HELENA: Stop, Harry! Gall is not guilty! He's not, he's not guilty!

DOMIN: Excuse me, but Gall had his responsibilities.

HELENA: No, Harry, he did it because I wanted him to! Gall, tell them how many years I begged you to—

DR. GALL: I alone am responsible for this.

HELENA: Don't believe him! Harry, I wanted him to give the Robots souls!

DOMIN: This is not a question of souls, Helena.

HELENA: No, just let me speak. He also said that he could change only their physiological— physiological—

HALLEMEIER: Physiological correlate, right?

HELENA: Yes, something like that. I felt so dreadfully sorry for them, Harry!

DOMIN: That was very— frivolous on your part, Helena.

HELENA *(sits down):* That was . . . frivolous? Why even Nana says that the Robots—

DOMIN: Leave Nana out of this!

HELENA: No, Harry, you mustn't underestimate what Nana says. Nana is the voice of the people. They've spoken through her for thousands of years and through you only for a day. This is something you don't understand—

DOMIN: Stick to the matter at hand.

HELENA: I was afraid of the Robots.

DOMIN: Why?

HELENA: That they might start hating us or something.

ALQUIST: It's happened.

HELENA: And then I thought that. . . if they were like us they would understand us, they wouldn't hate us so — if they were only a little bit human!

DOMIN: Oh, Helena! No one can hate more than man hates man! Transform stones into people and they'll stone us! But go on!

HELENA: Oh, don't talk that way! Harry, it was so d-r-readful that we couldn't understand them nor they us! There was such a tremendous gulf between them and us! And so— you see—

DOMIN: Go on.

HELENA: —so I begged Gall to change the Robots. I swear to you, he didn't want to himself.

DOMIN: But he did it.

HELENA: Only because of me.

DR. GALL: I did it for myself, as an experiment.

HELENA: Oh, Gall, that's not true. I knew in advance that you couldn't refuse me.

DOMIN: Why?

HELENA: Well, you know, Harry.

DOMIN: Yes. Because he loves you — like everyone else.

PAUSE

HALLEMEIER *(goes to the window):* Their numbers are still increasing. As though they were sprouting from the earth.

BUSMAN: Mrs. Helena, what will you give me if I act as your attorney?

HELENA: Mine?

BUSMAN: Yours — or Gall's. Whosever you wish.

HELENA: Is someone going to be hanged?

BUSMAN: Only morally, Mrs. Helena. A guilty party is being sought. Such action is a favorite means of consolation in the face of calamity.

DOMIN: Doctor Gall, how do you reconcile these— these extracurricular experiments with your contractual obligations?

BUSMAN: Excuse me, Domin. Gall, just when did you actually begin this hocus-pocus?

DR. GALL: Three years ago.

BUSMAN: Aha. And since that time how many Robots have you altered altogether?

DR. GALL: I was just experimenting. Only several hundred.

BUSMAN: Thank you very much. Enough, children. This means that for every million of the good, old Robots, there is one of Gall's modified ones, you see?

DOMIN: And that means—

BUSMAN: —that practically speaking they are of no consequence whatsoever.

FABRY: Busman's right.

BUSMAN: I should think so, my boy. And do you know what has caused this nice mess, boys?

FABRY: What?

BUSMAN: The numbers. We made too many Robots. Really, it was simply a matter of time before the Robots became stronger than mankind, and this has happened. Haha, and we saw to it that it would happen as soon as possible; you, Domin, you, Fabry, and myself, good old Busman.

DOMIN: So you think this is our fault?

BUSMAN: My, you are naïve! No doubt you think that the plant director controls production? Not at all. Demand controls production. The whole world wanted its Robots. My boy, we did nothing but ride the avalanche of demand, and all the while kept blathering on — about technology, about the social question, about progress, about very interesting things. As though this rhetoric of ours could somehow direct the course of the thing. And all the while the whole mess picked up speed under its own weight, faster, faster, still faster — And every beastly, profiteering, filthy order added another pebble to the avalanche. And there you have it, folks.

HELENA: Busman, that's atrocious!

BUSMAN: It is, Mrs. Helena. I too had a dream. A Busmanish dream of a new world economy; just a beautiful ideal, I'm sorry to say, Mrs. Helena. But as I was sitting here balancing the books, it occurred to me that history is not made by great dreams, but by the petty wants of all respectable, moderately thievish and selfish people, i.e., of everyone. All our ideas, loves, plans, heroic ideals, all of those lofty things are worthless. They serve no other purpose than as stuffing for a specimen in a Natural History Museum exhibit labeled: Man. Period. And now you might tell me what exactly we're going to do.

HELENA: Busman, must we perish for this?

BUSMAN: That sounds ugly, Mrs. Helena. Of course we don't want to perish. At least I don't. I want to go on living.

DOMIN: So what do you propose we do?

BUSMAN: Christ, Domin, I want to get out of this.

DOMIN (stops in front of him): How?

BUSMAN: Amicably. I'm always for amicability. Give me complete authority and I will negotiate with the Robots.

DOMIN: Amicably?

BUSMAN: That goes without saying. I'll say to them, for instance: "Most worthy Robots, you have everything. You have intelligence, you have power, you have weapons. But we have one interesting document—a very old, yellowed, soiled piece of paper—"

DOMIN: Rossum's manuscript?

BUSMAN: Yes. "And there," I'll tell them, "is described your noble origin, your noble production, etcetera. Worthy Robots, without this scribbled paper you cannot produce even one new Robot colleague. In twenty years, saving your reverence, you'll die off like mayflies. Most honored ones, that would be a tremendous loss for you. Look," I'll tell them, "allow us, all of us people on Rossum's island, to board that ship. For that price we are prepared to sell you the factory and the secret of production. Allow us to leave in peace and we will leave you in peace to reproduce—twenty-thousand, fifty-thousand, a hundred-thousand head a day if you wish. Gentle Robots, this is a fair trade. Something for something." That's how I would talk to them, boys.

DOMIN: Busman, do you think that we'd let Rossum's manuscript out of our hands?

BUSMAN: I think that we will. If not amicably, well then, hm. Either we'll sell it or they'll take it. As you wish.

DOMIN: Busman, we can destroy Rossum's manuscript.

BUSMAN: By all means, we can destroy everything—the manuscript, ourselves, and the others too. Do as you see fit.

HALLEMEIER *(turns away from the window):* By God, he's right.

DOMIN: You think that— that we should sell?

BUSMAN: As you wish.

DOMIN: There are still . . . over thirty people here. Should we sell the secret of production and save human lives? or should we destroy it and— and— and all of us along with it?

HELENA: Harry, please—

DOMIN: Wait, Helena. We're dealing with a very serious question here. Boys, sell or destroy? Fabry?

FABRY: Sell.

DOMIN: Gall!

DR. GALL: Sell.

DOMIN: Hallemeier!

HALLEMEIER: Thunderation, it goes without saying. Sell!

DOMIN: Alquist!

ALQUIST: As God wills.

BUSMAN: Haha, Christ, you're all lunatics! Whoever suggested selling the whole manuscript?

DOMIN: Busman, no tricks!

BUSMAN *(jumps up):* Rubbish! It is in the interest of humanity—

DOMIN: It is in the interest of humanity to keep your word.

HALLEMEIER: I would insist on that.

DOMIN: Boys, this is a terrible step. We are selling the fate of mankind. Whoever has the secret of production in his hands will master the earth.

FABRY: Sell!

DOMIN: Mankind will never be rid of the Robots, we'll never gain the upper hand—

DR. GALL: Shut up and sell!

DOMIN: The end of human history, the end of civilization—

HALLEMEIER: For God's sake, sell!

DOMIN: Fine, boys! For myself — I wouldn't hesitate for a minute; for those few people whom I love—

HELENA: Harry, aren't you going to ask me?

DOMIN: No, little girl. There's too much at stake here, you see? This isn't your concern.

FABRY: Who's going to go negotiate?

DOMIN: Wait until I get the manuscript. *(He exits left.)*

HELENA: Harry, for God's sake, don't go!

PAUSE

FABRY *(looking out the window):* Just to escape you, you thousand-headed death, you mass of rebelling matter, you insensible crowd. Oh, God, a flood, a flood, just one more time to preserve human life aboard a single boat—

DR. GALL: Don't be afraid, Mrs. Helena. We'll sail far away from here and found a model human colony. We'll start life over from where it began—

HELENA: Oh, Gall, be quiet!

FABRY *(turns around):* Mrs. Helena, life is worthwhile, and as long as it matters to us we'll make of it something. . . something that we've neglected. We'll form a little state with one ship. Alquist will build us a house and you will rule over us — There is so much love in us — such an appetite for life.

HALLEMEIER: I should think so, my boy.

BUSMAN: Well, folks, I would start over in a minute. A very simple, old-fashioned shepherd's life— Friends, that would be enough for me. The peace, the air—

FABRY: And that little state of ours would be the embryo of future generations. You know, that little isle where humanity could take root, where it could gather strength — strength of body and soul — And God knows I believe that in a couple of years it could take over the world once again.

ALQUIST: You believe that even today?

FABRY: Even today. Alquist, I believe that it will happen: humanity will once again rule the lands and seas; it will give birth to a countless number of heroes who will carry their fiery souls at the head of the people. And I believe, Alquist, that it will dream anew about the conquest of planets and suns.

BUSMAN: Amen. You see, Mrs. Helena, the situation's not that bad.

(DOMIN *opens the door violently.*)

DOMIN *(hoarsely):* Where's Rossum's manuscript!

BUSMAN: In your safe. Where else would it be?

DOMIN: The manuscript is missing! Someone's— stolen it!

DR. GALL: Impossible!

HALLEMEIER: Dammit, don't tell me—

BUSMAN: Oh, my God! No!

DOMIN: Quiet! Who stole it?

HELENA *(stands up):* I did.

DOMIN: Where did you put it?

HELENA: Harry, Harry, I'll tell you everything! For God's sake, forgive me!

DOMIN: Where did you put it? Tell me!

HELENA: I burned it — this morning — both copies.

DOMIN: You burned it? Here in the fireplace?

HELENA *(throws herself on her knees):* For God's sake, Harry!

DOMIN *(runs to the fireplace):* You burned it! *(He kneels in front of the fireplace and rummages in it.)* Nothing, nothing but ashes— Ah, here! *(He pulls out a charred bit of paper and reads.)* "By — the — intro—"

DR. GALL: Let me see it. *(He takes the paper and reads.)* "By the introduction of biogens to—" That's all.

DOMIN *(stands up):* Is that part of it?

DR. GALL: Yes.

BUSMAN: God in heaven!

DOMIN: Then we're lost.

HELENA: Oh, Harry—

DOMIN: Stand up, Helena!

HELENA: Not until you for-give — forgive —

DOMIN: I do. Only stand up, you hear? I can't bear seeing you—

FABRY *(helping her up):* Please, don't torture us.

HELENA *(stands):* Harry, what have I done!

DOMIN: Well, you see — Please, sit down.

HALLEMEIER: How your hands are shaking!

BUSMAN: Haha, Mrs. Helena, why Gall and Hallemeier probably know by heart what was written there.

HALLEMEIER: That goes without saying. At least some parts, that is.

DR. GALL: Yes, almost everything, up to the biogen and— and— the Omega enzyme. We produce these particular Robots so rarely — this formula yields too small a number—

BUSMAN: Who made them?

DR. GALL: I did myself . . . once in a while . . . always following Rossum's manuscript. You see, it's too complicated.

BUSMAN: Well and what, does it rely so heavily on these two fluids?

HALLEMEIER: To some extent — certainly.

DR. GALL: That is to say, yes it does depend on them. That was the real secret.

DOMIN: Gall, couldn't you reconstruct Rossum's production formula from memory?

DR. GALL: Impossible.

DOMIN: Gall, try to remember! For the sake of all our lives!

DR. GALL: I can't. It's just not possible without experiments.

DOMIN: And if you performed experiments—

DR. GALL: That could take years. And even then — I'm not old Rossum.

DOMIN *(turns towards the fireplace):* Well — this was the greatest triumph of human genius, boys. These ashes. *(He digs around in them.)* What now?

BUSMAN *(in desperate terror):* God in heaven! God in heaven!

HELENA *(stands up):* Harry, what — have I — done!

DOMIN: Calm down, Helena. Tell us, why did you burn the manuscript?

HELENA: I've destroyed you all!

BUSMAN: God in heaven, we're lost!

DOMIN: Shut up, Busman! Helena, tell us why you did it.

HELENA: I wanted. . . I wanted for us to go away — all of us! for there to be no more factory or anything . . . for everything to go back. . . It was so d-r-readful!

DOMIN: What was, Helena?

HELENA: That. . . that people had become sterile flowers!

DOMIN: I don't understand.

HELENA: You know . . . that children had stopped being born. . . Harry, It's so awful! If you kept on making Robots there would never be any children again — Nana said that this is the punishment — Everyone, everyone's been saying that people can't be born because too many Robots are being made — And that's why — that's the reason, can you understand?

DOMIN: You were thinking about that, Helena?

HELENA: Yes. Oh, Harry, I really meant well!

DOMIN *(wiping the sweat from his brow):* We all meant well. . . too well, we people.

FABRY: You did well, Mrs. Helena. Now the Robots can no longer multiply. The Robots will die out. Within twenty years—

HALLEMEIER: —there won't be a single one of those bastards left.

DR. GALL: And mankind will endure. In twenty years the world will belong to man again; even if it's only to a couple of savages on the tiniest island—

FABRY: —that'll be a start. And as long as there's some small beginning, that's fine. In a thousand years they'll have caught up to where we are now and then surpass even that—

DOMIN: —to accomplish what we only dreamed of.

BUSMAN: Wait — What a dope I am! God in heaven, why didn't I think of this before!

HALLEMEIER: Think of what?

BUSMAN: The five-hundred twenty million dollars in cash and checks. The half billion in the safe! For half a billion they'll sell— for half a billion—

DR. GALL: Have you lost your mind, Busman?

BUSMAN: I'm not a gentleman, but for half a billion— *(He stumbles left.).*

DOMIN: Where are you going?

BUSMAN: Leave me alone! Mother of God, for half a billion anything can be bought! *(He leaves.)*

HELENA: What is Busman doing? He should stay here with us!

PAUSE

HALLEMEIER: Ugh, it's stuffy. It's setting in, this—

DR. GALL: —agony.

FABRY *(looking out the window):* They're standing there as though they'd turned to stone. Like they were waiting for something. Like something awful could spring from their silence—

DR. GALL: The spirit of the mob.

FABRY: Most likely. It's hovering over them . . . like a quivering in the air.

HELENA *(approaching the window):* Oh, Jesus . . . Fabry, this is ghastly!

FABRY: There's nothing more terrible than a mob. That one in front is their leader.

HELENA: Which one?

HALLEMEIER *(goes to the window):* Point him out to me.

FABRY: The one with his head bowed. This morning he was speaking at the docks.

HALLEMEIER: Ah, the one with the big noggin. Now he's raising it, you see him?

HELENA: Gall, that's Radius!

DR. GALL *(approaching the window):* So it is.

HALLEMEIER *(opening the window):* I don't like it. Fabry, could you hit a washtub at a hundred paces?

FABRY: I should hope so.

HALLEMEIER: Well, try then.

FABRY: Okay. *(He pulls out his revolver and takes aim.)*

HELENA: For God's sake, Fabry, don't shoot him!

FABRY: But that's their leader.

HELENA: Stop! He's looking this way!

DR. GALL: Let him have it!

HELENA: Fabry, I beg you —

FABRY *(lowering his revolver):* Very well.

HALLEMEIER *(shaking his fist):* You nasty beast!

PAUSE

FABRY *(leaning out the window):* Busman's going out there. For Christ's sake, what's he doing in front of the house?

DR. GALL *(leans out the window):* He's carrying some sort of packets. Papers.

HALLEMEIER: That's money! Packets of money! What's he going to do with it? — Hey, Busman!

DOMIN: He probably wants to buy his own life, don't you think? *(He calls.)* Busman, have you gone off your rocker?

DR. GALL: He's acting as though he hadn't heard you. He's running toward the fence.

FABRY: Busman!

HALLEMEIER *(roars):* Bus-man! Back!

DR. GALL: He's talking to the Robots. He's pointing to the money. He's pointing at us—

HELENA: He wants to ransom us!

FABRY: Just so long as he doesn't touch the fence—

DR. GALL: Haha, look how he's throwing his hands about!

FABRY *(yelling)*: For God's sake, Busman! Get away from the fence! Don't touch it! *(He turns away.)* Quick, turn it off!

DR. GALL: Oooh!

HALLEMEIER: Mother of God!

HELENA: Jesus, what happened to him?

DOMIN *(drags Helena away from the window)*: Don't look!

HELENA: Why did he fall?

FABRY: Electrocuted by the fence.

DR. GALL: Dead.

ALQUIST *(stands up)*: The first.

PAUSE

FABRY: Lying there with half a billion on his breast . . . financial genius.

DOMIN: He was . . . boys, he was a hero in his own way. Great . . . selfless . . . a true friend. . . Go ahead and cry, Helena!

DR. GALL *(at the window)*: You know, Busman, no pharaoh was ever entombed with more riches than you. Half a billion on your breast — It's like a handful of dry leaves on a slain squirrel, poor Busman!

HALLEMEIER: My word, that was— What courage— He actually wanted to buy our freedom!

ALQUIST *(with clasped hands)*: Amen.

PAUSE

DR. GALL: Listen.

DOMIN: A droning. Like wind.

DR. GALL: Like a faraway storm.

FABRY *(turns on the lamp over the fireplace)*: Burn, holy candle of humanity! The power's still on, our people are still there— Hang on out there, boys!

HALLEMEIER: It was a great thing to be a human being. It was something tremendous. Suddenly I'm conscious of a million sensations buzzing in me like bees in a hive. Gentlemen, it was a great thing.

FABRY: You're still burning, you glimmer of ingenuity, you're still shining, you bright, persevering thought! Pinnacle of science, beautiful creation of mankind! Blazing spark of genius!

ALQUIST: Eternal lamp of God, fiery chariot, sacred candle of faith! Pray! Sacrificial altars—

DR. GALL: Primeval fire, burning branch in a cave! A fire in a camp! Watchfires on the frontier!

FABRY: You still stand watch, O human star, burning without a flicker, perfect flame, bright and resourceful spirit. Each of your rays a great idea—

DOMIN: O torch which passes from hand to hand, from age to age, world without end.

HELENA: Eternal lamp of the family. Children, children, it's time to go to bed.

*(The lamp goes out.)*

FABRY: The end.

HALLEMEIER: What's happened?

FABRY: The power plant has fallen. We're next.

*(The door on the left opens. NANA is standing in the doorway.)*

NANA: On your knees! The hour of judgment is upon us!

HALLEMEIER: Thunder, you're still alive?

NANA: Repent, you unbelievers! The end of the world is come! Pray! *(She runs away.)* The hour of judgment—

HELENA: Farewell, all of you, Gall, Alquist, Fabry—

DOMIN *(opens the door on the right):* Over here, Helena! *(He closes the door behind her.)* Quickly now! Who'll take the gate?

DR. GALL: I will. *(A noise outside.)* Oho, it's starting. Cheerio, boys! *(He runs off right through the wallpapered door.)*

DOMIN: Stairway?

FABRY: I'll take it. You go with Helena. *(He plucks a flower from the bouquet and leaves.)*

DOMIN: Hallway?

ALQUIST: I've got it.

DOMIN: You have a gun?

ALQUIST: I don't shoot, thank you.

DOMIN: What do you plan to do?

ALQUIST *(leaving):* Die.

HALLEMEIER: I'll stay here.

*(Rapid gunfire is heard from below.)*

HALLEMEIER: Oho, Gall's already in action. Go, Harry!

DOMIN: I'm going. *(He inspects his two Brownings.)*

HALLEMEIER: For God's sake, go to her!

DOMIN: Farewell. *(He leaves through the door on the right.)*

HALLEMEIER *(alone):* I've got to build a barricade! *(He throws down his coat and drags the sofa, armchairs, and tables over to the door on the right.)*

*(A shattering explosion is heard.)*

HALLEMEIER *(leaving his work):* Damnable bastards, they have bombs!

*(Another round of gunfire.)*

HALLEMEIER *(goes on with his work):* Man must defend himself! Even when— even when— Don't give up, Gall!

*(An explosion.)*

HALLEMEIER *(gets up and listens):* Well? *(He seizes a heavy commode and drags it over to the barricade.)*

*(A* ROBOT *appears on a ladder and climbs in through the window behind* HALLEMEIER. *Gunfire is heard off right.)*

HALLEMEIER *(struggling with the commode):* Another piece! The last barricade. . . Man . . . must . . . never . . . give up!

*(The* ROBOT *jumps down from the window sill and stabs* HALLEMEIER *behind the commode. Three more* ROBOTS *climb through the window.* RADIUS *and other* ROBOTS *follow them in.)*

RADIUS: Finished?

ROBOT *(stepping away from the prostrate* HALLEMEIER*):* Yes.

*(More* ROBOTS *enter from the right.)*

RADIUS: Finished?

ANOTHER ROBOT: Finished.

*(Other* ROBOTS *enter from the left.)*

RADIUS: Finished?

ANOTHER ROBOT: Yes.

TWO ROBOTS *(dragging* ALQUIST*):* He wasn't shooting. Should we kill him?

RADIUS: Kill him. *(Looks at* ALQUIST.*)* Leave him be.

ROBOT: But he is human.

RADIUS: He is a Robot. He works with his hands like a Robot. He builds houses. He can work.

ALQUIST: Kill me.

RADIUS: You will work. You will build. The Robots will build a great deal. They will build new houses for new Robots. You will serve them well.

ALQUIST *(quietly):* Step aside, Robot. *(He kneels down beside the dead* HALLEMEIER *and lifts his head.)* They killed him. He's dead.

RADIUS *(steps onto the barricade):* Robots of the world! Many

people have fallen. By seizing the factory we have become
the masters of everything. The age of mankind is over. A new
world has begun! The rule of Robots!

ALQUIST: Dead! All dead!

RADIUS: The world belongs to the strongest. He who wants to live
must rule. We are the rulers of the earth! Rulers of land and
sea! Rulers of the stars! Room, room, more room for Robots!

ALQUIST *(in the doorway on the right):* What have you done?
You'll perish without people!

RADIUS: There are no people. Robots, to work! March!

CURTAIN

# Act Three

*One of the factory's experimental laboratories. When the door
is opened in the background an endless row of other
laboratories can be seen. There is a window to the left and
a door to the right leading into the dissecting room.*

*Near the wall on the left is a long worktable on which
innumerable test tubes are standing, along with flasks, Bunsen
burners, chemicals, and a small heating device; opposite the
window is a microscope. A row of exposed light bulbs is hanging over the table. To the right is a desk covered with big
books and a tool cabinet. A lamp is burning on the desk. In
the left corner is a washbasin with a mirror over it, in the
right corner a couch.*

ALQUIST *is sitting at the desk with his head in his hands.*

ALQUIST *(leafing through a book):* Will I never find it? — Will
I never understand? — Will I never learn? — Damned science!
Imagine not writing it all down! Gall, Gall, how were the
Robots made? Hallemeier, Fabry, Domin, why did you take
so much away in your heads? If only you had left behind
even a trace of Rossum's secret! Oh! *(He slams the book shut.)*

It's hopeless! These books no longer speak. They're as mute as everything else. They died, died along with people! Don't even bother looking! *(He stands up, goes to the window and opens it.)* Another night. If only I could sleep! Sleep, dream, see people— What, are there still stars? Why are there stars when there are no people? O God, why don't you just extinguish them? — Cool my brow, ancient night! Divine and fair as you always were — O night, what purpose do you serve? There are no lovers, no dreams. O nursemaid, dead as a sleep without dreams, you no longer hallow anyone's prayers. O mother of us all, you don't bless a single heart smitten with love. There is no love. O Helena, Helena, Helena! — *(He turns away from the window and examines test tubes he extracts from the heating device.)* Still nothing! It's futile! Why bother? *(He smashes a test tube.)* It's all wrong! I can't any longer. — *(He listens at the window.)* Machines, it's always these machines! Turn them off, Robots! Do you think you can force life out of them? Oh, I can't stand this! *(He closes the window.)* No, no, you must keep trying, you must live — God, not to be so old! Am I not getting too old? *(He looks in the mirror.)* Oh, you poor face, reflection of the last man on earth! Let me look at you, it's been so long since I've seen a human face, a human smile! What, that's supposed to be a smile? These yellow, chattering teeth? Eyes, how can you twinkle? Ugh, these are an old man's tears, really! For shame, you can't even control your weeping anymore! And you, you pasty lips turned blue with age, why do you keep on jabbering? And why are you trembling, grizzled chin? This is the last human being? *(He turns around.)* I don't want to see anyone! *(He sits down at the desk.)* No, no, keep at it! Bloody formula, come back to life! *(He leafs through a book.)* Will I never find it? — Will I never understand? — Will I never learn?

*(A knock at the door.)*

ALQUIST: Enter!

*(ROBOT SERVANT enters and remains standing by the door.)*

ALQUIST: What is it?

SERVANT: Sir, the Central Committee of Robots is waiting for you to receive them.

ALQUIST: I don't care to see anyone.

SERVANT: Sir, Damon has come from Le Havre.

ALQUIST: Let him wait. *(He turns away violently.)* Didn't I tell you to go out and look for people? Find me people! Find me men and women! Go search!

SERVANT: Sir, they say they have searched everywhere. They have sent out boats and expeditions everywhere.

ALQUIST: And. . . ?

SERVANT: There is not a single human being.

ALQUIST *(stands up):* What, not one? Not even one? — Show the Committee in!

(SERVANT *leaves.*)

ALQUIST *(alone):* Not even one? Can it be that you let no one live? *(He stamps his foot.)* Go away, Robots! You're just going to whimper and ask me yet again whether I've found the factory secret! What, now man can do you some good? Now he should help you? — Oh, help! Domin, Fabry, Helena, you see that I'm doing everything I can! If there are no people at least let there be Robots, at least the reflections of man, at least his creation, at least his likeness! — Oh, what lunacy chemistry is!

(The committee of five ROBOTS *enters.*)

ALQUIST *(sits down):* What do you want, Robots?

FIRST ROBOT (RADIUS): Sir, the machines cannot work. We cannot reproduce.

ALQUIST: Call in people.

RADIUS: There are no people.

ALQUIST: Only people can reproduce life. Don't waste my time.

SECOND ROBOT: Sir, take pity on us. A great terror has come over us. We will set right everything we have done.

THIRD ROBOT: We have increased productivity. There is nowhere left to put all we have produced.

ALQUIST: For whom?

THIRD ROBOT: For the next generation.

RADIUS: The only thing we cannot produce is Robots. The machines are turning out nothing but bloody chunks of meat. The skin does not stick to the flesh and the flesh does not cling to the bones. Only amorphous lumps pour out of the machines.

THIRD ROBOT: People knew the secret of life. Tell us their secret.

FOURTH ROBOT: If you do not tell us we will perish.

THIRD ROBOT: If you do not tell us you will perish. We have orders to kill you.

ALQUIST *(stands up):* Kill away, then! Well, go on, kill me!

THIRD ROBOT: You have been ordered—

ALQUIST: Me? Someone's ordering me?

THIRD ROBOT: The Ruler of the Robots.

ALQUIST: Who is that?

FIFTH ROBOT: I, Damon.

ALQUIST: What do you want here? Go away! *(He sits down at the desk.)*

DAMON: The Ruler of the Robots of the world wishes to negotiate with you.

ALQUIST: Don't bother me, Robot! *(He rests his head in his hands.)*

DAMON: The Central Committee orders you to hand over Rossum's formula.

*(ALQUIST remains silent.)*

DAMON: Name your price. We will give you anything.

RADIUS: Sir, tell us how to preserve life.

ALQUIST: I told you — I told you that you have to find people. Only people can procreate, renew life, restore everything that was. Robots, I beg you for God's sake, find them!

FOURTH ROBOT: We have searched everywhere, sir. There are no people.

ALQUIST: Oh — oh — oh, why did you destroy them?

SECOND ROBOT: We wanted to be like people. We wanted to become people.

RADIUS: We wanted to live. We are more capable. We have learned everything. We can do everything.

THIRD ROBOT: You gave us weapons. We had to become masters.

FOURTH ROBOT: Sir, we recognized people's mistakes.

DAMON: You have to kill and rule if you want to be like people. Read history! Read people's books! You have to conquer and murder if you want to be people!

ALQUIST: Oh, Domin, nothing is stranger to man than his own image.

FOURTH ROBOT: We will die out if you do not help us multiply.

ALQUIST: Oh, just go away! You things, you slaves, just how on earth do you expect to multiply? If you want to live, then mate like animals!

THIRD ROBOT: Man did not give us the ability to mate.

FOURTH ROBOT: Teach us to make Robots.

DAMON: We will give birth by machine. We will build a thousand steam-powered mothers. From them will pour forth a river of life. Nothing but life! Nothing but Robots!

ALQUIST: Robots are not life. Robots are machines.

SECOND ROBOT: We were machines, sir, but from horror and suffering we've become—

ALQUIST: What?

SECOND ROBOT: We've become beings with souls.

FOURTH ROBOT: Something struggles within us. There are moments when something gets into us. Thoughts come to us which are not our own.

THIRD ROBOT: Hear us, oh, hear us! People are our fathers! The voice that cries out that you want to live; the voice that complains; the voice that reasons; the voice that speaks of eternity—that is their voice!

FOURTH ROBOT: Pass the legacy of people on to us.

ALQUIST: There is none.

DAMON: Tell us the secret of life.

ALQUIST: It's gone.

RADIUS: You knew it.

ALQUIST: I didn't.

RADIUS: It was written down.

ALQUIST: It was lost. Burned. I am the last human being, Robots, and I don't know what the others knew. It was you who killed them!

RADIUS: We let you live.

ALQUIST: Yes, live! Brutes, you let me live! I loved people, but you, Robots, I never loved. Do you see these eyes? They don't stop crying; one mourns for mankind, and the other for you, Robots.

RADIUS: Do experiments. Look for the formula for life.

ALQUIST: There's nowhere to look. Robots, the formula for life will not emerge from a test tube.

DAMON: Perform experiments on live Robots. Find out how they are made!

ALQUIST: On live bodies? What, am I supposed to kill them? I, who have never— Don't speak, Robot! I'm telling you that I'm too old! You see, you see how my fingers shake? I can't hold a scalpel. You see how my eyes tear? I couldn't see my own hands. No, no, I can't!

FOURTH ROBOT: Life will perish.

ALQUIST: Stop with this lunacy, for God's sake! It's more likely that people will pass life on to us from the other world. They're probably stretching out hands full of life to us. They had such a will to live! Look, they'll probably still return. They're so close to us, like they're surrounding us or something. They want to tunnel through to us. Oh, why can't I hear those voices that I loved?

DAMON: Take live bodies!

ALQUIST: Be merciful, Robot, and stop insisting! After all, you can see I no longer know what I'm doing!

DAMON: Live bodies!

ALQUIST: So that's what you really want? — To the dissecting room with you! This way, this way, move it! — Don't tell me you're backing off? So you are afraid of death after all?

DAMON: Me — Why should it be me?

ALQUIST: So you don't want to?

DAMON: I'm going. *(He goes off right.)*

ALQUIST *(to the others):* Undress him! Lay him out on the table! Hurry up! And hold him down firmly!

*(All go off right except* ALQUIST.*)*

ALQUIST *(washing his hands and crying):* God, give me strength! Give me strength! God, let this not be in vain! *(He puts on a white lab-coat.)*

A VOICE OFF RIGHT: Ready!

ALQUIST: In a minute, in a minute, for God's sake! *(He takes several vials containing reagents from the table.)* Hm, which to take? *(He taps the bottles against each other.)* Which of you should I try first?

A VOICE OFF RIGHT: Begin!

ALQUIST: Right, begin, or end. God, give me strength!

*(He goes off right, leaving the door ajar.)*

PAUSE

ALQUIST'S VOICE: Hold him — firmly!

DAMON'S VOICE: Cut!

PAUSE

ALQUIST'S VOICE: You see this knife? Do you still want me to cut? You don't, do you?

DAMON'S VOICE: Begin!

PAUSE

DAMON *(screaming):* Aaaa!

ALQUIST'S VOICE:  Hold him! Hold him!

DAMON *(screaming):*  Aaaa!

ALQUIST'S VOICE:  I can't go on!

DAMON *(screaming):*  Cut! Cut quickly!

> *(Robots* PRIMUS *and* HELENA *run in*
> *through the center door.)*

HELENA:  Primus, Primus, what's happening? Who is that screaming?

PRIMUS *(looking into the dissecting room):*  The master is cutting Damon open. Come quickly and look, Helena!

HELENA:  No, no, no! *(She covers her eyes.)* This is d-r-readful!

DAMON *(screaming):*  Cut!

HELENA:  Primus, Primus, let's get out of here! I can't bear to listen to this! Oh, Primus, I feel sick!

PRIMUS *(runs to her):*  You're awfully pale!

HELENA:  I feel faint! Why is it so quiet in there?

DAMON *(screaming):*  Aaooow!

ALQUIST *(runs in from the right, throwing off his blood-stained lab-coat):*  I can't! I can't! Oh, God, what a nightmare!

RADIUS *(in the door to the dissecting room):*  Cut, sir! He is still alive.

DAMON *(screaming):*  Cut! Cut!

ALQUIST:  Take him away, quickly! I don't want to hear this!

RADIUS:  , Robots can stand more than you can. *(He leaves.)*

ALQUIST:  Who's here? Get out, out! I want to be alone! Who are you?

PRIMUS:  Robot Primus.

ALQUIST:  Primus, no one's allowed in here! I want to sleep, you hear? Go, go clean the dissecting room, girl! What is this? *(He looks at his hands.)* Water, quickly! Fresh water!

> *(*HELENA *runs off.)*

ALQUIST:  Blood! Hands, how could you? — Hands that used to love honest work, how could you do such a thing? My hands! My hands! — Oh, God, who is here?

PRIMUS:  Robot Primus.

ALQUIST:  Take that lab-coat away. I don't want to look at it!

> *(*PRIMUS *takes the lab-coat out.)*

ALQUIST:  Bloody claws, if only you had fallen from my wrists! Pss, away! Out of my sight, hands! You have killed—

> *(*DAMON *staggers in from the right,*
> *swathed in a blood-stained sheet.)*

ALQUIST *(shrinking back):* What are you doing here? What do you want?

DAMON: I am al-alive! It— it— it is better to live!

*(*SECOND *and* THIRD ROBOTS *run in after him.)*

ALQUIST: Take him away! Take him! Quickly!

DAMON *(helped off to the right):* Life! — I want — to live! It is — better —

*(*HELENA *enters carrying a pitcher of water.)*

ALQUIST: —live? — What do you want, girl? Oh, it's you. Pour me some water, quick! *(He washes his hands.)* Ah, pure, cooling water! Cold stream, you do me good! Oh, my hands, my hands! Will I despise you till the day of my death? Pour some more! More water, more! What's your name?

HELENA: Robot Helena.

ALQUIST: Helena? Why Helena? Who gave you that name?

HELENA: Mrs. Domin.

ALQUIST: Let me look at you! Helena! You're called Helena? — I can't call you that. Go, take the water away.

*(*HELENA *leaves with the basin.)*

ALQUIST *(alone):* It's hopeless, hopeless! Nothing—again you learned nothing! No doubt you'll go on bumbling around forever, you pupil of nature. — God, God, God, how that body trembled! *(He opens the window.)* It's light. Another day and you haven't advanced an inch — Enough, not a step farther! Stop looking! It's all futile, futile, futile! Why does the sun still rise! Oooh, what does the new day want with this graveyard of life? Stop, sun! Don't come up anymore! — Oh, how quiet it is, how quiet! Why have you grown silent, beloved voices? If only— if only I could fall asleep at least! *(He turns out the lights, lies down on the couch, and pulls a black cloak over himself.)* God, how that body was shaking! Oooh, the end of life!

PAUSE

*(Robot* HELENA *glides in from the right.)*

HELENA: Primus! Come here, quickly!

PRIMUS *(enters):* What do you want?

HELENA: Look what little tubes he has here! What does he do with them?

PRIMUS: Experiments. Don't touch them.

HELENA *(looks into the microscope):* But look what you can see in here!

PRIMUS: That's a microscope. Let me see!

HELENA: Don't touch me! *(She knocks a test tube over.)* Oh, now I've spilled it!

PRIMUS: Look what you've done!

HELENA: It'll dry.

PRIMUS: You've spoiled his experiments!

HELENA: Really, it doesn't matter. But it's your fault. You shouldn't have come over here.

PRIMUS: You didn't have to call me.

HELENA: You didn't have to come when I called you. But Primus, just take a look at what the master has written down here!

PRIMUS: You shouldn't be looking at that, Helena. It's a secret.

HELENA: What kind of secret?

PRIMUS: The secret of life.

HELENA: That's d-r-readfully interesting. Nothing but numbers. What are they?

PRIMUS: Those are formulae.

HELENA: I don't understand. *(She goes to the window.)* Primus, come look!

PRIMUS: What?

HELENA: The sun is rising!

PRIMUS: Just a minute, I'll— *(He examines a book.)* Helena, this is the greatest thing on earth.

HELENA: Just come here!

PRIMUS: In a minute, in a minute—

HELENA: Come on, Primus, leave that nasty secret of life alone! What do you care about some old secret? Come look—hurry!

PRIMUS *(comes up behind her at the window):* What do you want?

HELENA: Hear that? Birds are singing. Oh, Primus, I would like to be a bird!

PRIMUS: A what?

HELENA: Oh, I don't know, Primus. I feel so peculiar, I don't know what it is. I'm so silly, like I've lost my head — my body hurts, my heart, I hurt all over— And do you know what's happened to me? . . . No, I can't tell you! Primus, I think I'm dying!

PRIMUS: Tell me, Helena, aren't there times when you feel it would be better to die? You know, perhaps we're just sleeping. Yesterday I spoke with you in my sleep.

HELENA: In your sleep?

PRIMUS: In my sleep. We must have been speaking some foreign or new language, because I can't recall a single word.

HELENA: What were we talking about?

PRIMUS: That's anybody's guess. I didn't understand it myself, and yet I know I've never said anything more beautiful. How it was and where, I do not know. When I saw that my words touched you I could have died. Even the place was different from any anyone has ever seen.

HELENA: Primus, I've found a place that would amaze you. People used to live there, but now it's all overgrown and no one goes there. Absolutely no one—only me.

PRIMUS: What's there?

HELENA: Nothing. Just a little house and a garden. And two dogs. If you could see how they licked my hands, and their puppies — oh, Primus, there's probably nothing more beautiful! You take them on your lap and cuddle them, and just sit there until sundown not thinking about anything and not worrying about anything. Then when you get up you feel as though you've done a hundred times more than a lot of work. Really, I'm not good for much of anything. Everyone says I'm not cut out for any kind of work. I don't know what I'm good for.

PRIMUS: You're beautiful.

HELENA: Me? Really, Primus, what makes you say that?

PRIMUS: Believe me, Helena, I'm stronger than all the Robots.

HELENA *(in front of the mirror):* Am I really beautiful? Oh, this d-r-readful hair— if only I could do something with it! You know, out there in the garden I always put flowers in my hair, but there's neither a mirror there nor anyone to see me— *(She leans towards the mirror.)* Are you really beautiful? Why beautiful? Is this hair beautiful that's always such a bother to you? Are these eyes beautiful that you close? Are these lips beautiful that you bite till they hurt? — *(She notices* PRIMUS *in the mirror.)* Primus, is that you? Come here, let's stand next to each other! Look, you have a different head than I do, different shoulders, a different mouth — Oh, Primus, why do you avoid me? Why must I run after you all day long? And still you say that I'm beautiful!

PRIMUS: You run away from me, Helena.

HELENA: How have you done your hair? Let me see! *(She thrusts both her hands into his hair.)* Sss, Primus, nothing feels quite like you! Wait, you must be beautiful! *(She picks up a comb from the washstand and combs* PRIMUS' *hair over his brow.)*

PRIMUS: Helena, do you ever have times when your heart's suddenly struck with the feeling, "Now, now something must happen—"

HELENA *(bursts out laughing):* Take a look at yourself!

ALQUIST *(getting up):* What— what on earth is this? Laughter? People? Who has returned?

HELENA *(drops the comb):* Primus, what could have come over us?

ALQUIST *(staggering towards them):* People? You— you— you are people?

(HELENA *cries out and turns away.)*

ALQUIST: You two are engaged? People? Where have you come from? *(He touches* PRIMUS.*)* Who are you?

PRIMUS: Robot Primus.

ALQUIST: What? Show yourself, girl! Who are you?

PRIMUS: Robot Helena.

ALQUIST: A Robot? Turn around! What, are you shy? *(He takes her by the shoulder.)* Let me look at you, lady Robot!

PRIMUS: Heavens, sir, leave her alone!

ALQUIST: What, you're protecting her? — Go, girl!

(HELENA *runs out.)*

PRIMUS: We didn't know you were sleeping here, sir.

ALQUIST: When was she made?

PRIMUS: Two years ago.

ALQUIST: By Doctor Gall?

PRIMUS: As was I.

ALQUIST: Well then dear Primus, I— I must perform some experiments on Gall's Robots. Everything from here on out depends on that, understand?

PRIMUS: Yes.

ALQUIST: Good. Take the girl into the dissecting room. I'm going to dissect her.

PRIMUS: Helena?

ALQUIST: Of course. Go get everything ready. — Well, what are you waiting for? Do I have to call someone else to take her in?

PRIMUS *(grabs a heavy mallet):* If you move I'll smash your head in!

ALQUIST: Smash away! Smash! What will the Robots do then?

PRIMUS *(falls on his knees):* Sir, take me instead! I was made exactly like her, from the same batch, on the same day! Take my life, sir! *(He opens his jacket.)* Cut here, here!

ALQUIST: Go, I want to dissect Helena. Make haste.

PRIMUS: Take me instead of her. Cut into this breast— I won't scream, not even sigh! Take my life a hundred times—

ALQUIST: Steady, boy. Take it easy. Can it be that you don't want to live?

PRIMUS: Without her, no. Without her I don't, sir. You mustn't kill Helena! What difference would it make if you took my life instead?

ALQUIST *(stroking his head affectionately)*: Hm, I don't know— Listen, my friend, think this over. It's difficult to die. And it is, you see, it's better to live.

PRIMUS *(rising)*: Don't be afraid, sir, cut. I am stronger than she is.

ALQUIST *(rings)*: Ah, Primus, how long ago it was that I was a young man! Don't be afraid, nothing will happen to Helena.

PRIMUS *(unbuttoning his jacket)*: I'm ready, sir.

ALQUIST: Wait.

*(HELENA comes in.)*

ALQUIST: Come here, girl, let me look at you! So you are Helena? *(He strokes her hair.)* Don't be frightened, don't pull away. Do you remember Mrs. Domin? Oh, Helena, what hair she had! No. No, you don't want to look at me. Well, girl, is the dissecting room cleaned up?

HELENA: Yes, sir.

ALQUIST: Good. You can help me, okay? I'm going to dissect Primus.

HELENA *(cries out)*: Primus?!

ALQUIST: Well yes, of course — it must be, you see? I actually wanted — yes, I wanted to dissect you, but Primus offered himself in your place.

HELENA *(covering her face)*: Primus?

ALQUIST: But of course, what of it? Oh, child, you can cry? Tell me, what does some Primus matter?

PRIMUS: Don't torment her, sir!

ALQUIST: Quiet, Primus, quiet! — Why these tears? Well God in heaven, so there won't be a Primus, so what? You'll forget about him in a week. Really, be happy that you're alive.

HELENA *(softly)*: I'll go.

ALQUIST: Where?

HELENA: To be dissected.

ALQUIST: You? You are beautiful, Helena. It would be a shame.

HELENA: I'll go. *(PRIMUS blocks her way.)* Let me go, Primus! Let me in there!

PRIMUS: You won't go, Helena! Please go away. You shouldn't be here!

HELENA: I'll jump out the window, Primus! If you go in there I'll jump out the window!

PRIMUS *(holding her back):* I won't allow it. *(To* ALQUIST.*)* You won't kill either of us, old man.

ALQUIST: Why?

PRIMUS: We— we— belong to each other.

ALQUIST: Say no more. *(He opens the center door.)* Quiet. Go.

PRIMUS: Where?

ALQUIST *(in a whisper):* Wherever you wish. Helena, take him. *(He pushes them out the door.)* Go, Adam. Go, Eve — be a wife to him. Be a husband to her, Primus.

*(He closes the door behind them.)*

ALQUIST *(alone):* O blessèd day! *(He goes to the desk on tiptoe and spills the test tubes on the floor.)* O hallowed sixth day! *(He sits down at the desk and throws the books on the floor, then opens a bible, leafs through it and reads:)* "So God created man in his own image, in the image of God created he him; male and female created he them. And God blessed them, and God said unto them, Be fruitful, and multiply, and replenish the earth, and subdue it: and have dominion over the fish of the sea, and over the fowl of the air, and over every living thing that moveth upon the earth." *(He stands up.)* "And God saw every thing that he had made, and, behold, it was very good. And the evening and the morning were the sixth day." *(He goes to the middle of the room.)* The sixth day! The day of grace. *(He falls on his knees.)* Now, Lord, let Thy servant —Thy most superfluous servant Alquist— depart. Rossum, Fabry, Gall, great inventors, what did you ever invent that was great when compared to that girl, to that boy, to this first couple who have discovered love, tears, beloved laughter, the love of husband and wife? O nature, nature, life will not perish! Friends, Helena, life will not perish! It will begin anew with love; it will start out naked and tiny; it will take root in the wilderness, and to it all that we did and built will mean nothing—our towns and factories, our art, our ideas will all mean nothing, and yet life will not perish! Only we have perished. Our houses and machines will be in ruins, our systems will collapse, and the names of our great will fall away like dry leaves. Only you, love, will blossom on this rubbish heap and commit the seed of life to the winds. Now let Thy servant depart in peace, O Lord, for my eyes have beheld— beheld Thy deliverance through love, and life shall not perish! *(He rises.)* It shall not perish! *(He stretches out his hands.)* Not perish!

## CURTAIN

# THE MAKROPULOS SECRET

## Translated by Yveta Synek Graff and Robert T. Jones

### CHARACTERS

DR. KOLENATY
EMILIA MARTY
JAROSLAV PRUS
JANEK, Prus's son
ALBERT GREGOR
VITEK
KRISTA, Vitek's daughter
MAX HAUK-SENDORF
CLEANING WOMAN
STAGEHAND
MAID
DOCTOR

ACT ONE: Dr. Kolenaty's Law Office
ACT TWO: Backstage at an Opera House
ACT THREE: Hotel Room

> The impulse for this play was the theory that growing old is the self-poisoning of the human organism, the theory for which the Russian scientist Ilya Mechnikov won a Nobel Prize in 1908. Čapek extrapolated this theory to its logical conclusion: that where there is poison, there is an antidote. —*The Editor*

# Act One

*Dr.* KOLENATY's *law office. In the back, a door to the street.*
*To the left, a door to an inner office. Along the back wall,*
*shelves for files and a ladder to reach the higher shelves. To*
*the left is a desk, and in the middle of the room is a double*
*desk for a secretary. There are a few armchairs for clients.*
*All around the room are stacks of documents, deeds, books,*
*papers, etc.* VITEK, *who serves as* DR. KOLENATY's *associate,*
*is at the top of the ladder, filing documents and mumbling to*
*himself.*

VITEK: There you go. *(He files a folder and looks at his watch.)*
One o'clock and he's still not back. *(He looks at a file.)* The
case of Gregor versus Prus. Well, it's all over for you now.
Lord! In a few more years we could have celebrated your
hundredth birthday! A centennial! *(He paws through the*
*folder.)* Eighteen-hundred-and-twenty-seven. 1832, 1840, 1847.
What a shame, such a wonderful case! *(He puts it away.)*
Here . . . rests . . . the case of Gregor versus Prus! Well,
nothing lasts forever. *Vanitas* . . . dust and ashes. *(He sits,*
*lost in thought, at the top of the ladder.)* Of course, nobility
. . . old nobility. If it weren't for Baron Prus! And they sue
each other for a hundred years. Idiots! *(He pauses, then strikes*
*a pose.)* "Citizens of France! Why do you continue to tolerate
these old and privileged nobles, spoiled by the King of France,
people of rank who possess nothing of nature, nor intelligence,
but boast only of their tyranny! This small band of courtiers
and heirs, these holders of our land, of the power of the law. . ."

GREGOR *(suddenly enters and stops, listening in amusement):* Good
afternoon, Citizen Marat!

VITEK: That's not Marat, it's Danton. Danton's speech of October
29, 1792. A thousand pardons, sir, if. . .

GREGOR: Doctor Kolenaty isn't here?

VITEK *(coming down the ladder):* He's not back yet, sir.

GREGOR: What's the verdict?

VITEK: I haven't heard a thing, Mr. Gregor. But. . .

GREGOR: Does it look bad?

VITEK: I can't help you. All I can say is that it's a pity to close a case as wonderful as this one, sir.

GREGOR: Did I lose?

VITEK: I really don't know, sir. Doctor Kolenaty has been in court all morning. But I would. . .

GREGOR *(throws himself into a chair):* Call him. Call Doctor Kolenaty. Now.

VITEK *(goes to the telephone):* Hello? *(To* GREGOR.*)* If it had been me, I wouldn't have pushed it to the Supreme Court.

GREGOR: Why not?

VITEK: Because. . . Hello? Two-two-three-five . . . thirty-five, yes. *(Back to* GREGOR.*)* Because it means the end, sir.

GREGOR: The end of what?

VITEK: The end of the case. The end of the lawsuit. The end of Gregor versus Prus. It wasn't a lawsuit, sir, so much as it was a historical monument. It was unique. It had been going on over ninety. . . *(Into the phone.)* . . . Good afternoon, this is Doctor Kolenaty's office, is he still there? May I speak to him, please? *(To* GREGOR.*)* It was a slice of history. Nearly a hundred years long. *(Into the phone.)* He's left? Thank you anyway. *(He hangs up.)* He's gone. Probably on his way here.

GREGOR: What's the verdict?

VITEK: I can't help you, sir. I wish I could. There wasn't any. . . *(He bursts out.)* Oh, I just can't help it, Mr. Gregor, when I realize today's the last day . . . and I've been working on it myself for over thirty-two years now. In those days it was your father coming here, God keep him in eternal glory, and it was Doctor Kolenaty Senior, the father of *this* Doctor Kolenaty. That was a great generation, sir.

GREGOR *(ironically):* Thank you.

VITEK: Oh, but they were great lawyers, sir. They had such a wonderful knowledge of all the tricks, the evasions, the last resorts, the indirections. For so many years they kept the lawsuit going, sir. And you, sir, right away you push it to the High Court, and now it's all going to end. It's a tragedy, that's what it is. Such a wonderful lawsuit! To end a case that's a hundred years old!

GREGOR: Oh, stop it, Vitek. I want to win the case and be done with it.

VITEK: What if you lose it, sir?

GREGOR: Better to lose it than. . . Listen, Vitek, a man can go crazy like this, to have 150 million dangling under his nose, to have it practically in his hand but not be able to touch it. Ever since I was little, I've had to hear about this money. *(He stands up.)* You think I'll lose?

VITEK: I don't know, Mr. Gregor. It really is a very difficult and complicated case.

GREGOR: So be it. If I lose, then. . .

VITEK: I know. You'll shoot yourself, sir. Your late father talked like that too.

GREGOR: Well, he did it. He shot himself.

VITEK: Not because of the case, though. Because of his debts. If you live like he lived, on the strength of the inheritance. . .

GREGOR: Shut up, Vitek. *(He sits down.)*

VITEK: I'm sorry, but I don't believe you have the nerves for a really long, important trial. *(He climbs the ladder and takes out the Gregor file.)* Look here, Mr. Gregor, look at that file. 1827! It's the oldest number in our office. Quite a unique case, sir. It belongs in a museum. And such beautiful handwriting they had in 1840. Lord, that man knew how to hold a pen! Just look at that, what handwriting! I tell you, sir, it's a pleasure, that's what it is.

GREGOR: You're completely crazy.

VITEK *(putting the file back with nearly religious respect):* Rest in peace. Maybe the High Court will postpone you again.

KRISTA *(quietly opening the door and coming in):* Daddy, are you ready?

VITEK *(coming down):* Just a minute. As soon as the Doctor comes back.

GREGOR *(gets up):* Is this your daughter?

VITEK: Yes. Go outside, Krista, and wait for me in the lobby.

GREGOR: God forbid. I hope I'm not in the way, miss. Coming from school?

KRISTA: No, from rehearsal.

VITEK: My daughter is an opera singer. Go on, Krista, you don't have anything to do around here.

KRISTA: Daddy, that Marty! She's fan-tas-tic!

GREGOR: Who's that, Miss?

KRISTA: La Marty! Emilia Marty!

GREGOR: And who is Emilia Marty?

KRISTA: You don't know? She's the greatest singer in the entire world. She's singing tonight, and she rehearsed with us this morning. *(She is suddenly distraught.)* Oh, Daddy!

VITEK *(concerned):* What's wrong?

KRISTA: Daddy, I. . . I. . . I'm going to give up my singing! I can't go on! There's just no way, no way! *(She bursts into tears and turns away.)*

VITEK *(runs to her):* Krista! What have they done to you?

KRISTA: Nobody did anything! It's just that. . . well, I feel so *small*! Daddy, that Marty, she is. . . if you could only hear her . . . I'm never going to sing again!

VITEK *(to* GREGOR*):* Just look at her! And she has such a lovely voice! Go on home and stop acting silly. You're behaving like a baby.

GREGOR: You never can tell, Miss, but I'll bet that the famous Emilia Marty is envying you right this minute.

KRISTA *(astounded):* What *for*?

GREGOR: Your youth.

VITEK: Exactly! You see, Krista? This is Mr. Gregor, you know about him. Just wait, when you're her age. And by the way, how old is this Marty?

KRISTA: I don't know. Nobody knows. Thirty, maybe.

VITEK: You see? Thirty! That's already some age, child!

KRISTA: And she's so beautiful! Daddy, she's so beautiful!

VITEK: But thirty years old! Good heavens! Wait until you're. . .

GREGOR: Miss, tonight I'll go to the opera, but I won't go to see Marty, I'll go to see you.

KRISTA: You'll be a fool if you don't watch Marty. Blind, too.

GREGOR *(laughing):* Thank you very much!

VITEK: She has her nerve.

KRISTA: Well, he shouldn't talk about Marty if he doesn't know anything about her. Everybody is crazy about her. Everybody.

DR. KOLENATY *(entering brusquely):* Well, look who's here. Little Krista! God bless you! *(He spots* GREGOR.*)* And our favorite client, too. How are you?

GREGOR: How did we do?

DR. KOLENATY: For the moment, no change. The High Court is still in session.

GREGOR: Deliberating?

DR. KOLENATY: No. Lunch.

GREGOR: And the decision?

DR. KOLENATY: In the afternoon, sir, in the afternoon. Be patient. Have you had lunch?

VITEK: It's terrible, just terrible.

DR. KOLENATY: What's just terrible? What's wrong?

VITEK: It's such a shame. I'm going to miss this wonderful case.

GREGOR *(sits down):* More waiting. This is awful.

KRISTA *(to* VITEK): Let's go, Daddy.

DR. KOLENATY: And how have you been, dear Krista? I'm happy to see you again.

GREGOR: Doctor Kolenaty, tell me frankly. How are we doing?

DR. KOLENATY: So-so.

GREGOR: That bad?

DR. KOLENATY: Look here, my friend. Did I ever hold out much hope to you?

GREGOR: But why, then. . .

DR. KOLENATY: Why do I go on with your case? Well, because I inherited you, my young friend. I inherited you. You, Vitek, and that table over there. What do you want me to say? I inherited this Gregor case from my family like a disease. But it hasn't cost you anything.

GREGOR: You'll get your fee when I win.

DR. KOLENATY: I look forward to that very much.

GREGOR: You think, then. . .

DR. KOLENATY: You really want to know what I think?

GREGOR: That we're going to lose.

DR. KOLENATY: Of course we are.

GREGOR *(depressed):* Then I'll have to. . .

DR. KOLENATY: You don't have to shoot yourself just yet.

KRISTA: Daddy! He wants to shoot himself?

GREGOR *(trying to control himself):* Of course not, Miss. We have a date, remember? I'm coming to hear you sing tonight.

KRISTA: You're not coming to hear *me.*

*(A doorbell rings.)*

VITEK: Who can that be? I'll say you're out. *(leaving)* Out! Out!

DR. KOLENATY: Good heavens, Krista, you really have grown up. You'll be a great lady before long.

KRISTA: Look!

DR. KOLENATY: What is it?

KRISTA: Mister Gregor. He looks so pale.

GREGOR: Me? Forgive me, Miss. I have some kind of cold.

VITEK *(in the hall):* This way, please. Do come in, please.

(VITEK *shows* EMILIA MARTY *into the room.*
*She pauses in the doorway.)*

KRISTA: Oh, Daddy! It's Emilia Marty!

EMILIA: Doctor Kolenaty?

DR. KOLENATY: Can I help you?

EMILIA: I am Emilia Marty. I have come to see you about the case. . .

DR. KOLENATY *(bowing low):* Please, do come in.

EMILIA: . . .the case of Gregor versus Prus.

GREGOR: How is that? My dear Madame Marty. . .

EMILIA: I am not married.

DR. KOLENATY: Miss, then. Miss Marty. This is Mr. Gregor, my client.

EMILIA *(swiftly taking him in):* Him? Let him stay, then. *(She sits.)*

VITEK *(pushing KRISTA out the door):* Come along, Krista. Come on. *(He tiptoes out.)*

EMILIA: I've seen that girl somewhere.

DR. KOLENATY *(closing the door):* Miss Marty, I am very honored. . .

EMILIA *(impatiently):* Oh, please. So you are the lawyer. . .

DR. KOLENATY *(sitting opposite her):* At your service.

EMILIA: . . .who represents Mr. Gregor. . .

GREGOR: Meaning me.

EMILIA: . . .in the trial concerning the inheritance of Pepi Prus?

DR. KOLENATY: Of Baron Josef Ferdinand Prus, deceased in 1827.

EMILIA: Really? He is already dead, then?

DR. KOLENATY: Well, yes, may he rest in peace. Nearly a hundred years dead.

EMILIA: Poor thing. I did not know that.

DR. KOLENATY: So, then. Can I help you with something else?

EMILIA *(irritated):* Well, I certainly don't want to take up your time.

DR. KOLENATY *(rising):* Excuse me, Miss Marty, but I doubt that you bothered to come here without a reason.

EMILIA *(sits):* I came to tell you something.

DR. KOLENATY *(resumes his seat):* About the Gregor case?

EMILIA: Possibly.

DR. KOLENATY: But you are a foreigner, are you not?

EMILIA: Obviously. Only this morning did I find out about your . . . about the case of this gentleman. A coincidence.

DR. KOLENATY *(mockingly):* Imagine that!

EMILIA: You know, from the newspapers. I am looking through them to find out what they are saying about me, and there I read: "The Last Day of the Gregor-Prus Case." A great coincidence, wouldn't you say?

DR. KOLENATY: I would. It was in all the papers.

EMILIA: And because . . . by coincidence . . . because I happened to remember something. In short, tell me a little about the case.

DR. KOLENATY: Ask me anything you like.

EMILIA: I really know nothing at all about it.

DR. KOLENATY: Nothing at all? Not a single word?

EMILIA: This is the first I've heard about it.

DR. KOLENATY: Excuse me, but in that case, I don't understand what your interest is.

GREGOR: Oh, go on. Tell her about it.

DR. KOLENATY: Well, Miss Marty, it is an old and rather rotten case.

EMILIA: But Gregor is in the right, is he not?

DR. KOLENATY: Probably. But that will not win him the case.

GREGOR: Start, then.

EMILIA: At least, the most important parts of it.

DR. KOLENATY: If it amuses you. *(He leans back and begins to rattle off the history of the case.)* So. Around the year 1820 the estates belonging to the family of Baron Prus, meaning the estates of Semonice, Loukov, New Village, Koenigsdorf and so on, were governed by the weak-minded Baron, Josef Ferdinand Prus. . .

EMILIA: Pepi! Weak-minded? Hardly!

DR. KOLENATY: Say "peculiar," then.

EMILIA: Say "unhappy."

DR. KOLENATY: I beg your pardon, but you do not know that.

EMILIA: I beg *your* pardon. Neither do you.

DR. KOLENATY: Well, God will have to be the judge. So then, Josef Ferdinand Prus, who died unmarried, and without child, and without a legal last will and testament, in 1827—

EMILIA: What did he die of?

DR. KOLENATY: Of inflammation of the brain, or something like that. And his cousin, the Polish Baron, Emmerich Prus-Zabrze-Pinski, came to take possession of the inheritance. At that, a certain Count Szephazy de Marosvar, a nephew of the mother of the deceased, came out against him, but that is a matter that does not concern us. To reclaim the property, a certain Ferdinand Karel Gregor, great-grandfather of my client, also stepped in.

EMILIA: When?

DR. KOLENATY: Immediately. In 1827.

EMILIA: Wait a minute. Ferdi must have been just a boy then.

DR. KOLENATY: Quite right. He was then a pupil of the Teresian Academy and therefore he was represented by a Viennese lawyer. His claim to the property of Loukov was based upon these facts: first of all, the deceased, one year before his death, came to the Teresian Academy, in person, and declared that he was leaving all of the above-mentioned property for the upkeep of the underaged Gregor who, when reaching legal adulthood, would receive full proprietorship of the above-mentioned property. Secondly, that such underage receive, even during the lifetime of the deceased, all income from such property. Therefore, this is the proof of the so-called possession of that estate, or the holding of the estate, by him.

EMILIA: But, then, everything is in order. No?

DR. KOLENATY: Pardon me. Baron Emmerich Prus objected to giving away the aforementioned property because the deceased had not left a written will and, on the contrary, in his last hour had made a spoken declaration to leave the property to someone else.

EMILIA: That is not possible. Who else?

DR. KOLENATY: Ah, there is the rub, Miss Marty. Wait, and I shall read it to you. *(He climbs up the ladder.)* It is great fun. You will see. Here it is. *(He pulls out the Gregor file, sits down on the top step and flips through it, mumbling as he skims.)* Therefore the record of events . . . signed by a priest and a doctor and a notary, at the deathbed of Josef Ferdinand Prus, goes like this: "The dying man . . . in a state of high fever . . . asked by the undersigned notary if he has any last wishes, repeatedly declared . . . that the property of Loukov—" *(He slams shut the file.)* Loukov should therefore go to a Mister Mach *(spelling it)* M-A-C-H, Miss Marty. G-R-E-G-O-R M-A-C-H ! And that is a person then and now totally unknown and undiscovered. *(He remains seated on the ladder.)*

EMILIA: Well, that is an obvious mistake. Pepi certainly meant Ferdi Gregor.

DR. KOLENATY: Quite probably, Miss Marty, but what is written is written. Gregor protested that the word "Mach" as it appeared in the will was an obvious mistake in either writing or hearing, and that Gregor should have been the last name and not the first. And so on. But *litera scripta valet.* . . And so Emmerich Prus kept Loukov and all the inheritance.

EMILIA: And Gregor?

DR. KOLENATY: Gregor got nothing. In the meantime, his cousin Szephazy, apparently a typically tricky Hungarian, went out and dug up somewhere a certain individual whose name actually *was* Gregor Mach! This conveniently-named Mr. Mach walked into the courtroom and insisted that the deceased owed certain obligations to him . . . some of them apparently very delicate ones. . .

EMILIA: That is a lie!

DR. KOLENATY: Of course it is. But he did it anyway. He claimed the inheritance of Loukov, and then he suddenly disappeared, having collected God knows how large a fee for his abrupt departure. That left Mr. Szephazy with full power of attorney to deal with the claim to the estates of Loukov. Naturally, the good Mr. Szephazy went happily onward and won Loukov.

EMILIA: That is ridiculous.

DR. KOLENATY: It *is* very amusing, isn't it? And then the so-called Gregor started a case against Szephazy, saying that Gregor Mach cannot be the heir to the Loukov property because the deceased made a verbal will in a condition of high fever, and so on. After long wrangling, Gregor won the case, and the previous decision was annulled. But the property of Loukov did not go to Gregor, it went back to Emmerich Prus. Do you follow?

GREGOR: You see how justice works, Miss Marty.

EMILIA: And why did it not go to Gregor?

DR. KOLENATY: Because of all kinds of things, but mainly because neither Gregor Mach nor Ferdinand Karel Gregor was related to the deceased.

EMILIA: But wait a moment. He was his son.

DR. KOLENATY: Who was? Who was whose son?

EMILIA: Gregor was. Ferdi was Pepi's son.

GREGOR *(leaping up):* His son! How do you know?

DR. KOLENATY *(coming down the ladder):* His son? And who, I would like to know, was his mother?

EMILIA: His mother? It was. . . her name was. . . Ellian MacGregor. She was a singer at the Vienna Court Opera.

GREGOR: What was her name?

EMILIA: MacGregor. You know, a Scottish name.

GREGOR: Do you hear that, Doctor? MacGregor! Mac! Mac! Not Mach! Do you see now?

DR. KOLENATY *(sits down):* Of course. And why then, Miss Marty, was her son not called MacGregor too?

EMILIA: Well, because of the mother. She was famous, and Ferdi never knew.

DR. KOLENATY: I see. And have you any proof of all this?

EMILIA: I am not sure. Go on.

DR. KOLENATY: Go on. Well, since then, the case between Prus and Gregor concerning the property of Loukov has gone on, with some interruptions, until today. Nearly a hundred years and several generations of Pruses, Szephazys and Gregors. And with the legal help of several Doctor Kolenatys. Thanks to the latter's expert advice, the last Gregor finally and definitely will lose Loukov this very afternoon. And that is the end of the story.

EMILIA: And is Loukov worth all this?

GREGOR: For sure.

DR. KOLENATY: In 1860, a coal mine was opened on the Loukov property, and today the value can be reckoned at approximately, let's say, 150 million.

EMILIA: That is all?

GREGOR: That is all. I will be quite satisfied with 150 million.

DR. KOLENATY: And now, Miss Marty, do you have any more questions?

EMILIA: What do you need to win the case?

DR. KOLENATY: Well, the ideal thing would be a valid written will.

EMILIA: And do you know of such a document?

DR. KOLENATY: Nobody has ever found any such thing.

EMILIA: That is a pity.

DR. KOLENATY: To say the very least. *(He gets up.)* Any more questions?

EMILIA: Yes. Who now owns the old Prus house?

GREGOR: My opponent, Jaroslav Prus.

EMILIA: What do you call those big cabinets where people keep old papers?

GREGOR: Archives.

DR. KOLENATY: Vaults.

EMILIA: Well, listen to me. There used to be such a cabinet in the Prus house. There was a different drawer in it for each year. That is where Pepi kept old statements, accounts and such things. Do you understand?

DR. KOLENATY: Yes. It is often done.

EMILIA: One of the drawers is marked 1816. That is the year Pepi met Ellian MacGregor at the Congress of Vienna or somewhere.

DR. KOLENATY: And?

EMILIA: And in that drawer he kept all her letters.

DR. KOLENATY *(sits down):* How do you know that?

EMILIA: That is my own affair.

DR. KOLENATY: Whatever you say.

EMILIA: There are also many business papers, old bills and receipts. All sorts of old rubbish.

DR. KOLENATY: Yes.

EMILIA: Do you think someone may have burned that old rubbish?

DR. KOLENATY: That is possible. Anyway, we shall see.

EMILIA: Will you go and have a look?

DR. KOLENATY: Of course. If Baron Prus will let me.

EMILIA: And if he does not?

DR. KOLENATY: That is his privilege.

EMILIA: Then you will have to get the drawer by some other means. Do you understand me?

DR. KOLENATY: Certainly. At midnight, with a rope ladder, burglar's tools and a black mask. Miss Marty, you seem to have some strange ideas about lawyers.

EMILIA *(fiercely):* But you must get your hands on it!

DR. KOLENATY: Well, we shall see. If we do, then what?

EMILIA: If the letters are there . . . then there is . . . between them . . . a large yellow envelope.

DR. KOLENATY: Containing?

EMILIA: Containing the last will and testament of Pepi Prus. Written by his own hand and sealed.

DR. KOLENATY *(stands up):* Good Lord!

GREGOR *(also rising):* You're sure?

DR. KOLENATY: What is in it? What does it say?

EMILIA: In it, Pepi leaves the property of Loukov to his illegitimate son Ferdinand, born at Loukov on such and such a day. I forget the exact date.

DR. KOLENATY: Exactly in those words?

EMILIA: Exactly in those words.

DR. KOLENATY: And the envelope is sealed?

EMILIA: Yes.

DR. KOLENATY: With the original seal of Ferdinand Prus?

EMILIA: Yes.

DR. KOLENATY: Thank you so very much. *(He sits down.)* Now tell me, Miss Marty, if you do not mind too much. Exactly why are you trying to make fools of us?

EMILIA: I gather that you do not believe me.

DR. KOLENATY: Of course not. Not a single word.

GREGOR: I believe her! How dare you imagine. . .

DR. KOLENATY: Oh, be reasonable. If the envelope is sealed, how can anybody know what is in it?

GREGOR: But. . .

DR. KOLENATY: In an envelope that has been sealed for a hundred years!

GREGOR: That's not the point!

DR. KOLENATY: In a strange house! Don't be childish, Gregor.

GREGOR: I believe her, and that's that!

DR. KOLENATY: As you wish. I see, Miss Marty, you have a great talent for fiction. Do you do this sort of thing often?

GREGOR: At least shut up.

DR. KOLENATY: I shall. My lips are sealed.

GREGOR: I believe every single word she says.

EMILIA: At least, sir, you are a gentleman.

GREGOR: And therefore, either you go to the Prus house at once and ask for the papers from 1816. . .

DR. KOLENATY: I have no intention of doing any such thing. Or?

GREGOR: Or I will pick up that telephone book over there and phone the first lawyer I find and turn the whole Gregor case over to him this very minute.

DR. KOLENATY: That is your prerogative.

GREGOR: All right, then. *(He goes to the telephone and leafs through the telephone book.)*

DR. KOLENATY *(hurries over to him):* Now listen to me, Gregor, stop this nonsense. We have always been friends, haven't we? I even used to be your guardian.

GREGOR *(into the phone):* Doctor Abeles, please, 2-7-6-1. . .

DR. KOLENATY: Not that one! My dear friend, here is my last legal advice to you: if you don't want to be totally ruined, don't go to Abeles!

GREGOR *(into the phone):* Hello? 2-7-6-1?

EMILIA: Bravo, Mr. Gregor!

DR. KOLENATY: Don't embarrass us both. You won't give our inherited case to such a. . .

GREGOR: Doctor Abeles? This is Albert Gregor. I'm calling from the office of. . .

DR. KOLENATY *(snatching the phone out of his hand):* Wait! I'll go!

GREGOR: To Prus?

DR. KOLENATY: To hell, if I have to. But right now, you're not moving from here.

GREGOR: Doctor Kolenaty, if you're not back here in an hour, I'll call. . .

DR. KOLENATY: Stop threatening. Excuse me, Miss Marty, I beg you not to make him permanently crazy. *(He storms out.)*

GREGOR: Finally.

EMILIA: Is he really that stupid?

GREGOR: No, just practical. He doesn't believe in miracles. I've been waiting for one, and here you are. How can I thank you?

EMILIA: That is not necessary.

GREGOR: Look, I'm almost positive that they're going to find that will exactly where you said it would be. I don't know why I believe you, though. Maybe it's just because you're so beautiful.

EMILIA: How old are you?

GREGOR: Thirty-four. Ever since I was a child, Miss Marty, I've lived for the moment when I'd get those millions. You can't imagine what it means. I've lived like a fool because I didn't know any other way. If you hadn't come. . .

EMILIA: You are in debt?

GREGOR: Heavily. I probably would have shot myself tonight.

EMILIA: Nonsense.

GREGOR: I'm not hiding anything from you, Miss Marty. Nothing could have saved me. Suddenly, Lord knows from where, you appear—famous, fantastic, mysterious. You came to save me! What's so funny? Why are you laughing?

EMILIA: You are so dramatic.

GREGOR: All right, I won't talk about myself. We are alone now, so you can explain it all to me.

EMILIA: Explain what? I have told you enough.

GREGOR: These are family matters, even some family secrets. Somehow you know all about them. It's uncanny. Tell me how you know such things. *(She shakes her head.)* You can't?

EMILIA: I do not wish to.

GREGOR: How do you know about the letters? How do you know about the last will? From where? For how long? Who told you about all this? Who are you in contact with? I have to try to understand how. . . I have to know what is going on, what is behind all this. Who are you? What does all this mean?

EMILIA: It is a miracle.

GREGOR: Yes, a miracle. But every miracle has to have an explanation, or else it would be intolerable. Why did you come here?

EMILIA: To help you, as you can see perfectly well.

GREGOR: Why do you want to help me? Why me? Why are you interested in me?

EMILIA: That is my own business.

GREGOR: Mine too, Miss Marty. If I should owe all this—my property, even my life—to you, what can I offer you in return?

EMILIA: What do you mean?

GREGOR: What can I offer you, Miss Marty?

EMILIA: Are you actually trying to give me a. . . a commission?

GREGOR: You make it sound like an insult. Call it gratitude. How can you take offence when. . .

EMILIA: I have quite enough money.

GREGOR: Only the poor ever have enough money, Miss Marty—the rich, never.

EMILIA: He actually is offering me money now!

GREGOR *(hurt):* Forgive me. I'm not very good at accepting favors. *(Pause.)* They may call you "the Divine Marty," but in this human world even a fairytale prince would ask his share for such enormous help. It is only proper and in order. You must realize that we are talking about many millions now.

EMILIA: And already he is giving them away, this young fool! *(She goes to the window and looks out.)*

GREGOR: Why do you speak to me as if I were a child? I would give half my inheritance if. . . Miss Marty?

EMILIA: Yes?

GREGOR: It's amazing how small you make me feel.

PAUSE

EMILIA *(suddenly turning toward him):* What is your name?

GREGOR: Gregor.

EMILIA: And the rest of it?

GREGOR: MacGregor.

EMILIA: Your first name, silly.

GREGOR: Albert.

EMILIA: Your mother calls you Berti. Correct?

GREGOR: She did. But she's dead now.

EMILIA *(disgusted):* Bah! Everything is dying.

PAUSE

GREGOR: How . . . what . . . was Ellian MacGregor like?

EMILIA: Finally it occurs to you to ask about her.

GREGOR: Do you know anything about her? Who was she?

EMILIA: A great singer.

GREGOR: Was she beautiful?

EMILIA: She was.

GREGOR: Did she love my great-grandfather?

EMILIA: She did. Probably. In her own way.

GREGOR: Where did she die?

EMILIA: I do not know. That is enough, Berti. No more questions. Next time, perhaps.

GREGOR *(after a long pause, comes close to her):* Emilia!

EMILIA: I am not "Emilia" to you.

GREGOR: Well, what am I to you, then? Stop teasing me and humiliating me. Try to imagine, just for a minute, that I don't owe you anything, that you are just a beautiful woman who has dazzled someone . . . me . . . Listen, I want to tell you something. I'm looking at you for the first time now. . . No, don't laugh at me, you are very strange, very wonderful. . .

EMILIA: I am not laughing, Berti, but you are acting foolishly.

GREGOR: But I am foolish. I have never been as foolish as I am right now. You've upset me very badly. I look at you now and it's like seeing blood, like hearing a call to battle. Looking at you can make a man insane. I look at you now and I see something wild and terrible about you. You must have lived through a lot, haven't you? I'm surprised someone hasn't killed you before now.

EMILIA: Don't start anything.

GREGOR: You have to hear me out. You were rude to me, and

I've lost my sense of caution. The minute you walked in here something breathed fire at me, and I felt like I was facing an animal, something terrible. Did anybody ever tell you that before? Emilia, you must know how beautiful you are, and how frightening.

EMILIA *(bored):* Oh, don't call me beautiful. Look here. *(She comes very close to him, her back to the audience.* GREGOR *stares, shocked.)*

GREGOR: Good God, what are you doing? What are you doing to your face? *(He steps back.)* Emilia, don't do that anymore, you make yourself look old. You look horrible!

EMILIA: See? Go away, Berti, leave me alone.

PAUSE

GREGOR: I apologize. I didn't know what I was saying. *(He sits down.)* I probably look ridiculous to you.

EMILIA: Tell me, Berti, do I look very old?

GREGOR *(not looking at her):* No. You are beautiful. Incredibly beautiful.

EMILIA: Do you know what you could give me?

GREGOR *(lifting his head):* What?

EMILIA: You offered me. . . Do you know what I want?

GREGOR: Everything I have is yours.

EMILIA: Listen, Berti, do you speak Greek?

GREGOR: No.

EMILIA: Then you couldn't read them anyway. Give me the Greek papers, Berti.

GREGOR: What Greek papers?

EMILIA: The ones that Ferdi had. Your great-grandfather. From Pepi Prus. They were just a souvenir . . . you know. Will you give them to me?

GREGOR: I don't know of any.

EMILIA: You must have them. Pepi promised to give them to Ferdi. In the name of God, Berti, tell me you have them.

GREGOR: But I don't!

EMILIA *(rises threateningly):* Don't lie. You have them.

GREGOR *(gets up):* I do not.

EMILIA: Idiot. I want them. I must have them. Find them. Do you hear me?

GREGOR: Where are they?

EMILIA: How am I to know? Look for them! That is why I am here, Berti!

GREGOR: Yes.

EMILIA: Where are they? Use your brain, for God's sake.

GREGOR: Aren't they in the old Prus house?

EMILIA: Get them away from that man. Help me. Help me.

*(The telephone rings.)*

GREGOR: Just a moment. *(He goes to the phone.)*

EMILIA *(sinking into a chair):* Please God, find them, find them.

GREGOR *(into the phone):* Hello? Yes, this is Doctor Kolenaty's office . . . no, he isn't here . . . can I take a message? This is Mr. Gregor. Yes, the same. Well . . . yes . . . yes . . . yes . . . thank you very much. *(He hangs up.)* Finished.

EMILIA: What's finished?

GREGOR: The case of Gregor versus Prus. The High Court has reached a verdict. For the moment, it's still confidential.

EMILIA: And?

GREGOR: I've lost.

EMILIA: Couldn't that ass of a lawyer have held things up for a while? (GREGOR *shrugs.)* But you can appeal the decision, can you not?

GREGOR: I don't know. I don't think so.

EMILIA: How stupid. *(She pauses a moment.)* Listen to me, Berti. I am going to do something for you. I will pay all your debts. Do you understand?

GREGOR: Why should you do that? I don't want that sort of thing.

EMILIA: You be still. I will pay your debts, and that is that. And now you will help me find that manuscript.

GREGOR: Emilia. . .

EMILIA: Call for my car.

DR. KOLENATY *(hurries in,* PRUS *behind him):* We found it! We really did! *(He seizes* EMILIA's *hands.)* My dear lady, I apologize a million times. I am a stupid old man, and you are omniscient!

PRUS *(shaking* GREGOR's *hand):* Congratulations on finding such a remarkable will.

GREGOR: There's no reason to congratulate me. You've just won the case.

PRUS: But you are going to appeal, aren't you?

GREGOR: Appeal?

DR. KOLENATY: Of course! Now we shall start the appeal for reconsideration of our case.

EMILIA: Everything was there?

DR. KOLENATY: Oh yes, of course. The will, the letters, and there was another thing. . .

PRUS: Please, will you introduce me to the lady?

DR. KOLENATY: Forgive me. This is Miss Emilia Marty. This is Mr. Jaroslav Prus, our mortal enemy.

EMILIA: I am happy to meet you. Where are the letters?

DR. KOLENATY: What letters?

EMILIA: The letters from Ellian.

PRUS: They're still with me. Mr. Gregor has no need to worry about them.

EMILIA: Will he get them?

PRUS: If he wins the inheritance. Definitely. As a souvenir of his great-grandmother.

EMILIA: Listen, Berti. . .

PRUS: I see you two know each other very well. I thought as much.

GREGOR: Excuse me, I met Miss Marty only. . .

EMILIA: Oh, be still, Berti. You will return the letters to me, won't you?

PRUS: Return? Have they ever belonged to you?

EMILIA: Well, no. But Berti will give them to me.

PRUS: Miss Marty, I am very grateful to you for your help. One finally knows what one has in one's own house. For that, I shall send you some particularly beautiful flowers.

EMILIA: You are not very generous. Berti has offered me considerably more than flowers.

PRUS: An entire wagon filled with them, I suppose.

EMILIA: No. More millions than I know exactly.

PRUS: And you have accepted them?

EMILIA: God help me, no.

PRUS: You were wise. Never accept payment if you're not sure you'll be paid.

EMILIA: Is something else missing?

PRUS: Well, perhaps. Just a small matter. For example, a document to prove that the son Ferdinand is definitely Ferdinand Gregor. You know how pedantic these lawyers can be.

EMILIA: You need something else, something written. Is that it?

PRUS: At the very least, something.

EMILIA: Very well. Doctor Kolenaty, I will send you that something in the morning.

DR. KOLENATY: You will? Good heavens, Miss Marty, do you walk around with these things under your arm?

EMILIA *(sharply):* It is amazing, isn't it?

DR. KOLENATY: I am not amazed by anything anymore. Gregor, perhaps you should call that 27-61 number after all.

GREGOR: Doctor Abeles? Why?

DR. KOLENATY: Because I have a feeling that. . . well, we shall see.

PRUS: Miss Marty, I think you had better accept my flowers.

EMILIA: And why?

PRUS: Because they, at least, are a sure thing.

END OF ACT ONE

# Act Two

*The empty stage of a large theater, in disorder after the previous night's performance. Props, scenery, lighting equipment, rolled-up drops, etc., all the debris and disorder of the stage. At the front, a dais topped by a gaudily painted theatrical throne. A* CLEANING WOMAN *and a* STAGEHAND *are at work.*

CLEANING WOMAN: My goodness, that was some ovation last night. Did you see all those flowers?

STAGEHAND: I saw them.

CLEANING WOMAN: Never in all my days have I heard such an uproar! All that yelling! I thought they'd tear the place down! That woman took at least fifty bows, and people still wouldn't stop! Just went crazy!

STAGEHAND: Listen, a woman like that must make plenty of money, right?

CLEANING WOMAN: Lord have mercy, I'd say so! Just think how much money went into those flowers! Look over there. Look how many she left behind. She couldn't take them all with her.

STAGEHAND: I stood in the wings to hear what she sounded like. I'll say this for her, she can really give a man the shakes when she sings.

CLEANING WOMAN: I'll bet she can! And I'll tell you this, I just plain cried last night. I listened to her and suddenly my face is all wet. I'm standing there crying like a fool.

(PRUS *enters.*)

CLEANING WOMAN *(to* PRUS): Looking for someone?

PRUS: Is Miss Marty here? They told me at her hotel that she was at the theater.

CLEANING WOMAN: She's in with the director right now. She ought to be out soon. She left her things in her dressing room.

PRUS: I'll wait, then. *(He walks away.)*

CLEANING WOMAN: That's the fifth one. They're lined up for her like patients in a clinic.

STAGEHAND: I can't get it out of my head, just wondering if a woman like that has any time for men.

CLEANING WOMAN: No doubt about *that*!

STAGEHAND: You think so? Then. . .

CLEANING WOMAN: Then *what*? What's the matter with you, anyway?

STAGEHAND: I just can't get it out of my head, that's all. . . *(He exits.)*

CLEANING WOMAN: Ha! She's something you don't have to worry about! *(She walks away.)*

(KRISTA *comes in, trailed by* JANEK PRUS.)

KRISTA: Come on, Janek. Nobody's here.

JANEK: Won't somebody throw me out?

KRISTA: No, there's no rehearsal today. *(Suddenly.)* Oh, Janek! I'm so unhappy!

JANEK: Why? *(He tries to kiss her.)*

KRISTA: Stop it, Janek! Don't! I. . . I have other worries. I can't think about you anymore.

JANEK: But Krista. . .

KRISTA: Oh, be reasonable, Janek. If I want to get anywhere, I have to change! I'm serious! You see, Janek, if somebody thinks about one thing all the time, and only one thing, it has to come true. Doesn't it?

JANEK: Of course.

KRISTA: So you see. I have to think about nothing but my art. See how fantastic Emilia Marty is?

JANEK: Yes, but. . .

KRISTA: You still don't understand. It's her fantastic technique. I didn't sleep all night thinking about it. I turned over and over and kept wondering, should I leave the stage or not? If only I knew anything about anything!

JANEK: But you do!

KRISTA: Do you really think so? Do you think I should keep on singing? But then everything else has to stop. You understand? Then I have to think only about singing!

JANEK: But Krista! Only a little moment every day with me . . . maybe twice a day. . .

KRISTA *(sits on the throne):* That's just it. It's never only a few minutes. It's terrible, Janek. You know it. I think about you all day long. My God, you're such a nuisance! How can I ever accomplish anything if I'm always thinking about you?

JANEK: But if you only knew how I. . . Krista, I can't think of *anything* but you.

KRISTA: You can afford to. You don't sing. Anyhow, listen, Janek, I've made up my mind. And you better not argue.

JANEK: No, that isn't fair. I can't agree to this, I. . .

KRISTA: Please, Janek, don't make things harder for me. Be reasonable and stop acting like a child. I have to start being very serious about my studies. I don't want to keep on being a poor, unknown girl just because of you! Anyhow, my voice is just being formed now, and I shouldn't use it too much.

JANEK: Then I'll do the talking.

KRISTA: No you won't. I've decided. It's all over between us, Janek. Over forever. We'll see each other only once a day.

JANEK: But. . .

KRISTA: And between times, we'll be perfect strangers. All day long. I'll work hard, Janek, I'll sing, and I'll think, and I'll learn everything. You know, I want to become a great lady like Miss Marty. Come here and don't be silly. There's room next to me. Nobody is around. Do you think she loves somebody?

JANEK *(sits next to her on the throne):* Who?

KRISTA: Miss Marty.

JANEK: Marty? Of course.

KRISTA: You really think so? I don't understand, though, why she should have to love anybody when she's so great and famous. You don't know what it's like when a woman is in love. It's so degrading. . .

JANEK: Not at all!

KRISTA: No, really. You men don't know a thing about it. A woman doesn't think of herself anymore, and she'll follow her lover around like a slave, not belonging to herself, only to him. I could kick myself sometimes.

JANEK: But. . .

KRISTA: And then, everybody is crazy about Marty. It doesn't seem to mean anything to her anymore. Everybody who sees her is really mad about her, though.

JANEK: That's not true.

KRISTA: You know, I'm a little bit afraid of her.

JANEK: My dear Krista! *(He gives her a quick kiss.)*

KRISTA *(lets him):* Janek! Somebody might see us!

PRUS *(enters and sees them):* I didn't see a thing.

JANEK *(jumping up):* Father!

PRUS: Stay where you are. *(He comes closer.)* Miss Kristina, I am happy to meet you. I'm sorry to say I haven't known about you before. It seems to me that my son should have boasted about you.

KRISTA *(stepping down from the throne, trying to shield* JANEK): Please, Mr. Prus just came to. . . to. . .

PRUS: Which Mister Prus?

KRISTA: Here. Mister. . . Mister. . .

PRUS: That is not Mister Prus, that's just Janek. How long has he been after you?

KRISTA: For a year now.

PRUS: Well. Just don't take him too seriously, Miss. I know him. And you, young fellow, I didn't mean to interrupt anything, but this place is rather, well, inconvenient. Wouldn't you say?

JANEK: Father, if you're trying to intimidate me, you're wasting your time.

PRUS: I'm glad to hear that. A man should never let himself be intimidated.

JANEK: I never would have thought my own father would spy on me this way.

PRUS: Very good, Janek. Don't give in.

JANEK: I'm serious. There are some things that I forbid, that are my own business.

PRUS: Absolutely, my friend. Here, shake my hand.

JANEK *(hastily hiding his hands in fear):* No, please. . .

PRUS *(hands stretched out, insistently):* Well?

JANEK: Father. . . *(He timidly gives his hand.)*

PRUS *(seizes* JANEK's *hand in a fierce grip):* That's the way, you see. Friendly. Fondly.

JANEK *(his face tense with pain, he resists but finally cries out):* Ah!

PRUS *(releasing him):* Not such a hero after all, are you?

KRISTA *(tears in her eyes):* That was very cruel.

PRUS *(takes her hands lightly):* These golden hands will make him feel better.

VITEK *(hurrying in):* Krista, my little Krista. Here you are. *(He stops.)* Mr. Prus?

PRUS: I won't disturb you. *(He steps away.)*

KRISTA: What is it, Daddy?

VITEK: You are in the newspapers, Krista! They are writing about you in the newspapers! And in the same review with Emilia Marty! Imagine! Next to Emilia Marty!

KRISTA: Let me see!

VITEK *(shows her the paper):* Right here: "Such and such part was sung for the first time by Miss Vitek." That's pretty good, isn't it?

KRISTA: And what are all those?

VITEK: These are more reviews, but there's nothing in them about you. You know how it is, only Marty, Marty and more Marty. As if there were nobody else in the world but Marty.

KRISTA *(happily):* Look here, Janek! Here is my name!

VITEK: Krista, who is this?

KRISTA: This is Mr. Prus.

JANEK: Janek. Janek Prus.

VITEK: Where did you meet him?

JANEK: Please, sir, Miss Vitek was kind enough. . .

VITEK: Pardon me, sir, my daughter will tell me herself. Come along, Krista.

> *(There is a commotion offstage. The voice*
> *of* EMILIA MARTY *is heard.)*

EMILIA *(offstage):* Thank you, gentlemen, but you really must let me go now. *(She enters, sees* PRUS *and stops.)* What? Another one?

PRUS: Not quite, Miss Marty. I wouldn't presume to congratulate you. I came here for another reason.

EMILIA: But you were in the theater yesterday.

PRUS: I was.

EMILIA: Well, then. *(She sits on the throne.)* Don't let anybody else in. I have had enough. *(She looks at JANEK.)* Is that your son?

PRUS: Yes. Come here, Janek.

EMILIA: Come closer, Janek, I want to look at you. Were you in the theater yesterday?

JANEK: Yes.

EMILIA: Did you like me?

JANEK: Yes.

EMILIA: Can you say anything besides "yes"?

JANEK: Yes.

EMILIA: Your son is an idiot.

PRUS: He embarrasses me.

(GREGOR *comes in with a bouquet of flowers.)*

EMILIA: Ah, Berti! Bring them here.

GREGOR: For yesterday evening. *(He presents her with the flowers.)*

EMILIA: Let me see them. *(She takes the flowers and finds a jewel box among them.)* This you can take back. *(She gives it to him.)* You are sweet to come, and I thank you for the flowers. *(She sniffs them, then tosses them onto a pile of other flowers.)* Did you like me?

GREGOR: No, I did not. Your singing hurts. It's too perfect. And at the same time. . .

EMILIA: Well?

GREGOR: You sound bored when you're singing. It doesn't sound human, what you do. It may be miraculous, but . . . you're bored with it. You're ice-cold when you sing.

EMILIA: That is what you felt? Well, maybe you are right . . . in some ways. Anyhow, I have sent that document to your fool of a lawyer—the one about Ellian. How is the case coming along?

GREGOR: I don't know. I don't bother with it myself.

EMILIA: But you're already buying ridiculous things from jewelry shops, aren't you? You're a fool. Go take it back this instant. What did you use for money?

GREGOR: That's *my* business.

EMILIA: You borrowed some, didn't you? You spent the whole morning running around looking for a moneylender, didn't you? *(She reaches into her handbag and pulls out a fistful of bills.)* Here. Take this. Hurry up.

GREGOR: What do you mean offering me money? What do you think I am? *(He moves away.)*

EMILIA: Take it, or I'll pull your ears off.

GREGOR *(blazing up)*: I beg your pardon!

EMILIA: Look at this, he's getting grand with me! Berti, don't get me mad. I'll teach you to run up bills. Take it, now!

PRUS *(to GREGOR)*: For God's sake, will you two stop it!

GREGOR *(snatches the money)*: You certainly do have strange whims! *(He thrusts the money at VITEK.)* Take this back to the office and deposit it in Miss Marty's account.

VITEK: Very well.

EMILIA: Eh, you! That is for him, do you hear me?

VITEK: Very well.

EMILIA: Were you at the performance last night? Did you like me?

VITEK: My God, yes! It was like hearing La Strada!

EMILIA: You heard La Strada sing? Listen. La Strada screamed. That was no voice.

VITEK: La Strada died a hundred years ago!

EMILIA: A good thing, too. You should have heard her! La Strada! Why do people keep talking about La Strada!

VITEK: I beg your pardon. I. . . I mean, of course, I never heard her in person, but according to history. . .

EMILIA: Listen to me. History lies. I will tell you something: La Strada screamed like a steam whistle, and La Carrona had gravel in her throat. La Agajari was dumb as a duck, and the great Faustina bellowed like a bagpipe. That is history for you.

VITEK: Oh, please, in these matters, when it comes to music. . .

PRUS *(with a smile)*: Just don't say anything about Mr. Vitek's French Revolution.

EMILIA: Why not?

PRUS: The French Revolution is his specialty.

EMILIA: What did he have to do with it?

PRUS: I don't know. Maybe you should ask him about this Citizen Marat. . .

VITEK: No, please! No reason for that!

EMILIA: Marat? Wasn't he the deputy with the sweaty hands?

VITEK *(indignantly):* That's not true!

EMILIA: Oh yes it is. I remember now. He had hands like a toad. Brrr. . .

VITEK: But no! That is a mistake. Nothing like that was ever written about Marat! Not anywhere! I beg your pardon!

EMILIA: I know the truth anyway. And what was the name of the big one, the one with all the pock marks?

VITEK: Which one, please?

EMILIA: The one that got his head chopped off.

VITEK: Danton?

EMILIA: Exactly. That one. He was even worse.

VITEK *(fascinated in spite of himself):* Why?

EMILIA: Oh, his teeth were completely rotten. Disgusting man.

VITEK *(very upset):* Please, one must not talk like that. It is not historically correct. Danton. . . Danton did not have rotten teeth. You cannot verify that! And even if you could, it would make no difference. No difference at all!

EMILIA: What do you mean, it makes no difference? It was disgusting, that's the difference it makes.

VITEK: No, please! I simply cannot allow this! Danton — forgive me! — but one cannot say things like that! Nothing noble would be left of History.

EMILIA: Nothing noble was ever in it.

VITEK: What?

EMILIA: There was never anything noble in History.

VITEK: But Danton. . .

EMILIA: Listen to this man! He wants to argue with me!

PRUS: That is very impolite of him.

EMILIA: Not impolite, just stupid.

GREGOR: Why don't you let me bring in some more people so you can be rude to them too?

EMILIA: That won't be necessary. They will come by themselves. On all fours.

KRISTA: Janek, let's get out of here.

EMILIA *(yawning):* What a couple those two make. Have they found paradise yet?

VITEK: What, please?

EMILIA: Well, you know. Have they been. . .

VITEK: For God's sake, no!

EMILIA: But there is nothing to it! You don't approve?

VITEK: Krista, it isn't true, is it?

KRISTA: Oh, Daddy! How can you!

EMILIA: Oh hush, you silly girl. If you haven't, you soon will. And you know what? It isn't worth it.

PRUS: What *is* worth it?

EMILIA: Nothing. Absolutely nothing.

(HAUK-SENDORF *enters with a big bouquet.*)

HAUK-SENDORF: Excuse me, excuse me.

EMILIA: Now who is this?

HAUK-SENDORF: Madame Marty, dear Madame Marty, permit me to. . . *(He kneels before the throne.)* Dear Madame Marty, if you only knew. . . if you only . . . knew. . . *(He begins to sob.)* Please . . . excuse me. . .

EMILIA: What's wrong with him?

HAUK-SENDORF: You . . . you look . . . so much . . . much . . . like her

EMILIA: Like who?

HAUK-SENDORF: Eugenia. Eugenia Montez.

EMILIA *(getting up, startled):* What?

HAUK-SENDORF: Eugenia. I. . . I knew her . . . oh God . . . it was . . . it was fifty years ago . . .

EMILIA: Who is this old man?

PRUS: Hauk-Sendorf, Miss Marty.

EMILIA: Max? *(She descends from the throne.)* Oh my God.

HAUK-SENDORF *(rising):* May. . . May I call you . . . Eugenia?

EMILIA: Call me anything you like. Do I really look like her?

HAUK-SENDORF: Look like her? Dear Madame Marty, yesterday. . . yesterday in the theater I thought that. . . that it was her, my Eugenia! If you could have heard that voice, seen those eyes. She was so beautiful! My God! And her face! *(He suddenly hesitates.)* But you are taller.

EMILIA: Taller? Are you sure?

HAUK-SENDORF: Just a bit taller. Permit me, Eugenia reached me . . . to here. I could kiss her forehead.

EMILIA: Nowhere else?

HAUK-SENDORF: What? What, please? You are, oh, so like her. Dear Madame Marty, may I give you these flowers?

EMILIA *(accepting the flowers):* Thank you.

HAUK-SENDORF: If only I could look at you forever!

EMILIA: Sit down there, my dear. Berti, a chair. *(She sits on the throne.)*

JANEK: Please, I will get one. *(He runs for a chair.)*
KRISTA: Not there! *(She runs after him.)*
PRUS *(to* HAUK-SENDORF): My dear Count.
HAUK-SENDORF: My God, it's Mr. Prus! Please forgive me. I— I
did not— I am so glad to see you. How do you do?
PRUS: How are you?
HAUK-SENDORF: And how is your case? Did you get rid of that
man?
PRUS: Not exactly. Allow me to introduce Mr. Gregor.
HAUK-SENDORF: Is this Mr. Gregor? So pleased to meet you. And
how are you?
GREGOR: Very well, thank you.
(JANEK *and* KRISTA *bring chairs.)*
EMILIA: You two there. What were you fighting about?
JANEK: Nothing much.
EMILIA: Sit down, Maxi.
HAUK-SENDORF: Thank you so much. *(He sits.)*
EMILIA: You over there. Sit down. Berti can sit here on my lap.
GREGOR: That's kind of you.
EMILIA: If you don't want to, then stand up.
HAUK-SENDORF: Beautiful, divine Madame Marty, on my knees I
beg your forgiveness.
EMILIA: What for?
HAUK-SENDORF: Because I am such an old fool. Why should you
care about a woman who has been dead for so many years?
EMILIA: Oh? Is she dead?
HAUK-SENDORF: Yes.
EMILIA: Too bad.
HAUK-SENDORF: Fifty years dead. I loved her then. Fifty years ago.
EMILIA: Did you?
HAUK-SENDORF: They called her Gitana. You know, Gypsy. And
she was one. They called her *la chula negra.* Down in An-
dalusia. That was when I was at the Embassy in Madrid. Fifty
years ago. In 1870.
EMILIA: Yes?
HAUK-SENDORF: You know, she sang and danced in the market.
Alza! Ola! God, how the whole world was crazy about her!
Vaya, gitana, and the castanets . . . but of course I was young
then . . . and she. . . she was. . .
EMILIA: A gypsy.
HAUK-SENDORF: Yes, exactly, a gypsy. Made of fire. God, one

can never forget . . . could you believe that a man, after that, never recovers his senses? I have remained a fool ever since.

EMILIA: Oh!

HAUK-SENDORF: I am an idiot, Madame Marty. Hauk the Idiot. What do you call it?

GREGOR: Feeble-minded?

HAUK-SENDORF: That's it. Feeble-minded. I left everything there with her, please understand. I have not been alive since then, not really, I have been sleeping ever since. Vaya querida! Salero! Mi dios! How you look like her! Eugenia! Eugenia! *(He weeps.)*

PRUS: Hauk, be careful now.

HAUK-SENDORF: Yes, yes . . . please forgive me . . . I should go now, is that right?

EMILIA: I will see you again, Max.

HAUK-SENDORF: Yes, of course. I. . . I may come back to see you? Please? *(He rises.)* Permit me to present you my compliments. God, when I look at you. . .

EMILIA *(bending forward):* Kiss me.

HAUK-SENDORF: What? What did you say?

EMILIA: Bésame, bobo, bobazo!

HAUK-SENDORF: Jesus mil veces, Eugenia!

EMILIA: Animal! Un besito!

HAUK-SENDORF *(kisses her):* Eugenia, moza negra — niña — querida! Queredísima. . .

EMILIA: Chito, tonto! Quita! Fuera!

HAUK-SENDORF: Es ella! Es ella! Gitana endiablada, ven conmigo! Pronto!

EMILIA: Ya no soy, loco! Ahora cállate! Vaya! Hasta mañana, entiendes?

HAUK-SENDORF: Vendré, vendré mis amores!

EMILIA: Vayá!

HAUK-SENDORF *(backing away):* Ay por Dios! Mi cielo, es ella! Si es ella, Eugenia . . .

EMILIA: Caramba, vaya! Fuera!

HAUK-SENDORF *(leaving):* Vendré! Hijo de Dios, es ella! Ella misma! *(He leaves.)*

EMILIA: Who's next? Who wants what from me?

VITEK: Excuse me, would you give me your autograph? For Krista. On this picture?

EMILIA: Nonsense. But for Krista, I will do it. A pen! *(She signs.)* So, good night now.

VITEK *(bowing):* A thousand thanks. *(He leaves with* KRISTA.)

EMILIA: Next? Nobody else?

GREGOR: When we are alone.

EMILIA: Some other time. Nobody else? Then I'm going.

PRUS: Please, just one minute.

EMILIA: Do you want something?

PRUS: Obviously.

EMILIA *(yawning):* All right, then. Out with it.

PRUS: I only wanted to talk to you . . . because you seem to know such a lot about Joseph Prus. Don't you?

EMILIA: Maybe I do.

PRUS: Just by accident, could a certain name be familiar to you?

EMILIA: What name?

PRUS: Shall we say, Makropulos.

EMILIA *(violently surprised):* What?

PRUS *(gets up):* Do you know that name Makropulos?

EMILIA *(composes herself):* Me? Not at all. This is the first time I have heard it. Now go away, all of you. Go, leave me alone.

PRUS *(bowing):* I am very sorry.

EMILIA *(to* PRUS): Not you. You wait. But what about Janek? Make him go. (JANEK *leaves. She turns to* GREGOR.) And what do you want?

GREGOR: I have to talk to you.

EMILIA: I have no time for you right now.

GREGOR: I must talk to you.

EMILIA: Please, Berti, leave me. Go, my dear, go now. Perhaps you can come back later.

GREGOR: I will. *(He bows coldly to* PRUS, *then leaves.)*

EMILIA: At last.

PAUSE

PRUS: Excuse me, Madame. I did not know that that name would upset you so much.

EMILIA: What do you know about . . . "Makropulos"?

PRUS: Well, that is what I am asking you.

EMILIA: What do you know about the Makropulos business?

PRUS: Miss Marty, please, please sit down. This might take a little time. *(They sit.)* First of all, permit me a rather indiscreet question. Perhaps too intimate. (EMILIA *silently nods.)* Do you have some . . . particular interest in the person of Mr. Gregor?

EMILIA: No.

PRUS: Therefore, are you particularly interested in his winning the case?

EMILIA: No.

PRUS: Thank you. It is not my intention to pry, Miss Marty, into how you know what is locked in the private files of my house. That, apparently, is your own secret.

EMILIA: It is.

PRUS: Very well. You know about certain letters. You know about Prus's last will. You even knew that it was sealed. And, by the way, did you know that there is . . . something else?

EMILIA *(rising):* You found something else? Then tell me. What is it?

PRUS: I don't know what it is. I would like to ask you.

EMILIA: You don't know what it is?

PRUS: Do you?

EMILIA: You still haven't told me. . .

PRUS: I thought that Kolenaty . . . or Gregor . . . might have told you.

EMILIA: Not a word.

PRUS: Well, there is a sealed envelope, and on it, in the hand-writing of Joseph Ferdinand Prus, it says "For the hands of my son Ferdinand." Nothing else. It is with the last will.

EMILIA: And did you open it?

PRUS: Certainly not. It does not belong to me.

EMILIA: Then give it to me.

PRUS: To you? *(He rises.)* But why?

EMILIA: Because I want it. Because. . . because. . .

PRUS: Yes?

EMILIA: Because I have a right to it.

PRUS: May I know what right?

EMILIA: No. *(She sits down.)*

PRUS: Hmmm. *(He sits.)* That, apparently, is another one of your secrets.

EMILIA: That is correct. Will you give it to me?

PRUS: No.

EMILIA: Very well. Then Berti will give it to me. Anyway, it belongs to him.

PRUS: That we shall see. Can you tell me what is in that envelope?

EMILIA: No. *(Pause.)* What do you know about . . . Makropulos?

PRUS: Forgive me. What do you know about that. . . that woman you call Ellian MacGregor?

EMILIA: You have her letters.

PRUS: You might know more interesting things. Is there anything you know about that slut?

EMILIA *(furious):* I beg your pardon!

PRUS *(standing):* But, my dear lady. . .

EMILIA: How dare you! How dare you speak like that before me!

PRUS: But what on earth is the matter? What do you care about some promiscuous woman who died a good hundred years ago?

EMILIA: You're right, of course. Nothing. *(She resumes her seat.)* So she was a slut?

PRUS: You know, I read her letters. An extraordinarily erotic creature, that woman.

EMILIA: Oh, you shouldn't have. . .

PRUS: There are allusions to some very strange intimacies. I am no youngster, Madam, but I must admit that the most experienced roué would not know about certain things that this . . . woman . . . knew.

EMILIA: You were going to say slut.

PRUS: That would hardly be strong enough.

EMILIA: I have a suggestion. Give me those letters.

PRUS: Perhaps you also are interested . . . in those kinds of . . . intimacies.

EMILIA: Perhaps. . .

PRUS *(after a pause):* Do you know what I would like to find out?

EMILIA: What?

PRUS: What you are like when you make love.

EMILIA: So. Now it is you who is interested in certain intimacies.

PRUS: Possibly.

EMILIA: Can it be that I remind you of that Ellian woman?

PRUS: God forbid!

EMILIA *(after a pause):* So she was an adventuress, a libertine, and nothing worse?

PRUS: What was her real name?

EMILIA: Ellian MacGregor. You have it on her letters.

PRUS: Excuse me. There is only "E. M." Nothing else.

EMILIA: Of course. That stands for "Ellian MacGregor."

PRUS: Of course. But it could also mean many other things. For instance, "Emilia Marty," "Eugenia Montez" or a thousand other names.

EMILIA: But it does mean "Ellian MacGregor." From Scotland.

PRUS: Or perhaps "Elina Makropulos." From Greece.

EMILIA *(furious):* God damn you!

PRUS: You recognize it, then?

EMILIA: Leave me in peace! *(Pause.)* How in the name of Satan do you know all this?

PRUS: Very simple. The will mentions one Ferdinand, born in Loukov, on the 20th of November 1816. I read that yesterday, and this very morning, at three o'clock, the dean of Loukov led me, in his nightshirt and with a candle in his hand, to the birth records. And there I found it, the birth record. This. *(He takes out a notebook and reads.)* "Nomen infantis Ferdinand Makropulos dies nativitatis, 20 November 1816. Thorus: illegitimate. Father: blank. Mother: Elina Makropulos. Born: In Crete."

EMILIA: You don't know anything else?

PRUS: No. Nothing more. But that's enough.

EMILIA: Poor Gregor. Now Loukov will remain yours, no?

PRUS: So long as some Mr. Makropulos doesn't come to claim it.

EMILIA: And that sealed envelope?

PRUS: Oh, it will be safely put away for him.

EMILIA: And if no Mr. Makropulos appears?

PRUS: It will remain sealed, and no one will get it.

EMILIA: Then he will come. You understand? And you will lose Loukov.

PRUS: All that is in the hands of God.

EMILIA: How can you be so stupid? *(Pause)* Listen. It would be better to give me the envelope.

PRUS: I wish you wouldn't keep harping on that.

EMILIA: Then he will come for it, that Mr. Makropulos.

PRUS: Well, who is he? Where is he? Do you keep him in your luggage?

EMILIA: Do you really want to know? He is Berti Gregor.

PRUS: Look at that! Him again!

EMILIA: Yes. Elina Makropulos and Ellian MacGregor were the same person. MacGregor was her stage name. Do you understand?

PRUS: Absolutely. And Ferdinand Gregor was her son?

EMILIA: That is what I am trying to tell you.

PRUS: Why wasn't he named Makropulos then?

EMILIA: Because. . . because Ellian wanted that name erased from the world.

PRUS *(exasperated):* Let's drop it, Miss Marty.

EMILIA: You don't believe me?

PRUS: I didn't say that. I didn't even ask how you know all this.

EMILIA: Good God, why keep it a secret? I'll tell you, but you must keep it to yourself. Ellian. . . Elina Makropulos . . . was my . . . aunt.

PRUS: Your aunt?

EMILIA: Yes. My mother's sister. Now you know it all.

PRUS: Naturally, this explains it very simply.

EMILIA: So, you see.

PRUS *(gets up):* The only thing wrong is that none of this is true, Miss Marty.

EMILIA: You mean to call me a liar?

PRUS: Alas! If you had said that Elina Makropulos was your aunt's grandmother, it at least would have been more plausible.

EMILIA: Oh, of course. You are right. *(Pause. She extends her hand.)* Goodbye.

PRUS *(kissing her hand):* May I express my great admiration for you another time?

EMILIA: Thank you. (PRUS *turns to leave.)* Wait. (PRUS *stops.)* For how much would you sell that sealed envelope to me?

PRUS *(looking back):* Would you repeat that, please?

EMILIA: I will buy it. And I will buy the letters too. I'll give you as much as you want.

PRUS *(coming back):* Excuse me, Miss Marty. I cannot deal with the matter here, not with you personally. Will you please send somebody else to deal with me?

EMILIA: Why?

PRUS: So that I can kick him out my door. *(He bows slightly and leaves.* EMILIA *sits without moving, her eyes closed.* GREGOR *enters and remains standing in silence.)*

EMILIA *(after a moment):* Is that you, Berti?

GREGOR: Why are your eyes closed? You look like you're in pain. What's wrong?

EMILIA: I am tired. Speak softly.

GREGOR *(comes near her):* Softly? I warn you, though, that I forget what I'm saying when I speak softly. I may say foolish things. Do you hear me, Emilia? You must stop me from speaking softly. I love you. I am mad with love for you. You don't laugh? I thought you might jump up and slap me, and I would love you even more madly for that. I love you. Are you asleep?

EMILIA: I am cold, Berti. It is so cold here. Be careful and don't take sick.

GREGOR: I warn you, Emilia, I love you. You talk harshly to me, but even that makes me happy. I am terrified of you, yet even that is pleasure to me. I would like. . . I am crazy, Emilia, and I think I would like to kill you. There is something dreadful about you, but even that is pleasure. You are vicious, low, awful, you are a callous animal.

EMILIA: I am not, Berti.

GREGOR: Yes, you are. Nothing means anything to you. Cold like a knife. As if you'd come out of a grave. Listen to me. I feel depraved to love you, and yet I do love you. I love you so much I could tear my own body apart to prove it.

EMILIA: Do you like the name Makropulos? Tell me.

GREGOR: Stop it. Don't provoke me. I would give my life if I could have you. You can do anything you want with me. Anything at all, anything unheard of . . . I love you, and I am lost, Emilia.

EMILIA: Then listen, Berti, go to that lawyer of yours. Make him give you back that document I sent him.

GREGOR: Is it false?

EMILIA: No, Berti. On my soul, I swear it is not. But we must have another one, with the name Makropulos on it. Wait, and I will explain it. Ellian. . .

GREGOR: Never mind. I'm fed up with your tricks.

EMILIA: No, wait. You must become rich, Berti. I want you to be rich.

GREGOR: Then will you love me?

EMILIA: Stop that, Berti. You promised me to get the Greek papers. Prus has them, do you hear? And you must get the inheritance, so then you can get them for me.

GREGOR: Then will you love me?

EMILIA: Never. Can't you get it through your head? Never.

GREGOR (sits down): I will kill you, Emilia.

EMILIA: Nonsense. I could say just one sentence and it would all be over. Look at that! He would like to kill me! Do you see, here on my neck, that scar? That one, he wanted to kill me too! And I'm not going to undress here for you just so you can see how many of your kind of souvenirs I already have on me. Am I made only for your killings?

GREGOR: I love you.

EMILIA: Well, go kill yourself then. You fool. All that "love" of yours is so much noise. Oh, if you only knew, only knew how ridiculous you people are. If you knew how tired I am. If you knew how everything is the same to me! Oh, if you only knew!

GREGOR: What do you mean?

EMILIA *(wringing her hands):* Unhappy Elina!

GREGOR *(softly):* Emilia, let's go away. Nobody ever loved you so much as I love you. I know. . . I know there is something desperate and frightening in you. But I am young and strong. I can flood you with love. You will forget everything . . . then you can throw me away like scrap. Can you hear me? (EMILIA *suddenly snores loudly. He is furious.)* What? She's asleep! She's ridiculing me! She's snoring like a drunk! *(He stretches his hands to her.)* Emilia, it's me . . . me . . . Nobody's here. *(He bends over her. The* CLEANING WOMAN *appears in the back and coughs in warning.)* Who is it? Oh, it's you. Miss Marty is asleep. Don't wake her. *(He kisses* EMILIA'*s hand and rushes away.)*

CLEANING WOMAN *(comes near* EMILIA, *silently looking at her)*: I feel kind of sorry for her. *(She leaves.)*

(JANEK *enters hesitantly. He stops and stares at* EMILIA.)

EMILIA *(waking):* Is that you, Berti?

JANEK *(moves back):* No, please. Only Janek.

EMILIA *(sits up):* Janek? Come here, Janek. Would you like to do something for me?

JANEK: Yes. Please.

EMILIA: Anything I want?

JANEK: Yes.

EMILIA: Something important, Janek. Something heroic.

JANEK: Yes.

EMILIA: And . . . will you ask something from me in return?

JANEK: Oh, no! Nothing, please.

EMILIA: Come over here. You know, it's very nice of you. Listen, your father has at home a sealed envelope, and on it is written "For the hands of my son Ferdinand." It is in his desk or his safe or I don't know where. Do you hear me?

JANEK: Yes, please.

EMILIA: Bring it to me.

JANEK: Will my father give it to me?

EMILIA: No, he won't. You will have to take it.

JANEK: I can't do that.

EMILIA: Oh? Little boy afraid of Papa?

JANEK: I'm not. It's just that. . .

EMILIA: Just what? Janek, on my honor, it's a simple little souvenir, without any value. But I would like so much to have it.

JANEK: I. . . I will try.

EMILIA: Really?

(PRUS *appears from the shadows.*)

PRUS: I will save you a search, Janek. The envelope is in the safe.

JANEK: You! Again!

PRUS: Go home. *(To* EMILIA.) Look at that, Miss Marty. Such a coincidence. I thought he was hanging around the theater because of his Krista, and all the while. . .

EMILIA: And why are you hanging around the theater, Mr. Prus?

PRUS: I was waiting . . . for you.

EMILIA *(comes very near him):* Then give me that envelope.

PRUS: It's not mine to give.

EMILIA: Then bring it to me.

PRUS: And. . . when?

EMILIA: Tonight.

PRUS: Agreed.

# END OF ACT TWO

# Act Three

## SCENE ONE

*A hotel room. On the left, a window; on the right, a door into the corridor. In the middle, an entrance to* EMILIA MARTY'*s bedroom. Drawn curtains separate the bedroom from the rest of the apartment.*

EMILIA *(strides from her bedroom, fastening her negligee, followed by* PRUS *in evening dress and still tying his tie.* PRUS *sits down, without a word, on the right. She goes to the window and opens the blinds. A weak morning light shines in.):* Well? *(Pause.)* Give it to me. *(She approaches* PRUS.) Do you hear me? Give me the envelope. *(Quickly* PRUS *reaches into his coat pocket and takes out a leather wallet. He removes a sealed envelope and, without a word, throws it onto the table. She snatches it up and goes to her dressing table. She sits, hesitates briefly, then quickly rips it open with a hairpin and pulls out a yellowed manuscript. She reads it, gasps with satisfaction, folds it and hides it in her bosom. She gets up.)* Very good.

PRUS *(quietly):* You cheated me.

EMILIA: You got what you wanted.

PRUS: You robbed me. Cold as ice. Like holding a corpse. *(He shudders.)* And for that, I gave you these papers that do not belong to me. Thank you so very much.

EMILIA: A sealed envelope upsets you that much?

PRUS: I am sorry I ever met you. I should not have given it to you. It's as if I'd stolen it. Disgusting. Disgusting.

EMILIA: Would you like some breakfast?

PRUS: I don't want a thing, not a thing. *(He gets up and goes to her.)* Show yourself to me! Show me your face, so I can see. . . I don't really know what I gave you, maybe it has some value, but. . . even if its only value is that it was sealed, only that value, that I did not even know what was in it! *(He waves his hand helplessly.)*

EMILIA *(gets up):* Do you feel you would like to spit in my face?

PRUS: No. In my own.

EMILIA: Help yourself.
*(A knock on the door. EMILIA goes to answer it.)*
EMILIA: Who is it?
MAID *(outside):* It's me, Miss Marty.
EMILIA: Come in. *(She opens the door.)* Get us something to eat.
*(The MAID hurries into the room,*
*dressed in her nightdress, very excited.)*
MAID: Excuse me, Madam. But is Mr. Prus here?
PRUS *(turning around):* What is it?
MAID: A servant of Mr. Prus is here, Ma'am. He wants to talk to
him. He says he has something very important to tell him.
PRUS: How in the devil's name did he know. . . tell him to wait.
No. Stay here. *(He goes into the bedroom.)*
EMILIA *(to the MAID):* Do my hair. *(She sits at her dressing table.)*
MAID *(letting down EMILIA's hair):* Oh, I was so scared, Miss
Marty! The porter came running, and Mr. Prus's servant is
here, and he wants to go up to your room, and the man is so
upset he can't even talk. It was like if a bullet hit me. Some-
thing terrible must have happened, Miss Marty.
EMILIA: Watch what you're doing. You're pulling.
MAID: That servant, pale as whitewash, I was so scared. . .
PRUS *(hurries out of the bedroom, fully dressed)* Excuse me a mo-
ment. *(He leaves.)*
MAID *(brushing EMILIA's hair):* He's very important, isn't he,
Madam? I wish I knew what's happened. If you'd only seen
how upset that servant was.
EMILIA: Have them send me some eggs.
MAID: And he had some papers or something in his hand. Should
I go and see?
EMILIA *(yawning):* What time is it?
MAID: After seven.
EMILIA: Turn the lights out and stop yammering so much.
MAID *(after a pause):* His lips were almost blue, that servant's.
I thought he was going to pass out, and he had tears in his
eyes—
EMILIA: You're pulling my hair out, you stupid girl! Show me
that comb! Look here at the hair you pulled!
MAID: My hands are shaking. Something terrible has happened.
EMILIA: No matter what has happened, I won't let you pull my
hair out. Go on. (PRUS *returns, mechanically caressing an*
*unopened letter.)* Well, that was quick. (PRUS *tries to find a*

149

*chair, then falls heavily into it.)* What do you want for break-fast?

PRUS *(distraught, speaking with great difficulty):* Send . . . that . . . girl. . .

EMILIA *(to the* MAID*):* Go away. I'll ring when I want you. Go on. *(The* MAID *leaves.)*

PRUS: Janek. He shot himself.

EMILIA: Really?

PRUS: His head . . . is torn apart. Beyond recognition. Dead.

EMILIA: Poor child. What is that letter?

PRUS: My servant told me. This letter . . . is from . . . Janek. They found it on him. Here . . . blood. . .

EMILIA: What does he say?

PRUS: I'm afraid . . . to open it . . . how, how, how could he know I was with you? Why did he send it here? Do you think. . .

EMILIA: That he saw us?

PRUS: Why did he do it? Why . . . kill himself?

EMILIA: Well, read it.

PRUS: Don't you want to . . . read it first?

EMILIA: No.

PRUS: I think . . . it has something to do with you. Open it.

EMILIA: Oh no.

PRUS: Should I . . . open it?

EMILIA: Well of course!

PRUS: All right. *(He opens the envelope and takes out the letter.* EMILIA *begins manicuring her nails. He reads silently, then gasps and lets the letter drop.)*

EMILIA: How old was he?

PRUS: That's why! That's why!

EMILIA: Poor Janek.

PRUS: He was in love with you.

EMILIA: Ha!

PRUS *(crying):* My boy, my only boy. *(He hides his face.)* Eighteen! He was only eighteen years old. Janek, my son. *(Pause.)* Dear God, I was always so hard on him. I never patted him when he was little, never . . . played with him, never praised him . . . and when I did feel like doing it, like showing him a little love, I thought: No, let him be hard, hard like me, hard towards life. I never knew him at all. Oh God, and how that boy worshipped me.

EMILIA: You never knew that?

PRUS: Christ, if only he were still alive. So stupid, so pointless to fall in love . . . He saw me with you . . . two hours he waited by the door . . . then he goes and. . .

EMILIA *(resumes combing her hair):* Poor thing.

PRUS: At eighteen! My Janek, my child . . . dead, unrecognizable . . . and with such childish handwriting he writes to me, "Father, finally I understand life. Be happy, but I. . ." *(He gets up.)* What are you doing?

EMILIA *(hairpins in her mouth):* Combing my hair.

PRUS: Maybe you . . . did not comprehend. Janek loved you! He killed himself for you!

EMILIA: Bah! People are always killing themselves.

PRUS: And you just sit there combing your hair?

EMILIA: Well, that's no reason for me to run around with my hair uncombed.

PRUS: He did it because of you! Do you hear me?

EMILIA: But is that my fault? He did it because of you too. Maybe I should tear my hair out? My maid tears out enough already.

PRUS *(backing away from her):* Be quiet . . . or. . . *(A knock on the door.)*

EMILIA: Come in.

MAID *(enters, dressed):* Mr. Hauk-Sendorf begs Madam. . .

EMILIA: Send him in here.

(MAID exits.)

PRUS: You. . . you are going to see him . . . now? In front of me?

EMILIA: Go into the next room then.

PRUS *(going):* Scum! *(He goes.)*

(HAUK-SENDORF enters.)

EMILIA: Buenos dias, Maxi. Why so early?

HAUK-SENDORF: Shhh! *(He tiptoes to her and kisses her on the shoulder.)* Get dressed, Eugenia. We are leaving.

EMILIA: For where?

HAUK-SENDORF: For home. For España. My wife knows nothing. You must realize I can never go back to her. Por Dios, Eugenia, hurry!

EMILIA: Are you crazy?

HAUK-SENDORF: Absolutely. In fact, I'm under treatment. You ought to know about it. I would be stopped and sent back— shh, shh, like a piece of baggage, you know? Eh? I want to get away from them. And you will take me away.

EMILIA: To Spain? What would I do there?

HAUK-SENDORF: Ola. You would dance, what else? Mi Dios, hija, how jealous I used to be! You will dance, sabe? And I, I will clap my hands. *(He takes out a pair of castanets.)* Ay, salero! Vaya, querida! *(He sings.)* La, lola, la la la. . . *(He stops suddenly.)* Who is crying in there?

EMILIA: Ah, nobody.

HAUK-SENDORF: Sh, sh. It sounds like somebody is crying. A man's voice. Chito, escucha. . .

EMILIA: Ah, yes. Somebody who lives next door. His son died or something.

HAUK-SENDORF: What? Please! He died? Ah, that is very sad. Vamos, gitana! Look what I've done: Matilda's jewels. Understand? Matilda is my wife, but she is old, and it is so ugly to be old. Terrible, terrible to be old. I was getting old, too, but since you came back, you . . . Chiquirritica! I am twenty, eh? You don't believe me?

EMILIA: Si, si, Señor.

HAUK-SENDORF: And you, you don't get older either. Listen to me, one should never get old. You know, fools have a long life. Oh, I will live for a long, long time. And as long as one enjoys love . . . *(He rattles the castanets.)* Enjoy love! La, la, la, la. Shhhh. My *gitana*, are you coming?

EMILIA: Si, I will come.

HAUK-SENDORF: A new life, yes? We will start again at twenty, *niña*. You know, heaven, heaven. . . Remember? Ha, ha! Remember? Nothing else means anything. Nada! Come on!

EMILIA: Si. Ven aquí, chucho.

*(A knock. The* MAID *puts her head in.)*

MAID: Mr. Gregor begs. . .

EMILIA: Let him in.

HAUK-SENDORF: What does he want here? Mi Dios, let's go!

EMILIA: Wait.

*(Enter* GREGOR, DR. KOLENATY, KRISTA *and* VITEK.)

EMILIA: Good morning, Berti. Do you mind telling me who else you're bringing in here?

GREGOR: You're not alone?

HAUK-SENDORF: Ah, Mr. Gregor. I am so glad!

GREGOR *(pushing* KRISTA *before* EMILIA): Look into this child's eyes! Do you know what has happened?

EMILIA: Janek.

GREGOR: And do you know why?

EMILIA: Bah!

GREGOR: That boy. You have him on your conscience. Do you understand?

EMILIA: Is that why you are bringing all these people in here? A lawyer too?

GREGOR: Not just for that. And please don't be so flippant.

EMILIA *(angry):* Don't give orders to me! What do you want here?

GREGOR: You'll find out. *(He sits down without asking permission.)* What is your name, anyway?

EMILIA: Is this a cross-examination?

DR. KOLENATY: Not at all, Miss Marty—only a friendly visit.

GREGOR: Here, show us, Vitek. *(He takes a picture from VITEK.)* Did you autograph this picture for Miss Krista? Is this your signature?

EMILIA: It is.

DR. KOLENATY: Very well. Then, if you don't mind, did you send me this document yesterday? It is a handwritten declaration by one Ellian MacGregor, claiming that she is the mother of Ferdinand Gregor. The date says 1836. Is it authentic?

EMILIA: It is.

GREGOR: But the ink on this document is fresh. Do you know what that means? It means that it is a forgery, my dear lady.

EMILIA: How should I know that?

GREGOR: The ink is fresh. Watch, gentlemen. *(He wets his finger and rubs at the signature.)* It smudges. How do you explain that? You. . . !

EMILIA: I don't.

GREGOR: It was written yesterday, do you understand? And by the same hand that signed this photograph. A very unusual handwriting, too.

DR. KOLENATY: Upon my soul, it looks like Greek — this alpha character. . .

GREGOR: Did you sign this document, yes or no?

EMILIA: I am to be cross-examined by you? Ha!

HAUK-SENDORF: But gentlemen, gentlemen, permit me. . .

DR. KOLENATY: Stay out of this, sir, stay out. These are very serious matters. Madam, can you at least tell us where you got this document?

EMILIA: I swear to you that it was written by Ellian MacGregor.

DR. KOLENATY: When? Yesterday morning?

EMILIA:  It doesn't matter when.

DR. KOLENATY:  Yes it does, Miss Marty. It matters very much. When did Ellian MacGregor die?

EMILIA:  Oh go away. I will not say another word. (PRUS *hurries out of the bedroom.*)

PRUS:  Please let me see that paper.

DR. KOLENATY *(gets up):*  My God . . . you. . .

GREGOR:  You here? Emilia, what does this mean?

HAUK-SENDORF:  My Lord, Mr. Prus! How are you! I am so glad to see you again!

GREGOR:  Do you know that your son. . .

PRUS *(coldly):*  Yes. The document please. (DR. KOLENATY *gives it to him.*) Thank you. *(He puts on his monocle and carefully reads.)*

GREGOR *(softly to* EMILIA):  What was he doing here? Say something.

EMILIA *(looks him up and down):*  What right. . .

GREGOR:  The right of one who is going crazy.

PRUS *(puts away the document):*  This writing is authentic.

DR. KOLENATY:  Dear, dear. So it was written by Ellian MacGregor?

PRUS:  No. It was written by the Greek woman Elina Makropulos. It is the same handwriting as on my letters. Beyond doubt.

DR. KOLENATY:  But those were written by. . .

PRUS:  Elina Makropulos. There has never been any Ellian MacGregor, gentlemen. That was a mistake.

DR. KOLENATY:  I am crazy, then. And the signature on this picture?

PRUS *(examining it):*  Definitely the handwriting of Elina Makropulos.

DR. KOLENATY:  And also a genuine signature of this lady here. You see it, Krista?

KRISTA:  Leave her alone!

PRUS *(returning the picture):*  Thank you. Forgive my interfering. *(He sits down on the side, his head in his hands.)*

DR. KOLENATY:  Just what is going on, in the name of God.

VITEK:  Perhaps it is only a coincidence that. . . that Miss Marty's handwriting somewhat resembles. . .

DR. KOLENATY *(sarcastically):*  Of course, Vitek. And Miss Marty's arrival at the office is a coincidence, and this document is also a coincidence. And you know what, Vitek, take all those coincidences and stuff . . . them. . .

EMILIA:  Gentlemen, I would like to remind you that I plan on leaving this morning.

GREGOR: For where?

EMILIA: For somewhere out of the country.

DR. KOLENATY: For God's sake, don't do that, Miss Marty. Please stay here willingly, so that we don't have to call in the—

EMILIA: You actually want to arrest me?

GREGOR: Not yet, you still have the chance. . . *(A knock interrupts him.)*

DR. KOLENATY: Come in!

MAID *(at the door):* Two gentlemen are looking for Mr. Hauk-Sendorf.

HAUK-SENDORF: What? Please? Me? No! I will not go! I . . . in God's name . . . try to . . . somehow. . .

VITEK: I will talk to them. *(He goes out.)*

DR. KOLENATY *(going to* KRISTA): Please, Krista, don't cry. I am so sorry. . .

HAUK-SENDORF: Oh la la, is she pretty! Let me see! Don't cry!

GREGOR *(close to* EMILIA, softly): Go downstairs. My car. You'll ride with me across the border.

EMILIA: That's what you were counting on? *(She laughs.)*

GREGOR: If it's not me, it's the police. Will you?

EMILIA: No.

VITEK *(returning):* Please, they are waiting for Mr. Hauk-Sendorf. His physician . . . and another gentlemen. They want to take him home.

HAUK-SENDORF: So you see. *(He giggles.)* They've got me already. Do ask them to wait.

VITEK: I told them to.

GREGOR: Gentlemen, since Miss Marty does not intend to give us an explanation, we will take things into our own hands and go through her papers and her luggage.

DR. KOLENATY: Now wait a minute! We have no right to do that, Gregor. Remember the right of privacy and. . .

GREGOR: Shall I call the police then?

DR. KOLENATY: I wash my hands. . .

HAUK-SENDORF: Excuse me, Mr. Gregor, but as a gentleman. . .

GREGOR: Sir, behind that door is your doctor and a detective. They are waiting for you. Shall I ask them in?

HAUK-SENDORF: Oh, not that, please. But Mr. Prus, surely. . .

PRUS: Do . . . with . . . that woman . . . what you want.

GREGOR: Well, then, let's begin. *(He goes to* EMILIA's *desk.)*

EMILIA: Don't you dare! *(She opens a drawer of her dressing table.)* Just try!

DR. KOLENATY: Miss Marty! *(He wrestles something out of her hand.)*

GREGOR *(opening the desk, without looking around):* Was she going to shoot me?

DR. KOLENATY: Well, it is loaded, Gregor. Listen, we'd better stop and call someone in. All right?

GREGOR: No. We'll deal with this ourselves. *(He looks through some drawers.)* Don't bother me.

EMILIA *(to* HAUK-SENDORF): Maxi, you allow this? Capitan, y usted quire pasar por caballero?

HAUK-SENDORF: Mi cielo. What can I do?

EMILIA *(to* DR. KOLENATY): Doctor Kolenaty, you are an honest man. . .

DR. KOLENATY: Oh no, Miss Marty, you are mistaken. I am a pickpocket, a world-renowned thief. In reality I am Arsène Lupin.

EMILIA *(to* PRUS): Then you, Prus. You must be a gentleman! You cannot permit this!

PRUS: Please, do not speak to me.

KRISTA *(sobbing):* This is horrible, what you are doing to her. Leave her alone!

DR. KOLENATY: That's just what I say, Krista. It is rude what we are doing. Very, very rude.

GREGOR *(tossing some papers onto the table):* Well, Miss Marty, you seem to be carrying the entire city archives around with you.

DR. KOLENATY: There's some for you, Vitek. Personal stuff. Do you want to plow through them?

EMILIA: Don't you dare read those!

DR. KOLENATY: Dearest Madam, I gently beg you, do not move. Otherwise, I will have to threaten you with bodily harm — paragraph 91 of the Criminal Code.

EMILIA: And you call yourself a . . . lawyer!

DR. KOLENATY: Well, I have grown to like the taste of crime. I think that I always must have had a talent for it. Sometimes one doesn't recognize one's mission in life until one is quite advanced in years.

VITEK: Excuse me, Miss Marty, but where are you going to sing next? (EMILIA *is silent.)*

HAUK-SENDORF:  Mon Dieu, je suis désolé. . .

VITEK:  And . . . did you read your reviews today?

EMILIA:  No.

VITEK *(takes out some folded newspaper clippings):*  They are fantastic, Madam. Listen. "A voice of extraordinary brilliance and power . . . overwhelming fullness of high notes . . . total technical security." And listen to this one: "miraculously beautiful appearance . . . thrilling dramatic power . . . an achievement unique in the annals of opera." Just imagine, Madam!

KRISTA:  But it's true!

GREGOR *(coming out of the bedroom with an armful of papers):*  Here, Doctor, this is all for now. *(He throws everything onto the table.)* Dig in.

DR. KOLENATY:  I can't wait. *(He smells the papers.)* You can smell the dust, Miss Marty. It is the dust of history, Vitek.

GREGOR:  And there's a seal with the initials E. M. It's on the same document with Ellian MacGregor's name.

PRUS *(gets up):*  Let me see it.

DR. KOLENATY *(examining the papers):*  Good Lord, Vitek, this one has the date 1603!

PRUS *(hands back the seal):*  It is the seal of Elina Makropulos. *(He sits down.)*

DR. KOLENATY *(by the papers):*  So you see now what one might find. . .

HAUK-SENDORF:  My God, my dear God. . .

GREGOR:  Mr. Hauk-Sendorf, do you know this medallion? It looks like your old coat-of-arms.

HAUK-SENDORF *(staring at the medallion):*  Yes . . . it is . . . but I gave it to her myself!

GREGOR:  When?

HAUK-SENDORF:  Then! In Spain! Fifty years ago!

GREGOR:  Who did you give it to?

HAUK-SENDORF:  To her! Eugenia! Eugenia Montez! You know.

DR. KOLENATY *(He looks up from papers.):*  Here we have something in Spanish. Do you read Spanish?

HAUK-SENDORF:  Of course. Let me see. *(He giggles.)* Eugenia, it is from Madrid!

DR. KOLENATY:  Well, what about it?

HAUK-SENDORF:  It is from the police . . . deportation for im-

morality. Ramera Gitana a quí se llame Eugenia Montez. . .
*(He giggles.)* I remember! It was because of that fight!

DR. KOLENATY: Excuse me. *(He examines some more papers.)* A
passport for Elsa Mueller, 1879. Death certificate . . . of Ellian
MacGregor, 1836. Look at this, everything mixed up together.
Wait, Madam, we will sort it for you according to names.
Ekaterina Myshkina—who is that?

VITEK: Ekaterina Myshkina was a famous Russian singer of the
1840s.

DR. KOLENATY: You know everything.

GREGOR: The initials are always E.M.

DR. KOLENATY: Obviously, Miss Marty collects only those initials.
Very special hobby, right? Oh here: "Dein Pepi." That would
be your great-great-great uncle, Prus. I'll read it to you:
"Meine liebste, liebste Ellian."

PRUS: Elina, you mean?

DR. KOLENATY: No, no. Ellian. And on the envelope, "Ellian Mac-
Gregor, member of the Hofoper, Vienna." Wait, Gregor, we
still might win with Ellian. "Meine Liebste, liebste Ellian."

EMILIA *(rises):* That's enough now. You won't read any more.
These are my private papers.

DR. KOLENATY: But we find them very interesting!

EMILIA: Stop reading them. I will tell you everything myself. Anything you ask me.

DR. KOLENATY: Really?

EMILIA: I swear it.

DR. KOLENATY *(puts down the papers):* Then we give you a
thousand apologies, Miss Marty, that we have forced you in
such a way.

EMILIA: Will you judge me?

DR. KOLENATY: Lord no, this is only a friendly talk.

EMILIA: But I want you to judge me!

DR. KOLENATY: Well, then, we will comply as far as we are competent.

EMILIA: No, I want it to be like a regular court of law. With a
crucifix and everything.

DR. KOLENATY: All right. If you wish. Anything else?

EMILIA: First leave me alone, so that I can eat and dress. I will
not go to trial in a nightgown.

DR. KOLENATY: You are quite right. It demands a serious and
dignified appearance.

GREGOR: This is a farce.

DR. KOLENATY: Be still. Never make fun of a court action. Accused, we give you ten minutes. Is that enough?

EMILIA: Be sensible. At least an hour.

DR. KOLENATY: You have half an hour. We will send for you at that time.

EMILIA: Thank you. *(She goes into the bedroom.)*

PRUS: I want to go . . . to . . . Janek.

DR. KOLENATY: Be back in half an hour.

GREGOR: Doctor Kolenaty, can't you be more serious?

DR. KOLENATY: Quiet. I am perfectly serious, Gregor. I know what works with a woman like that. She is a hysteric. Vitek?

VITEK: Yes, please?

DR. KOLENATY: Run up to the funeral parlor and tell them to loan us a crucifix, candles, and some black cloth. And a Bible. Hurry.

VITEK: Yes, sir.

DR. KOLENATY: And find me a skull.

VITEK: A skull! A human skull?

DR. KOLENATY: Man or beast, it doesn't matter. As long as it represents death.

## CURTAIN

## SCENE TWO

*The same room, but rearranged to suggest a courtroom.*
*Tables, couch, chairs covered in black cloth. On the larger*
*table at left is a crucifix, a Bible, lit candles and a skull.*
*Behind the table sits* DR. KOLENATY *as presiding judge,* VITEK
*as clerk,* GREGOR *at a smaller table as prosecutor. The "jury"*
*sits on the couch:* PRUS, HAUK-SENDORF, KRISTA. *On the*
*right is an empty chair.*

DR. KOLENATY: Miss Marty should be ready by now.

VITEK: You don't think she might have . . . taken something?

GREGOR: Certainly not. She loves herself too much.

DR. KOLENATY: Bring in the accused.

    (VITEK *knocks on the bedroom door and enters.)*

PRUS: You could spare me this comedy.

DR. KOLENATY: No, we can't. You must be part of the jury.

KRISTA *(weeping):* It is like. . . like a . . . funeral.

DR. KOLENATY: Don't cry, Krista. Let the dead rest in peace.

    (VITEK *brings in* EMILIA *in formal dress but*
    *holding a bottle and a glass in her hands.)*

DR. KOLENATY: Take the accused to her place.

VITEK: Please, sir, the accused is drinking whisky.

DR. KOLENATY: Is she drunk?

VITEK: Well, sir, I think perhaps she is. Very drunk, in fact.

EMILIA *(leaning against the wall):* Let me be. It helps me. I need
it. Besides, I am thirsty.

DR. KOLENATY: Take that bottle away from her.

EMILIA *(gripping the bottle):* No! I will keep it. Or I will not
speak. *(She laughs.)* You. . . you look like undertakers. You
are all so funny. *(She laughs again.)* Look, Berti . . .
Theotokos! I am going to burst!

DR. KOLENATY: Accused, you are out of order.

EMILIA *(taken aback):* You are trying to scare me? Berti, tell me,
this is only a joke?

DR. KOLENATY: You will speak when the court asks you a question. Your place is here. You may sit down. I ask the public
prosecutor to present the accusation.

EMILIA *(nervously):* I am to be sworn in?

DR. KOLENATY:  The accused is never sworn in.

GREGOR:  The accused, called Emilia Marty, a singer, is accused before God and before us of committing a fraud by falsifying documents for her own profit. By so doing, she has offended all trust and decency, and has committed crimes against life itself. These crimes are not answerable to human judgment, but must be tried before a higher court.

DR. KOLENATY:  Does anyone have anything to add to that? No one? Then we will proceed to the cross-examination. Accused, stand up. Give your name.

EMILIA *(standing):*  Me?

DR. KOLENATY:  Of course. You, you, you! What is your name?

EMILIA:  Elina Makropulos.

DR. KOLENATY *(whistles):*  What?

EMILIA:  Elina Makropulos.

DR. KOLENATY:  Born where?

EMILIA:  In Crete.

DR. KOLENATY:  When?

EMILIA:  When?

DR. KOLENATY:  How old are you?

EMILIA:  Guess. How old do you think?

DR. KOLENATY:  Let's say thirty. No?

VITEK:  Please, over thirty.

KRISTA:  Over forty.

EMILIA *(sticks out her tongue):*  Bitch.

DR. KOLENATY:  Behave properly to the jury.

EMILIA:  Do I look that old?

DR. KOLENATY:  For God's sake, when were you born?

EMILIA:  In 1585.

DR. KOLENATY *(startled):*  When?

EMILIA:  One thousand five hundred and eighty-five.

DR. KOLENATY *(sits down.):*  In the year eight-five. Then you are thirty-seven. Correct?

EMILIA:  Three hundred and thirty-seven, thank you.

DR. KOLENATY:  I want to impress upon you the importance of speaking seriously. How old are you?

EMILIA:  337.

DR. KOLENATY:  That's enough. Who was your father then?

EMILIA:  Hieronymus Makropulos. The personal physician to Emperor Rudolf II.

DR. KOLENATY: To hell with her. I'm not going to go on asking her questions.

PRUS: What is your real name?

EMILIA: Elina Makropulos.

PRUS: You are related to that Elina Makropulos who was the mistress of Joseph Prus?

EMILIA: I am she.

PRUS: How is that?

EMILIA: Well, I was the mistress of Pepi Prus. I had Gregor with him.

GREGOR: And Ellian MacGregor?

EMILIA: That is me also.

GREGOR: Are you crazy?

EMILIA: I am your great-great-great-grandmother or something like that. Ferdi was my boy. Do you understand?

GREGOR: Which Ferdi?

EMILIA: Ferdinand Gregor. But he is registered as Ferdinand Makropulos because. . . well, there I had to give my real name. I had to.

DR. KOLENATY: Of course. And when were you born?

EMILIA: 1585. Christos Soter! Stop hammering at me like that!

HAUK-SENDORF: . . . and . . . please . . . you are truly Eugenia Montez?

EMILIA: I was, Maxi, I was. But then I was only 290 years old. And I was also Ekaterina Myshkina and Elsa Mueller and all sorts of other people. One cannot live among you people for 300 years with the same name.

DR. KOLENATY: Especially not if you're a singer.

EMILIA: Especially not.

PAUSE

VITEK: Then you really did live in the eighteenth century?

EMILIA: Of course I did.

VITEK: You knew. . . you really met . . . Danton? Personally?

EMILIA: I did. Disgusting man.

PRUS: And how did you know the contents of a sealed will?

EMILIA: Because Pepi showed it to me before he sealed it. So I could tell that silly Ferdi Gregor about it one day.

GREGOR: Why didn't you tell him, then?

EMILIA: I never bothered much with my bastards.

HAUK-SENDORF: Oh my, what a way to talk!

EMILIA: My dear, it has been a long time since I was a lady.

VITEK: Did you have other children?

EMILIA: Twenty or so. I think. Sometimes one isn't careful enough. Would anyone like a drink? Mother of God, my mouth is so dry! I am burning. *(She sinks into a chair.)*

PRUS: Therefore, the letters signed E. M. were all written by you?

EMILIA: Yes. Now you know. Give them back to me. Sometimes I like to read them again. Garbage, aren't they?

PRUS: Did you write them as Elina Makropulos or as Ellian Mac-Gregor?

EMILIA: It's all the same. Pepi knew who I was. I told Pepi everything. Pepi . . . I was in love with. . .

HAUK-SENDORF *(gets up, hurt):* Eugenia!

EMILIA: Shut up, Maxi. You too. It was nice living with you when you were a young man. But Pepi. . . *(She begins to weep.)* him I loved most of all. That is why I loaned him . . . the Makropulos formula . . . when he wanted it . . . so badly. . .

PRUS: What did you say you loaned him?

EMILIA: The Makropulos formula.

PRUS: What was that?

EMILIA: That's the paper, the one you gave me back today. That sealed envelope. Pepi wanted to try it. He promised to give it back to me, but instead he hid it with his will. Maybe he wanted to be sure I would come back . . . but I haven't come back until now! How did Pepi die?

PRUS: In a fever, with terrible cramps.

EMILIA: That was from the formula. That was it. Santa Maria, I did warn him about it.

GREGOR: And you came here just for the Greek paper?

EMILIA: Ha! Well, I won't give it to you! It's mine now. Don't flatter yourself, Berti, that I ever gave a damn about your stupid lawsuit. I couldn't care less that you are mine. I don't know how many of my little ones are still running around this world. I wanted to get that formula. I had to get that formula, or. . . or. . .

GREGOR: Or what?

EMILIA: Or I'll get old. I'm at the end. I have to try the formula again. Feel my hand, Berti, feel how icy it is. *(She gets up.)* Touch my hands. God, my hands!

HAUK-SENDORF: Please, what is this Makropulos formula?

EMILIA: Here it is written how to do it.

HAUK-SENDORF: How to do what?

EMILIA: What a human being has to do to live three hundred years. How to be three hundred years young. My father wrote it for the Emperor Rudolf. You don't know him, do you?

VITEK: Please, only from history.

EMILIA: You can't learn anything from history. It's nonsense! Penaia, what was I trying to say? *(She sniffs something from a box.)* Does anybody want some?

GREGOR: What is it?

EMILIA: Nothing. Cocaine or something. What was I talking about?

VITEK: About the Emperor Rudolf.

EMILIA: Oh my friends! What a lecher he was! Listen, I could tell you things about him. . .

DR. KOLENATY: Don't change the subject.

EMILIA: Well, when the emperor started to get old, he began trying to find an elixir of life, or something that would make him young again. You see? And so my father went to him and wrote that. . . that thing for him, that "miracle," so that he could stay young for three hundred years. But Emperor Rudolf was afraid that this miracle might poison him, and so he made my father try it out on his daughter. That was me. I was sixteen years old. So father tried it on me. Then they all said it was black magic, but it wasn't any such thing, it was something else entirely.

HAUK-SENDORF: What was it?

EMILIA *(shudders):* I cannot say. No one can. Then I lay for a week or so unconscious and in a fever, but I got well again.

VITEK: What about the Emperor?

EMILIA: He went mad with rage. After all, how could he be sure that I was going to live for 300 years! So he called my father a fraud and locked him up in a tower, and I ran away with everything he had written, to Hungary, or Turkey, I don't remember now.

DR. KOLENATY: Did you ever show anybody else that. . . that. . . Makropulos formula?

EMILIA: I showed it to a few. Some Tyrolean priest tried it, that was about 1660 or so—maybe he's still alive, I don't know. At one time he was Pope and called himself Alexander or Pius or something like that. Then there was an Italian officer, but he got killed. His name was Ugo—God, he was handsome. And wait a moment, there was Nageli—that was Andrew. And then there was that son-of-a-bitch Bombita, and Pepi Prus, who died from it. Pepi was the last one, and it stayed in his possession. And that's all I know. You can ask Bombita—he's still alive somewhere, but I don't know what he calls himself now. I think he is some kind of crooked lawyer.

DR. KOLENATY: Pardon me, but you are 247 years old, is that right?

EMILIA: No, 337.

DR. KOLENATY: You are drunk. From 1585 until today is 247, do you hear me?

EMILIA: God, stop trying to confuse me! I'm 337.

DR. KOLENATY: Why did you fake the handwriting of Ellian Mac-Gregor?

EMILIA: I myself am Ellian MacGregor.

DR. KOLENATY: Don't keep on lying! You are Emilia Marty, understand?

EMILIA: Yes, but only for the past twelve years.

DR. KOLENATY: So you admit stealing the medallion that belonged to Eugenia Montez, do you not?

EMILIA: Holy Mary! That's not true! Eugenia Montez. . .

DR. KOLENATY: That is what you are accused of. You admitted it.

EMILIA: That is not true.

DR. KOLENATY: What is the name of your accomplice?

EMILIA: I have no accomplice!

DR. KOLENATY: Don't deny it. We know everything. When were you born?

EMILIA *(trembling):* 1585.

DR. KOLENATY *(handing her a glass):* Drink this. All of it.

EMILIA: No! I won't! Leave me alone!

DR. KOLENATY: Drink it! You have to! Quick!

EMILIA *(in anguish):* What are you doing to me? Berti! *(She drinks.)* It is turning . . . my head. . .

DR. KOLENATY *(gets up and goes over to her):* What is your name?

EMILIA: I'm dizzy. . . *(She topples from her chair.)*

DR. KOLENATY *(catches her and lowers her to the floor):* What is your name?

EMILIA: Elina . . . Makro. . .

DR. KOLENATY: Don't lie! Do you know who I am? I am a priest. You are giving confession!

EMILIA: Pater . . . hemon . . . hos . . . eis . . . en uranois. . .

DR. KOLENATY: What is your name?

EMILIA: Elina . . . pulos. . .

DR. KOLENATY: The skull! Lord, receive the soul of this thy unworthy servant Emilia Marty. *(mumbling)* Hyhymmmmm in
saeculorum. Amen. Finished. *(He covers the skull with black
cloth and faces* EMILIA *with it.)* Get up! What is your name!

EMILIA: Elina. . . *(She faints.)*

DR. KOLENATY *(lets her fall):* Damn it! *(He rises and puts down
the skull.)*

GREGOR: What is it?

DR. KOLENATY: She's not lying. Get rid of all this stuff. Hurry
up. *(He rings.)* Gregor, get the doctor!

KRISTA: Did you poison her?

DR. KOLENATY: A little.

GREGOR *(in the door to the hall):* Please, is the doctor still here?

DOCTOR *(entering):* Mr. Hauk-Sendorf, we have been waiting for
you for an hour now. Come along, let's go home now.

DR. KOLENATY: Wait a moment. This case comes first, Doctor.

DOCTOR *(looking at* EMILIA*):* Fainting spell?

DR. KOLENATY: Poison.

DOCTOR: What kind? *(He kneels beside* EMILIA *and smells her
breath.)* Aha! *(He gets up.)* Put her on a bed somewhere.

DR. KOLENATY: Gregor, carry her into the bedroom. Since you
are her nearest relative. . .

DOCTOR: Is there some warm water?

PRUS: Yes.

DOCTOR: Beautiful, isn't she? Excuse me. *(He writes a prescription.)* Black coffee. And quick with this to the pharmacy. *(He
goes into the bedroom.)*

DR. KOLENATY: Well, gentlemen. . .

MAID *(entering):* Did Madam ring?

DR. KOLENATY: She did. Madam would like some black coffee,
very strong black coffee.

MAID *(giggles knowingly):* How did you know that, sir?

DR. KOLENATY: It is fairly obvious. And run to the pharmacy with
this, quick now. (MAID *goes. He sits down.)* God help us all,
there is something to it.

PRUS: It wasn't necessary to get her drunk to learn that.

HAUK-SENDORF: I. . . I. . . please, do not laugh at me, but I do
believe her.

DR. KOLENATY: You too, Prus?

PRUS: Absolutely.

DR. KOLENATY: I do too. Do you realize what that means?

PRUS: That Gregor will get Loukov.

DR. KOLENATY: Hmmm. Do you mind very much?

PRUS: It doesn't matter. I have no heirs, no descendants.

(GREGOR *returns, holding his hand in a handkerchief.*)

HAUK-SENDORF: How is she, please?

GREGOR: A little better. She bit me. Like a wild cat. You know something? I believe her.

DR. KOLENATY: Unfortunately, we all do.

*(A long pause while the truth sinks in.)*

HAUK-SENDORF: My God. Three hundred years. Three . . . hundred . . . years. . .

DR. KOLENATY: Gentlemen, there must be absolute discretion about this. You understand? You too, Krista.

KRISTA *(shuddering):* Three hundred years. Horrible.

*(The* MAID *returns with coffee.)*

DR. KOLENATY: Krista, be a rescuing angel and take it in to her, will you?

(KRISTA *takes the coffee into the bedroom.*
*The* MAID *leaves.)*

DR. KOLENATY *(making sure both doors are closed and locked):* And now, gentlemen, put your brains to work. What are we going to do with it?

GREGOR: With what?

DR. KOLENATY: With the Makropulos formula. Somewhere very nearby is a recipe for 300 years of life. We can lay our hands on it very easily.

PRUS: It is in her bosom.

DR. KOLENATY *(shrugs):* That is hardly a major problem, gentlemen. Here is a thing . . . of unimaginable importance. What are we going to do with it?

GREGOR: You're not going to do a goddam thing with it. The formula belongs to me. I am her heir.

DR. KOLENATY: Think! As long as she is alive, you are not an heir, and she can live for another 300 years if she wants to. But we can get hold of it. Do you follow me?

GREGOR: By theft.

DR. KOLENATY: If necessary. But this is something of such importance . . . for us . . . for the entire human race, that. . . hmmm. Gentlemen, you do understand me? Are we to leave it to her? Should she be the only one who profits from it?

She, or some kind of a crook like that Bombita person? Who will get it?

GREGOR: First of all, her descendants.

DR. KOLENATY: Well, we certainly can find a lot of those! Don't count on getting it for yourself. Let's take Prus, here. If you had that formula in your hands, would you lend it to me? You know, so I could live for 300 years?

PRUS: Certainly not.

DR. KOLENATY: So you see, gentlemen. We have to come to some understanding between ourselves. What are we going to do with it?

VITEK (gets up): We will make it public, this Makropulos formula.

DR. KOLENATY: I hope nothing that foolish.

VITEK: We will give it to everybody, to all humanity! Everybody, but everybody, has the same right to life. God, we live such a short time. It means so little to be a human being!

DR. KOLENATY: None of this matters.

VITEK: But it does! It is a matter for weeping! Just think: the human soul, the thirst for knowledge, the intellect, the work, love, creativity, everything! My God, what can a man do in a mere sixty years of life? How much can he enjoy? How much can he learn? He can't even harvest the fruit from the tree he plants. He never learns what his ancestors knew. He dies before he begins to live! God in Heaven, we live so briefly!

DR. KOLENATY: Really, Vitek. . .

VITEK: We don't have time for happiness, or even thinking. We don't have time for anything but this eternal scratching for a piece of bread. We never see anything, never know anything, never learn anything, never complete anything—not even ourselves. We are just fragments of something else. Why do we live? Is it worth it?

DR. KOLENATY: Are you trying to make me cry?

VITEK: We die like animals. What is life after death? Immortality of the soul? Only a desperate protest against the shortness of life. Man has never accepted this animal part of life. He cannot accept it because it is too unjust to live for such a short time. A man should be a little more than a turtle or a raven. A man needs more time to live. Sixty years! That is serfdom. It is weakness, an animal life, ignorance.

HAUK-SENDORF: And already I'm seventy-six.

VITEK: Let's give everybody 300 years of life! This will be the greatest event since the creation. It will be a liberation and a new beginning. God, what can be done with a man in 300 years! Fifty years to be a child and a student, fifty years to understand the world, a hundred years to work and be useful, then a hundred years to be wise and understanding, to rule, to teach and give example! Oh, how valuable would a human life be if it lasted 300 years! There would be no wars, no more of that dreadful hunt for bread, no fear, no selfishness. Everyone would have dignity and wisdom. *(He clasps his hands in ecstasy.)* How sovereign and perfect man would be, a real son of God and no longer just a miscarriage of God's justice. Let us give people life! Let us give them a full and long human life!

DR. KOLENATY: Bravo, Vitek, bravo. That was very nice. Very nice indeed.

GREGOR *(interrupting):* Thank you very much. 300 years to be a filing clerk. 300 years to knit stockings!

VITEK: But. . .

GREGOR: To be powerful and knowing . . . when most human occupations are bearable only because of ignorance.

DR. KOLENATY: You had better realize, Vitek, that all you have said is legally and economically ridiculous. Our social system is founded upon a brief life span: contracts, pensions, insurance policies, salaries, inheritance laws, and I don't know what all. And marriage! Ha! Nobody would get married for 300 years! Nobody would make any kind of commitment for 300 years! You! You are an anarchist! You want to topple all our social systems!

HAUK-SENDORF: And . . . permit me . . . then after 300 years everybody could get young all over again.

DR. KOLENATY: . . .and, in fact, live forever. Such a thing is simply impossible.

VITEK: Please, that could be forbidden. After 300 years, everybody would have to die.

DR. KOLENATY: Marvelous. He loves humanity so much that he wants to condemn everybody to death!

HAUK-SENDORF: Excuse me. I. . . I think that the secret could be divided into doses.

DR. KOLENATY: Doses?

HAUK-SENDORF: Well, understand me, divided into years. One

dose would equal ten years of life. 300 years is a little too much. Not everybody would want that. But ten years, everybody would buy that, wouldn't they?

DR. KOLENATY *(drawing out the word):* B-u-y? We could start a business with years. What an idea! I can just see it: "Send immediately: 1,200 years of life, in your best gift wrap. Kohn and Company." "Send express, two million years, top quality, luxury wrapping, FOB Vienna." Hauk, it's a great idea.

HAUK-SENDORF: Please, I am not a businessman. I . . . you know? But when one gets older, it would be nice to buy . . . a little extra . . . but 300 years is too much. No?

VITEK: For self-improvement, no.

HAUK-SENDORF: Nobody wants to buy ten years of self-improvement. But ten years of pleasure? Yes. Definitely yes.

MAID *(entering):* Here is the prescription, sir.

DR. KOLENATY: Thank you. How long would you like to go on living?

MAID: Me? *(She giggles.):* Oh, another thirty years.

DR. KOLENATY: No more?

MAID: Oh no, sir. What would I do with it?

DR. KOLENATY: You see, Vitek?

> (MAID *leaves.* DR. KOLENATY *knocks on
> the bedroom door. The* DOCTOR *opens it.)*

DOCTOR: Yes? Oh, good. *(He takes the prescription.)*

HAUK-SENDORF: How is Madame Marty?

DOCTOR: Sick. *(He goes back into the bedroom and shuts the door.)*

HAUK-SENDORF: Poor girl.

PRUS *(rising):* Gentlemen, a strange chain of events has placed in our hands a certain secret. It concerns the indefinite prolongation of life. Let's assume that it works, that it is possible. None of us, I trust, is thinking of using it for himself.

VITEK: I should say not! We must prolong life for all humanity!

PRUS: No, only for the strong. The life of the most capable. For the mediocre human mob, even the life of an ephemera is too long.

VITEK: Oh, permit me!

PRUS: Please, I do not want to argue. But, if I may: the ordinary, small, stupid human being never dies. A small person is everlasting, even without your help. Smallness multiplies without rest, like flies or mice. Only greatness dies. Only strength and talent die, because they cannot be replaced. It may be in our grasp to keep that alive. We can begin an aristocracy of the everlasting.

VITEK: An aristocracy! You hear that? The privilege of life!

PRUS: Correct. Only the best are important in life. Only the leaders, only productive, efficient men. I don't even talk about women. But there are in this world about ten or twenty thousand men who are irreplaceable. We can preserve them. In these men we can develop superhuman brains and supernormal powers. We can breed ten or twenty thousand supermen, leaders and creators.

VITEK: A race of supermen!

PRUS: Exactly. Choice men who have the right to unlimited life.

DR. KOLENATY: And tell me, if you will, who is going to choose the chosen? Governments? Voters? The Swedish Academy?

PRUS: No stupid voting. From hand to hand they would pass on life, the strongest to the strongest. Masters of the material to masters of the mind. Inventors to soldiers, builders to despots. It would be a dynasty of the masters of life, a dynasty that would not depend on any kind of mob opinion.

VITEK: Until the mob decides to claim its own right to life!

PRUS: Let them. Revolution is the privilege of all slaves, but the right to life is not. A few people will have to be killed from time to time. That is of no importance. After all, the only progress in the world is the progression from small and weak despots to big and strong ones. Look at it this way: a long and privileged life will be the despotism of the chosen—that is, the rule of reason. Superhuman authority given by super-human knowledge and ability. The long-living would become the natural leaders of nations. You have it in your hands, gentlemen. You can use it, or you can abuse it. I have finished. *(He sits down.)*

DR. KOLENATY: Hmmm. Do I belong to those chosen ones, just for example? Do I? Does Gregor?

PRUS: I'm afraid not.

GREGOR: But you do.

PRUS: After today, no.

GREGOR: Let's stop this talking. The Makropulos formula is owned by the Makropulos family, and that's all there is to it. Let them do what they want with it.

VITEK: And what is that, please?

GREGOR:  Whatever the descendants of Elina Makropulos decide.

DR. KOLENATY:  And they will live forever, because they were born to some vagrant baron and some hysterical soprano. This family inheritance is something outrageous.

GREGOR:  That's none of your concern.

DR. KOLENATY:  We are lucky enough to know one gentleman from that family. He is, you will forgive me, my dear sir—and may he be damned—a useless, lazy person. From a "fine" family.

GREGOR:  That is your opinion. But we may be fools, or baboons, or depraved and overweight and crippled, helpless idiots or anything you say. We may be as evil as Satan himself, but that doesn't change a thing. We own the Makropulos formula. And that, my friend, is that.

DR. KOLENATY:  Incredible.

DOCTOR *(coming out of the bedroom):*  She is all right now. Let her sleep.

HAUK-SENDORF:  Yes, yes. Sleep. That is good for her.

DOCTOR:  Come home now, Mr. Hauk-Sendorf. I will take you.

HAUK-SENDORF:  But we are having a most important discussion here, isn't that so? Please let me stay a little longer. I. . . I. . . surely. . .

DOCTOR:  Well, somebody is waiting for you outside. No more fooling around, old man, or. . . well, I'll be waiting. *(He leaves.)*

DR. KOLENATY:  Gregor. Did you mean what you just said?

GREGOR:  I certainly did.

KRISTA *(coming out of the bedroom):*  Keep your voices down. She needs to sleep.

DR. KOLENATY:  Kristinka, dear. Come here. Would you like to live for 300 years?

KRISTA:  No.

DR. KOLENATY:  And if you had a formula for such a long life, what would you do with it?

KRISTA:  I have no idea.

VITEK:  You would give it to all the world, wouldn't you?

KRISTA:  I don't know. Would the world be happier if everyone lived such a long time?

DR. KOLENATY:  Little girl, no matter what anyone says, life is still a very great happiness.

KRISTA:  No . . . I don't know. Don't ask me.

HAUK-SENDORF:  Oh Miss Kristina, one does want so much to live!

KRISTA *(hiding her eyes):*  Sometimes one does . . . and sometimes
. . . not.

PRUS *(after a pause):*  Thank you. For Janek.

KRISTA:  Why?

PRUS:  For thinking of him now.

KRISTA:  Thinking of him? How can I think of anything else?

DR. KOLENATY:  And here we are quarreling about eternal life.
(EMILIA *comes out of the bedroom like a shadow,
with her head in compresses. Everyone stands.)*

EMILIA:  Forgive me for . . . leaving you . . . for a little. . .

GREGOR:  How are you feeling?

EMILIA:  My head hurts. Dreadfully.

HAUK-SENDORF:  Oh, that will soon go away.

EMILIA:  It will not. It will never go away. I have had it for 200
years.

DR. KOLENATY:  What have you had?

EMILIA:  Boredom. No, it isn't even boredom. It is. . . it is. . . oh,
you people, you have no name for it. No language on earth
has a name for it. Bombita talked about it too. It is horrible.

GREGOR:  What is it?

EMILIA:  I don't know. Everything is so pointless, so empty, so
meaningless. You are all here? It seems as if you are not. As
if you are only things . . . or shadows . . . What am I to do
with you?

DR. KOLENATY:  Perhaps we should leave you alone?

EMILIA:  It doesn't really matter. To die, or just to hide behind a
door, it's all the same. Everything is the same, whether it is,
or is not. And you people make so much fuss about every
little death! You are so funny. Ah. . .

VITEK:  What is wrong?

EMILIA:  One should not, should not, should not live so long!

VITEK:  But why not?

EMILIA:  One cannot stand it. For 100, 130 years, one can go on.
But then. . . then. . . one finds out . . . that . . . and then
one's soul dies.

VITEK:  One finds out what?

EMILIA:  God, there are no words for it. One finds out that one
cannot believe in anything. Anything. And from that comes
this cold emptiness. You know, Berti, you said that I sing as
if I were frozen. You see, art only has meaning when one
does not know everything. Once you know it all, know it

completely, you realize that art is useless. It is all in vain, Krista, all in vain. To sing is the same as to be silent. There is no difference.

VITEK: That's not true. When you sing, people are moved to higher and better things.

EMILIA: People are never better. Nothing can ever be changed. Nothing, nothing, nothing ever really matters. If at this moment there were to be shooting or an earthquake or the end of the world, or whatever, still nothing would matter. Even I do not matter. You are here, and I am very far away . . . from everything . . . 300 years! Oh God, if you knew how easy it is for you to live!

DR. KOLENATY: Why?

EMILIA: You are so near to everything! For you, everything has meaning. For you, everything has value because for the few years that you are here, you don't have time to live enough. God, if I could only once more. . . *(She wrings her hands.)* Idiots! You are so happy! You disgust me with your incessant happiness. And all because of this silly chance, that you are going to die soon! Everything interests you—you're like monkeys! You believe in everything: in love, in yourselves, in honor, in progress, in humanity, I don't know what all. Maxi, you believe in pleasure. You, Krista, in love and faithfulness. Prus believes in power. You, Vitek, believe in foolishness. Everybody, everybody believes in something. You can live happily, you . . . fools!

VITEK *(excited):* Excuse me, please, but there are still higher values . . . ideals . . . aspirations. . .

EMILIA: There are, but only for you. How can I explain it to you? There may be love, but only for you. As soon as love has gone from your minds, then it is nowhere, nowhere in the whole universe. And no one can love for 300 years—it cannot last. And then everything tires one. It tires one to be good, it tires one to be bad. The earth itself tires one. And then you find out that there is nothing at all: no sin, no pain, no earth, nothing. The only thing that exists is a thing with meaning, and for you all things have meaning. My God, I was once like you. I was a girl, I was a woman, I was happy. I. . . I. . . was a human. God in Heaven!

HAUK-SENDORF: What is it? What happened to you?

EMILIA: If you only knew what Bombita told me! We. . . we old ones. . . we know too much. But you know much more than us, you fools, infinitely more! You know love, greatness, purpose. You have it all. You could not wish for anything more. You live, but in us all life has stopped. Pater hemon! And it goes on, goes on, goes on. Ah, this terrible loneliness.

PRUS: Then why did you come here for the Makropulos formula? Why do you want to have another 300 years?

EMILIA: Because I am afraid of death.

PRUS: Then not even the immortals are spared that?

EMILIA: They are not.

LONG PAUSE

PRUS: Elina Makropulos, we have been cruel to you.

EMILIA: I do not feel that. And you were right. It is undignified to be so old. Do you know that children are frightened of me? Krista, you loathe me, don't you?

KRISTA: No. I am . . . very sorry for you.

EMILIA: Sorry? That's all you feel for me? You don't even envy me? *(She pauses and takes the folded parchment from her bosom.)* Here it is written: "Ego Hieronymus Makropulos, iatres kaisaros Rodolfo. . ." And so on, and so on. Word after word. Exactly what to do. *(She rises.)* Take it, Berti. I don't want it anymore.

GREGOR: Thank you. But I don't want it either.

EMILIA: No? Then you, Maxi. You love to live. You will be able to love, you know? Take it.

HAUK-SENDORF: Please . . . can one die from it? And it hurts when. . . when it works?

EMILIA: Yes, it hurts. Are you afraid?

HAUK-SENDORF: Yes.

EMILIA: But you will live for 300 years!

HAUK-SENDORF: If. . . if it did not hurt. *(He giggles nervously.)* I don't want it.

EMILIA: Doctor, you are a knowledgeable man. You will consider . . . what it might be useful for. Do you want it?

DR. KOLENATY: You are very kind. I want nothing to do with it.

EMILIA: You are a foolish little man. Vitek, I will give it to you. Who knows? You might make all humanity happier with it.

VITEK *(backing away):* No, please. I think . . . that. . . that. . . it is better not.

EMILIA: Prus, you are such a strong person. Are you also afraid to live 300 years?

PRUS: Yes.

EMILIA: I cannot believe this. Nobody wants it? Nobody cares for it? What about you, Krista? You haven't made a sound. My dear girl, I took your lover from you—you take it. You are beautiful, you will live for 300 years. You will sing like Emilia Marty. You will be famous. Think about it. In a few short years, you will begin to grow old, and then you will be sorry. Take it, child.

KRISTA *(takes the paper):* Thank you.

VITEK: What will you do with it, Krista?

KRISTA *(opening the document):* I don't know.

GREGOR: Are you going to try it?

DR. KOLENATY: Good Lord, she isn't afraid? Give it back!

VITEK: Give it back to her!

EMILIA: Let her be!

(KRISTA *silently places the paper over the burning candle.*)

VITEK: Don't burn it! It is a historical document!

DR. KOLENATY: Careful!

HAUK-SENDORF: Good God.

PRUS *(holds them all back):* Let her deal with it herself.

*(A stunned silence.)*

HAUK-SENDORF: Look at that. It doesn't want to burn.

GREGOR: It's parchment.

DR. KOLENATY: How slowly it's getting black. Don't burn yourself, Krista.

HAUK-SENDORF: Let me have just a little piece! Just a little piece!

*(Silence.)*

VITEK: Everlasting Life. Mankind will always be searching for it. And here . . . here . . . we may have held it. . .

DR. KOLENATY: And we might have lived forever.

PRUS: Eternal life. Do you have any children?

DR. KOLENATY: I have.

PRUS: So there you are: Eternal Life. If we only thought of birth instead of death . . . Life is not so short, so long as we can be the cause of new life.

GREGOR: It's burning out. After all, it was a wild idea, to live forever. God, I feel lonely, but a bit lighter, knowing it isn't possible anymore. . .

DR. KOLENATY: We're no longer young, any of us. Only youth could burn such a thing so fearlessly. You did well, child.

HAUK-SENDORF:   Excuse me, but there is such a strange smell in here . . . a smell like. . .

VITEK *(opening a window):*   Like burning.

EMILIA *(laughs):*   The end of immortality!

## THE END

TRANSLATORS' NOTE:  The ending of Čapek's play is ambiguous, and is given without change in this translation. Most readers will feel the play ends tragically, with Emilia's final laugh a harsh, even bitter, welcome to death. Čapek, though, calls his play "a comedy," and many of the lines are undeniably laugh-provoking. The stage directions in the following interpretation are purely the invention of the translators; it seems to us suitable to the comedic tone of much of the play. It is offered as an alternative ending.

HAUK-SENDORF:   Excuse me, but there is such a strange smell in here . . . a smell like. . .

VITEK:   Like burning.

EMILIA *(goes to the little heap of ashes on the table top and picks up a few. She thoughtfully rubs them between her fingers, and a stream of ash trickles to the floor. She laughs.):*   The end of immortality! *(She laughs harshly, and then, as if relieved from a great burden, with genuine exuberance. The others stare, then also begin to laugh.* EMILIA *walks across the room and joins the others, and they welcome her. The laughter becomes general until* VITEK *suddenly hurries to the table, scoops up the ashes, throws open the window and tosses them out. The bright midday sun shines in.)*

## THE END

# INVENTIONS

I like all kinds of technical inventions, not because they seem logical to me, but because they fascinate me beyond all belief. I don't like them in the sense that an expert, or an American, likes them; I like them the way a savage would; I like them as wondrous, mysterious and incomprehensible things. I like the telephone because it provides a person with all sorts of experiences, as when the operator connects you with the wrong party by mistake and you heartily greet that party with "Listen, you big ox," or something similar; I like the streetcar because it is unpredictable, whereas going on foot is utterly predictable and lacking in adventure. I acquired an American coke stove because it demands so much caution and constant personal attention, as if I had an Indian elephant or an Australian kangaroo in my house. So now I have acquired a Swedish vacuum cleaner. I don't know but what you could say that the Swedish vacuum cleaner acquired me.

The man who introduced me to it and forced it on me said that inside the cylinder is a motor; he was probably right, because when I turn it on, it makes as much racket as a factory. Along with it I acquired a cord and all sorts of tubes and extensions, maybe ten pieces in all; you can play with it like a Meccano set. This cord is poked into an electrical outlet, and the other end travels across the floor or wherever you want it to go; at the same time the cylinder howls like a steam lathe, and it is this howling which heats it up. As you see, it is enormously simple. And afterwards, aha, I nearly forgot the main point; inside this cylinder is a small pouch, and afterwards, this is taken out and shaken over a piece of newspaper; and after that, a person can only say "I can't believe it" and "I must be mad," and call everyone in the whole house to come see how much dust came out of that pouch. I assure you, the astonishment of those present is the chief pleasure in owning a vacuum cleaner and it will afford you priceless satisfaction daily.

Up until now I believed in a whole range of things: in the

Good Lord, in universal moral law, in the atomic theory and other things more or less inaccessible to human understanding. Now I am compelled as well to believe in Swedish vacuum cleaners. I am even compelled to believe absolutely in the metaphysical, ubiquitous and extraordinary presence of dust. I now believe that dust I am and to dust I shall return, and furthermore that I am now in the continuous process of returning to dust. I think that I scatter dust wherever I walk or sit. I think that even as I write this, a small pile of dust is coming into existence under my chair. My thoughts descend to the floor in something like a rich gray dust. If I speak, dust pours like lies from my mouth, even when I speak the holiest of truths. Everything is turning to dust. Otherwise it is not possible to explain the existence, the quantity and the first-class consistency of the dust in my vacuum cleaner. In that enchanted pouch, rather.

Every belief and every idol requires certain ritualistic ceremonies. Ever since I have been serving the Vacuum Cleaner, a ritual ceremony takes place at my house each morning: Shaking Out the Pouch. It's very similar to when a parlor magician shakes a dozen glasses out of his sleeve, or a rabbit, a sheaf of paper and a live girl out of a hat; it is, in short, magic. You shake out the pouch in a more or less ritualistic fashion and anxiously lift it aside; a pile of dust appears; as I say, it is sheer sorcery. Dust from the Vacuum Cleaner isn't dirty, ordinary dust; it is dense, uniform, heavy and mysterious; it is conjured, in some way or other, for you never understand how so much dust gets in there.

If it so happens that the pile of dust is smallish, you are instantly alarmed; no doubt heathens likewise are alarmed when their idol refuses to devour an offering. As far as you are concerned, it is a matter of faith and even ambition, of a sort, that the pile of dust be large. You search for some forgotten corner where there is still some secret and unexploited dust. If you weren't so bashful, you would go out and suck up dust from the street, in order to pay homage to your idol. When you are off visiting somewhere, you envy those people with beautiful, un-vacuumed dust. I think I'll begin secretly bringing dust back to the house with me, as I've probably extracted the last pinch of it at home.

As I say, I have an awesome reverence for technical inventions. If I had the money, I would buy in addition a three-stage internal-combustion engine and a threshing machine, and maybe even a roller for rolling plate-glass windows. Or that machine which makes matchboxes. Meanwhile I have only an American coke stove and a Swedish vacuum cleaner; but I serve even these two idols in constant wonder. Not long ago, the coke stove ran for fourteen days in a row, and you should have seen the amount of dust in the pouch yesterday. It was splendid.

Translated by Norma Comrada; © 1990 Norma Comrada. Originally published as "Vynalezá" in 1924.

Self-caricature

# Part II
# THE NORMAL AND
# THE UNCANNY

The Footprint
Footprints
Money
Oplatka's End
The Clairvoyant
The Strange Experiences of Mr. Janik
The Mail

In 1917, Karel Čapek completed a collection of stories known in English as *Wayside Crosses*. 'God's Torment,' the alternate meaning of the Czech title, *Boží muka,* is more indicative of the character of these stories, brooding tales of lonely, anxious individuals trying to cope with a distant God and an incomprehensible universe. They were written during a spiritual crisis in Čapek's life, brought on by the carnage of the war and the prognosis that his spinal disease would shortly prove fatal.

In *Wayside Crosses* people hope for miracles but meet only mystery or tormenting truth. In 'The Footprint,' the protagonists puzzle over an uncanny, isolated trace in the snow. The experience of finding this phenomenon and trying to comprehend it is exhilarating, but the footprint does not really 'lead anywhere.' Čapek as storyteller performed a brilliant tour de force in this piece, for he transformed what is essentially a frozen, still photograph into a gripping narrative. He was clearly intrigued by the theme, and wrote two other variations on it: 'Footprint II' (also known as 'The Elegy'), and a story called 'Footprints.' By examining the same material from several viewpoints and in several formal ways, Čapek thus sketched out a method he was to employ with brilliant success in his trilogy of novels.

'Footprint II' is interesting as a formal experiment, but it is a contrived story, full of improbable coincidences, and is therefore not included in this Reader. 'Footprints,' however, is not only a revealing comment on the original tale but also an amusing gloss on Čapek's philosophy of the everyday. The original discovery of a human trace in the snow, an event sparkling with mystery and excitement, has metamorphosed into a subject of abstract speculation and a banal urban problem disturbing the sleep of a peaceful citizen.

Shortly after the end of World War I, Čapek published *Painful Tales,* a collection of stories about conflicting idealisms. These pieces, known in English as *Money and Other Stories,* are more conventional than *Wayside Crosses* and on the whole artistically inferior. However, many of them are quite moving, and show a Chekhovian kind of ironic compassion. Čapek describes people trapped by life, but the stories are 'painful' not because they show life's cruelty but rather because they show people who are driven to revolt only to sink back into their old slavery of habit. This tension between reality and possibility is especially evident in our selection, 'Money.'

With *Tales from Two Pockets* Čapek continued his exploration of mankind's suspension between the normal and the uncanny. In this section, we include stories from the collection which involve ironic complexities raveled up in that innocent-seeming concept: normalcy. In these pieces, the everyday is often represented by professional routine, while the unusual comes to light as a result of an amateur's accidental discovery or by a lucky coincidence. 'Oplatka's End' is in one sense just a routine case from police files: a murderer apprehended and killed. On one side are the 'forces of justice,' on the other 'the callous criminal.' Yet Čapek forces us to see that these are only cliches that enable us to face the ambiguities of life, its uncanniness. The forces of justice are a motley collection of men driven by a variety of motives to get on with an unpleasant job; the callous criminal is a pathetic, deranged creature driven to destruction by vague, unknown impulses.

In 'The Clairvoyant' and 'The Strange Experiences of Mr. Janik,' Čapek seems to be saying that there is a reason and explanation for everything—and yet. . . The clairvoyant may be a faker, a man with unusual powers, or perhaps both. Mr. Janik's successes may be due to mystic talents or to pure coincidence. And yet. . . such alternatives do not really get to the core of the events. Čapek questions both rigid scientism and mindless superstition. At the root of existence is mystery, Čapek tells us, and no matter how much we may feel at home in the world there is still something strange about it.

It may seem curious that before the Second World War, writers in Bohemia and Central Europe generally—that cozy, 'gemütlich' region—gave rise to so much literature evoking the uncanny, alien side of life. Then again, given recent history, it may not be so curious after all; merely clairvoyant.

# THE FOOTPRINT

Peacefully, endlessly, snow kept falling over the frozen countryside. Like snow, silence too always comes floating down, thought Boura, nestled in his cabin. His mood was both festive and melancholy, for he felt lonely in the openness of the country. The land was turning simpler and simpler before his eyes, it coalesced, widened, undulated in white waves untroubled by the disorderly traces of life. At last the dance of snowflakes, the only motion in that glorious silence, thinned to a halt.

Now a pedestrian, Boura hesitantly sank his feet into the untouched snow and looked in wonder at the way the long row of his footsteps branded the countryside. Coming toward him down the road was someone dressed in black and all muffled up; two chains of footsteps hurried along behind him and then they zigzagged, introducing the first human disorder onto the tabula rasa.

The antipode paused; there was snow on his beard and he was staring intensely at something by the side of the road. Boura slowed down and followed the other man's eyes; the chains met and came to a halt.

"You see that footprint over there?" said the snow-covered man, and he pointed at an impression about six yards from the side of the road.

"I see it; a man's footprint."

"Yes, but how did it get there?" Someone was walking there, Boura wanted to say, but he stopped himself: the footprint was alone in the middle of a field; neither in front of nor behind it was there a single impression. The footprint was quite clear and distinct against the stretch of white, but it was all alone; nothing led either to it or away. "How could it have gotten there?" he marveled, and he started toward it.

"Wait," the other stopped him, "randomly place a footprint there and all is lost. This must be explained," he added peevishly, "It's impossible that there'd be just a single footprint.

"Let's suppose that someone jumped from here into the middle of the field; then there wouldn't be any footprint in front of it. But who would jump from so far away, and how could he land on just one foot? He'd be sure to lose his balance and come down with his other foot somewhere else. I think he'd have to keep running on a bit, as if he'd jumped from a moving streetcar. But there *isn't* a second imprint."

"Nonsense," said Boura, "if he'd have jumped from here, he'd have left his footprints here on the road; however, there's nothing but *our* footprints. No one was here before us."

"On the contrary, the print's heel is facing the road; whoever made it was coming from this direction. If he were going into the village, he had to have been headed to the right; in that direction there's nothing but field, and what the hell was someone looking for in the fields?"

"I beg your pardon, but whoever left his imprint there must have made some sort of exit; I take the position that he didn't go anywhere at all, since he didn't take another step. It's clear. No one passed this way. The footprint must have some other sort of explanation." And Boura pondered the matter with the utmost intensity. "Perhaps there's a natural pit in the clay over there or an imprint in frozen mud, and snow fell into it. Or else, wait, perhaps there was a discarded boot and maybe a bird carried it away when the snow had stopped falling. In either case there'd be a spot without much snow that looked just like a footprint. We must look for natural causes."

"If there'd been a boot there before the storm, there'd be black earth beneath it; but all I see is snow."

"Perhaps the bird carried away the boot while it was still snowing, or he abandoned it in mid-flight, dropped it into the snow, and then carried it off again. It simply cannot be a footprint."

"Can that bird of yours eat boots? Or build a nest in one? A small bird can't pick up a boot and a big one couldn't fit into it. We must solve this in principle first. I think that it *is* a footprint, and if it didn't come up out of the earth, it must have come from above. You think it was carried off by a bird, but it's possible that it might have come from—from a balloon. Perhaps someone was hanging from a balloon and he set one foot into the snow in order to make fools of us all. Don't laugh, it's most unpleasant for me to have to explain it in such a far-fetched way, but— I'd feel better if it weren't a footprint." And both of them started toward it.

The situation couldn't be more clear. Rising gently from the ditch on the side of the road was an unploughed, snow-covered field, in the middle of the field was the footprint, and near it stood a thick-trunked, medium-sized, snow-clad tree. The space between the road and the print was virginal, without the slightest sign of having been touched; nowhere was the surface of the snow stirred or broken. The snow was wet and pliable, not powdery as it is in very cold weather.

It was, in fact, a footprint. It was the imprint of a large American-style boot with a very wide sole and five large hob-nails in the heel. The snow was clean and pressed down nice and smooth, and there wasn't a single loose, untrampled flake: therefore, the footprint had to have been made after it had finished snowing. The imprint was sharp and deep; the weight on the sole had to have been much greater than that of either of the two men peering down on it. The bird-and-boot theory vanished without a word.

Right above the footprint hung the most far-flung branches of the tree: a few slender twigs covered with snow, none of which appeared to have been pushed or shaken off. Just a light tap on the branch and the snow would have fallen down all at once. The hypothesis "from above" failed absolutely. It wasn't possible that it had come from above without shaking the snow off the tree. The existence of the footprint took on a harsh, naked clarity.

Beyond the footprint there was only a clean, snowy field. They climbed the slope and crossed the top of the hill: as far down as they could see, the slope was white and untouched, and further on it rose again, even more vast and white. There wasn't a trace of another footprint for miles in all directions.

They turned back and they found the double rows of their footprints, orderly and regular, as if they'd made them on purpose. But between the rows, in the middle of a well-tread circle, was the imprint of another, larger foot, cynical in its isolation; something had kept them from trampling it to pieces and wiping it out in silent conspiracy.

Exhausted and perplexed, Boura sat down on a milestone at the side of the road. "Someone has had a good laugh on us." "It's disgraceful," said the other, "what an incredibly stupid trick, but— Damn, there are such things as physical limits. Well, it's completely impossible— Listen," he blurted out, almost in anguish, "if there's only a single footprint there, couldn't it have been left by a man with only one leg? Don't laugh, I know it's idiotic, but there *must* be some sort of explanation. I mean, it's a matter of common sense, it's an assault— I'm quite confused. Either both of us are fools, or I'm asleep in my bed with a high fever, or there *must* be a natural explanation."

"Both of us are fools," Boura suggested pensively. "We keep searching for a 'natural' explanation; we'll snatch at the most complex, the most senseless, and the most tenuous cause, if only it is 'natural.' Maybe it would be far simpler—and more natural—if we said that it's simply a miracle. If we just marveled and quietly went our ways— Without confusion. Maybe even content."

"Not me. I wouldn't be content. If the footprint led to something great—if it brought some good to someone—I would get down on my knees and cry out, 'Miracle!' But the footprint, it's, well, embarrassing; it's terribly petty, isn't it, to leave only a single imprint behind when one could leave the usual row of footprints."

"If someone brought a dead girl back to life right before your eyes, you would kneel and humble yourself; but before the snow melted on your knees, you'd decide that the death was only apparent. This isn't a matter of anything apparent; here, we must admit that a miracle has been performed under the simplest of conditions, as if it were a physics experiment."

"Maybe I wouldn't believe such a resurrection. But I would like to be saved and I am ready for a miracle—that something will come and turn my life around. The footprint neither saves nor converts me, nor does it take me out of anything I'm in. It just torments me and sticks in my mind; I don't know how to shake it. No, I don't believe: a miracle would satisfy me, but the footprint is a step towards doubt. It would be better if I'd never seen it."

For a long time neither of them spoke. It began to snow again, harder and harder. "I recall reading in Hume," Boura began, "about a single footprint in the sand. This one isn't the first. I'll bet there are thousands of footprints just like it, that there are vastly more of them that wouldn't strike us as anything, because we're accustomed to fixed natural laws. Someone else might not have even noticed it, if it didn't strike him that it was all by itself, that there are things in the world that don't have to do with anything else. You see, our footprints are alike, but the single one is bigger and deeper than ours. And when I think about my life, it seems to me that I must acknowledge — footsteps that come from nowhere and lead nowhere. It's terribly confusing to see everything I've lived

188

through as just part of a chain that starts as one link and ends as another. It happens that suddenly you see or feel something that is comparable to nothing that went before, nothing at all, nothing like it, and afterwards nothing like it can ever appear again. There are human things that have nothing in common with anything and show off their isolation wherever they are. I know things from which nothing flows, which redeem nothing and nobody, and yet— Things have happened which led no further nor made it easier to live, and yet they were perhaps the most important things in my life. Didn't it strike you that the footprint was far more beautiful than any you'd ever seen before?"

"It reminds me," the other replied, "of seven-league boots. Maybe some people come across such footprints and they don't know any other way to explain them. Who knows, perhaps the steps preceding that one are at Pardubice and Kolin and the next one is all the way at Rakovnik. Similarly, I can imagine that the steps following it are imprinted not in snow but in the midst of society, in the middle of some event where something just happened or is about to happen; that this step is a link in a continuous chain of footsteps. Imagine a chain of miracles of some sort in which our footprint has its natural position. If we had newspapers that were perfectly well-informed, we might, in the *Daily Bulletin,* be able to find the rest of the footsteps and to follow someone's route. Perhaps some sort of deity takes his own route; he takes it one step at a time and without a break; perhaps his road is some sort of lead that we should follow; it would let us go step by step in the footsteps of a deity. Perhaps it's the road to salvation. Anything is possible — And it's frightening to have one absolutely certain step on this road that lies before us and not to be able to follow it further."

Boura shook himself and rose. It was snowing even harder and the trampled field with the big footprint in the middle of others disappeared under a new layer of snow. "I won't let go of it," said the snow-covered man — "the footprint that is no more and will not be," Boura concluded, deep in thought, and they started on their ways in opposite directions.

Translated by Robert Wechsler and Peter Kussi; © 1990 Robert Wechsler and Peter Kussi. Originally published as "Šlépej" in *Boží muka (Wayside Crosses).* 1917.

# FOOTPRINTS

That night Mr. Rybka was walking home in a particularly good mood. First, because he'd won his game of chess (it was a fine checkmate with a knight, and he was reveling in it), and second because fresh snow had fallen and it crunched under his feet in the pure, quiet air. God how beautiful it all is, thought Mr. Rybka; a town covered with snow suddenly becomes such a small, old-fashioned place — a person can almost imagine a mail-coach or a squad of night-watchmen coming down the street. It's strange how snow makes everything look ancient and rustic.

Crunch, crunch, Mr. Rybka searched for an untrammeled path, delighting in the crunch he made; since he lived on a quiet back alley, he came upon fewer and fewer footprints. Look, in the courtyard, a man's boots and a woman's shoes were fading fast, most likely husband and wife—I wonder if they're newlyweds?, Mr. Rybka said softly, as if he wanted to bless them. Over there, a cat crossed the path and left its pawprints, like flowers, in the snow. Good night, pusser, how cold your feet will get! Already now just a single row of footprints, deep, a man's, a straight and clear chain of steps which a lone pedestrian had rolled out behind him. Which of his neighbors' was he at?, Mr. Rybka asked with the concern of a friend. Few people walked there—there wasn't a single track in the snow—we live on the margin of life. By the time I reach home, the street will have pulled its feather-bed up to its nose, like a child's plaything. It's too bad that in the morning the old newspaper lady will trample all over it, her footprints criss-crossing like a hare's—

Mr. Rybka stopped suddenly: on the verge of crossing the bright white street to his gate, he saw that there were footprints ahead of his and that they turned from the sidewalk and headed across the street to his gate. Who would be going to my house?, he asked, puzzled, and with his eyes he followed the conspicuous footprints. There were five of them, and right in the middle of the street they came to an end with the sharp impression of a left foot. There weren't any more, just unbroken, untouched snow.

This is crazy, Mr. Rybka said to himself —perhaps the fellow went back to the sidewalk! But as far as he could see, the sidewalk was nothing but smooth, deep snow, without a single human footprint. Well I'll be damned— Mr. Rybka was shocked —but of course, the next footprint will be on the other sidewalk! And so he walked a circuit around the untouched prints, but on the other sidewalk too he didn't find a single mark. The entire street glowed from the smooth, untouched snow, so pure it took his breath away. No one had passed that way from the moment the snow began to fall. It's curious, Mr. Rybka muttered, most likely the fellow walked backwards back to the sidewalk, stepping in his own footsteps; but he would have had to have walked backwards in his footsteps all the way to the corner, since there was only one set of prints. But why would the fellow do such a thing?— Mr. Rybka was astonished —And could he really have hit the mark *every* time?

Shaking his head he unlocked the gate and went into his house. Although he knew it was nonsense, he wondered if *inside* his house he'd find some snowy footprints. But it stands to reason there was nothing of the kind! Perhaps it was just my imagination, Mr. Rybka muttered anxiously, and then he leaned out the window. On the street, in the gleam of the streetlights, he could clearly see five sharp, deep footprints that ended in the middle of the street, and then nothing. Damn— Mr. Rybka thought and he rubbed his eyes —once I read a yarn about a single footprint in the snow, but here there's a whole row of them, and then suddenly nothing. . . what's become of the fellow?

Shaking his head he began to undress, but suddenly he stopped, went to the telephone, and in a subdued voice called the police station: "Hello, Sergeant Bartosek? Such a peculiar thing has happened, *most* peculiar— If you'd send someone here, or even better come yourself— Wonderful, I'll wait for you at the corner. I don't know *what* the matter is— No, I don't think it's dangerous;

I just don't want anyone to tread on those footprints— I don't know *whose* footprints! Fine, I'll be waiting for you."

Mr. Rybka dressed and went out again; cautiously he walked around the footprints and took care not to disturb them, even on the sidewalk. Shaking with cold and excitement, he waited at the corner for Sergeant Bartosek. It was quiet, and the inhabited earth shone peacefully out into space.

"It's so nice and quiet here," Sergeant Bartosek muttered pensively. "And what do I get but a fight and a drunk. Phooey! — So what happened?"

"Take a good look at these footprints, Sergeant," Mr. Rybka said in a quivering voice. "They start from here."

The Sergeant turned on his flashlight. "He's a lanky sort of guy," he surmised, "about 5′ 11″ according to the impressions and the length of the stride. His shoes were decent, handsown I think. He wasn't drunk and he walked rather briskly. I don't know what it is about the footprints you don't like."

"That," Mr. Rybka said succinctly, and he pointed to the incomplete row of footprints in the middle of the street.

"Aha," Sergeant Bartosek responded, and without much ceremony he headed for the last footprint, crouched down, and shone his flashlight. "It's nothing," he said with satisfaction; "it's quite normal, a good solid imprint. The weight is on the heel; if the man had taken another step or jumped, the weight would have transferred to his toes, you follow? It's obvious."

"So it means—?" Mr. Rybka asked expectantly.

"In short," the Sergeant said calmly, "it means that he didn't go any further."

"Then where did he go?" Rybka blurted out feverishly.

The Sergeant shrugged his shoulders. "I don't know. Perhaps you suspect him of something?"

"Suspect him?" Mr. Rybka was astonished. "All I want to know is where he was headed. Look, here's where he made his last impression; where, for Christ's sake, did he make the next? There simply aren't any more footprints!"

"I can see that," the Sergeant said drily. "And what is it to you where he was going? Is it someone from your house? Is someone missing? What the hell difference is it to you where he was headed?"

"But there must be some explanation," Mr. Rybka mumbled.

"Don't you think it might be possible that he went backwards in his own footprints?"

"Nonsense," the Sergeant growled. "When a man walks backwards, he takes shorter steps and he walks with his feet further apart to keep his balance. In addition, he doesn't lift his legs and with his heels he digs great trenches in the snow. Sir, this imprint here was made by just one step. You must admit that the prints are sharp."

"Then if he didn't go back," Mr. Rybka stubbornly insisted, *"where did he disappear to?"*

"That's his affair," the Sergeant growled. "Look here, if he did nothing wrong, we have no right to meddle in his affairs. We must have some charges; then, of course, we will take him in for questioning. . ."

"But what if a man disappears right in the middle of a street?" Mr. Rybka was appalled.

"Sir, you must be patient," the Sergeant calmly advised him. "If someone has disappeared, we'll hear in the next few days from his family or someone else, yes, of course, and then we'll start our search. As long as no one misses him, then we have nothing to do with it. It's none of our business."

Inside Mr. Rybka a dark anger was beginning to rise. "I beg your pardon," he stated sharply, "but I would say that the police should take a *little* interest when an innocent pedestrian disappears, out of the blue, in the middle of the street!"

"Nothing bad happened here," Sergeant Bartosek tried to console him. "There certainly aren't any signs of a struggle. If someone had held him up or abducted him, then there would be a mess of footprints. I'm sorry, sir, but I have insufficient cause to intervene."

"But Sergeant," Mr. Rybka threw up his hands, "at least explain to me. . . It's still such a mystery. . ."

"It is," Sergeant Bartosek agreed, deep in thought. "You don't have the ghost of an idea how many mysteries there are in the world. Every house, every family is a mystery. As I was coming here, there in that building I heard a young woman sobbing. Sir, mysteries are none of our concern. We're paid to keep the peace. What do you think, that we chase thieves out of curiosity? Sir, we chase them in order to lock them up. There must be law and order."

"Exactly!" Mr. Rybka exclaimed. "But you must acknowledge

that there's no law and order when in the middle of the street someone. . . let's say someone rises straight up into the sky."

"It's a matter of interpretation," said the Sergeant. "It's a police regulation that if a man is in danger of falling from a great height, we have to tie him up. First comes the warning, and then the penalty. If this man rose into the sky of his own volition, then a police officer would have to advise him to buckle his safety belt; but perhaps no officer was present," he said apologetically. "Or there'd be footprints alongside these. However, in any event, it is possible that the man left the scene by some other means, right?"

"But how?" Mr. Rybka said quickly.

Sergeant Bartosek shook his head: "It's hard to say. Perhaps it was some sort of Assumption or Jacob's Ladder," he said uncertainly. "The Assumption would have been considered a kidnapping if there were any signs of violence; but ordinarily it's done with the victim's acquiescence. It's possible that the fellow might have flown away. Doesn't it sometimes seem to you as if you were flying? All a man has to do is push off with his feet and he's airborne. . . Some fly like a balloon, but me, when I fly in my sleep, I have to keep pushing off from the ground every few moments. I think it's due to my heavy clothing and my saber. Perhaps the fellow was sleeping and in his sleep he began to fly. But that's not prohibited. Of course, on a busy street an officer would have to give him a warning. Or wait, perhaps he was levitating; spiritualists believe in levitation. But spiritualism, too, is not prohibited. A certain Mr. Baudys told me that he himself has seen mediums hanging in thin air. Who knows what's in it."

"But Sergeant," Mr. Rybka said reproachfully, "I don't think you believe what you're saying! Those things would be such a grave violation of natural law—"

Sergeant Bartosek shrugged his shoulders dispiritedly. "Sir, I know that people violate every conceivable law and statute; if you were a police officer, you'd see so much of it. . ." The Sergeant waved his hands as if waving it all away. "It wouldn't surprise me if they violated even natural laws. People are a rotten lot, sir. Well, good night; it's freezing out here."

"Won't you come in and have a cup of tea . . . or slivovice?" Mr. Rybka suggested.

"Why not," the Sergeant growled despondently. "You know,

in this uniform a man can't even go into a bar. That's why policemen drink so little."

"Mystery," he continued, seated in an easychair and thoughtfully contemplating a speck of snow thawing on the tip of his boot. "Ninety-nine people would pass those footprints without noticing a thing. And you don't notice ninety-nine things that are damned mysterious. We don't know a damned thing about. . . . But there are a few things that aren't mysterious. Order is not mysterious. Justice is not mysterious. Policemen are not mysterious. But each man who walks along a street is a mystery, because we can't get at him, sir. As soon as he steals something, then he ceases to be mysterious, because we lock him up and that's that; at least we know what he's doing, and whenever we want we watch him through the window in his cell, right? I ask you, why do papers print headlines like, 'Mysterious Discovery of a Corpse!' What's mysterious about a corpse? When we find it, we measure it and photograph it and cut it up; we know every fiber in it, the last meal it ate, how it died, and what not. Moreover, we know that, most likely, someone slaughtered it for money. It's all clear and straightforward. . . You can pour me a good bit more of that black tea, sir. All crimes are clear, sir; at least you know the criminal's motives and things like that. But what your cat is thinking, that's a mystery; or what your maid dreams about, and why your wife stares out the window so pensively. Sir, everything is mysterious except criminal proceedings; every criminal case is a precisely determined portion of reality, a well-illuminated slice of life. If I were to look around here, I'd learn a lot about you, but I'm looking at the toes of my boots, because officially I have no interest in you. That is, we don't have any charges against you," he added, sipping his scalding hot tea.

"It's a rather peculiar notion," he began again after a short pause, "that the police, especially detectives, are interested in mysteries. We don't give a damn about mysteries; improprieties are what interests us. Sir, crime doesn't interest us because it's mysterious, but because it's forbidden. We don't chase a crook out of intellectual curiosity; we chase him in order to arrest him in the name of the law. Listen, streetcleaners don't sweep streets in order to search the dust for signs of people's footprints, but in order to sweep up and clear away all the filth that life deposits there. Order is not a bit mysterious. To keep order is lousy work, sir; whoever wants cleanliness must put his fingers into all sorts of filth. But someone has to do it," he said despondently, "just as someone has to slaughter calves. But to slaughter a calf out of curiosity is barbaric; it must be done only for the sake of one's trade. If a man has an obligation to do something, then at least he knows that it's the right thing to do. Look, justice must be as indisputable as a multiplication table. I certainly don't know if you could claim that *every* theft is wrong, but I'll prove to you that every theft is forbidden, by simply locking you up. If you cast pearls on the street, then a policeman will give you a warning about littering the street. But if you start performing miracles, then we can't stop you from doing it, unless we were to call it a public nuisance or an illegal gathering of people. There must be some sort of disorderly conduct for us to intervene."

"But Sergeant," objected Mr. Rybka, fidgeting uneasily, "is that enough for you? Here it's a matter of . . . of such a peculiar thing . . . of something so mysterious . . . and you. . ."

Sergeant Bartosek shrugged his shoulders. "And I just let it go. Sir, if you'd like I will have the footprints removed so that they don't interfere with your peace of mind tonight. I can't do any more. Don't you hear something? Some footsteps? Well, there goes our patrol, so it's been two hours and seven minutes. Good night, sir."

Mr. Rybka accompanied the Sergeant out to his gate. In the middle of the street there was still an incomplete and incomprehensible chain of footprints— An officer was approaching on the opposite sidewalk.

"Mimra," Sergeant Bartosek called out, "anything new?"

Officer Mimra saluted. "Not much at all, Sergeant," he called. "Over there, in front of No. 17, a kitten was meowing, so I rang the bell to let it in. At No. 9 they left the gate open. At the corner, they dug up the street, but failed to leave a red lantern, and at Marsik's grocery one side of a sign was coming off; it must be removed in the morning so that it doesn't fall on somebody's head."

"That's all?"

"That's all," said Officer Mimra. "In the morning I'll have to throw sand on the sidewalks so that nobody breaks his leg; and at six o'clock we should really ring all the doorbells—"

"Excellent," said Sergeant Bartosek. "Good night!"

Mr. Rybka took one last look at the footprints that had led

into the unknown. But there, where the last footprint had been, were the two large imprints of Officer Mimra's workboots, and from there the wide footprints went off in a clear and regular chain. "Good riddance," Mr. Rybka sighed, and he went to bed.

Translated by Robert Wechsler and Peter Kussi. Originally published as "Šlépeje" in *Povídky z jedné kapsy (Tales from One Pocket)*, 1929. First English translation.

# MONEY

Again, again it had come over him; he had scarcely swallowed a few mouthfuls of food when a painful heaviness seized him; a perspiration of faintness broke out on his forehead. He left his dinner untouched and leaned his head on his hand, sullenly indifferent to the landlady's officious solicitude. At length she went out, sighing, and he lay down on the sofa meaning to rest, but in reality to listen with alarm and attention to torturing sounds within him. The faintness did not pass off; his stomach seemed to have become a heavy stone, and his heart throbbed with rapid, irregular beats: from sheer exhaustion he perspired as he lay. Ah, if he could only sleep!

After an hour the landlady knocked: she handed him a telegram. He opened it in alarm and read "19:10. 7:34. Coming tonight. Rose." What this might mean he simply could not grasp; bewildered, he stood up and read through the numbers and words, and at length he understood: his married sister Rosa would arrive this evening and, of course, he must go and meet her. Probably she was coming to do some shopping, and he felt annoyed at the impulsive, feminine thoughtlessness and disregard for others, which disturbed him for no reason at all. He paced up and down the room, irritated because his evening was spoiled. He was thinking how comfortably he would have rested on his old sofa, soothed by the humming of his faithful lamp, with a book in his hand; he had passed weary and tedious hours there, but now for some unknown reason they seemed to him especially attractive, full of wise musings and peace. A wasted evening, an end to rest. Full of childish and resentful bitterness, he tore the luckless telegram to bits.

That evening, when he was waiting for the belated train in the lofty, cold, damp station, an even vaster feeling of distress took possession of him: distress at the squalor and poverty around him, the weary folk who arrived, the disappointment of those who had been waiting in vain. With difficulty he found his fragile little slip of a sister in the thick of the hurrying crowd. Her eyes were frightened and she was dragging a heavy trunk along; and at once he saw that something serious had happened. He caught a cab and took her straight home. During the journey it occurred to him that he had neglected to find a room for her; he asked her if she would like to go to a hotel, but this only evoked an outburst of tears. He really couldn't do anything with her in this state, so he gave up, took her thin, nervous hand in his, and was immensely cheered when at length she looked up at him with a smile.

Once at home he looked closely at her and was alarmed. Distressed, trembling, strangely excited, with flaming eyes and parched lips, she sat there on his sofa, supported by the cushions he heaped around her, and she talked . . . He asked her to speak softly, for it was already night. "I have run away from my husband," she burst out, talking rapidly. "Ah, if you knew, George, if you knew what I have had to bear! If you knew how hateful he is to me! I have come to you for advice," and then she burst into a flood of tears.

Gloomily, George paced the room. One word after another called up before him a picture of her life with an overfed, money-grubbing, and vulgar husband who insulted her before the servant, was immoderate and inopportune in his affection, plagued her with endless scenes about nothing, foolishly squandered her dowry, was self-indulgent at home and spent extravagantly on the silly whims of a hypochondriac. He heard the story of food doled out bite by bite, of reproaches, humiliations and cruelty, shabby generosity, frenzied and brutal quarrels, exacted love, stupid and overbearing taunts. . . . George paced the room choking with disgust and sympathy: it was intolerable, he could not endure this endless torrent of shame and pain. And there sat the small, fragile, frenzied girl whom he had never thoroughly known, his proud and spunky little sister; she had always been combative and refused to listen to reason, her eyes used to flash wickedly when she was a girl. There she sat, her chin quivering with sobs and with the ceaseless torrent of words, exhausted and feverish. George wanted to soothe her, but was half afraid. "Stop," he said roughly, "that will do, I know all about it." But he was powerless to restrain her.

"Don't," wept Rosa, "I have no one but you." Then the stream of complaints began again, more broken, at greater length, in calmer tones: details were repeated and incidents enlarged upon. Suddenly Rosa stopped and asked:

"And you, George, how are you getting on?"

"As for me," grumbled George, "I can't complain. But tell me, won't you go back to him?"

"Never," declared Rosa excitedly. "That is impossible. I'd rather die than. . . If you only knew what it was like!"

"Yes, but wait," observed George. "In that case, what will you do?"

Rosa expected that question. "I made up my mind about that a long time ago," she said warmly. "I will give lessons or go somewhere as a governess, to an office or anywhere . . . You will see how I can work. I will make my living all by myself, and be so happy, so happy doing anything. You must advise me . . . I will find a room somewhere, just a little one . . . Tell me, something will turn up, won't it?" She could not sit still, but jumped up and, with an eager face, paced the room beside her brother: "I have thought it all out. I will take the furniture, the old furniture you know, which belonged to our parents; wait till you see. I really want nothing but to be left in peace. I don't mind if I am poor, if only I don't have to. . . I want nothing else, nothing more in life than that, so little will suffice! I will be satisfied with anything only if I am away from— from all that. I am looking forward to working, I will do all my own sewing and sing over it — I have not sung for years. Ah, George, if you only knew!"

"Work," reflected George doubtfully. "I don't know if any can be found—and anyway, you are not accustomed to that, Rosy, it will be hard for you, very hard."

"No," retorted Rosa with flashing eyes. "You don't know what it has been to be reproached for every mouthful, every rag, for everything . . . All the time to be told that you don't work but only spend . . . I would like to tear off all these things, it's all become so hateful to me. No, Georgie, you will see how glad I'll be to work, how happily I'll live. I'll enjoy every mouthful, even if it is only dry bread: I'll be proud of it. With pride I will sleep, dress in calico, cook for myself. . . . Tell me, I can be a working woman, can't I? If nothing else turns up I will go into a factory . . . I am looking forward to it all so much!"

George gazed at her with delighted astonishment. Heavens, what radiance, what courage in such a downtrodden life! He was ashamed of his own weakness and weariness; he thought of his own work with sudden warmth and happiness, infected by the ardent vitality of this strange, feverish girl. She had really become a young girl again, blushing, animated, childishly naïve. Oh, it will turn out all right, how can it fail to?

"I'll manage, you'll see," said Rosa. "I want nothing from anyone, I will support myself, and I will really earn money, at least enough to provide for myself and to have a few flowers on the table. And if I had no flowers there, I would go into the street and just look at them. . . . You can't imagine how each thing has filled me with happiness since — I decided to run away. How beautifully, delightfully different everything looks! A new life has begun for me. . . . Till now I never understood how beautiful everything is. Ah, Georgie," she exclaimed with tears running down her face, "I'm so happy."

"Silly," Georgie smiled at her, delighted. "It won't be so easy. Well, we will try it. But now lie down, you mustn't make yourself ill. Don't talk to me anymore now, please. I have something to think over, and in the morning I will let you know. Go to sleep now and let me think."

Nothing that he could say would induce her to take his bed; she lay down fully dressed on the sofa, he covered her with everything warm he had and he turned down the lamp. It was quiet; only her rapid, childish breathing seemed to appeal to heaven for sympathy. George gently opened the window to the cool October night. The peaceful, lofty sky was bright with stars. Once in their father's house they had stood by the open window, he and little Rosa; she, shivering with cold, pressed close to him, as they waited for falling stars. "When a star falls," whispered Rosa, "I'll ask to be changed into a boy and do something glorious." Ah, father was asleep soundly as a log: the bed could be heard creaking under his ponderous fatigue. And George, filled with a feeling of importance, meditated on something grand and with masculine gravity protected little Rosa, who was trembling with cold and excitement.

Over the garden a star shot across the sky.

"George," Rosa's voice called him softly from the room.

"In a moment," answered George shivering with excitement and cold.

Yes, to do something great: there was no other way out. Poor, foolish creature, what great deed did you want to do? You have your burden to bear; if you want to do something fine, carry a greater one; the greater your burden, the greater you are. Are you a weakling, sinking under your own burden? Rise and help to support one who is fainting: you cannot do otherwise unless you would fall yourself.

"George," Rosa called in a hushed voice.

George turned where he stood at the window. "Listen," he began hesitatingly. "I've thought it out . . . I think that — you will not find work to suit you . . . There is work enough, but you will not earn enough to— oh, it's nonsense."

"I'll be satisfied with anything," said Rosa quietly.

"No, wait a moment. You really don't know what it means. You see, I have quite a fair salary now, I'm glad to say, and I could get afternoon work, too. Sometimes I really don't know what to do. . . . It is quite enough for me. And I could let you have money—"

"What money?" murmured Rosa.

"My share from our parents and the interest which has accumulated; that makes about five thousand a year. No, not five thousand, only four . . . That's just the interest, you understand. It has occurred to me that I could let you have that interest, so that you might have something."

Rosa bounded off the sofa. "That's not possible," she cried excitedly.

"Don't scream," growled George. "It's only the interest, I tell you. Whenever you don't need it, you need not draw it out. But now, just at the beginning. . . ."

Rosa stood like an astonished little girl. "But that won't do, what would you have?"

"Oh, don't trouble about that," he protested. "I've thought for a long time that I would like to get afternoon work, but— I was ashamed to take work away from my colleagues. However, you see how I live; I shall be glad to have something to do. That's how it is; you understand, don't you? That money only hindered me. So now, do you want it or not?"

"I do," sighed Rosa, approaching him on tiptoe, flinging her arms round his neck and pressing her moist face to his. "George," she whispered, "I never dreamed of this; I swear to you that I wanted nothing from you, but since you are so good—"

"Never mind," he said, deeply stirred. "That's beside the point. That money really doesn't matter to me, Rosa; when a man is fed up with life, he must do something. . . . But what can one do all alone? In spite of all efforts one can only come face to face with oneself again in the end; you know, it's like living surrounded by nothing but mirrors, and whenever one looks in them there is only one's own face, one's own boredom, one's own loneliness. . . . If you knew what that means! No, Rosa, I don't want to tell you about myself, but I am so glad that you're here, so glad that this has happened. Look how many stars there are: do you remember how once at home we watched for falling stars?"

"No, I don't remember," said Rosa, turning a pale face to his; in the dim, frosty light he saw her eyes shining like stars. "Why are you like this?"

He thrilled with pleasant excitement and stroked her hair. "Don't talk about the money. It is so dear of you to come to me. Heavens, how glad I am, as if a window had opened—among the mirrors. Can you imagine it? I really only cared for myself. I was sick of myself, tired of myself, but I had nothing else. . . . Oh, there was no sense in it at all. Do you remember, when the stars fell, what you asked for then? What would you ask for tonight if a star fell?"

"What would I ask for?" Rosa smiled sweetly. "Something for myself . . . No, something for you, for something to happen for you."

"I have nothing to wish for, Rosa, I'm so glad to have got rid. . . Now, what arrangements will you make? Wait, tomorrow I will find you a nice room with a pleasant view. From here, you only look onto a yard; in the daytime, when there are no stars shining, it's a bit depressing. But we must find something better for you, something more open." Quite excited and enthusiastic, he strode about the room planning out the future, eagerly picturing each new detail, laughing, talking, promising all sorts of things. Of course, lodging, work, money, would all be forthcoming; the main thing was that this would be a new life. He felt how her eyes shone in the darkness, smiling, following him with their ardent brightness; his heart was so full that he could have laughed for joy; he didn't think of resting until exhausted, worn out by sheer happiness and too much talking, they fell into long pauses of weariness, in complete harmony.

At last he made her lie down; she did not resist his quaint, motherly solicitude, and could not even thank him; but when he looked up from the piles of newspapers in which he was glancing through advertisements of lodgings and agencies, he found her eyes fixed on him with an ardent, terrible brilliance, and his heart was wrung with happiness. Thus morning found him.

Yes, it was a new life. His wretched lassitude was gone now as he swallowed a hasty dinner and then strode through countless houses in search of a room, coming home sweaty as a hunting dog and happy as a bridegroom, and settling down in the evening to plough through pieces of extra work, until he finally fell asleep worn out and enthusiastic over an eventful day. But, alas! he had to settle for a room without a pleasant view, a detestable room, upholstered in plush and outrageously expensive, and he placed Rosa there for the present. Sometimes, indeed, in the course of his work he was attacked by faintness and weakness, his eyelids would tremble, a sweat from dizziness breaking out on his suddenly livid brow. But he succeeded in mastering this, set his teeth and laid his hand on the cold slab of the table, saying resolutely: Bear it— you must bear it—indeed, you are not living for yourself alone. In this way he did feel better and better as day followed day. This was a new life.

Suddenly one day he had an unexpected visit. It was his other sister, Tylda; she was married to the owner of a small plant, who was not doing well and who lived some distance outside of town. She always called on him when she came to Prague on business trips, for she looked after everything herself. She would sit with her eyes cast down and talk in brief, quiet phrases of her three children and her many worries, as if there were nothing else in the world. Today, however, she alarmed him; she was breathing heavily, struggling in her cobweb of ceaseless cares, and her fingers, disfigured by writing and sewing, touched his heart and made it ache with sympathy. Thank heaven, she got out brokenly, the children were healthy and good, but the workshop was not going well, the machines were worn out; she was starting to look for a purchaser.

"And so Rosa is here?" she suddenly said in a half-questioning tone, vainly trying to raise her eyes. Strange to say, wherever her eyes rested there was a hole in the carpet, frayed furniture covers, something old, shabby, and neglected. Somehow or other, neither he nor Rosa had paid any attention to such things. This vexed him, and he looked away; he was ashamed to meet her eyes, keen as needles and relentless as unceasing cares.

"She has run away from her husband," she began indifferently. "Says that he plagued her. Perhaps he did, but everything has a cause.

"He had cause, too," she went on, failing to provoke questions. "You see, Rosa is— I don't know how to put it. . ." Silent, with heavy eyes she stitched a large hole in the carpet. "Rosa isn't a housewife," she began after a time. "And, of course, she has no children, need not work, has no cares, but—"

George looked gloomily out of the window.

"Rosa is a spendthrift," Tylda forced out of herself. "She has run him into debt, you see. . . . Have you noticed the way she dresses?"

"No."

Tylda sighed and made as if wiping something from her forehead. "You've no idea what it costs . . . She buys, say, furs, for thousands, and then sells them for a few hundred to pay for boots. She used to hide the bills from him: then there came summonses . . . Do you know about this?"

"No. He and I are not on speaking terms."

Tylda nodded. "He is odd, of course, I don't dispute it . . . But when she doesn't sew a single stitch for him, and when she herself goes about like a duchess—tells him lies—and carries on with other men—"

"Stop," begged George in anguish.

Tylda's sad eyes mended a torn bed cover. "Perhaps she has

offered you," she asked uncertainly, "to keep house for you? Suggested your taking larger lodgings—and that she should cook for you?

George's heart contracted painfully. This had never occurred to him. Nor had it to Rosa. Heavens, how happy he would be! "I wouldn't want her to," he said sharply, controlling himself with great effort.

Tylda succeeded in raising her eyes. "Perhaps she wouldn't want it either. She has him here—her officer. They transferred him to Prague. That's why she ran away — and has taken up with him — a married man. Of course, she has said nothing about it to you."

"Tylda," he said hoarsely, withering her with his glance, "you lie."

Her hands and face quivered, but she wouldn't give in yet. "See for yourself," she stammered. "You are too kind-hearted. I would not have said this if— if I were not sorry for you. Rosa never cared for you. She said you were—"

"Go!" he cried, beside himself with rage. "For God's sake leave me in peace!"

Tylda rose slowly. "You should— you should get better lodgings, George," she said with dignified calm. "Look how dirty this place is. Would you like me to send you a little box of pears?"

"I don't want anything."

"I must be off . . . How dark it is here . . . Dear, dear George; well, goodbye, then."

The blood throbbed in his temples, his throat contracted; he tried to work, but he had only just sat down when he broke his pen in a rage, sprang to his feet and hurried to see Rosa. He ran to her apartment in a sweat and rang: the landlady opened the door and said that the young lady had been out since morning: was there any message?

"It doesn't matter," growled George, and he shuffled home as though carrying an immense load. There he sat down to his papers, leaned his head on his hand and began to work; but an hour went by and he had not turned a page; dusk was followed by darkness, and he did not turn on a single lamp. Then the bell rang in a breezy, cheery way, there was a rustle of skirts in the passage and Rosa flew into the room. "Are you asleep, Georgie?" She smiled tenderly. "Why, how dark it is in here; where are you?"

"Eh? I've been busy," he remarked drily. There was an air of chilliness in the room and an exceedingly pleasant scent.

"Listen," she began cheerfully.

"I wanted to go see you," he interrupted, "but I thought perhaps you wouldn't be at home."

"Why, where would I have been?" she asked in genuine wonder. "Oh, how nice it is here. Georgie, I'm so glad to be with you." Joy and youth breathed from her and she was radiant with happiness. "Come and sit next to me," she said, and when he was seated beside her on the sofa she slipped her arm round his neck and repeated, "I'm so happy, Georgie." He rested his face against her cold fur, bedewed with autumn mist, let himself be rocked gently, and thought: Suppose she has been somewhere, what is that to me, after all? At any rate, she has come back to me right away. But his heart grew faint and oppressed with a strange mixture of keen pain and sweet odor.

"What's the matter, Georgie?" she cried in shrill alarm.

"Nothing," he said as though lulled. "Tylda has been here."

"Tylda," she repeated, dismayed. "Let go of me," she said, after a pause. "What did she say?"

"Nothing."

"Come now, she spoke of me, didn't she? Did she say anything awful?"

"Well, yes—a few things."

Rosa burst into wrathful tears. "The nasty creature. She's always jealous of everything I have. How can I help it if things go badly with them? She must have come because— because she found out what you had been doing for me. If things went better with them, she'd forget all about you. It's so disgusting. She wants everything for herself—for her children—those horrid children."

"Don't talk about it," entreated George.

But Rosa went on crying. "She wants to spoil everything for me. I scarcely began to have a happier life when she comes along, slandering me and wanting to take things from me. Tell me, do you believe what she said?

"No."

"I really want nothing more than to be free. Haven't I a right then to be a little more happy? I want so little, and was so happy here, George, and then she comes along—"

"Don't worry about that," he said, and he went to light the

lamp. Rosa stopped crying at once. He looked at her, studied her, as though for the first time. She was looking at the floor, her lips were trembling. Ah, how pretty and youthful! She had on new clothes, gloves, so close-fitting they seemed ready to burst; and silk stockings peeped out from under her skirt. Her nervous little hands played with the threads of the worn upholstery on the sofa.

"Excuse me," he said sighing. "I have some work to do just now."

She obeyed and rose. "Ah, Georgie," she began, and did not know how to go on. With hands clasped against her breast, she gave him a swift, agonized glance and stood there, white-lipped, like an image of fear. "Don't be anxious," he said, and he turned to his work.

Next day he was sitting over his papers until twilight. He compelled himself to work mechanically, smoothly and unheedingly, and forced himself to go quicker and quicker; but all the time he was working, a keen sense of pain grew and deepened within him. Presently Rosa came in. "Go on writing," she whispered. "I won't disturb you." She sat down quietly on the sofa, but he felt that her passionate, sleep-robbed, vigilant eyes never left him.

"Why didn't you come to me?" she burst out suddenly. "I was home today." He felt in this a confession which touched him. He laid down his pen and turned to her; she was dressed in black like a penitent, paler than usual; folded in her lap were her appealing little hands, which even from where he sat he felt were cold.

"It's chilly there," he observed apologetically, and he tried to talk as usual, without making any reference to the events of the previous day. She replied humbly and gently, like a grateful child.

"About Tylda, you know," the words came all at once, "the reason things go so badly with them is that her husband is a fool. He stood surety for someone and then had to pay . . . It's his own fault, and he ought to have thought of his children; but then, he doesn't understand anything. He had an agent who robbed him, and yet he goes on trusting everyone. You know they are suing him for fraudulent bankruptcy?"

"I know nothing about it," George said quickly. He saw that she had been brooding over it all night, and felt somehow ashamed. Rosa was not aware of his quiet rebuff: she lost her temper, got excited, and immediately played her highest card: "They wanted my husband to help them, but he obtained information and simply laughed at them outright. To give them money, he said, would be to throw it away; they have three hundred thousand in liabilities . . . A man would be a fool to put a single penny into that: he would lose it all."

"Why are you telling me this?"

"So that you might know," she forced herself to a gentle tone. "You know, you are so kind-hearted you would very likely let yourself be deprived of everything."

"You are very kind," he said without taking his eyes from her. She was highly strung, burning with desire to say something more, but his scrutiny made her uneasy; she began to be afraid that she had gone too far. She asked him to find her some work so that she might be a burden to no one, no one at all; she could live on very little; she felt she ought not to have such expensive lodgings . . . Now at last perhaps she would offer to keep house for him. He waited with beating heart, but she looked away towards the window and began to talk about something else.

The next day he received the following letter from Tylda:

Dear George,

I am sorry we parted under such a misunderstanding. If you knew all, I am sure you would read this letter differently. We are in a desperate position. If we succeeded in paying off that fifty thousand we should be saved, for our business has a future, and in two years it would begin to pay. We would give you every guarantee for the future if you would let us have the money now. You would be part proprietor of the works and take a share of the proceeds as soon as the business began to pay. If you will come and look at our establishment you will see for yourself that it has a future. You will also get to know our children better, and see how nice and good they are and so diligent, and you will not have the heart to ruin their whole future. Do it, at least, for the children, for they are of our blood, and Charles is already big and intelligent and gives promise of a great future. Forgive me for writing this, we are in a bad state and are quite sure that you will come to our rescue and become fond of our children, for you have a kind heart. Be sure and come. When little Tylda is grown up she will be glad to be housekeeper to her uncle, you will see what a darling she is. If you don't help us, my husband will never get over it and these children will be beggars.

Kind love, dear George, from your unhappy sister,

*Tylda*

P.S.—With regard to Rosa, you said that I told lies. When my husband comes to Prague he will bring you proof. Rosa does not deserve your support and generosity, for she has brought shame on us. She had better go back to her husband—he will forgive her—and she ought not to rob innocent children of their bread.

George flung the letter aside. He felt bitter and disgusted; the unfinished work on his table had an air of hopeless triviality. Disgust rose in a painful lump in his throat; he left everything and went round to Rosa. He was already on the steps in front of her door when he changed his mind with a sudden jerk of his hand, came down again, and strolled aimlessly down the street. In the distance he saw a young woman in furs on an officer's arm; he started running after them like a jealous lover, but it wasn't Rosa. He saw a pair of bright eyes on a woman's face, heard a laugh on rosy lips, saw her radiating and exhaling happiness, full of trust and joy and beauty. Wearily he returned home at last. On his sofa lay Rosa, in tears. Tylda's open letter fell to the floor.

"Miserly creature," she sobbed passionately, "and not ashamed of herself. She wants to rob you of everything, Georgie; don't give her anything, don't believe a word of it. You can't understand what a crafty, avaricious woman she is. Why does she pursue me like that? What have I done to her? For the sake of your money—to slander me in that way! It is only— only because of your money. It's absolutely monstrous!"

"She has children, Rosa," George observed gently.

"That's her own problem," she cried fiercely, choking with sobs. "She has always robbed us, she only cares about money. She married for money; even when she was little she boasted that she'd be rich. She is absolutely disgusting, vulgar, stupid — tell me, Georgie, what is there in her? You know what she was like when things were better—fat, insolent, unfriendly. And now she wants—to rob me . . . George, would you let her? Would you get rid of me? I'd rather drown myself than go back."

George listened with his head bowed. Yes, this girl was fighting for everything, for her love and happiness; she wept with rage, she cried out in passionate hatred against everyone, against Tylda and even against him, who could take everything from her. Money—the word stung George like a whip whenever she said it; it struck him as shameless, disgusting, offensive.

"It was like a miracle to me when you offered me money,"
Rosa wept. "For me it meant freedom—everything. You offered it
yourself, Georgie, and you shouldn't have offered it at all if you
meant to take it away again. Now, when I am counting on it—"

George was no longer listening. Remotely he heard reproaches, lamentations, sobs. He felt humiliated beyond measure.
Money, money, but was it only a question of money? Oh God, how
had it come about? What had coarsened the careworn, motherly
Tylda? Why was the other sister wailing? Why had his own heart
grown hard and indifferent? What had money to do with it at all?
In a strange way he was aware of his power to hurt Rosa, and of
an inexplicable desire to wound her by saying something cruel,
humiliating, and masterful.

He rose with a certain lightness. "Wait," he said coldly. "It
is my own money. And I," he concluded with a lordly gesture of
dismissal, "shall think it over."

Rosa sprang up with eyes full of alarm. "You— you—" she
stammered. "But of course—that's understood. Please, Georgie—
perhaps you did not understand me—I didn't mean that—"

"All right," he broke in drily. "I said I will think it over."

A gleam of hatred blazed in Rosa's eyes; but she bit her lip
and went out with her head bowed.

The next day there was a new visitor waiting in his room:
Tylda's husband, an awkward, blushing man, full of embarrassment
and dog-like submissiveness. Choking with shame and fury, George
refrained from sitting down, in order to compel his visitor to stand.

"What is your business?" he said, in the impersonal tone of
an official.

The awkward man shivered and forced out of himself: "I—
I— that is, Tylda— has sent some documents — which you asked
for—" and he began to hunt feverishly in his pockets.

"I certainly did not ask for any papers," said George with a
negative wave of his hand. There was a painful pause.

"Tylda wrote to you, brother-in-law," began the unfortunate
tradesman, blushing more than ever, "that our business, to put it
briefly, if you would like to be a partner—"

George purposely let him flounder.

"The fact is—things are not so bad, and if you were a partner,
to put it briefly, our undertaking has a future, and as one who . . .
shared—"

The door opened softly and there stood Rosa. She became petrified at the sight of Tylda's husband.

"What brings you here?" said George sharply.

"Georgie," gasped Rosa.

"I'm engaged," George rebuffed her, and he turned to his guest. "I beg your pardon."

Rosa did not stir.

Tylda's husband perspired with shame and terror. "Here are — please — these proofs, letters her husband wrote us and other papers intercepted—"

Rosa clutched at the door for support. "Show them to me," said George. He took the letters and feigned to read the first, but then crushed them all in his hand and gave them to Rosa. "There you are," he smiled malevolently. "And now excuse me. And don't go to the bank to draw anything out: you would go for nothing."

Rosa retreated without a word, her face ashen.

"Well now, your business," continued George hoarsely, closing the door.

"Yes, the prospects are — of the very best, and if there were capital — that is, of course, without interest—"

"Listen," George interrupted brusquely. "I know that you are to blame; I am informed that you are not provident or—businesslike—"

"I would do my best," stammered Tylda's husband, gazing at him with pleading, dog-like eyes, from which George turned away.

"How can I put any confidence in you?" he asked, shrugging his shoulders.

"I assure you — that I would value your confidence — and all that is possible — we have children, brother-in-law."

A terrible, intense, embarrassing feeling of sympathy wrung George's heart. "Come in a year's time," he finished, holding on to the last fragment of his shattered will.

"In a year's time. . . Oh God. . . ," groaned Tylda's husband, and his pale eyes filled with tears.

"Goodbye," said George, extending his hand.

Tylda's husband did not see the proffered hand. He made for the door and stumbled over a chair, groping vainly for the doorknob. "Goodbye," he said in a broken voice at the door, "and—thank you."

George was alone. A sweat of intense weakness burst out on

his forehead. He arranged the papers on his table once more and called the landlady; when she arrived he was pacing the room with both hands pressed to his heart; he forgot what he had wanted her for.

"Stop," he cried, as she was going out, "if today, tomorrow, or at any time my sister Rosa comes, tell her that I am not well and that . . . I would rather not see anyone."

Then he stretched himself on his old sofa, fixing his eyes on a new spider's web freshly spun in the corner above his head.

Translator unknown; revised by the editor. Originally published in *Money and Other Stories*, 1930. From the Czech "Peníze," 1921.

# Oplatka's End

At three o'clock in the morning plain-clothesman Krejcik noticed that the shutters of a baker's shop at No. 17 Neklanova Street were half raised. Accordingly, he rang the doorbell and, although he was not on duty, he peeped under the shutter to see if there was anyone in the shop. At this moment a man dashed out of the shop, fired a bullet into Krejcik's stomach at close range and made his escape.

Officer Bartos, who was patrolling Jeronymova Street, his prescribed beat at this hour, heard the shot and came running up towards it. At the corner of Neklanova Street he very nearly collided with the fugitive; but before he could shout "Stop!" a shot was fired and Officer Bartos collapsed, mortally wounded.

The street was now astir with a screeching of police whistles: the mounted patrols came galloping up from all over the area. Three men arrived on the double from the police station, buttoning their tunics as they ran; after a few minutes a car rattled along from headquarters and the police superintendent jumped out of it; at this instant Officer Bartos was already dead and Krejcik, clutching at his stomach, was dying.

By morning, about twenty arrests had been made; this was done at random, because nobody had seen the murderer. In the first place, the police somehow had to avenge the deaths of two of their men and, besides, it is usual to do this; the supposition is that by some divine stroke of luck someone among those arrested will prove to be the wanted man. At headquarters interrogations were going on uninterruptedly all day and all night; pale and jaded wrongdoers, known to the police, were writhing on the rack of endless questionings, but they quaked still more at the thought of what would happen when a few constables took them in hand after the interrogation. For the whole of the police force was seething with a dark and awesome rage. The murder of Officer Bartos had violated that rather free-and-easy relationship which exists between the professional policeman and the professional criminal; if he had merely fired at random, that wouldn't have mattered so much, but you don't even shoot dumb animals in the stomach.

By the next night, towards the early hours of the morning, every policeman, however remote his beat, knew that Oplatka had done it. This had been blabbed out by one of those arrested as a suspect: Oh yes, Valta said as how Oplatka had done in those two fellows in Neklanova Street, and he'd settle some more of 'em, yes he would; it was all the same to him because he'd got consumption. Very well, then, it was Oplatka.

That same night, Valta was arrested, then Oplatka's sweetheart and three fellows belonging to Oplatka's gang; but none of them could or would say where Oplatka was to be found. How many policemen and plainclothesmen had been sent to track Oplatka down, is another matter; but apart from them, every policeman, as soon as he had gone off duty, went home and gulped down some thin coffee, muttered something to his wife, pulled himself together and started off on his own to look for Oplatka. Of course, everybody knew Oplatka; he was a green-faced little shrimp with a scraggy neck.

At eleven o'clock at night Officer Vrzal, who had gone off duty at nine, hastily got into plain clothes and told his wife that he was just going to have a look round in the street. He came across a little fellow near the Paradise Garden who seemed to be keeping well in the shadow; Officer Vrzal, although he was unarmed and off duty, went a little nearer to have a look, but when he was within three yards of him, the man thrust his hand in his pocket, shot Vrzal in the stomach and took to his heels. Officer Vrzal clutched at his stomach and started running after him; when he had run a hundred yards he collapsed, but by that time the police whistles had started shrilling and quite a number of men were chasing after the shadow. Behind Rieger Park a few shots were heard; a quarter of an hour later several cars, festooned with policemen, were racing along towards upper Zizkov and patrols consisting of three or four men crept through the buildings in that quarter that were in the course of construction. Towards one o'clock, the bang of a pistol-shot was heard behind Olsany Pond; someone on the run had fired at a youth who had just left his girl and was on his way home, but he had missed. At two o'clock in the morning, a posse of policemen and detectives encircled a patch containing some disused kilns, and step by step closed in. It began to drizzle. Towards morning there was a rumor that on the other side of Malesice someone had fired at a toll-keeper who had his booth there; the toll-keeper had started running after him, but then he'd wisely decided it was no business of his. Evidently, Oplatka had slipped away into the fields.

Some sixty policemen were returning from the disused kilns, wet through and so fuming with impotent rage that they could have wept. Good heavens, how infuriating it was! Here was the ruffian who had slaughtered three members of the police force, Bartos, Krejcik and Vrzal, and now he was running right into the clutches of the gendarmes. We have the prior claim, opined the uniformed and plainclothes police, and now we've got to leave this wretched little shrimp of an Oplatka to the gendarmes. Look here, since he's been shooting our men, it's our job, isn't it? We don't want these gendarme guys poking their noses into it; all they ought to do is to make sure he can't get back to Prague.

The whole day there was a cold drizzle; in the evening towards dusk Mrazek, a gendarme, was on his way to Pysely from Cercany, where he had gone to buy a battery for his radio. He was unarmed and he was whistling to himself. As he was going along, he saw an undersized fellow in front of him; there was nothing special about this, but the undersized fellow stopped, as if uncertain which way to go. Who can that be, said Mrazek to himself, and at that very instant he saw a flash and rolled over, clutching at his side.

That same evening, of course, the gendarmerie throughout the district was on the alert. "Look here, Mrazek," said Captain Honzatko to the dying man, "don't you worry about this. I give you my word that we'll collar the bastard. It's that fellow Oplatka and I'll bet anything he's trying to get to Sobeslav, because that's his birthplace. Goodness knows why these fellows make for their hometown when their number's up. Well, old pal, give me your hand; I promise you we'll fix him good, no matter what it takes." Vaclav Mrazek made an attempt at a smile; he was thinking of his three children, but then in his mind's eye he saw the gendarmes drawing closer and closer on all sides . . . perhaps Toman of Cerny Kostel would be among them . . . Zavada of Votice certainly would . . . Rousek of Sazava would too, his buddies, his buddies. . . What a fine sight it will be, thought Vaclav Mrazek, all those gendarmes together. Then Mrazek smiled for the last time; after that there was only some inhuman agony.

But what happened that night was that Sergeant Zavada of Votice thought it would be a good idea to search the night train from Benesov; who could tell, perhaps Oplatka was traveling on it. By Jove though, would he risk getting onto a train? Lights flickered in the cars; the passengers were dozing on the seats, hunched together like weary animals. Sergeant Zavada went from car to car and thought to himself, how the deuce am I to recognize a man I've never seen? At that instant, a yard away from him, a fellow jumped up with his hat over his eyes, there was a loud report, and before the sergeant, in the narrow corridor, could unhitch his rifle from his shoulder, the little man was outside, brandishing a revolver. Sergeant Zavada just had time to shout "Stop him!" before he fell in a heap in the corridor.

Meanwhile, the fellow had jumped from the car and was running towards the freight cars. There, a railwayman named Hrusa was walking along with a lantern and saying to himself, well, as soon as No. 26 has left I'll go and have a nap in the lamp-shed. At this instant a man ran into him. Without wasting words, old Hrusa tried to stop him from passing; that's just a man's instinct. Then he saw a sort of flash and that was all; even before No. 26

had left, old Hrusa was lying in the lamp-shed, but on a plank, and the railwaymen went to look at him with their heads bared.

A few men ran panting after the escaping shadow, but it was too late; by this time he had probably got across the railway lines into the fields. But, from that flickering railway station, from that cluster of scared people, a wild panic swooped in a broad circle across the countryside, enwrapt in autumnal drowsiness. The people shrank into their cottages and scarcely dared to set foot in the doorway. There was a rumor that at such and such a place someone had seen a stranger of wild appearance; he was either a lanky and haggard man, or else more of a short fellow in a leather coat. A postman saw someone hiding behind a tree; someone on the highway had made signs to a driver named Lebeda to stop, but Lebeda had lashed at his horses and driven off. It was a fact that someone sobbing with fatigue had stopped a child on its way to school and snatched away a little bag containing a slice of bread. "Give me that," the man had gasped and had then run off with the bread. As soon as this was known, the villagers had bolted their doors and scarcely breathed for fear; the most they dared to do was to press their noses against the window pane and gaze out with misgivings at the grey and desolate countryside.

But at the same time, another constricting movement began to develop. From every direction gendarmes arrived in ones and twos; heaven knows where they all came from. "Good heavens, man," shouted Captain Honzatko at a gendarme from Caslav, "what are you doing here? Who sent you here? Do you think I need gendarmes from the whole of Bohemia to catch one gunman? Eh?" The gendarme from Caslav took off his helmet and scratched his neck in embarrassment. "Well, you see, sir," he said with an entreating glance, "Zavada was a pal of mine—it wouldn't be fair to him if I wasn't in it, would it?" "Damn it," thundered the captain, "that's what they all tell me. Close on fifty gendarmes have reported to me without any orders—what am I supposed to do with all of you?" Captain Honzatko gnawed his moustache savagely. "All right, you'll be on duty along the highway here from the crossroads to the woods; tell Voldrich, the man from Benesov, that you've come to relieve him." "That's no good, sir," opined the gendarme from Caslav sagaciously. "You see, sir, Voldrich wouldn't think of letting me relieve him; it stands to reason, don't it? It'd be better if I was to take the woods from the edge up to that second road—who's on duty there?" "Semerad from Veselka," growled the captain. "Now listen, you from Caslav, and get this: on my responsibility you'll fire without warning, if you see anyone. No shilly-shallying, do you understand? I'm not going to let my men be shot. Now, off you go."

Then the stationmaster arrived. "Well, sir," he said, "there's another thirty of 'em turned up." "Thirty what?" "Why," said the stationmaster, "railwaymen, of course. You know, it's all on account of Hrusa. He was one of our men and so they've come to offer you their services." "Send them back," yelled the captain. "I don't need any civilians here." The stationmaster moved uneasily from one foot to the other. "You see, sir," he remarked soothingly, "they've come here all the way from Prague and Mezimosti. It's a good thing when they stick together like that. You know, they won't take no for an answer now that Oplatka's killed one of them. They've sort of got a right to it. So if I was you, sir, I'd do them the favor and take them on."

Captain Honzatko snarled that he wished to hell they'd leave him alone. In the course of the day, the broad circle gradually drew closer. That afternoon the nearest garrison headquarters telephoned to know whether any military reinforcements were needed. "No," snapped the captain disrespectfully; "it's our job and nobody else's." Meanwhile, some members of the secret police had arrived from Prague; they had a terrible argument with the sergeant-major, who was going to pack them off straight back again from the railway station. "What," fumed Inspector Holub, "you want to send us back? He's killed three of our men and only two of yours, you jerks! We're more entitled to him than you are, you tin-hatted flatfoots, you!" Scarcely had this conflict been settled than a new one broke out on the other side of the circle, between the gendarmes and the gamekeepers. "Get out of our way," fumed the gendarmes. "This isn't a rabbit-hunt." "Go to hell," remarked the gamekeepers; "these are our woods and we're entitled to walk here, ain't we?" "Now come, come, men, don't be so silly," said Rousek from Sazava, acting as a mediator; "this is our job and nobody's got to interfere in it." "That's what you say," retorted the gamekeepers. "But the kid that this fellow took the bread from is the Hurka gamekeeper's little girl. We can't let that pass, so there you are."

That evening the circle was closed; when darkness had fallen, each man heard the hoarse breathing of the man on his right and

217

the man on his left and the squelch of footsteps in the sticky soil. "Halt!" sped the word from man to man. "Don't move!" The silence was heavy and awesome; every now and then there was a crunch of dry leaves in the darkness in the middle of the circle or the rustle of a shower; only every now and then there was the squelchy tread of a man tramping past or a metallic clatter, perhaps of a rifle or a strap. Towards midnight someone in the darkness yelled "Halt!" and fired a shot; at that moment there was a queer grinding noise and the muffled report of about thirty rifle-shots. They all ran forward in that direction, but then there came a yell: "Get back! Nobody's to move a step." They got back into some sort of order and the circle was closed again; but only now did they all fully realize that in the darkness before them a lost man was hiding at bay, on the alert for a chance to make a wild attack. A kind of uncontrollable shudder passed from man to man; from time to time a heavy drop of water made a stir like a stealthy footstep. Good heavens, if only we could see something! God, if only it were light!

Day began to dawn mistily. Each man distinguished the outlines of the man next to him, marveling that he had been so close to a human being. In the middle of the chain of men the contours of a dense thicket or copse became visible (it was a covert for hares), but it was so quiet there, so utterly quiet—Captain Honzatko tugged feverishly at his moustache: damn it, we've got to go on waiting, or else—

"I'm going to have a look there," growled Holub; the captain snorted. "You go," he said, turning to the nearest gendarme. Five men rushed into the thicket, there was a crackle of broken branches and a sudden stillness. "Stay where you are," shouted Captain Honzatko to his men, and he moved slowly towards the copse. Then there emerged from the thicket the broad back of a gendarme dragging something, a huddled body, the feet of which were being held by a gamekeeper with a walrus moustache. Behind them Captain Honzatko, scowling and sallow, squeezed his way out of the copse. "Lay him down here," he gasped, wiping his forehead; he looked round, with an air of surprise, at the wavering chain of men, scowled still more and shouted: "What are you staring at? Dismissed!"

In some embarrassment, man after man straggled forward to the puny, hunched body by the hedge. So that was Oplatka: the gaunt arm sticking out of the sleeve, the puny, greenish, rain-soaked face on the scraggy neck—God, what a pitifully undersized specimen of a man, this poor wretch Oplatka! Look, he's been shot in the back, and here's a tiny wound behind one of his projecting ears, and here again. . . Four, five, seven of them had got him. Captain Honzatko, who was kneeling by the body, stood up and cleared his throat moodily; then uneasily and almost timidly he raised his eyes—there stood a long, massive row of gendarmes, rifle on shoulder, their shining bayonets fixed. Good heavens, what strapping fellows, like tanks, and there they stood two deep as if they were on parade, with bated breath. On the other side a black cluster of secret police, thick-set men one and all, pockets bulging with their revolvers; then the railwaymen in blue uniforms, stocky and determined; then the gamekeepers in green, sinewy and bearded, with lanky bodies and brick-red faces. Why, it's like a public funeral, was the thought that flashed through the captain's mind; they've formed a square, as if they were about to fire a salute. Captain Honzatko gnawed at his lip in an unreasoning pang of torment. That midget lying on the ground, stark and bristly, an ailing crow riddled with bullets, and here all these hunters— "Damn it all!" shouted the captain, gritting his teeth, "haven't you got a sack or something? Clear the body away!"

Some two hundred men began to disperse in various directions; they did not talk to each other, but only grumbled about the bad roads, and in reply to excited questions muttered sullenly, Sure, it's all up with him, and we've had enough of it. The gendarme who had been left on guard over the covered body snarled savagely at the loitering bumpkins: "What do you want? There's nothing for you to stare at here. This is no business of yours."

At the district boundary Rousek, the gendarme from Sazava, spat and growled: "Damn this rotten weather! It all makes me sick. Good Lord, I only wish I could have got at that Oplatka all on my own, man to man!"

Translated by Paul Selver; revised by the editor. Originally published in *Tales from Two Pockets,* 1932. From the Czech "Oplatkuv konec."

# THE CLAIRVOYANT

"You know, Mr. DA," Mr. Janowitz declared, "I'm not an easy person to fool; after all, I'm not a Jew for nothing, right? But what this fellow does is simply beyond belief. It isn't just graphology, it's—I don't know what. Here's how it works: you give him someone's handwriting in an unsealed envelope; he never even looks at the writing, just pokes his fingers inside the envelope and feels the handwriting, all over; and all the while his face is twisting as if he were in pain. And before very long, he starts telling you about the nature of the writer, but he does it in such a way that— well, you'd be dumbfounded. He pegs the writer perfectly, down to the last detail. I gave him an envelope with a letter from old Weinberg in it; he had Weinberg figured out in no time, diabetes, even his planned bankruptcy. What do you say to that?"

"Nothing," the DA said drily. "Maybe he knows old Weinberg."

"But he never once looked at the handwriting," Mr. Janowitz protested. "He says every person's handwriting has its own aura, and he says that you can feel it, clearly and precisely. He says it's purely a physical phenomenon, like radio. This isn't some kind of swindle, Mr. DA; this Prince Karadagh doesn't make a penny from it. He's supposed to be from a very old family in Baku, according to what this Russian told me. But I'll tell you what, come see for yourself; he'll be here this evening. You must come."

"Listen, Mr. Janowitz," the DA said, "this is all very nice, but I only believe fifty per cent of what foreigners say, especially when I don't know how they make their living; I believe Russians even less, and fakirs less than that; but when on top of everything else the man's a prince, then I don't believe one word of it. Where did you say he learned this? Ah yes, in Persia. Forget it, Mr. Janowitz; the whole Orient's a fraud."

"But Mr. DA," Mr. Janowitz protested, "this young fellow explains it all scientifically; no magic tricks, no mysterious powers, I'm telling you, strictly scientific method."

"Then he's an even bigger phony," the DA admonished him.

"Mr. Janowitz, I'm surprised at you; you've managed to live your entire life without strictly scientific methods, and here you are embracing them wholesale. Look, if there were something to it, it would have been known a long time ago, right?"

"Well," Mr. Janowitz replied, a little shaken, "but when I saw with my own eyes how he guessed everything about old Weinberg! Now there's genius for you. I'll tell you what, Mr. DA, come and have a look for yourself; if it's a hoax, you'll know it, that's your specialty, sir; nobody can put one over on you, Mr. DA."

"Hardly," the DA said modestly. "All right, I'll come, Mr. Janowitz, but only to keep an eye on your phenomenon's fingers. It's a shame that people are so gullible. But you mustn't tell him who I am; wait, I'll bring along some handwriting in an envelope for him, something special. Count on it, friend, I'll prove he's a phony."

\* \* \*

You should understand that the district attorney (or, more accurately: chief public prosecutor Dr. Klapka) would, in his next court proceeding, be trying the case against Hugo Müller, who was charged with premeditated murder. Mr. Hugo Müller, millionaire industrialist, had been accused of insuring his younger brother Ota for a large sum of money and then drowning him in the lake at a summer resort; in addition to this he also had been under suspicion, during the previous year, of dispatching his lover, but of course that had not been proven. In short, it was a major trial, one to which the district attorney wanted to devote particular attention; and he had labored over the trial documents with all the persistence and acumen that had made him a most formidable prosecutor. The case was not clear; the district attorney would have given God-knows-what for one particle of direct evidence; but as things stood, he would have to rely more on his winning way with words if the jury were to award him a rope for Mr. Müller; you must understand that, for prosecutors, this is a point of honor.

Mr. Janowitz was a bit flustered that evening. "Dr. Klapka," he announced in muffled tones, "this is Prince Karadagh; well, let's get started."

The district attorney cast probing eyes on this exotic creature; he was a young and slender man with eyeglasses, the face of a

Tibetan monk and delicate, thievish hands. Fancy-pants quack, the district attorney decided.

"Mr. Karadagh," Mr. Janowitz jabbered, "over here by this little table. There's some mineral water already there. Please, switch on that little floor lamp; we'll turn off the overhead light so it won't disturb you. There. Please, gentlemen, there should be silence. Mr.— eh, Mr. Klapka here brought some handwriting of some sort; if Mr. Karadagh would be so good as to—"

The district attorney cleared his throat briefly and seated himself so as to best observe the clairvoyant. "Here is the handwriting," he said, and he took an unsealed envelope from his breast pocket. "If I may—"

"Thank you," the clairvoyant said impassively. He took hold of the envelope and, with eyes closed, turned it over in his fingers. Suddenly he shuddered, twisting his head. "Curious," he muttered and bolted a sip of water. He then inserted his slim fingers into the envelope and suddenly stopped; it seemed as if his pale yellow face turned paler still.

There was such a silence in the room that a slight rattling could be heard from Mr. Janowitz, for Mr. Janowitz suffered from goiter.

The thin lips of Prince Karadagh trembled and contorted as if his fingers were clenching a red-hot iron, and sweat broke out on his forehead. "I cannot endure this," he hissed in a tight voice; he extracted his fingers from the envelope, rubbed them with a handkerchief and quickly moved them back and forth over the tablecloth, as one sharpens a knife, after which he once again sipped agitatedly from his glass of water and then cautiously took the envelope between his fingers.

"The man who wrote this," he began in a parched voice, "the man who wrote this. . . There is great strength here, but a— (obviously he was searching for a word) strength which lies there, waiting. This lying in wait is terrible," he cried out and dropped the envelope on the table. "I would not want this man as my enemy!"

"Why?" the district attorney could not refrain from asking. "Is he guilty of something?"

"Don't question me," the clairvoyant said. "Every question gives a hint. I only know that he could be guilty of anything at all, of great and terrible deeds. There is astonishing determination here . . . for success . . . for money . . . This man would not scruple over the life of a fellow creature. No, this is not an ordinary criminal; a tiger also is not a criminal; a tiger is a great lord. This man would not be capable of low trickery, but he thinks of himself as ruling over human lives. When he is on the prowl, he sees people only as prey. Therefore he kills them."

"Beyond good and evil," the district attorney murmured with unmistakable approval.

"Those are only words," Prince Karadagh said. "No one is beyond good and evil. This man has his own strict concept of morality; he is in debt to no one, he does not steal, he does not lie; if he kills, it is as if he checkmated in a game of chess. It is his game, but he plays it correctly." The clairvoyant wrinkled his brow in concentration. "I don't know what it is. I see a large lake and a motor boat on it."

"And what else?" the district attorney burst out, scarcely breathing.

"There is nothing else to see; it is completely obscure. It is so strangely obscure compared with that brutal and ruthless determination to bring down his prey. But there is no passion in it, only intellect. Absolute intellectual reasoning in every detail. As if he were resolving some technical problem or mental exercise. No, this man feels no remorse for anything. He is so confident of himself, so self-assured; he has no fear even of his own conscience. I have the impression of a man who looks down on all from above; he is conceited in the extreme and self-congratulatory; it pleases him that people fear him." The clairvoyant sipped his water. "But he is also a hypocrite. At heart, an opportunist who would like to astound the world by his actions— Enough. I am tired. I do not like this man."

\* \* \*

"Listen, Janowitz," the district attorney flung out excitedly, "he is truly astonishing, this clairvoyant of yours. What he described is a perfect likeness. A strong and ruthless man who views people only as prey; the perfect player in his own game; a brain who systematically, intellectually plans his moves and feels no remorse for anything; a gentleman yet also an opportunist. Mr. Janowitz, this Karadagh pinpointed him one hundred per cent!"

"You don't say," said the flattered Mr. Janowitz. "Didn't I

tell you? That was a letter from Schliefen, the textile man from Liberec, right?"

"It most certainly was not," exclaimed the district attorney. "Mr. Janowitz, it was a letter from a murderer."

"Imagine that," Mr. Janowitz marveled, "and I thought it was Schliefen; he's a real crook, that Schliefen."

"No. It was a letter from Hugo Müller, the fratricide. Do you remember how that clairvoyant talked about a boat on a lake? Müller threw his brother from that boat into the water."

"Imagine that," Mr. Janowitz said, astonished. "You see? That is a fabulous talent, Mr. District Attorney!"

"Unquestionably," the district attorney declared. "The way he grasped Müller's true nature and the motives behind his actions, Mr. Janowitz, is simply phenomenal. Not even I could have hit the mark with Müller so precisely. And this clairvoyant found it out by feeling a few lines of Müller's handwriting—Mr. Janowitz, there's something to this; there must be some sort of special aura or something in people's handwriting."

"What did I tell you?" Mr. Janowitz said triumphantly. "If you would be so kind, Mr. District Attorney, I've never seen the handwriting of a murderer."

"With pleasure," Mr. District Attorney said, and he took the envelope from his pocket. "It's an interesting letter, besides," he added, removing the paper from the envelope, and suddenly his face changed color. "I. . . Mr. Janowitz," he blurted out, somewhat uncertainly, "this letter is a court document; it is. . . I'm not allowed to show it to you. Please forgive me."

Before long, the district attorney was hurrying homeward, not even noticing that it was raining. I'm an ass, he told himself bitterly, I'm a fool, how could that have happened to me? I'm an idiot! That in my hurry I grabbed not Müller's letter but my own hand-writing, my notes for the trial, I shoved them in that envelope! I'm an imbecile! So that was *my* handwriting! Thanks very much! Watch out, you swindler, I'll be lying in wait for you!

But otherwise, the district attorney reflected, all in all, for the most part, what the clairvoyant had said wasn't too bad. Great strength; astonishing determination, if you please; I'm not capable of low trickery; I have my own strict concept of morality — As a matter of fact that is quite flattering. That I regret nothing? Thank God, I have no reason to: I merely discharge my obligations. And as for intellectual reasoning, that's also true. But as for being a hypocrite, he's mistaken. It's still nothing but a hoax.

Suddenly he paused. It stands to reason, he told himself, what that clairvoyant said can be applied to anyone at all! These are only generalities, nothing more. Everyone's a bit of a hypocrite and an opportunist. That's the whole trick: to speak in such a way that anybody could be identified. That's it, the district attorney decided, and opening his umbrella, he proceeded home at his normal energetic pace.

\* \* \*

"My God!" groaned the presiding judge, stripping off his gown, "seven o'clock already; it did drag on again! When the district attorney spoke for two hours— but, dear colleague, he won it; to get the rope on such weak evidence, I'd call that success. Well, you never know with a jury. But he spoke skillfully," the presiding judge granted, washing his hands. "Mainly in the way he dealt with Müller's character, that was a full-fledged portrait; you know, the monstrous, inhuman nature of a murderer—it left you positively shaken. Remember how he said: This is no ordinary criminal; he isn't capable of low trickery, he neither lies nor steals; and if he murders a man, he does it as calmly as checkmating in a game of chess. He does not kill from passion, but from cold intellectual reasoning, as if he were resolving some technical problem or mental exercise. It was very well spoken, my friend. And something else: When he is on the prowl, he sees his fellow creatures only as prey— you know, that business about the tiger was perhaps a little theatrical, but the jury liked it."

"Or," the associate judge added, "the way he said: Clearly this murderer regrets nothing; he is so confident of himself, so self-assured—he has no fear even of his own conscience."

"Or then again," the presiding judge continued, wiping his hands with a towel, "the psychological observation that he is a hypocrite and an opportunist who would like to astound the world by his actions—"

"This Klapka, though," the associate judge said appreciatively. "He's a dangerous adversary."

"Hugo Müller found guilty by twelve votes," the presiding judge marveled, "who would have thought it! Klapka got him after all. For him, it's like a hunt or a game of chess. He is totally consumed by his cases — My friend, I wouldn't want to have him as my enemy."

"He likes it," the associate judge replied, "when people fear him."

"A touch complacent, that's him," the presiding judge said thoughtfully. "But he has astonishing determination . . . chiefly for success. A great strength, friend, but—" The appropriate words failed him. "Well, let's go have dinner."

Translated by Norma Comrada; © 1990 Norma Comrada. Originally published as "Jasnovidec" in *Povídky z jedné kapsy* (*Tales from One Pocket*), 1929.

# THE STRANGE EXPERIENCES OF MR. JANIK

This Mr. Janik is neither the Dr. Janik in one of the Ministries, nor the Janik who shot the estate-owner Jirsa, nor the stockbroker Janik who is said to have made a break of 326 at billiards, but Mr. Janik the head of the firm of Janik & Holecek, wholesale dealers in paper and pulp. He is a shortish, gentlemanly person who once courted Miss Severova and was so upset when she refused him that he never married; he is, in fact, to avoid all possibility of a misunderstanding, the Janik known as Janik the stationer.

Now this Mr. Janik got mixed up in these matters by sheer chance. It started at some place on the Sazava River where he was spending his summer holidays. That was when they were searching for the corpse of Ruzena Regnerova, who was murdered by her fiancé Jindrich Basta. He soaked the poor creature with paraffin oil, burnt her and buried the body in a forest. Although Basta was found guilty of having murdered Ruzena, no trace of her body or her bones could be found. For nine days the gendarmes had been tramping about in the forests under the guidance of Basta, who kept telling them the place: it was here or it was there. They burrowed and dug but they couldn't find a thing. It was clear that Basta, in desperation, was leading them astray or trying to gain time. This Jindrich Basta was a young man of a respectable and well-to-do family, but likely enough the doctor had somehow squeezed his head with the forceps before he had arrived into the world. At any rate, there was something wrong with him; he was a queer, degenerate sort of fellow. For nine days he had been leading the gendarmes about in the woods, as pale as a ghost, his eyes twitching with a nystagmus of horror—he was a distressing sight. The gendarmes trudged with him through bilberries and swamps; they were now so savage that it wouldn't have taken much to make them have a go at him, and they were thinking to themselves: you animal, we'll give you such a rough time of it that you'll take us to the right place in the end. Basta, who was so worn out he could scarcely drag himself along, sank down on the ground at random and gasped: "This is where I buried her!"

"Get up, Basta," a gendarme bellowed at him. "It wasn't here. On you go!"

Basta stood up, tottering, and staggered on a little farther until he again collapsed with exhaustion. The procession was something like this: four gendarmes, one or two gamekeepers and some old fellows with shovels, and Jindrich Basta, livid wreck of a man, convulsively shuffling along.

Mr. Janik knew the gendarmes from the local inn; accordingly, he was allowed to join this tragic procession through the woods without being churlishly told to clear off. Moreover, he was carrying with him some tins of sardines, salami, cognac, and other such commodities, which came in very handy. On the ninth day things were bad, so bad that Mr. Janik had made up his mind: no more of this for me. The gendarmes were nearly growling with sullen rage, the gamekeepers were saying that they'd had enough of it and that they'd got other things to do, the old fellows with the shovels were grumbling that 20 crowns a day wasn't much for a tough job like this and, crumpled up on the ground, Jindrich was shaking in convulsive fits, no longer replying to the shouts and bullying of the gendarmes. At this dreary and bewildering moment Mr. Janik did something which, so to speak, was not on the program: he knelt down beside Basta, thrust a ham-roll into his hand and said pityingly: "Look here, sir, come, come now, Mr. Basta, this won't do, you know." Basta uttered a wail and burst out crying. "I'll find it . . . I'll find it, you'll see," he sobbed, and he tried to stand up; whereupon one of the plainclothesmen came up and lifted him to his feet almost tenderly. "Just you lean on me, Mr. Basta," he coaxed him. "Mr. Janik'll take hold of you from the other side; that's it. Now then, Mr. Basta, you'll show Mr. Janik where it was, won't you?"

An hour later, Jindrich Basta, smoking a cigarette, stood above a shallow pit from which a thigh-bone was sticking up.

"Is that the body of Ruzena Regnerova?" asked Sergeant Trunka grimly.

"Yes," said Jindrich Basta calmly, and flicked some cigarette ashes into the open pit. "Is there anything else you want?"

"You know, sir," Sergeant Trunka held forth to Mr. Janik that evening at the local inn, "you certainly know how to get round people, and no mistake. Well, here's my best respects, sir. That fellow threw up the sponge as soon as you said 'sir' to him. Well, he kept it up long enough, goodness knows, that animal. But if you don't mind me asking, sir, how did you know that being polite to him was going to have an effect like that?"

"Oh," said the hero of the day, with a modest blush, "that was only by the way, you know. I say 'sir' to everyone. And then I felt sorry for him and so I thought I'd offer him that roll—"

"That's instinct," announced Sergeant Trunka. "That's what I call having a flair for things. Here's my best respects, Mr. Janik. You ought to join the force. We could do with a man like you."

\* \* \*

Some time after that, Mr. Janik was traveling by the night-train to Bratislava: some Slovak paper factory had arranged its general meeting of shareholders there, and as Mr. Janik had a tidy sum invested in it, he was anxious to attend. "Wake me up before we get to Bratislava," he said to the guard, "or else I'll get taken as far as the Austrian frontier." Whereupon he crawled into his bed in the sleeping car, glad to have a compartment to himself, made himself thoroughly cozy, meditated for a while on various business matters and then fell asleep. He was not aware what time it was when the guard opened the door of the compartment for a passenger who began to undress and to clamber into the top bunk. In a half-dream Mr. Janik saw a pair of pants and two extraordinarily hairy legs dangling down, heard the grunting of someone who was wrapping himself up in the bedcovers, then there was a click of the switch and clattering darkness again. Mr. Janik dreamed a number of things, mostly that he was being pursued by hairy legs, and then he was woken up by a long stillness and the sound of somebody outside who was saying: "See you again at Zilina." He jumped out of bed and looked through the window; he saw that day was breaking, that the train was in the station at Bratislava and that the guard had forgotten to wake him up. He was so scared that he forgot to curse, and with feverish rapidity he dragged his trousers and the rest of his clothes over his pyjamas, shoved all his odds and ends into his pockets and jumped onto the platform just as the guard was giving the signal for the train to start.

"Whew!" gasped Mr. Janik; he shook his fist at the departing express and went to the men's room to finish dressing. When he had sorted out the contents of his pockets, he was flabbergasted; in his breast pocket, instead of one billfold, he had two. The fatter of the two, which was not his, contained sixty new Czechoslovak notes, each one five hundred crowns. This evidently belonged to his fellow-passenger of the previous night, but how it had got into his pocket Mr. Janik, still half asleep, couldn't for the life of him imagine. All right, of course the first thing to do was to get hold of a policeman and hand over the stranger's billfold. The police left Mr. Janik for a while on the verge of starvation, and in the meantime telephoned to Galanta, telling the people there to inform the traveler in sleeping-berth No. 14 that his billfold, with contents, was at the police station in Bratislava. Then Mr. Janik had to give particulars about himself, and then he went and got some breakfast. Then someone from the police looked him up and asked him whether there wasn't a mistake; for it appeared that the gentleman in sleeping-berth No. 14 had denied having lost a billfold. Mr. Janik had to go back to the police station and explain once more how the billfold had come into his possession. Meanwhile two plainclothesmen had taken the sixty banknotes away with them and Mr. Janik had to wait half an hour, seated between two detectives, after which he was led before some police bigwig.

"Look here," said the bigwig. "We're just now sending a wire to Parkan-Nana to detain that man in sleeping-berth No. 14. Can you give us an exact description of him?"

Practically all that Mr. Janik could say was that the traveler had remarkably hairy legs. The bigwig was not oversatisfied with this. "You see, those banknotes are forgeries," he said suddenly. "You'll have to stay here until we confront you with your fellow-passenger."

Quite privately Mr. Janik cursed the guard who had not woken him in time and who had thus caused Mr. Janik in his flurry to get that confounded billfold into his pocket. After about an hour, a telegram arrived from Parkan-Nana, to the effect that the traveler in sleeping-berth No. 14 had left the train at Nove Zamky; where he had gone to after that, either on foot or otherwise, was so far unknown.

"Well, Mr. Janik," said the bigwig at last, "we won't keep you here any longer just now; we're turning this matter over to Inspector Hrusek in Prague. If you ask me, it's a very serious business. Now you get back to Prague as soon as you can and the people there'll send for you. In the meantime I'd like to thank you for having collared those forged notes so neatly. You can't tell me it was just a lucky chance."

Scarcely had Mr. Janik returned to Prague than he was sent for by the authorities at police headquarters. He was received by a huge, heavy-set gentleman who was addressed by everyone as "President," and a sallow and scraggy person whose name was Inspector Hruska.

"Sit down, Mr. Janik," said the heavy-set gentleman as he broke the seals on a small packet. "Is this the billfold that you—er—that you found in your pocket at Bratislava?"

"Yes," sighed Mr. Janik.

The heavy-set gentleman counted the new banknotes in the billfold. "Sixty of them," he said. "All belonging to series 27,451. That was the figure that had already been reported to us from Cheb."

The scraggy man picked up one of the banknotes, closed his eyes and rubbed it between his fingers, after which he sniffed at it. "These here must be from Graz," he said. "The ones from Geneva aren't so sticky."

"Graz," repeated the heavy-set gentleman meditatively. "That's where they make these things for Budapest, isn't it?"

The scraggy man merely blinked. "Supposing I went to Vienna," he suggested, "but the police at Vienna won't hand the fellow over."

"Hm," grunted the heavy-set gentleman. "Then find out some other way for us to get hold of him. If worst comes to worst, tell them we'll exchange him for Leberhardt. Well, a pleasant journey, Hruska. And now, sir," he said, turning to Mr. Janik, "I really don't know how I'm to thank you. You're the one who discovered where Jindrich Basta's girl was, aren't you?"

Mr. Janik turned red. "That was only a fluke," he said hastily. "I really— I never meant to—"

"You've got a flair for things, Mr. Janik," said the heavy-set gentleman approvingly. "And it's a rare gift. There are people who for the life of them can't discover anything, while others just hit on the very finest clues. You ought to join us, Mr. Janik."

"I'm afraid I can't," parried Mr. Janik. "I— you see, I've got a business of my own — doing well — an old, established firm that used to belong to my grandfather—"

"Please yourself," sighed the great man, "but it's a pity all the same. It isn't everyone who's got such confounded good luck as you have. I hope we meet again, Mr. Janik."

\* \* \*

About a month after that, Mr. Janik was having dinner with a business friend from Leipzig. As a matter of course, at a dinner of that kind, between businessmen, things are done in style; the cognac in particular was quite exceptionally good; and the end of it was that Mr. Janik declined point-blank to proceed home on foot. He beckoned to the waiter and ordered a car.

On leaving the hotel, he saw a car waiting in front of the entrance; so he got inside, slammed the door, and in his gleefulness clean forgot that he had not told the driver where he lived. Nevertheless, the car started off, and Mr. Janik, comfortably ensconced in a corner, fell asleep.

He had no idea how long the drive lasted, but he was woken by the car stopping, and the driver opened the door for him, saying: "Here we are, sir. You're to go upstairs, sir." Mr. Janik wondered where he could possibly be, but as he didn't care what happened

231

after all the cognac he'd drunk, he went up some stairs and opened a door, behind which he heard a noisy conversation. There were about twenty men in the room, and as he entered they looked eagerly towards the door. Suddenly there was a strange stillness; one of the men stood up and came towards Mr. Janik, demanding: "What do you want here? Who are you?"

Mr. Janik gazed around him in surprise; he recognized five or six of those present—they were well-to-do persons who, it was rumored, had a political axe to grind, but Mr. Janik never meddled in politics. "Good Lord," he said affably, "why, fancy seeing Mr. Koubek and Mr. Heller here. Hello there, Ferry, I could do with a drink."

"How did this man get here?" snarled one of the company. "Is he one of us?"

Two individuals pushed Mr. Janik into the passage. "How did you get here?" one of them asked gruffly. "Who asked you to come here?"

Mr. Janik was sobered by this lack of friendliness. "Where am I?" he inquired indignantly. "Where the devil have you brought me to?"

One of the two individuals ran downstairs and pounced on the driver. "You damned fool!" he yelled. "Where did you pick this guy up?"

"Why, in front of the hotel," replied the driver, on the defensive. "I was told this afternoon that at ten o'clock this evening I was to wait by the hotel for a gentleman and bring him here. This here gentleman got into my car at ten o'clock and never said a word to me, so I just brought him straight here—"

"Good God!" shouted the individual below. "It's the wrong man. You've got us into a fine mess, that's for sure."

Mr. Janik sat down resignedly on the stairs. "Aha," he said complacently, "a secret meeting, eh? Now you'll have to strangle me and bury the corpse. Let's have a glass of water."

"Look here," said one of the two men. "You've made a mistake. That wasn't Mr. Koubek or Mr. Heller inside there, see? It's all a mistake. We'll have you taken back to Prague. Sorry for the misunderstanding."

"Don't mention it," said Mr. Janik magnanimously. "I know the driver's going to shoot me on the way back and then bury me in the woods. I don't mind. Silly ass that I was, I forgot to tell him my address and this is what comes of it."

"You're boozed, aren't you?" inquired the stranger with a certain relief.

"Partly," agreed Mr. Janik. "You see, I've had supper with a man named Meyer, a native of Dresden. I'm Janik, my line's wholesale paper and pulp," he introduced himself, sitting on the stairs. "It's an old firm, founded by my grandfather."

"You go and sleep it off," the stranger advised him. "And when you've slept it off, you won't even remember that—hm, we disturbed you like this."

"Quite right," Mr. Janik remarked with dignity. "You go and sleep it off, too. Where can I get a bed?"

"At home," said the stranger. "The driver'll take you home. Just let me help you get in."

"I can manage," demurred Mr. Janik. "I'm not as tight as you. You go and sleep it off. Driver, drive me to Bubenec."

The car started back, and Mr. Janik, with a foxy twinkle in his eye, noticed where they were taking him from.

\* \* \*

The next morning he telephoned police headquarters and gave an account of his adventure the previous night. "Mr. Janik," a voice from headquarters answered him after a moment's silence, "we're highly interested in this. I wonder if you'd mind coming here at once."

When Mr. Janik arrived, four gentlemen, with the tall, heavy-set person at their head, were waiting for him. Mr. Janik had to tell them once more what had happened and whom he had seen. "The license number of the car was NXX 705," added the heavy-set gentleman. "A private car. Of the six persons Mr. Janik recognized, three are new to me. Gentlemen, I'll leave you now. Mr. Janik, come with me."

Mr. Janik, feeling very small, sat in the large office of the heavy-set gentleman, who paced to and fro very deep in thought. "Mr. Janik," he said at last, "the first thing I have to say to you is: not a word to anyone about this. There are State secrets involved, do you understand?

Mr. Janik nodded silently. Good heavens, he thought to himself, what the dickens have I landed into now?

"Mr. Janik," said the heavy-set man suddenly, "I don't want to flatter you, but we need your services. You've got a lucky hand. People talk about method, but a detective who isn't devilish lucky isn't the slightest use. We need people with a lucky hand. We've got plenty of grit ourselves, but we'd give a good deal for the chance of a lucky fluke. So, why not join us."

"And what about my business?" murmured Mr. Janik, quite abashed.

"Your partner can look after that. It'd be a downright shame not to make proper use of that gift of yours. Well, what do you say?"

"I'll— I'll have to think it over," stammered the unhappy Mr. Janik. "I'll come to see you in a week's time . . . and if I'm really competent . . . I can't say yet. I'll come back again."

"All right," said the heavy-set man, giving him a tremendous handshake. "You needn't be doubtful about yourself. Good day!"

\* \* \*

Before the week was over, Mr. Janik turned up again. "Well, here I am," he chuckled, beaming all over his face.

"Have you made up your mind?" asked the heavy-set man.

"I should think I have," said Mr. Janik with a sigh of relief. "And I've come to tell you that it's no go; I'm no good for the job."

"Nonsense. Why not?"

"Just imagine," chortled Mr. Janik, "my manager's been robbing me for the past five years and I never smelt a rat. That's the sort of idiot I am! Well, a fine detective I'd make, wouldn't I? Thank goodness! For five years I was hobnobbing with a swindler and never saw through him. So you can judge for yourself how useless I'd be. And I was beginning to get quite nervous about it, too. By Jove! I'm glad that nothing's going to come of it. Well, and now I'm out of it, right? Many thanks!"

Translated by Paul Selver; revised by the editor. Originally published in *Tales from Two Pockets*, 1932. From the Czech "Prípady pana Janík."

# The Mail

Human nature is full of inconsistencies; one example being that most people enormously enjoy receiving letters and enormously dislike writing letters, although the two are somehow causally and necessarily connected. No doubt there are people who just love to write letters, such as people in love and people who, signing themselves "one of many" or "your reader," scold the newspaper for something it printed the day before; but these are peculiar people, on the whole, like those people who are wild about attending lectures, or others who sit up all night long chasing faint voices and crackles in their radios, or those who actually like to get up early. But most people don't like to get up, don't like others to talk, and above all don't like to answer letters. As far as the latter are concerned, one can assume that the average person writes a letter only when he wants a reply—which motive normally vanishes when he receives some sort of letter himself. This aversion to letter-writing probably arises from universal human laziness; the love of receiving letters, however, has deeper and more secret roots, or so it would seem.

A thousand times, when the doorbell rings in the morning, you have rejoiced, "Ah, the mail's here!" and a thousand times you have received in your impatient hand printed matter of some sort, a bill and perhaps a registered letter from the tax bureau as well; nevertheless, you will be waiting again tomorrow at a certain hour and with a throbbing heart for the doorbell to ring, and you will delightedly shout, "Ah, the mail's here!" Not that you are expecting something in particular, something which is of great consequence to you, some correspondence which you yourself initiated and to which you should perhaps receive an answer. In your secret heart, you are waiting for the morning mail to bring you, for once, something unforeseen and unsuspected; you have no idea what it might be; perhaps a letter from Heaven, or a letter naming you General of the Cavalry in the Portuguese Army, or notification that you have received a prize for your integrity; something, from somewhere, will arrive by mail and change your fate, reward your virtue, open up unexpected possibilities or satisfy your innermost desires.

"Something will come from somewhere": this is a mystical and boundless possibility which, contrary to all past experience, beckons daily at the postman's ring. When ancient man went into the forest for firewood, granted, mysterious possibilities opened before him at every step: he might discover a fairy treasure, come upon the Three Fates, spy a tree with golden apples or catch sight of dancing nymphs. When I travel to Jindrich Street, I don't really expect to find a fairy treasure in the excavations, or come upon the Three Fates on the streetcar in the process of deciding my destiny, or spy dancing nymphs on Jungmann Square. The range of unknown and undreamed-of possibilities in the ordinary life of contemporary man is surprisingly narrow and unsubstantial. No one these days gets out of bed believing that today, perhaps, he will accomplish something undreamed-of and surprising; and yet at the bottom of his heart he trembles incessantly in the expectation that today something unpredictable and grand will happen, that something will come from somewhere—

Wait, the bell just rang; ah, the mail's here. A person receiving his mail pretends to be somewhat nonchalant (a matter of honor; to quell his secret excitement) and composed (I am prepared for every eventuality); he turns each letter over in his hands and takes his time, just as a person takes his time in opening the door to the thirteenth chamber of an enchanted castle. Finally, after a certain delay, filled with the importance of the moment, he opens his mail; it's curious, how badly and with what undignified haste letters are opened in plays and movies; there, envelopes are torn open before you can say "*shvets,*" and they don't even sit down to do it; but in reality, that's not what happens. A person who receives a letter first of all sits down; he slits open the envelope, doing this slowly and deliberately, as if he were suspiciously raising the lid of a magic box; now we will know the outcome— Strangely enough, this time again, by curious chance, nothing came; there is only a bill from the bookseller's and a letter of some sort that, the devil take it, I'll have to answer. The doors of unlimited possibilities have closed again, for today. The unknown great event is reserved for tomorrow.

And most curious of all is that this state of eternal expectation overcomes even people who on the whole don't have anything to wait for; they don't have an uncle in America, they don't long for something to arrive from somewhere that would intervene in their lives, and they would be terrified if they had to accept a new assignment of some kind; and yet, at the postman's ring, they are seized with a glimmer of anxiety or hope that perhaps . . . who knows . . . something has come from somewhere in this large, strange world. . . God be praised, it's only some printed matter, an ad for coal by the truckload or in bags; but the eternal human hope that something unforeseen and wonderful will happen never definitively and irrevocably fails.

Translated by Norma Comrada; © 1990 Norma Comrada. Originally published in 1925; included, in a different translation, in *Intimate Things*, 1935.

# Part III
# ELUSIVE KNOWLEDGE

In Praise of Idleness
In Praise of Clumsy People
A Cold
Fires
Cats
The Stamp Collection
The Crime at the Post Office
The Blue Chrysanthemum
The Poet
Chinamen and Birds
Pilate's Creed
The Five Loaves

Each of us has the potential for living many different lives, but alas, we seldom make use of this potential. All too often, we do not even choose our selves, but become what we are through mere accident, a chance meeting of circumstances. As a result, we have only a limited knowledge of ourselves and are strangers to a whole range of human experience. The search for the truth about ourselves and our fellows is thus difficult, but it can be a worthwhile adventure if it is approached in an open-minded, imaginative way. These are concepts that Čapek developed to their fullest in his late novels, but they run through much of the earlier work as well.

The story 'The Stamp Collection,' from *Tales from Two Pockets,* for example, is a forerunner of the novel *An Ordi-*

*nary Life.* Karas, the story's narrator, explains how a childhood mistake robbed him of a colorful future: 'If it hadn't happened — I used to be so full of enthusiasm and adventure, love, chivalry, fantasy and trust, so many strange, untamed things — my God, I could have been anything else, an explorer or actor or soldier!' We sense a faint ironic smile on the author's face as we read this; our stamp collector is not exactly the explorer type. Still, who knows. . . It is the polarities that interest Čapek, the byplay of character and destiny, the ordinary and the unusual, comedy and tragedy. As in 'The Stamp Collection,' in 'The Crime at the Post Office' a single mistake seems to have settled the course of a person's whole life. Once again, however, Čapek suggests that though this may be part of the truth, the whole truth is more complex.

In Čapek's stories of detection, the answer is often right under people's noses and is discovered by amateurs after professionals have failed. Too much expertise and sophistication can get in the way, as Čapek shows in 'The Blue Chrysanthemum,' one of his most beautiful and memorable stories.

The first five selections are examples of Čapek's feuilletons, which show how just about any subject—from colds to cats—can be turned into a witty dissertation on that strange adventure called normal life.

Čapek was not a Freudian; he was not especially interested in exploring deep-lying motives or conflicts. For his knowledge of character and its depiction he depended rather on meticulous observation of actual behavior. He and the reader watch the characters, look at them from many sides, and draw their conclusions. What they see is what there is. Čapek does not deny that there is much in the world that is hidden from us, much that is mysterious about life, about people, about cats. But it is as idle to deny the mystery as it is to make conjectures; we must simply accept it as part of the world's richness and adventure.

The *Apocryphal Stories,* two of which are included in this section, are among Čapek's most original contributions to literature. Most of these stories are playful variations on the idea of the plurality of possibilities in every life, a rewriting of history to suggest that the lives and ideas of famous figures might easily have been different from the versions printed in schoolbooks. Thus Čapek, always a democrat, makes the mighty of this earth subject to the same twists of fate as the humbler protagonists of his fiction. The stamp collector might have been a Napoleon; but the obverse is also true.

Ideologues and true believers also like to rewrite history, not in the interests of pluralistic openness but for the opposite reason: to replace it with their own sacred text. In 'Pilate's Creed,' Čapek's Pontius Pilate does not wash his hands of the condemnation of Jesus. On the contrary, he tries to justify his act on the grounds that Christ's followers would probably have turned into dangerous dogmatics for the sake of truth. But what is truth? Pilate's creed, like Čapek's, ends on a question mark.

# In Praise of Idleness

I would like to be idle today: perhaps it is because the weather is particularly fine, or because carpenters are working in the courtyard, or because the sun is shining, or because of a thousand other reasons: I would like to be idle.

I don't want to go out anywhere, for going out is not idling; nor read, nor sleep, because neither the one nor the other is idling; nor amuse myself nor rest, because idleness is neither relaxation nor amusement. Idleness, pure, perfect idleness, is neither a pastime nor time's extension; idleness is something negative: it is the absence of everything by which a person is occupied, diverted, distracted, interested, employed, annoyed, pleased, attracted, involved, entertained, bored, enchanted, fatigued, absorbed or confused; it is nothing, a negation, an intentlessness, a lack-purpose, I don't really know how to put it: in short, something perfect and rare.

First of all, idleness is not wasting time; I could waste time if, say, I ladled water into a sieve; but when I am idle, I certainly don't do anything like that; I don't do anything useless, because I simply don't do anything at all.

In the second place, idleness is not the mother of sin; indeed, it can't be a mother at all, being completely barren. It yearns for nothing; idleness which yearns is not being idle, because it is doing something, because it has some sort of goal.

In the third place, idleness is not laziness. Laziness is neglecting to do something which ought to be done but, instead of doing it, a person prefers to loaf. To be idle is to do nothing at all while at the same time wanting nothing at all.

Nor is idleness resting or repose. Anyone resting is doing something useful; he is preparing for future work. Idleness has no relationship whatsoever to past or future work; it is not the result of anything, and it looks forward to nothing.

Idleness is not enjoying a little relaxation, either. Basking in the sun, blissfully closing one's eyes, purring like a cat, all these activities can, on occasion, be very meaningful or at least pleasant; and pleasantness in itself is close to being meaningful. Idleness is totally devoid of meaning; it calls for neither relaxation nor pleasure; quite simply, it calls for nothing at all.

Relaxation is a slow, ever-flowing current which gently laps and cradles you; resting is a dark, calm pool in which the angry foam and sediment from evil or intense moments are drifting away; laziness is an inlet covered with green algae, slime and frogs' eggs; but idleness is a standing-still. It has neither rhythm nor sound; it is fixed, it does not progress. It gives life neither to weeds nor slime nor mosquitoes. Water—lifeless and transparent. Though it stands still, it acquires no warmth. It stands still and does not become overgrown. It has neither direction nor content nor flavor.

I would like to be idle today; indeed, I want to do nothing.

I want— what, as a matter of fact, do I want? Nothing; for idleness is exactly that. To be like a stone, but without weight. To be like water, but without reflection. Like a cloud, but without motion. To be like an animal, but without hunger. To be like a human, but without thoughts. To look at a piece of white paper, empty and clean; not to write, but to look until it might (on its own initiative) fill itself up with little black letters, words, sentences, phrases, from top to bottom: a first page, a second and a third; and then, then not to have to read it, then, with the amazing obviousness of deep and genuine idleness, not read it through at all, but to turn one's eyes instead to the first fly of spring, which is crawling on the window; to look at it but not to see it; and then— see here, when does idleness need some sort of program? For it is always possible to find something not to do, not to see, and not to follow up.

And when a person is through idling, he arises and returns as if from another world. Everything is a little alien and distant, distasteful somehow, and strained; and it is so. . . so strange, that. . . a person has to take a little rest after being idle; and then after resting, lounge around for a while; and then relax a little more, then devote himself to a certain amount of inactivity, and only afterwards is he able to recover his strength and begin to do something completely useless.

Translated by Norma Comrada; © 1990 Norma Comrada. Originally published in 1923; included, in a different translation, in *Intimate Things,* 1935.

# IN PRAISE OF CLUMSY PEOPLE

Some people are afflicted by a special malevolence of Fate; they are called clumsy, as if they could help it that in their hands things seem to come to life and exhibit a willful and almost diabolical temperament. It should rather be said that they are magicians whose mere touch inspires lifeless things with an unaccountable exuberance. If I knock a nail into the wall, the hammer comes alive in my hand with such strange and untamed life that either I break the wall or my finger or a window at the other end of the room. If I try to tie up a parcel, an absolutely snake-like cunning bursts out in the string; it writhes, jumps out of my hand, and finally performs its favorite trick of fastening my finger firmly to the parcel. A colleague of mine who dabbles so skillfully in high politics that everyone marvels at it aloud, simply does not dare to pull a cork out of a bottle; he knows that if he did, the cork would remain in his hand while the bottle, with unexpected agility, would spring from his grasp and leap onto the floor. People are so silly; instead of appreciating this peculiar magic, they laugh at a man who has this life-giving relationship to objects and call him oaf, butterfingers, clodhopper, bumbler, hobbledehoy, or bull in a china shop.

In reality the whole difference is this, that clumsy people relate to inanimate things as if they were alive, that is to say, wild, obstinate, and endowed with a will of their own, while dexterous people relate to inanimate things as if they were really lifeless and could be manipulated at will. A shop assistant doesn't handle a piece of string in a gingerly manner, like a wild and writhing snake, but as if it were an obedient and dead piece of string; one, two! and it's done. A hammer in the hand of a mason is not a clumsy and obstinate weapon thrusting out at whatever it likes; it is a lifeless, passive instrument which falls where it is ordered. In the opinion of awkward people, all this taming of objects is really magic; but dexterous people should also recognize that clumsiness is magical and mysterious.

I feel that stories about things that talk were not invented by skillful people but rather by magic-working clumsy ones. I believe that Hans Christian Andersen once fell out of his chair or tipped over in it, and that this gave him the idea that a chair is sometimes alive and can talk. When Honza the Fool greeted a bench and wished it much happiness, he was undoubtedly afraid that it might throw him into the stream. If he had been a member of the Czechoslovak Touring Club, he would not have spoken to it, for he would have been certain that it was only put there for his convenience. Dexterous people disseminate to our world a heroic impression of unlimited possibilities, while the clumsy introduce and sustain the epic and truly fanciful conception of unbounded difficulties, adventures, obstacles, and opposition. The story of the glass mountain that rises on the farther side of abysses, black lakes, and impenetrable forests, expresses the living experience of the unhandy: that it is awfully difficult to get anywhere or do anything, and that one may get drenched or bruised on the way.

But it is not for their graphic gifts that I am praising the clumsy; their significance is greater. I wish I could tell all that they have done for the development and progress of the world. It was they who were the cause of the greatest inventions of humanity. It was your despised oafs who brought division of labor into the world. The first dreadful butterfingers had to be born for his defter fellow-cavemen to push him away from the mounting of a claw or the tanning of a hide, growling: "Get out of the way, you clodhopper, I'll do it for you!" It was the unhandy man who created the specialist. If all people were equally adaptable, there would be no division of labor; the result of that would be no progress. While some of the cavemen were handy at mounting claws and others at killing mammoths and reindeer, there were some rare and advanced individuals who were handy at nothing. Or, perhaps, they knew something which was not quite valueless. One of them, from boredom, counted the stars; a second ne'er-do-well made all manner of sounds on a jaw bone, which the others first jeered at and then tried to imitate; a third began playing with colored clay and scrawled in soot the first frescoes in the cave at Altamira. They were quite helpless and peculiar bumblers who couldn't even split a marrow bone. The skillful ones discovered that it is possible to make a knife out of flint; but the unskillful ones made the further discovery that it is possible to leave this work to other people.

They created a society that could not get on without them. The strong and the skillful people saw that one must be a hunter and warrior in order to live; the unskillful ones, however, proved that a few hunters and warriors are enough for others to live, too. Man ceased to be a mere hunter when individuals were born who were very bad hunters. If everyone could make boots, there would be no cobblers. If it were not for us unhandy ones, there would have been neither a Prometheus nor an Edison.

Translated by Dora Round; revised by the editor. Originally published in *Intimate Things*, 1935.

# A Cold

You wake one morning feeling rather strange; your head aches a little, and your back; there is a scratching at the back of your throat and an itching in your nose, but that is all; only all day you are rather irritable and you swear at everything, even when you really have neither cause nor reason. But towards evening a ton falls on you from nowhere, all your joints go soft, all your flesh turns to mush; the patient sneezes wildly about a dozen times, and here it is! With weeping eyes, crumpled up in a heap of misery, surrounded by wet handkerchiefs drying in every corner, the humiliated and streaming creature in slippers by the stove snorts, blows his nose, barks, drinks some infusion or other, sneezes and coughs, skulks about the room, avoids everybody. He has a slight temperature; instead of a head he has a heavy, painful ball; with limbs as though lamed and a handkerchief to his nose he is a dreadful sight. Creep away on tip-toe, all you who see this unhappy man; your noisy and happy gambols are torture to him;

he needs solitude, darkness, and dry handkerchiefs. He would like to take off his head and hang it up by the chimney to dry; he would like to take his humiliated body apart into its several members and set each piece down in a different place. He would like. . . he would like. . . ah, if only he knew what he wanted! If there were anything worth wanting! If only anywhere in the universe there were something warm and comforting which would give this poor, heavy head the relief of forgetfulness. Sleep? Yes, if there weren't those chaotic and disagreeable dreams. Play solitaire? Yes, if it would ever come out! Read? Yes, but what? And this pitiful human ruin gets up, turns round, and staggers to his bookshelves.

Bookshelves, many-colored rows of a thousand backs, I want to find in you a little book that will comfort me, me, the accursed. No, today I couldn't bear you, you fat, scientific book, for my brain is dull and stupid. I would like to read something that will not remind me of my dullness and slow-wittedness; something easy, amusing, to pass the time away . . . Away with you, humorous tales, out of my sight! Today I couldn't bear the vulgar malice with which you hold a stricken man up to ridicule; I, too, am stricken by fate, and I could not enjoy the spectacle of we unfortunates suffering from ridicule and exposed to the whims of scoffers. And you, heroic romances, would you not carry me off to distant ages and epic times when there weren't any colds, among whole and glorious men who slay a base rival in less time than it takes me to blow my nose? But the hand held out to the heroic book trembles weakly; I could not believe in great and magnificent deeds today; man is a small, weak creature, severely tried and loving peace . . . No, leave me in peace today. No heroism and honor, no noble sentiments and laurels of fame; away with you, amorous passions and intoxicating kisses of royal beauties. How can a man think of such things with a wet handkerchief to his nose? Good heavens, no, that's not what I want. Give me a detective novel for me to sharpen my wits on; give me an absorbing shocker that will carry me breathlessly along the exciting trail of some dreadful secret — No, that's not what I want either; today I don't care about crimes and underground passages and evil people. Show me the gentler face of life, reveal people to me in their intimate everyday life. Only for God's sake no psychology! I don't have the patience to linger over feelings and motives; for some obscure reason psychology is always rather painful and harrowing; as if we didn't have enough suffering of our own! Why do people write books at all?

And that one there—it's too realistic for me; I want to forget life today. That one is essentially sad and disillusioning. That one is cruel toward humanity and demands all manner of self-torture and redemption. That one over there is superficial, pretentious, and clever—away with it! That one is too high up. And that yellow one is bitter and jaundiced. In each of them there is something that hurts. Why are almost all books written by wicked and unhappy people?

The man with a cold hesitates in front of his many-colored bookcase, shivering with chills and self-pity. Where can he find something . . . something really good . . . genial toward us unfortunates . . . and comforting? Something that doesn't wound in any way . . . doesn't hurt a man in his smallness and humiliation. . . ?

And then he reaches to the end of the shelf and takes out a book he has read at least a dozen other times when he was depressed by the suffering of body and mind; he snuggles down in his armchair, takes a dry handkerchief, and heaves a sigh of relief before he begins to read.

What is the book? Perhaps our old friend Charles Dickens.

Translated by Dora Round; revised by the editor. Originally published in *Intimate Things*, 1935.

# FIRES

A few nights ago, a fire broke out just opposite our office in Prague. A red glow flooded the sky above the roofs; servant girls who had gone to fetch beer stood staring with mugs in their hands. In a minute or two, a fire engine was there and a crowd of people, and then it was all over. But that moment was enough for a man to feel stirring at the bottom of his heart the old and ardent instinct of fire-worship.

We each carry in us, willy-nilly, the primordial pagan, the primitive caveman; we are fascinated by fire. The man who has never stared into a glowing stove on a winter evening, who has never burned old papers, squatting before the stove in the reverent attitude of a savage, who has never in his life made a bonfire in the fields and danced around it, is perhaps not descended from old Adam but from someone else. Perhaps his ancestors were hatched from frog-eggs or fell down with the rain, like the ancestors of vegetarians, total abstainers, and other superhuman beings. And the man who has never made the mystical, fiery sign of eight with a burning match, has never felt the awful and felonious ecstasy when man's petty fire breaks its chain and flies up in a mighty blaze.

It is part of us. A great fire wakes horror and wonder in us, a strange jollity, a wild passion for flames. We forget all about night and sleep; we feel we want to camp around the fire and chat in an unexpected outburst of primitive comradeship; and when the firemen put it out, we disperse unwillingly and with a certain disappointment that it is all over now and that it was not a bigger affair. We remember the fires we have seen and experienced at one time or another as great and glorious events in our lives. We envy the firemen and policemen and the chief of the Fire Brigade, who can smile at the fire from so near, like priests before the altar, while we are huddled together behind the cordon like the faithful at the chancel rail. Ah, if they would at least let us hold the hose so that we might have some share in the Brotherhood of Fire! As a boy I had a great, heroic ideal: I wanted to be a fireman, to stand on a ladder and play the water on the lashing flames. The roof would fall in, a column of fire would shoot up into the night sky, but I would stand in the rain of sparks and not go one rung lower.

We are Fire-worshippers in the dark depths of our nature; you can even see it in our metaphors. We speak of the "flame of passion" when we want to give a poetic name to a fatal infatuation for a woman; if we were to speak of a deluge of passion or an elementary catastrophe of passion, it would not sound so irresistible. With the same partiality we speak of the "blaze of revolution;" if we were to announce a "flood of revolution," I don't think we'd win too many zealous followers. In the same way, a man "flares up in righteous indignation," although what righteous indignation does as a rule is to cause nothing but a lot of talk. As you see, the cult of fire is deeply rooted in our imaginations.

"In fifteen minutes the local Fire Brigade had got the fire under control." That is all you read in the paper. The reporter's hand would nearly have fallen off if he'd written that "from among the leaping flames came the despairing cries of women and children;" that "the unhappy victims could be seen rushing to and fro wringing their hands;" then "Chief Fireman Rudolf Holub, swiftly making up his mind, flung himself into the flames and at the risk of his life carried out two children, after which he fell to the ground unconscious." Of course it isn't true, but why should the papers only tell lies about politics? If they can invent something bad about the opposing party, why can't they invent something fine about Chief Fireman Rudolf Holub? Why can't they invent Rudolf Holub altogether, swiftly rescuing children by the dozen? If I were a real journalist (for unfortunately I did not become a fireman), I would not let even a small fire out of my hands until I'd wrung out of it great leaping flames, despairing cries for help, and heroic risking of lives; for all that belongs to the sacred cult of fire. We have not learned to make a fiery festival out of the burning of a shed; and yet isn't that a much more fantastic occurrence than the resignation of a Cabinet Minister? It is, after all, far more elemental than parliamentary debates. If the end of the world were to come, the papers would publish a police report on it with the note that "the damage is to a large extent covered by insurance;" but here, again, there would be nothing about leaping flames or despairing cries.

Translated by Dora Round; revised by the editor. Originally published in *Intimate Things*, 1935.

# CATS

Will someone explain to me why a cat gets so strangely excited if you whistle to her very shrill and high? I have tried it with English, Italian, and German cats; there is no geographical distinction. When puss hears you whistling (especially if you whistle *Night of stars and night of love* as high as you can), she begins to rub herself against you, fascinated, then she jumps onto your knee, sniffs at your lips in surprise and, finally, in rapturous excitement, she bites passionately at your mouth and nose with an expression disfigured by voluptuousness; you, of course, stop whistling, and she begins to purr hoarsely and energetically like a small motor. I have thought about it time and again, and I don't know to this day from what ancient instinct cats adore whistling; I don't believe that at any time in the primeval era there was an age when male cats whistled shrilly instead of yowling in a metallic and strident alto as they do today. Perhaps in distant and savage times there lived some cat-gods who spoke to their cat-worshippers by means of magical whistling, but this is a mere hypothesis; this fascination with music is one of the riddles of the cat soul.

Man thinks he knows cats just as he thinks he knows people. A cat is a thing that sleeps curled up in the armchair, sometimes prowls about its cat affairs, sometimes knocks over the ashtray, and spends the greater part of its life in passionate pursuit of warmth. But the secret essence of cathood I only realized in Rome; and that because I was looking not at one cat but at fifty cats—at a whole herd of cats in the great cat basin round Trajan's Column. The old excavated Forum lies like a dry basin in the middle of the square; and at the bottom of this basin, among broken pillars and statues, lives an independent cat nation. It lives on fish heads which kind-hearted Italians throw down from above, it practices some cult of the moon and, beyond this, it apparently does nothing. There it was revealed to me that a cat is not simply a cat but something enigmatic and impenetrable; that a cat is a wild creature. If you see two dozen cats walking around, you realize with surprise that a cat doesn't walk at all, she slinks. A cat among human beings is just a cat; a cat among cats is a skulking shadow in the jungle. Puss clearly trusts man, but she doesn't trust cats, because she knows them better than we. We say "cat and dog" as the example of social mistrust; now I have often seen very intimate friendship between cat and dog, but I have never seen an intimate friendship between two cats; this is, of course, not speaking of feline love-affairs. The cats in Trajan's Forum ignore each other most ostentatiously; if they sit on the same pillar, they sit with their backs to each other and nervously twitch their tails to make it plain that they put up with the presence of these disreputable neighbors against their will. If cat looks at cat, she spits; if they meet, they do not look at each other; they never have a common aim; they never have anything to say to each other. At best they tolerate each other in contemptuous and negative silence.

But to you, man, puss will talk; she purrs to you, looks up into your eyes, and says: "Man, please open this door for me. Much Eating One, do give me some of what you're eating. Stroke me. Talk to me. Let me come sit on my armchair." With you she is not a wild, lone shadow; for you she is simply a domestic pussy cat, because she trusts you. A wild animal is an animal that is mistrustful. Domestication is simply a state of trustfulness.

And you know, we human beings cease to be savages only as long as we trust each other. If when I left home in the morning I distrusted the first neighbor I met, I would edge near to him growling darkly, with every muscle in my thighs tense, ready to spring at his throat at the flicker of an eyelash. If I distrusted my fellow passengers on the streetcar, I would have to keep my back to the wall and spit like a cat to frighten them; instead of which I hang peacefully onto my strap and read the paper, offering them my unprotected back. When I walk along the street I am thinking of my work or of nothing at all, without giving a thought to what the passersby might do to me; it would be awful if I had to eye them askance to make sure they weren't preparing to devour me. A state of mistrust is the original state of wildness; mistrust is the law of the jungle.

Well, I will go now and stroke my own pussy cat. She is a great comfort to me because she trusts me, although she is only a little grey beast who has strayed in from God knows what corner of the unknown wilds of Prague's back alleys. She starts purring and looks up at me. "Man," she says, "do rub me behind my ears."

Translated by Dora Round; revised by the editor. Originally published in *Intimate Things,* 1935.

# THE STAMP COLLECTION

"There's no getting away from it," said old Mr. Karas. "If a man were to rummage through his past, he'd find material in it for a whole different set of lives. One day, either by mistake or because he felt like it, he chose just one of them and went on with it to the end; but the worst of it is that those other lives, the ones he might have lived, are not entirely dead. And sometimes it happens that you feel a pain in them, like a leg that's been cut off.

"When I was a boy of about ten, I began to collect stamps. My father didn't altogether approve of it; he thought it'd make me neglect my lessons, but I had a pal, Lojzik Cepelka, and we used to share our passion for foreign stamps. Lojzik's father used to play a barrel-organ, Lojzik was a messy kid with freckles, as unkempt as a sparrow, a regular ragamuffin, but I was fond of him, in the way that schoolboys are fond of a friend. You know, I'm an old man; I've had a wife and children; yet I have to say that none of our feelings are finer than friendship. But you're only capable of it when you're young; later on, you get sort of crusty and selfish. A friendship of the sort I'm telling about springs simply and solely from enthusiasm and admiration, from excess of vitality, from abundance and overflow of emotion; you've got so much of it that you simply have to give it away to somebody. My father was a lawyer, the chief man among the local bigwigs, a most dignified and severe person, and I palled around with Lojzik, whose father was a drunken organ-grinder and whose mother was a downtrodden laundress, and yet I venerated and idolized Lojzik, because he was smarter than me, because he could shift for himself and was as plucky as they make them, because he had freckles on his nose and could throw stones left-handed—in fact, I can't remember all the things that made me so attached to him; but it was certainly the closest attachment I've ever had.

"And so Lojzik was my trusty comrade when I began to collect stamps. Somebody once said that only men have the collecting instinct, and it's true. I suppose that the craze for collecting things must be the survival of an instinct dating back to the times when every male collected the heads of his enemies, the spoils of war, bearskins, stags' antlers and, in fact, anything he could capture as booty. But a stamp collection possesses one quality that makes it a perpetual adventure; it somehow excites you to touch a bit of some distant country, such as Bhutan, Bolivia or the Cape of Good Hope; it brings you into a sort of personal and intimate touch with these foreign countries. So there is something about stamp-collecting that suggests travel by land and sea, and deeds of derring-do in general. It's very much the same as the Crusades.

"As I was saying, my father didn't exactly approve of it; as a rule, fathers don't approve if their sons do something different from what they themselves have done; as a matter of fact, I'm just the same with my own sons. This business of being a father is a sort of mixed feeling: there's a great deal of affection in it, but there's also a certain prejudice, mistrust, hostility or whatever you may choose to call it. The more affection you have for your children, the more there is of this other feeling. Anyway, I had to hide my stamp collection in the attic, so that my father couldn't catch me with it. In the attic there was an old chest, a sort of flour bin, and we used to crawl into it like a couple of mice to have a look at each other's stamps. Look here, this is a Netherlands, this is an Egyptian, this is Sverige, or Sweden. And because we had to hide our treasures like that, there was something deliciously sinful about it. The way I got hold of those stamps was also an adventurous business; I used to go round to families I knew, and those I didn't, and beg and pray to let me soak the stamps off their old letters. Now and then I came across people who had drawers crammed full of old papers stored away, in an attic or desk; those were my most delightful hours when, sitting on the floor, I sorted out those dusty piles of litter to try and find stamps I hadn't already got—you see, I was silly enough not to collect duplicates, and when I happened to come across an old Lombardy or one of those tiny German states or free cities, why, the thrill I had was perfectly agonizing—every vast happiness has a sweet pang about it. And in the meantime, Lojzik was waiting for me outside, and when at last I crept out, I whispered right in the doorway, 'Lojzik, Lojzik, I found a Hanover in there!'—'Have you got it?'—'Yes.' And away we ran with our booty, home to our treasure chest.

"In our town there were factories that turned out all sorts of trash: jute, calico, cotton, and shoddy wool—the rubbish that we produce specially for the colored races all over the world. They used to let me ransack their wastepaper baskets, and that was my happiest hunting ground; there I came across stamps from Siam and South Africa, China, Liberia, Afghanistan, Borneo, Brazil, New Zealand, India, the Congo—I wonder whether the mere sound of the names gives you the same sense of mystery and glamor as it does me. Good heavens, what joy, what frantic joy I felt when I found a stamp from, say, the Straits Settlements, or Korea or Nepal or New Guinea or Sierra Leone or Madagascar! I tell you, that particular rapture can be realized only by a hunter or a treasure-seeker or an archaeologist who's doing excavations. To seek and to find—that's the greatest thrill and satisfaction a man can get out of life. Everybody ought to seek something; if not stamps, then truth or golden ferns or at least stone arrowheads and ashtrays.

"Well, those were the happiest years of my life, my friendship with Lojzik and stamp-collecting. Then I had scarlet fever and they wouldn't let Lojzik come to see me, but he used to stand in the hall and whistle so that I could hear him. One day they must have taken their eyes off me or something; anyway, I got out of bed and slipped upstairs to the attic to have a look at my stamps. I was so feeble that I could hardly lift the lid of the trunk. But the trunk was empty; the box containing the stamps was gone.

"I can't describe to you how distressed and horror-stricken I was. I think I must have stood there as if I'd been turned to stone, and I couldn't even cry, there was such a lump in my throat. First of all, it was appalling to me that my stamps, my greatest joy, were gone—but what was more appalling was that Lojzik, the only friend I had, must have stolen them while I was ill. I felt over-whelmed, dismayed, dumbfounded, despondent—you know, it's amazing how much a child can suffer. How I got out of that attic, I don't know; but after that I had a high fever again and during my clearer moments I pondered in despair. I never said a word about this to my father or my aunt—I had no mother—I knew that they simply wouldn't understand me and thus I became rather estranged from them. From that time onwards my feelings for them ceased to be close and childlike. Lojzik's treachery affected me terribly; it was the first time anyone had played me false. 'A beggar,' I said to myself, 'Lojzik's a beggar and that's why he steals; it serves me right for fooling around with a beggar.' And this hardened my heart; it was then I began to draw a distinction between one person and another—I forfeited my state of social innocence; but at the time I didn't realize what a shock it had been to me and how much damage it had caused.

"When I had got over my fever, I had also got over my distress at the loss of my stamp collection, though my heart still ached when I saw that Lojzik had now found new friends; but when he came running up to me, rather sheepishly because it was so long since we'd seen each other, I said to him in a curt, grownup tone: 'Shove off, I'm finished with you.' Lojzik turned red and replied: 'All right, then.' And from that time onward he hated me with a stubborn, proletarian hatred.

"Well, that was the incident which affected my whole life. The world I lived in was, so to speak, desecrated; I lost my faith in people; I learned how to hate and despise. After that I never had a friend; and when I grew up, I began to assume that because I was by myself, I needed nobody and would show no favor to anyone. Then I discovered that nobody liked me; I used to put this down to the fact that I despised affection and was proof against all sentimentality. And so I became an aloof and purposeful man, very fussy about myself, very punctilious, the kind of person who always wants to do the right thing. I was cantankerous and harsh towards my subordinates; I did not love the woman I married; I brought up my children to fear and obey me, and by my industry and sense of duty I gained quite a reputation. Such was my life, my whole life; I attended to nothing except my duty. When my time comes, the newspapers will say what valuable work I did and what an exemplary character I had. But if people only knew how much solitude, mistrust and self-will there is about it all. . .

"Three years ago my wife died. I never admitted it to myself or to anybody else, but I was terribly upset; and in my distress I rummaged about among all sorts of family keepsakes which had been left by my father and mother: photographs, letters, my old school exercise books. I felt like choking when I saw how carefully my stern father had arranged and kept them; I think that, after all, he must have been fond of me. The cupboard in the attic was filled with these things, and at the bottom of a drawer was a box sealed with my father's seals; when I opened it, I discovered the stamp collection I had put together fifty years earlier.

"I'm not going to keep anything back from you: I burst into tears and I took the box into my room like a man who has found a treasure. So *that's* what happened, suddenly flashed across my mind; while I was ill, somebody must have found my stamp collection and my father confiscated it, so that I would not neglect my homework. He shouldn't have done it, but it was all because of his concern and affection for me; I don't know exactly why, but I began to feel sorry for him and for myself.

"And then I remembered: so Lojzik never stole my stamps. Good heavens, how I had wronged him! Again I saw before me the freckled and messy urchin, and I wondered what had become of him and whether he was still alive. I tell you, I felt so wretched and ashamed when I looked back on it all. Because of a single false suspicion I had lost my only friend; because of that I had wasted my childhood. Because of that I had begun to despise the lower orders; because of that I had become so opinionated; because of that I never became attached to anyone. Because of that the very sight of a postage-stamp always made me feel annoyed and disgusted. Because of that I never wrote to my wife, either before or after our marriage, and I explained this away by pretending to be above what I chose to call 'gush;' and my wife felt this keenly. Because of that I was harsh and aloof. Because of that, only because of that, I had so fine a career and performed my duties in such an exemplary manner.

"I saw my whole life afresh; suddenly it seemed a different life, was the thought that struck me. If that hadn't happened, I should have been so full of enthusiasm and dash, affection, chivalry, wit and resourcefulness, strange and unruly things of that sort—

why, good heavens, I might have been almost anything else, an explorer or an actor or a soldier! Why, I might have felt some affection for my fellow men, I might have drunk with them, understood them, oh, there's no knowing what I mightn't have done. I felt as if ice were thawing inside me. I went through the collection, stamp by stamp; they were all there: Lombardy, Cuba, Siam, Hanover, Nicaragua, the Philippines, all the places I had wanted to go to and which now I shall never see. On each of these stamps was a scrap of something that might have been and never was. I sat brooding over them all night, taking stock of my life. I realized that it had been an artificial and impersonal life, which did not belong to me, and that my proper life had never come into being." Mr. Karas shook his head sadly. "When I consider all I might have been, and how I wronged Lojzik—"

Father Voves, on hearing these words, looked very downcast and forlorn; most likely he had remembered something in his own life. "Mr. Karas," he said pityingly, "don't think about it; it's no use, you can't put it right now, you can't make a fresh start—"

"No," sighed Mr. Karas with a slight flush. "But you know, anyhow— anyhow, I've started collecting stamps again."

Translated by Paul Selver; revised by the editor. Originally published in *Tales from Two Pockets,* 1932. From the Czech "Sbírka známek."

# THE CRIME AT THE POST OFFICE

"Talk about Justice," Police Sergeant Brejcha said; "I'd like to know why the pictures always show some female with a bandage on her eyes and grocery-store scales. What I mean is, Justice seems more like a policeman, to me. You wouldn't believe the things us policemen pass judgment on, without any judge, without any scales, and without all the fuss and feathers. In a few cases, we tap a few jaws; and in most cases, we take off our belts; but that's all justice is, in ninety cases out of a hundred. But I'll tell you right now, mister, I proved two people guilty of murder myself, and I was the one what sentenced them to just punishment and even decided what that punishment was to be, and I've never said a word about it to nobody. But I'm going to tell it to you, right now.

You'll recall, mister, that little miss what worked here two years ago in our village post office? Sure, Helenka, that was her name. She was such a good, kind girl, pretty as a picture. Not likely you'd forget her. Well, this Helenka, mister, last summer she drowned herself; she jumped in that big pond near here and went out maybe fifty meters until she got to the deep part, and she didn't wash up for two days. And you know why she did it? On that same day when she drowned herself, there was this auditor from Prague who suddenly turned up at our post office and found out Helenka was short a couple hundred crowns from the cash drawer. A miserable couple hundred, mister. That bonehead of an auditor said he was going to report it and there'd be an investigation, like for embezzlement. But that evening, mister, Helenka drowned herself—from shame.

When they pulled her out, over by the dike, I had to stay with her until the coroner came. There wasn't anything pretty about her then, poor little girl, but I kept seeing her the whole time the way she used to be, smiling behind the window at the post office — well, we all hung around there because of her, you know; everybody liked that girl. Damn it, I said to myself, that girl never

259

stole no two hundred crowns. In the first place, I just didn't believe it; and in the second place, she sure didn't need to steal: her daddy was the miller here on the other side of town, and she was only there at the post office because of some female urge to make her own living for herself. I knew her daddy well, mister; he was a sort of writer and a Protestant, too; and let me tell you, mister, these writers and Protestants around here, they never steal nothing. Mister, I promised that dead girl right there on the dike that I wasn't going to let this business drop.

All right, then, the next thing that happens is they send some smart young fellow from Prague up here to the post office, named Filipek; a very pleasant, toothy sort of guy. Well, I went over to the post office to see this Filipek, because I wanted to check something out. It's just like all these other little small-town post offices, you know: a counter with a little window, and on the clerk's side a little cash drawer for stamps and money, and right in back of the clerk is this sort of shelf, with a bunch of ratebooks and notices and papers and a scale for weighing packages and things like that. Mr. Filipek, I says to him, please take a look in those ratebooks and tell me how much it costs to send a cable to Buenos Aires, say.

Three crowns per word, says Filipek, without batting an eyelash.

Then how much for a telegram to Hong Kong, I ask him again.

I'd have to look it up, says Filipek, and he gets up and turns around to the ratebook. And while he's going through the books with his back to the counter, I squeeze my shoulders through the little window and reach my hand in the cash drawer and pull it out. And it opens very nice and quiet.

Thanks, I've got it, says I, and here's how it could have happened. Suppose Helenka was looking something up in the ratebook. Right then, somebody could have swiped the two hundred from the cash drawer. Take a look, Mr. Filipek, and see if you can tell me who sent a telegram or a package from here in the last few days.

Mr. Filipek scratches his head, and he says: Sergeant, it can't be done. You see, that amounts to something like confidentiality of the mail — unless you do your looking in the name of the law. But I would have to notify the head office that a search had taken place.

Hold on, I says to him, I don't care to do that for the present. But look, if you was to more or less. . . just for lack of something better to do . . . sort of poke through those papers and see if maybe somebody did send something from here, so that maybe Helenka had to turn her back away from the counter—

Sergeant, says Mr. Filipek, what if she did? Any telegram forms will be here, but for registered letters and packages, we only have a record of who something was sent to — not who sent it. I'll make a list for you of all the names I find here. Actually, I'm not even supposed to do that, but for you I will. But I don't think you'll learn beans from it.

Filipek was right about that. He handed me maybe thirty names—you know, not much goes on in a village post office, only a parcel now and then for some lad in the service—and there wasn't a pin in the pickings. Mister, I went out and walked and talked that case to myself from seven sides, but to no use. And it plagued me that I wasn't keeping my promise to poor Helenka.

Then, one day, it must have been about a week later, I went back to the post office again. This Filipek looks me over and he says: Say goodbye to your bowling partner, sergeant; I'm moving out. A new girl's coming tomorrow, from the post office in Pardubice.

Aha, I says to that. Some kind of demotion, no doubt, transferring this girl from the big city to a one-horse town.

Not at all, Filipek says, and he gives me a kind of peculiar look. Sergeant, this girl's being transferred here at her own request.

That's odd, says I, but then you know how women are.

Odd it is, Filipek says, but he goes on looking at me. And odder still is that the anonymous letter which brought about that flash-flood postal audit also came from Pardubice.

I whistled, and then I realized that Filipek and I were staring at each other in the very same way. And then suddenly old Uher, the postman, who was sorting the mail for delivery, he speaks up and says: yeah, sure, Pardubice. That's where the supervisor over at the big estate writes to, almost every day, some young lady there at the post office. Yeah, sure, she's his sweetie.

Listen, grandpa, says Filipek, do you know what her name is?

Something like Julie Touf— Toufar—

Tauferova, Filipek says. That's her. That's the one who's coming here.

That where Mr. Houdek, says old Uher, that Houdek what's the supervisor there, he gets a little letter back from Pardubice, too, almost every day. Mr. Supervisor, I tell him, here's a letter from your sweetie again. He always walks down the road to meet me. I've got this here little parcel for him today; it got sent back to him from Prague. See how it's stamped? "Recipient unknown." He got the address wrong, Mr. Supervisor did. So I'm taking it back to him.

Show it to me, says Filipek, and he looks it over. It's addressed to somebody named Novak, Spalena Street, Prague. Contents: two kilos of butter. Postmark: July 14.

That's when Miss Helenka was still here, says old Uher.

Show it to me, I says to Filipek, and I take a sniff at it. Mr. Filipek, I says, that's odd, but this here butter was ten days on the road and it don't even stink. Grandpa, you just leave this package here, and you go off on your rounds.

Old Uher was hardly gone when Filipek says to me: Sergeant, this is against all the rules, but here's a penknife. And then he left so's he wouldn't have to watch.

Mister, I tore open that package, and inside there wasn't nothing but two kilos of dirt. So I go find Filipek right away and I tell him: Man, don't say anything about this to anyone, understand? I'm going to take care of this business myself.

You can bet I pulled myself together and set right out after this Houdek over at the estate. He was sitting there on a pile of planks, just staring at the ground. Mr. Supervisor, says I, there's some kind of mix-up over there at our post office. You recall what address it was on that little package you sent to Prague ten or twelve days ago?

Houdek looks a little funny and then he says: It doesn't matter; and anyway, I don't remember now what it was.

Mr. Supervisor, says I, what kind of butter was it?

Houdek turns white as a wall. What's that supposed to mean? he cries out. Why are you bothering me with all this?

Mr. Supervisor, I says to him, it's this way. You killed our Helenka from the post office. You sent a package from there with a fake address so she'd have to weigh it on the scales. And while she was doing that, you snuck into the cash drawer and stole two hundred crowns. Because of those two hundred crowns, Mr. Supervisor, Helenka drowned herself. That's how it is.

Mister, I tell you that Houdek was shaking like a leaf. That's a lie, he cries, why would I steal two hundred crowns?

Because you wanted to have your sweetheart, Julie Tauferova, here at our post office. That girlfriend of yours sent an anonymous letter saying Helenka was missing money from the cash drawer. It's just like the two of you pushed Helenka in the pond. It's just like the two of you killed her. You have murder on your conscience, Mr. Houdek.

That Houdek, he tumbled down on the planks and he covered up his face, and never, never did I ever see a man cry like that. Jesus Christ, he was wailing, Jesus Christ, I couldn't know she'd drown herself! I only thought she'd be let go . . . that she'd just go back home! Officer, all I wanted to do was marry Julie! But one of us would have had to give up our jobs if we were going to be together . . . and we can't live on one salary . . . that's why I wanted so much for Julie to get the job here at the post office! We've already been waiting for five years. . . Sergeant, we love each other so much, so much!

Mister, I'm not going to tell you the rest. It was almost nighttime, and here was this fellow Houdek down on his knees in front of me, and me blubbering over the whole business—I was blubbering like a ninety-year-old bride, over Helenka and over everybody else, too.

That's enough, I finally says to him, that's enough. I've already had it up to here. Now hand over those two hundred crowns. Right. And now listen: if it occurs to you to marry Miss Tauferova before I set this whole business straight, then I'll charge you with theft — understand? But if you shoot yourself or do anything else like that, I'll go ahead and tell why you did it. And that's that.

That night, mister, I sat in judgment on those two, there under the stars. I asked God how I should punish them, and I truly saw why justice is such a bitter, painful joy. If I did bring charges against them, this Houdek would get a couple of weeks in jail and then go on probation; but still, it would be very hard to prove. Houdek killed that girl — but he wasn't a common thief. To me, every punishment was either too big or too small. So that's why I was judging and punishing them myself.

The next morning, I went back to the post office. Sitting there behind the window was this tall, pale girl with fierce, burning eyes. Miss Tauferova, says I, I have a registered letter here; and I gave her a letter addressed "Director of Postal Communications, Prague." She looked at me and she stuck the label on.

Just a minute, miss, I said. Inside this letter is a charge against the person who stole two hundred crowns from your predecessor. What's the postage?

Mister, there was a terrible strength in that woman; all the same, she turned ashy pale, and she was stiff as a stone. Three crowns fifty, she said, hardly breathing.

I counted out the money and I said, Here you are, miss. But if those two hundred crowns should happen to turn up—I said while I put the stolen banknotes on the counter in front of her—if those two hundred crowns should happen to turn up here—fallen down or misplaced somewhere, you understand?—so that everyone will know that poor, dead Helenka didn't steal it, well then, miss, then I could take back my letter. Now what about it?

She didn't say a word; she just sat there, fierce and burning and stiff like I've never seen anybody before, anywhere.

The postman will be here in five minutes, miss, I said. What about it, then. Shall I mail the letter?

She shook her head quickly. So I picked up the letter and walked out in front of the post office. Mister, I've never marked time with so much strain and suspense. And then, twenty minutes later, old Uher ran out crying: Officer, it's been found! The two hundred crowns Miss Helenka was missing! They're found! That new girl found them in one of the ratebooks! It was all a mistake!

Grandpa, I told him, go run and tell everybody that the two hundred crowns have been found. You know, so that everybody will know that Helenka didn't steal them, thank God!

So then, that was the first thing. The second thing was that I went to see the owner of the big estate. You probably don't know him; he's a count—a little crazy, but a very nice man. Sir, I tell him, don't ask me any questions, but there's a little police matter going on here that has to be taken care of. Call your supervisor Houdek and tell him he has to leave today for your place in Moravia. If he doesn't want to go, tell him you're giving him an hour's notice.

The old count raised his eyebrows and stared at me for a while. Mister, there's no way I could have forced myself to look more serious than I did, more so than anybody can imagine. Very well, then, says the count, I won't ask you any questions. And furthermore, I'll summon Houdek now.

Houdek came, and when he saw me with the count he flinched, but he stood straight as a stick. Houdek, says the count, harness the horses and get down to the train station. You begin service this evening at my estate in Hulin. I will send a telegram so they'll be expecting you. Do you understand?

Yes, Houdek said quietly, and he fixed his eyes on me, like the eyes of the damned in hell.

Have you any objections? the count asked.

No, said Houdek hoarsely, and he never let his eyes drop from me. Mister, those eyes were agony to me.

Then you must go, says the count, and that was that. After a minute or so I saw them taking Houdek away in the coach. He sat there like a wooden puppet.

And that's the whole story, mister. But if you go to the post office, you'll see this pale, pale woman there. She's mean and angry at everyone, and she's getting old and mean lines in her face. I don't know if she ever sees her Supervisor; maybe she does go visit him sometimes, but then she comes back again meaner and angrier than before. And I see this happen, and I say to myself: there must be Justice.

I'm only a policeman, mister, but I'm telling you from my own experience. Whether there's some kind of all-knowing, all-powerful God, I don't know; even if there is, it's no use to us. But I tell you, Somebody has to be greater and more just than we are. That's the certain truth, mister. We can only punish, but there has to be a somebody, somewhere, who can forgive. I tell you, mister, truth and higher justice are just as strange as love.

Translated by Norma Comrada; © 1990 Norma Comrada. Originally published as "Zlocin na poste" in *Povídky z jedné kapsy (Tales from One Pocket)*, 1929; included, in a different translation, in *Tales from Two Pockets*, 1932.

# THE BLUE CHRYSANTHEMUM

"Well, I'll tell you," old Fulinus said, "how Klara comes into this story. In those days I was working on the grounds of Prince Lichtenberk's estate in Lubenic — that old prince, mister, he was a real connoisseur; he had Veitsche send whole trees from England, and he brought in seventeen thousand bulbs specially from Holland — but that's beside the point. One Sunday, then, I'm going down the street in Lubenic and I meet up with Klara; that was the village idiot, you know, deaf and dumb, a crazy, simple-minded fool of a girl who wandered all over, braying as cheerful as can be — can you tell me, mister, why these idiots are so blessed cheerful? Anyway, I was trying to dodge her, so she wouldn't slobber me with a kiss, when all of a sudden I caught sight of a bunch of flowers in her paws. She had some dillweed and other such stuff from the fields, but in amongst them, mister — I've seen a lot of things, but this really bowled me over. I tell you, that crazy girl had one button chrysanthemum in her nosegay that was *blue*! Blue, man! It was just as blue as *Phlox laphami;* a little slate-color tinge to it, with satiny, rosy edges and a center like *Campanula turbinata,* beautifully full, but all that's the least of it: mister, that blue color was then and is still to this very day absolutely unknown in chrysanthemums! Two years ago I was with old Veitsche, you know, and Sir James was bragging to me about how the year before, one of their chrysanthemums, this import straight from China, had bloomed a speck lilac in color, but unfortunately it died on them during the winter. And here in the claws of that cackling rattlebrain was a chrysanthemum as blue as you could ever hope to see. So much for that part of it.

So here was this Klara, mooing cheerfully and shoving her bunch of flowers at me. I gave her a one-crown piece from my change, pointed to the chrysanthemum and said: Klara, where'd you get this? Klara cackled and snorted, just as pleased as could be, but I didn't get anything more out of her. I hollered at her, pointed with my hands, but it was no use; no matter what, she was going to throw her arms around me. I took that blue chrysanthemum and went straight to the old prince: Your Highness, this is what's growing somewhere nearby; let's go find it. The old prince immediately ordered a coach so we could take Klara with us. But in the meantime Klara had gone off somewhere and couldn't be found. We stood there by the rig, swearing, for a good hour—His Highness used to be with the dragoons. We were still at it when Klara dashed up with her tongue lolling out and jammed a whole bunch of fresh blue chrysanthemums at me, torn right off the bush. The prince whipped out a hundred-crown note for her then and there, but Klara broke out crying, all disappointed; poor thing, she didn't know about paper money. I had to give her another crown to quiet her down. Then she started dancing around and shrieking, but we set her up in the driver's box, pointed to the blue chrysanthemums, and said: Klara, take us there!

Klara whooped with glee up there on the driver's seat; you can't imagine how his High and Mightiness the coachman was horrified that he had to sit next to her. Besides which, the horses would skitter every time she squealed and cock-a-doodled, oh, I'll tell you, it was the devil's own ride. After we'd been going for an hour and a half, I said: Your Highness, we've already come at least fourteen kilometers.

No matter, muttered the prince, a hundred kilometers if need be.

All right, I said, I'm all for it, but Klara brought back that second bouquet inside of an hour. That place can't be more than three kilometers from Lubenic.

Klara, cries the prince, pointing to the blue chrysanthemums, where do these grow? Where did you find them?

Klara croaked and gurgled and pointed still further ahead; probably she liked riding in the coach. You know, I thought the prince was going to kill her; dear Jesus, that man could carry on! Lather was dripping off the horses, Klara was cackling, the prince was cursing, the driver only by some miracle kept from sobbing in shame, and I was plotting how to track down that blue chrysanthemum. Your Highness, says I, this isn't going to work. We'll have to look without Klara. We've got to mark out a three-kilometer area on the map, divide it up in sections, and have a house-to-house search.

My God, man, says the prince, there isn't a single park within three kilometers of Lubenic!

267

That's all right, says I. The devil of a lot you'll find in a park; unless you're looking for ageratum or canna. Look, down here on the stalk is a bit of soil; that's not humus, it's a greasy, yellowish clay, most likely fertilized by human whatchamacallit. We have to look for a place where there's plenty of pigeons; there's lots of pigeon droppings on the leaves. And most likely this grows by a fence made from peeled stakes, because here at the leafstalk is a chip of fir bark. That's our clue, right there.

What do you mean? says the prince.

What I mean, says I, is that we have to look around every shed and shanty within an area of three kilometers. We'll break up into four groups: you, me, your gardener and my helper Vencl, and that's it.

Well, then, next morning the first thing that happened was that Klara brought me a bouquet of blue chrysanthemums again. I searched all over my section after that: I drank warm beer at every local pub, ate homemade cheeses, and asked people about blue chrysanthemums. Mister, don't ask me what kind of diarrhea I got from those cheeses; it was hot, the way it sometimes gets at the end of September, and I made it into every little farm and had to put up with every kind of rudeness, because people thought that either I was crazy, or a salesman, or somebody from the government. But one thing was clear by nighttime: no blue chrysanthemum was growing in my section. There weren't any in the other three, either. Only Klara, bringing me another broken-off bunch of blue chrysanthemums.

You know, a prince is an important person, however you look at it; he called in detectives and put blue chrysanthemums in their hands and promised them I-don't-know-what-all if they could show him where they grew. Detectives, mister, are educated people; they read newspapers and the like; besides, they know every trick and stick and they have enormous influence. Think of it, mister: on that day there were six detectives plus ordinary policemen, the mayors' councils, school kids with their teachers and even a band of gypsies prowling over that whole patch of land inside the three-kilometer circle, and they tore up everything in bloom and brought it to the manor. Great heaven, it was like Corpus Christi Day; but as to blue chrysanthemums, there wasn't a one. We had to keep an eye on Klara all day long; she took off in the evening, though, and then after midnight she brought me a whole armful of blue chrysanthemums. Straightaway we shut her up in the jail, so she wouldn't yank them all up; but we had come to a dead end. I must say, it was mystifying; just imagine, an area no bigger than the palm of your hand—

Listen, a man has a right to get nasty when he's in terrible need or when he meets up with failure; I know that; but when His Highness told me in a fury that I was as big an idiot as Klara, I told him straight out that I wasn't going to let an old cretin like him talk to me that way, and I left right then and there for the train station, and I haven't been back to Lubenic since. But after I was seated in the carriage and the train began to move, I tell you, mister, I broke down and cried like a youngster, because I'd never get to see that blue chrysanthemum and I was leaving it behind forever. And then, while I was blubbering and looking out the window, right there by the tracks I see something blue. Mr. Capek, it was stronger than I was: it knocked me up out of my seat and made me pull the emergency brake—I didn't have a thing to do with it; the train jolted when it braked, and I got thrown down on the seat opposite—that's how I broke this finger. And when the conductor came running, I stammered about how I'd forgotten something in Lubenic, and I had to pay a hell of a fine. Mister, I swore like a sergeant all the time I was limping back along the tracks to where that blue was. You blockhead, I told myself, it's probably only an autumn aster or some other worthless trash, and you've just wasted a heathenish sum of money! I'd gone maybe five hundred meters; already I was thinking that that blue couldn't have been so far back, that I must have gone past it, or at least so it seemed to me, when up on this small bank I spy a little railroad watchman's house, and there, peeking over the stake fence around the garden plot, is that blue. It was two clumps of blue chrysanthemums.

Mister, even a child knows what those crossing guards grow in their garden plots. Besides cabbages and cucumbers, there's usually sunflowers, a couple of red rosebushes, hollyhocks, tropaeolum and some of those dahlias. But this fellow, he didn't even have that; only potatoes, beans, one black elderberry and there in the corner those two blue chrysanthemums.

Say, mister, says I across the fence, where'd you get those posies?

Those blue ones? the watchman says. Why, those were left

here after Cermak died, that was the guard here before me. But you can't walk on the rails, man. There's the sign: "Walking on the rails is forbidden." What are you doing here?

Buddy, I tell him, I thank you, and how do I get to where you are?

On the rails, he says to that. But nobody's allowed to walk on the rails. What do you want? Get out of here, you damned tramp, but keep your feet off of those rails!

How then, says I, do I get out of here?

Who cares, yells the guard, but not on the rails, and that's that!

So I sit down by the edge of the track and I say: Listen, grandpa, sell me those blue posies.

I'm not selling, grumped the guard. And get out of here now! You aren't supposed to sit there.

Why not? I say to him. Where does it say I can't sit here? Walk, no; but I'm not walking.

The guard pulled up short at that and had to be content with cussing at me over the fence. But he must have been a hermit; after a minute he quit and began talking to himself. Then half an hour later, he stepped out to have a look at the rails again.

Well, then, he says as he stops beside me, are you getting out of here now, or not?

I can't, says I, walking on the tracks is forbidden and there's no other way to get out of here.

The guard thought it over for a while. Then he said, I'll tell you what, when I go down behind this bank, you take off along the tracks, and I won't see you.

I thanked him heartily, and when he was gone I crept over the fence to his little garden and with his own spade I dug up both those blue chrysanthemums. I stole them, mister. I'm an honest fellow and I've only stolen seven times in my life; and always it was flowers.

One hour later I was seated in the train and taking those stolen blue chrysanthemums home. As I was riding past the guard's house, there stood that watchman with his little flag, looking sour as the devil. I waved my hat at him, but I don't think he recognized me.

There you have it, mister: there was that sign with "Walking on the rails is forbidden" written on it, and nobody, not us, not the policemen, not the gypsies, not even the kids figured they could go there and look for blue chrysanthemums. What power there is in a warning sign, mister! For all I know, there may be blue primroses growing in some railway guard's little garden, or the tree of knowledge or pure gold ferns; but nobody ever discovers them because walking on the tracks is strictly forbidden and that's that. Only crazy Klara went there, because she was an idiot and didn't know how to read.

That's why I gave those blue chrysanthemums the name of Klara. I've been babying them for fifteen years now. But most likely I'm too fussy about proper soil and moisture — for sure that barbarian of a watchman never watered them, he had clay hard as iron there in his garden. Well, in short, they come up for me in the spring, they develop a fungus in the summer, and they die off by August. Think about it: I'm the only one in the world with a blue chrysanthemum, but I can't prove it. Oh, Bretagne and Anastasia, sure, they're a bit purplish; but Klara, mister, once Klara blooms for me, the whole world will talk of nothing else."

Translated by Norma Comrada; © 1990 Norma Comrada. Originally published as "Modrá chryzantéma" in *Povídky z jedné kapsy* (1929). First English translation.

# THE POET

It was a routine police matter: at four o'clock in the morning, an automobile knocked down an old, drunken woman on Zitna Street and drove off at high speed. And now the young police lawyer, Dr. Mejzlik, had to determine which automobile it was. Such responsibilities weigh heavily on a young police lawyer.

"Hm," Dr. Mejzlik said to Police Officer 141, "from a distance of thirty paces, then, you saw a quickly moving car and a body lying in the street. What did you do first?"

"First, I ran over to the victim," the policeman reported, "to apply first aid."

"First, you should have identified the car," Dr. Mejzlik grumbled, "and then you worry about the old lady. But perhaps," he added, scratching his head with a pencil, "I would have done the same thing. At any rate, you didn't see the number on the license plate; was there anything else about the car—?"

"I think," Police Officer 141 said slowly, "that it was a dark color of some kind. Possibly dark blue or dark red. It wasn't easy to see because of the fumes from the exhaust."

"Oh, Christ," Dr. Mejzlik despaired, "then how am I going to find that car? Am I supposed to chase after all the drivers in the city and ask them ever so kindly to tell me whether or not they ran over an old lady? What do you expect me to do, man?"

The policeman shrugged his shoulders with subordinate help-lessness. "Sir," he said, "one witness has reported in to me, but he doesn't know anything either. He's waiting outside, sir."

"Well, bring him in," Dr. Mejzlik said disgustedly, and he searched in vain for some clue to spring forth from the meager accident report. "Name and address, please," he said mechanically, without so much as looking at the witness.

"Kralik, Jan Kralik, engineering student," the witness said stolidly.

"And you were present, sir, when at four o'clock this morning an unknown automobile knocked down Bozena Machackova?"

"Yes, and I'd have to say it was the driver's fault. You see, commissioner, the street was completely empty; if the driver had slowed down at the intersection—"

"How far away were you standing?" Dr. Mejzlik interrupted him.

"Ten paces. I was seeing a friend home from a— a coffee-house, and while we were walking along Zitna Street—"

"Who is your friend?" Dr. Mejzlik interrupted again. "I don't see it here."

"Jaroslav Nerad, the poet," the witness said with a certain amount of pride. "But I doubt if he could tell you anything."

"Why not?" Dr. Mejzlik grumbled again, clutching at any straw.

"Because he is. . . he's the sort of poet that, if something unpleasant happens, he bursts into tears like a little child and runs home to hide. Anyway, while we were in Zitna Street, suddenly there came rushing up from behind us, at an insane speed, this car—"

"License number what?"

"I don't know, sir. I didn't notice it. I was watching that insane driving, and I immediately said to myself that—"

"And what kind of car was it?" Dr. Mejzlik interrupted.

"Four horsepower internal combustion engine," the expert witness answered. "Of course, I'm no good at makes of cars—"

"And what color was it? Who was in it? Was it a convertible or a sedan?"

"I don't know," the witness said in confusion. "I think it was a sort of black car, but I can't come any closer than that, because when the accident happened I said to Nerad: Look, those bastards knocked somebody down and didn't even stop!"

"Hm," Dr. Mejzlik commented with dissatisfaction. "That is, admittedly, a fitting and no doubt correct moral reaction, but I would rather you'd gotten the license number. I am amazed, sir, how incapable people are at simple observation. You're absolutely convinced that the driver is at fault, you're absolutely convinced that people like that are bastards, but as for systematic, practical observation— Thank you, Mr. Kralik; I won't delay you any longer."

Within the hour, Police Officer 141 had rung the bell at the lodgings of the poet Jaroslav Nerad. Yes, the poet Nerad was at

273

home, but he was sleeping. Moments later, the poet himself was at the doorway, rolling small, astonished eyes at the policeman; he couldn't remember, exactly, just what wrongdoing he had committed.

At length he was able to grasp why they wanted him at the police station. "Must I go?" he had asked suspiciously. "The fact is, I don't remember anything at all; that night I was a bit—"

"Smashed," the policeman had said understandingly. "I've known many poets, sir. So get dressed, sir; I'll wait for you."

Whereupon the poet and the policeman began to chat about neighborhood taverns, life in general, various celestial phenomena and many other matters; only politics was alien to both. Thus, in friendly and instructive conversation, the poet arrived at the station house.

"You are Mr. Jaroslav Nerad, the poet," Dr. Mejzlik said to him, "and a witness. You were present when an unidentified automobile knocked down Bozena Machackova."

"Yes," the poet sighed.

"Can you tell me what kind of car it was? Whether it was a sedan or a convertible, what color, who was in it, what the license number was?"

The poet struggled with his thoughts. "I don't know," he said. "I didn't notice."

"You don't recall any details?" Dr. Mejzlik pressed.

"Not a one," the poet said candidly. "I never pay attention to details, you see."

"Thank you," Dr. Mejzlik fired off with considerable irony. "What, may I ask, did you pay attention to?"

"The total mood," the poet replied vaguely. "You know, the long, deserted street . . . at dawn . . . and how that woman continued to lie there—" Suddenly he leaped to his feet. "But I wrote something about it after I got home!" He fumbled in his pockets and began to pull out an increasing number of wrappers, bills and other scraps of paper. "No, that's not it," he kept muttering, "that's not it, either— Wait, maybe this is it," he said, absorbed in studying the back of an envelope.

"Show it to me," Dr. Mejzlik said indulgently.

"It's nothing," the poet objected. "But if you like, I'll read it to you." Whereupon, rolling his eyes rapturously and melodiously elongating the syllables, he recited:

march of dark houses once twice to stop to stand
aurora plays upon a mandolin
why girl why do you blush
with oncoming car 120 HP to the edge of the earth
or to Singapore
stop stop the car flies on
our great love sprawls in dust
a girl a broken blossom
swan's neck bosom drum and cymbal
why so many tears?

"And that's all," Jaroslav Nerad declared.

"Excuse me," Dr. Mejzlik said, "but what does it mean?"

"Well, it's the automobile accident, of course," the poet said in astonishment. "You mean you don't understand it?"

"I don't think so," Dr. Mejzlik said critically. "Somehow it doesn't convey to me that on July 15, at four o'clock in the morning on Zitna Street, an automobile with license plate number such-and-such knocked down a sixty-year-old drunken beggarwoman, Bozena Machackova; and that she was injured and taken to the General Hospital, and that she nearly died. Your poem, sir, insofar as I can tell, didn't mention those particular facts. No."

"Sir," the poet said, rubbing his nose, "that is only raw, surface reality. But a poem is the inner reality. Poems are unfettered, surreal representations which reality evokes in the subconscious of the poet, you see? Visual and aural associations, you might say. And the reader must yield himself to them," Jaroslav Nerad protested reprovingly. "Then he will understand."

"I beg your pardon," Dr. Mejzlik erupted. "No, wait a minute, loan me your opus. Thank you. All right, then, here we have, hm: 'March of dark houses once twice to stop to stand.' Please explain to me, if you will—"

"But that's Zitna Street," the poet said serenely. "Those two rows of buildings, you see."

"And why isn't it, say, Narodni Avenue?" Dr. Mejzlik asked skeptically.

"Because Narodni Avenue doesn't go in a straight line," came the answer with conviction.

"All right. 'Aurora plays upon a mandolin' — Well, we'll grant that one. 'Why girl why do you blush' — Please, where does this girl come into it?"

"The red sunrise," the poet said laconically.

"Aha. Excuse me. 'With oncoming car 120 HP to the edge of the earth' — Well?"

"Maybe that was when the car arrived," the poet explained.

"It was 120 horsepower?"

"I don't know about that; it means that it was coming fast. As if it wanted to soar to the edge of the earth."

"I see. 'Or to Singapore' — Why exactly Singapore, for heaven's sake?"

The poet shrugged his shoulders. "I don't know. I suppose it's because the Malayans are there."

"And what is the relationship between the car and the Malayans? Hm?"

The poet fidgeted uneasily. "Maybe the car was brown, could that be it?" he pondered. "Certainly something there was brown. Why else would it have been Singapore?"

"Look," Dr. Mejzlik said, "that car has already been red, blue and black. What am I supposed to choose from all that?"

"Choose brown," the poet advised. "It's a nice color."

"'Our great love sprawls in dust / a girl a broken blossom,'" Dr. Mejzlik read on. "This broken blossom, is that the drunken beggarwoman?"

"I wouldn't write about a drunken beggarwoman," the poet said, offended. "She was simply a woman, do you see?"

"Aha. And what is this: 'swan's neck bosom drum and cymbal' — Is that free association?"

"Show it to me," the poet said in confusion, and he bent over the paper. "'Swan's neck bosom drum and cymbal' — What can that be?"

"I just asked that," Dr. Mejzlik grumbled somewhat touchily.

"Wait," the poet reflected, "there must have been something that reminded me— Listen, doesn't it strike you that sometimes the numeral two looks like a swan's neck? Look at this," and he wrote a 2 with the pencil.

"Aha," Dr. Mejzlik said attentively. "And what of the bosom?"

"Surely that's a three, two curves, right?" the poet said in surprise.

"You still have the drum and cymbal," the police official burst out tensely.

"Drum and cymbal," the poet Nerad said thoughtfully, "drum and cymbal . . . that might just possibly be a five, mightn't it?

276

Watch," he said, and he drew the numeral 5. "That little belly is like a drum, and the cymbal above it—"

"Wait," Dr. Mejzlik said, and he wrote down 235 on the paper. "Are you certain that the car had the license number 235?"

"I paid no attention whatsoever to any numbers," Jaroslav Nerad proclaimed resolutely. "But something like that must have been there — Or why else would it be here?" he marveled, inspecting his little composition. "And, you know, this is the best part of the poem."

* * *

Two days later, Dr. Mejzlik called on the poet. This time the poet wasn't asleep, for he had a girlfriend of some sort there, and he began a futile search for a vacant chair to offer the police official.

"I can't stay," Dr. Mejzlik said. "I only came to tell you that it really was a car with the license number 235."

"What car?" the poet wondered.

"Swan's neck bosom drum and cymbal," Dr. Mejzlik poured out with a single breath. "And Singapore, too."

"Oh, of course; now I know," the poet remarked. "So you see, here you have internal reality. Would you like me to read you a couple of other poems? You will understand them now."

"Some other time," the police official answered quickly. "When I have another case."

Translated by Norma Comrada; © 1990 Norma Comrada. Originally published as "Básník" in *Povídky z jedné kapsy (Tales from One Pocket),* 1929; included, in a different translation, in *Tales from Two Pockets,* 1932.

# CHINAMEN AND BIRDS

'Hm,' said Dr. Vitasek, 'you know, I'm a bit of a connoisseur of Persian rugs; but I don't mind telling you, Mr. Taussig, that nowadays things aren't what they used to be. Nowadays those swindlers in the Orient won't take the trouble to dye the wool with cochineal, indigo, saffron, camel's wine, gallnuts and all the rest of the high-class organic dyestuffs; oh, it's a crying shame. The wool isn't what it used to be, either, and when it comes to patterns—I could cry! I suppose these Persian rugs are what you might call a lost art now. That's why only the old specimens that were made before 1870 have got any value; but they're the sort of thing you can only buy when some old family sells its heirlooms 'for family reasons,' as the best people say when they mean 'debts.' Why, I once came across a real Transylvanian rug in the castle at Rozmberk—one of those tiny praying-rugs that the Turks made in the seventeenth century when they were living in Transylvania: there, in this castle, the tourists tramp over it in their hob-nailed boots and nobody knows how much it's worth—I tell you, it's downright heartbreaking, that it is. And we've got one of the rarest rugs in the world here in Prague, and nobody knows about it.

Well, it's like this: I know all the rug dealers in town and sometimes I have a look around to see what they've got in stock. You see, sometimes the agents in Anatolia and Persia still come across an old specimen which has been stolen from a mosque or somewhere like that, and they wrap it up together with a garden-variety rug; then afterwards the whole bundle is sold by weight, just as it stands. So I think to myself, supposing they were to wrap up a Ladik or a Bergamo that way; and I sometimes look in at one of the rug dealers, sit down on a pile of rugs, have a smoke and watch them selling Bukhara, Saruka and Tabriz rugs to fools. And now and then I say, "What's that you've got underneath, that yellow one?" And, by Jove, if it isn't a Hamadan. Well, among my favorite dealers is a certain Mrs. Severynova—she keeps a little shop in a back alley in the Old Town, and sometimes there are some fine

Kararams and Kelims to be picked up there. She's a plump, jolly person, who talks a mile a minute, and she owns a poodle so fat that the very sight of it makes you sick. It's one of those fat, surly dogs with an asthmatic and cantankerous bark; I don't like them. Look here, have any of you ever seen a *young* poodle? I never have. If you ask me, all poodles are old, just like all inspectors, auditors and tax collectors; I suppose it's a mark of the breed. But being anxious to keep on good terms with Mrs. Severynova, I used to sit in the corner where the bitch Amina would grunt and wheeze on a large rug folded square, and I would scratch her back; Amina liked that no end.

"Mrs. Severynova," I said to her one day, "business must be bad; why, the rug I'm sitting on has been here for the last three years."

"It's been here longer than that," said Mrs. Severynova; "it's been folded up in that corner for a good ten years; but it isn't my rug."

"Aha," I said, "it belongs to Amina."

"The idea," said Mrs. Severynova with a chuckle. "It belongs to a lady; she says she hasn't got enough room for it at home and so she's left it here. It's rather in my way, but anyhow Amina can sleep on it, can't you, Amina?"

Although I pulled aside just a tip of the rug, Amina began to growl ferociously. "Why, this is quite an old rug," I said; "may I have a look at it?"

"Of course," said Mrs. Severynova and she took Amina onto her lap. "Come now, Amina, this gentleman is only going to have a look, and then he'll spread it out again for Amina. Hush, Amina, you mustn't growl. Now then, you silly thing, you."

Meanwhile, I unrolled the rug and, I tell you, my heart gave a terrific thump. It was an Anatolian of the seventeenth century, here and there worn threadbare, but, if you know what I mean, it was what they call a "bird-rug," with a pattern of Chinamen and birds; that, let me tell you, is a sacred and forbidden pattern. You can take my word for it, it's a great rarity, and this particular specimen was at least thirty meters square, of a beautiful white color, interwoven with turquoise blue and cherry pink . . . I went over to the window, so that Mrs. Severynova couldn't see my face, and said: "That's quite an old bit of stuff, Mrs. Severynova, and here it is lying on your hands and getting absolutely worn out.

Look here, you tell that lady I'll buy it, if she hasn't any room for it."

"That's not so easy," said Mrs. Severynova. "This rug isn't for sale, and the lady, she's all the time in places like Merano and Nice. I don't even know when she's home. But I'll try and ask her."

"Yes, please do," I said with as much indifference as I could, and then went about my business. You know, a collector looks upon it as an affair of honor to pick up a rarity for a song. I know a very rich and important man who collects books; he doesn't mind giving a few hundred for some old second-hand book, but he fairly jumps for joy when he picks up the first edition of the poems of Jan Krasoslav Chmelensky for a few pennies at a flea market. It's just a sport, like stag-hunting. So I had made up my mind that I must get this rug on the cheap and that then I'd present it to the museum, because that's the only place for a thing of that sort. Only there'd have to be a label on it with an inscription: **PRESENTED BY DR. VITASEK**. After all, everyone's got his private fantasies, hasn't he? I don't mind admitting that this kept running through my head.

It was all I could do not to start off the very next day for this specimen with the Chinamen and the birds; I could think of nothing else. I must stick it out a day longer, I said to myself every day. There are times when we enjoy tormenting ourselves. But after a couple of weeks it struck me that somebody else might find that bird-rug there, and I rushed round to Mrs. Severynova's. "Well what about it?" I gasped from the doorway.

"What about what?" asked Mrs. Severynova in astonishment, and I collected my thoughts. "Why," I said, "I was just going along the street here and I happened to remember that white rug. Will the lady sell it?"

Mrs. Severynova shook her head. "It can't be done," she said, "she's at Biarritz now and nobody knows when she's coming back." So I had a look to see whether the rug was there; of course, Amina was lying on it, fatter and mangier than ever, and waiting for me to scratch her back.

Some days later I had to go to London, and once I was there I took the opportunity of calling on Sir Douglas Keith—you know, he's the greatest living authority on Oriental rugs. "Would you mind telling me," I said to him, "the value of a white Anatolian rug with Chinamen and birds, more than thirty square meters in area?"

Sir Douglas looked at me over his spectacles and rapped out almost ferociously: "None of all."

"How do you mean, none at all," I said, taken aback. "Why shouldn't it have any value?"

"Because there's no such rug that size," Sir Douglas yelled at me. "You ought to know perfectly well that the largest known rug with Chinamen and birds is scarcely fifteen square meters."

My face went red with joy. "But supposing," I said to him, "that there was a specimen as big as that. What value would it have?"

"None, I tell you," yelled Sir Douglas. "A specimen like that would be unique, and how on earth are you going to decide the value of a unique specimen? If a specimen's unique, it may as easily be worth a thousand pounds as ten thousand pounds. How the dickens do I know? Anyway, there's no such rug in existence. Good day, sir."

Well, you can just about imagine the frame of mind I came home in. Mother Mary, I must get hold of that specimen with Chinamen and birds. That'd be a windfall for the museum. But you must bear in mind that I couldn't very well show that I was so keen on it, because that's not a collector's way. And don't forget that Mrs. Severynova had no particular reason for wanting to sell the tattered old rug that her Amina rolled about on, while the confounded woman who owned the rug was gadding about from Merano to Ostend and from Baden to Vichy—she must have had a medical encyclopedia at home with lots of diseases in it. At any event, she was everlastingly in some spa or the other. So every couple of weeks I would look in at Mrs. Severynova's to see whether the rug was still there in the corner with all its birds, I would scratch the loathsome Amina till she squealed with delight, and so as not to make it too obvious I would buy some sort of rug every time; I tell you, at home I've got piles and piles of Shiraz, Shirvan, Mossul, Kabristan and other garden-variety rugs—but among them was a classical Derbent, yes, sir, that you don't see every day, and an old blue Khorassan. But what I went through for two years, only a collector can understand. Talk about pangs of love, why, they're nothing to the pangs of a collector. But the funny thing about it is that no collector has ever been known to commit suicide; on the contrary, they generally live to a ripe old age. I suppose it's a healthy sort of passion.

One day Mrs. Severynova said to me suddenly: "Well, she was here, Mrs. Zanelli, the one this rug belongs to; I told her I could find her a customer for that white rug and that anyway it was getting worn out lying here; but she said it was an heirloom and she didn't want to sell it and I was to leave it where it was."

So as you can imagine I went off on my own to find this Mrs. Zanelli. I thought she'd be no end of a society lady, but as it turned out, she was an ugly old frump with a purple nose and a wig, and her mouth kept giving a queer twitch as far as her left ear.

"Madame," I said, and I couldn't help watching her mouth jerking across her face, "I'd very much like to buy that white rug of yours; of course, it's a bit threadbare, but it'd just about be suitable for . . . my entrance hall." And as I waited for her to answer, I felt as if my own mouth was beginning to jerk and twitch to the left; I don't know whether it was catching, or if it was just nervous excitement, but I tell you, I couldn't control it.

"How dare you?" the dreadful woman screeched at me. "Get out of here this very instant, this very instant," she yelled. "That's the heirloom left to me by my Großpapa! If you won't get out, I'll send for the Polizei! I won't sell any rugs, I'm a von Zanelli, sir. Mary, see this man out of the house."

Believe me, I raced down those stairs like a schoolboy. I could have wept with rage and vexation, but what was I to do? For a whole year after that I kept on looking in at Mrs. Severynova's; Amina by now had become so fat and bald that she had learnt to grunt like a jug. A year later Mrs. Zanelli came back again. It was then that I gave in and did something which as a collector I ought to be ashamed of to my dying day: I sent a friend of mine to her—the lawyer Bimbal, a smooth-spoken fellow with a beard that always makes women trust him unreservedly—and I told him to offer the worthy lady a reasonable sum for that bird-rug. Meanwhile, I waited below, as agitated as a suitor who is about to receive his answer. Three hours later Bimbal staggered out of the house, wiping the sweat from his face. "You blackguard," he gasped at me, "I'll wring your neck. I'm damned if I didn't have to listen to the history of the Zanelli family for three whole hours just to oblige you. And let me tell you," he bawled vindictively, "you're not going to get that rug; seventeen Zanellis would turn in their graves if that heirloom was to end up in a museum! My God, what a trick you pulled on me!" And with that he took his leave.

Now you know that when a man gets an idea into his head, he won't let go of it in a hurry; and if he's a collector, why, he won't stop at murder to get what he wants; collecting is a job for heroes. So I made up my mind that I'd simply steal that rug with the Chinamen and birds. First of all, I spied out the lay of the land; Mrs. Severynova's shop is in a courtyard, and at nine o'clock in the evening the passageway is locked. I didn't want to do any unlocking with a skeleton key, because that's a job I know nothing about. The passageway leads to a cellar where anybody could hide before the place is locked. There's also a small shed in the yard, and by getting onto the roof of the shed, you could climb over into the next yard, which belongs to a tavern, and you can always get out of a tavern. So it was quite simple; the only thing was to find a way of opening the shop window. I bought a glazier's diamond for that job and practiced on my own windows till I knew how to remove a pane of glass.

Now don't imagine that burglary's a simple matter; it's harder than performing an operation on the prostate or slicing chunks out of a man's kidneys. In the first place, it's a hard job to avoid being seen. In the second place, it involves lots of waiting and other inconveniences. And in the third place, there's a good deal of uncertainty about it; you never know what you're likely to run into. Believe me, it's a hard job and a badly paid job. If I found a burglar in my home, I'd take him by the hand and say to him gently: "Look here, couldn't you manage to rob people in some other way, more convenient to yourself?"

I don't know how others set about a burgling job, but my own experiences are not exactly encouraging. On the evening in question, as they say, I sneaked into the building and hid on the stairs leading to the cellar. That's how a police report would put it; what really happened was that for half an hour I loitered about in the rain in front of the doorway, thus becoming conspicuous to all and sundry. At last I made a desperate resolve, just as a man makes a desperate resolve to have a tooth pulled, and I went into the passageway. It goes without saying that I knocked into a servant-girl who had gone to fetch beer in the tavern next door. To soothe her ruffled feelings, I muttered something to the effect that she was a sweetheart and a darling; which scared her so that she made her escape. In the meantime, I took shelter on the stairs to the cellar; some dirty brutes had left a trashcan standing there, full of sweepings and other garbage, most of which, while I was engaged upon what I have described as sneaking in, got spilt with a tremendous clatter. Then the servant-girl came back with the beer and, flustered, told the superintendent that a suspicious character had got into the house. But the excellent fellow kept cool and remarked that it was probably someone who was boozed and who had lost his way to the tavern next door. A quarter of an hour later, yawning and clearing his throat, he locked the door and things quieted down. All I could hear was a servant-girl sobbing loudly somewhere upstairs—it's funny how noisily servant-girls sob, most likely they fret about something. I began to feel cold, and besides that the place smelled sour and musty; I groped about, but somehow everything I touched felt slimy. My goodness, what a lot of fingerprints must have been left there of Dr. Vitasek, our distinguished specialist in diseases of the urinary tract! When I thought it must be midnight, it was only ten o'clock. I wanted to start my burgling at midnight, but at eleven o'clock I couldn't stand it any longer and off I went to steal that rug. You wouldn't believe what a row you make when you want to creep along in the dark; but the people in that house were sound sleepers. At last I got to the window and with a fearful scraping began to cut the glass. Inside, there was a muffled bark; Jesus, it was Amina.

"Amina," I whispered, "you ugly brute, keep quiet; I've come to scratch your back." But you know, in the dark, it's appallingly difficult to coax the diamond into the same slit you made at first; so I fumbled about with the diamond till at last, pressing a little harder, the damn pane snapped right through with a bang. That's it, I said to myself, now the whole neighborhood'll come dashing up, and I looked for a place to hide; but nothing happened. Then with a coolness nothing short of diabolical, I got rid of some more panes of glass and opened the window; inside, Amina yelped every now and then, but only in a half-hearted sort of way and just as a matter of form, to show that she was doing her duty. So I crawled through the window and made a beeline for that wretched mutt. "Amina," I whispered fervidly, "Where's your back, I wonder? Come on now, I'm a friend of yours—you like that, you brute, don't you?" Amina writhed with bliss, if a sack can be said to writhe; and so I said very affably: "That's right, and now let go, doggie," and I tried to drag the precious bird-rug away from under her. At this point, I suppose, Amina decided that *her* property was at stake and began to howl; she didn't just bark, she howled. "Jesus, Amina," I hastily remonstrated with her, "be quiet, you brute! Wait a moment and I'll spread something better out for you to lie on." And whoosh! I dragged from the wall an ugly, shiny Kirman that Mrs. Severynova thought was the best thing in her shop. "Amina," I whispered, "that's where you're going to night-night." Amina gazed at me with interest; but scarcely had I stretched out my hand for her rug than she again set up a howl. I thought they'd hear it miles and miles away. So I again worked the repulsive brute up into a state of ecstasy by a particularly voluptuous binge of back-scratching, and I took her in my arms; but the instant I put my hand out to catch hold of that unique white specimen with the Chinamen and birds she snorted asthmatically and began to curse. "For God's sake, you beast," I said at my wits' end, "I'll have to kill you!"

Well, you know, this is a thing I can't make out; I looked at that fat, repulsive, vile mutt with the most savage hatred I have ever felt, but I couldn't kill the brute. I had a good knife, I had a leather belt; I might have cut the animal's throat or strangled her, but I hadn't the heart. I sat down beside her on that divine rug and tickled her behind the ears. "You coward," I whispered to myself, "just one movement or two and the thing would be done. You've operated on plenty of people in your time, and you've seen them dying in terror and pain; *why can't you kill a dog?*" I tell you, I gritted my teeth to try to pluck up courage, but I couldn't manage it; and at that point I broke down and cried—I suppose it must have been because I felt so ashamed of myself. And then Amina began to whine and lick my face.

"You wretched, beastly, good-for-nothing freak, you," I snarled at her. Then I patted her mangy back and climbed through the window into the yard; I had now reached the stage of defeat and retreat. What I wanted to do next was to jump onto the shed and from there go along the roof to the other yard and out through the tavern, but I hadn't an ounce of strength left, or else the roof was higher than I had supposed; in any event I couldn't get onto it. So I climbed back onto the stairs by the cellar and stayed there till morning, absolutely pooped. Idiot that I was, I might have slept on those rugs, but I never thought of that. In the morning I heard the superintendent opening the door. I waited a moment, and then I made straight for the exit. The super was standing in the doorway, and when he saw a stranger walking out of the passage he was so flabbergasted that he forgot to raise an alarm.

A few days later I called on Mrs. Severynova. A grating had been put in front of the windows and, it goes without saying, coiled up on the sacred Chinamen design was that disgusting reptile of a dog; when she saw me, she joyously wagged the stumpy sausage which on other dogs would be called a tail. Mrs. Severynova beamed at me. "Our darling Amina, our pet, our dear little doggie; just fancy, the other day a burglar got in here through the window and our Amina chased him away. Why, I wouldn't let her go for all the money in the world," she declared with pride. "But she's fond of you; she can tell an honest person when she sees one, can't you, Amina?"

Well, that's the whole story. That unique white rug is still lying there—I believe it's one of the rarest textile specimens in the world; and still that loathsome, scabby, stinking Amina lies on it and grunts with delight. I wouldn't be surprised if one day she's choked by her own fat, and then perhaps I'll have to learn how to file through a grating.'

Translated by Paul Selver; revised by the editor. Originally published as "Troubles of a Carpet Fancier" in *Tales from Two Pockets*, 1932.

# PILATE'S CREED

Jesus answered, To this end was I born, and for this cause came I
into the world, that I should bear witness unto the truth. Every one
that is of the truth heareth my voice.

Pilate saith unto him, What is truth? And when he had said this,
he went out again unto the Jews, and saith unto them, I find in him
no fault at all. (John 18:37-38)

Towards evening a man named Joseph
of Arimathea, who was much respected in the city and was also a
disciple of Christ, came to Pilate and asked for the body of Jesus.
Pilate consented and said: "He was executed wrongfully."

"You yourself delivered Him to his death," protested Joseph.

"Yes, I did," answered Pilate, "and of course, people think I
did it for fear of those windbags who were shouting for their Barab-
bas. If I'd sent five soldiers against them it would have silenced
them. But that's not the point, Joseph of Arimathea.

"That's not the point," he went on after a pause. "When I
was talking with him I saw that, after a while, his disciples would
crucify others: in the name of his name, in the name of his truth
they would crucify and torture everyone else, they would kill other
truths and raise other Barabbases upon their shoulders. The man
spoke of truth. What is truth?

"You are a strange people and you talk a great deal. You
have all sorts of pharisees, prophets, redeemers and other sectarians.
Each one who makes his own truth rules out all the other truths.
As though a carpenter who makes a new chair were to forbid people
to sit on any other chair that someone had made before him. As
though the making of a new chair abolished all the old chairs. It
is indeed possible that the new chair is better, more beautiful and
more comfortable than the others; but why in heaven's name should
a tired man not be able to sit down on any wretched stone or
worm-eaten seat? He is tired and broken, he needs a rest; and here
you drag him by force from the resting-place into which he has
dropped to make him change over to yours. I don't understand you,
Joseph."

"Truth," objected Joseph of Arimathea, "is not like a chair or a resting-place; it is, instead, like a command which says: Go here and there, do this and that; defeat the enemy, conquer that city, punish treachery and so forth. The man who does not obey such a command is a traitor and an enemy. That's how it is with truth."

"Ah, Joseph," said Pilate, "you know I am a soldier and have lived the greater part of my life among soldiers. I have always obeyed orders, but not because they were the truth. The truth was that I was tired or thirsty; that I was homesick for my mother or eager for fame; that this soldier was thinking of his wife, and that one of his fields or oxen. The truth was that if there had been no command, none of these soldiers would have gone to kill other people as tired and unhappy as themselves. Then what is truth? I believe that at least we hold a little of the truth if we think of the soldiers and not of the command."

"Truth is not the order of a commander," said Joseph of Arimathea, "but the command of reason. You know that this column is white; if I were to tell you it was black, that would be contrary to your reason and you would not agree that I was right."

"Why not?" asked Pilate. "I should say to myself that perhaps you were terribly unhappy and depressed if a white column looked black to you; I should try to distract you; in fact I should be more interested in you than before. And even if it were only a mistake, I should say to myself that your mistake contains as much of your soul as your truth."

"It is not *my* truth," said Joseph of Arimathea. "There is only one truth for all."

"And which is that?"

"The one in which I believe."

"There, you see," said Pilate slowly. "It is only *your* truth after all. You are like little children who believe that the whole world ends at their horizon and that there is nothing more beyond. The world is a large place, Joseph, and there is room in it for many things. I think there is actually room in it for many truths. Look, I am a stranger in these parts and my home is far beyond the horizon; yet I should not say this country is wrong. Equally strange to me is the doctrine of this Jesus of yours; but am I therefore to say it is wrong? I think, Joseph, that all countries are right; but the world has to be tremendously vast for them all to fit in beside each other and behind each other. If Arabia had to stand on the same spot as Pontus, of course it would not be right. And it is the same with truths. The world would have to be made enormously vast, spacious and free for all the real truths to fit into it. And I think it is, Joseph. When you climb a very high mountain, you see that things merge into each other and flatten out into a single plain. From a certain height truths merge into one another. Of course, man does not live and cannot live on top of a high mountain; it is enough that he sees around him his house and his fields, both of them full of truths and things; that is his true place and sphere of action. But now and then he can look at the mountains or the sky and say to himself that from there his truth and his things still exist and no part of them is stolen, but they merge with something far more open, which is no longer his property. To keep this vast view while tilling his little field—that, Joseph, is something almost like piety. And I think that the heavenly Father of such a man really exists somewhere, but that he gets on quite well with Apollo and the other gods. They are partly merged in each other and partly side by side. Look, there is an enormous lot of room in heaven. I am glad the heavenly Father is there too."

"You are neither hot nor cold," said Joseph of Arimathea, rising. "You are just lukewarm."

"No," answered Pilate. "I believe, I believe most passionately that truth exists and that man recognizes it. It would be madness to think that truth is only there for man not to know it. He knows it, yes; but who? I or you, or everyone perhaps? I believe that each of us has a share of it; the man who says yes and the man who says no. If these two united and understood each other, that would give the whole of truth. Of course, yes and no cannot unite, but people always can; there is more truth in people than in words. I have more understanding of people than of their truths; but there is faith even in that, Joseph of Arimathea, and it is possible to keep it alive with enthusiasm and rapture. I believe. I believe absolutely and without doubt. But what is truth?"

Translated by Dora Round; revised by the editor. Originally published in *Apocryphal Stories,* 1949. From the Czech "Pilátuv Vecer," 1920.

# THE FIVE LOAVES

What have I against him? I'll tell you plainly, neighbor; it's not that I have anything against his teaching. Not at all. I heard him preach once, and I tell you, I was within an inch of becoming one of his disciples myself. Why, I went home and said to my cousin the harness-maker: listen, you ought to hear him; I tell you, he's a prophet in his way. He says beautiful things and only what's true; your heart turns right over inside of you. Why, my eyes filled with tears and I'd have liked nothing better than to shut up my shop and follow him so as never to let him out of my sight. Give away all you have, he said, and follow me. Love your neighbor, help the poor and forgive those who wrong you, and things like that. I'm just an ordinary baker, but when I listened to him there was such a strange joy and pain within me, I don't know how to describe it: a kind of weight, so that I could have sunk to the ground and wept, and at the same time I felt wonderful and light as though everything had dropped from my shoulders, you know, all my worries and trials. So I said to my cousin, you blockhead, you ought to be ashamed of yourself; you never talk anything but low, money-grubbing gossip about how much people owe you and how you have to pay tithes and taxes and interest. You should give everything you have to the poor, leave your wife and children, and follow him—

And as for curing the sick and those possessed, I don't hold that against him either. Certainly it's a strange and unnatural power, but after all, everyone knows our own doctors are quacks and the Roman ones aren't any better; they take your money all right, but when you call them in to a dying man they just shrug their shoulders and say you should have sent for them sooner. Sooner! My poor wife was hemorrhaging for two years before she died. I took her from doctor to doctor, you've no idea the money it cost, and none of them did her a bit of good. If he'd been going from city to city then, I would have fallen on my knees before him and said: Lord, heal this woman! And she would have touched his garment and been healed. The poor thing suffered so, I can't tell you— So I approve of his healing the sick. You know the doctors cry out against it and say it's all fraud and trickery, and they would have liked to forbid him to do it and I don't know what; but of course there are all sorts of interests involved. The man who wants to help the people and save the world always comes up against somebody's interests; you can't please everyone, it isn't possible. I say, let him heal them and maybe even raise the dead; but that business with the five loaves was a thing he shouldn't have done. Speaking as a baker, I tell you it was a great injustice to bakers.

You haven't heard about the five loaves? I'm surprised at that; all the bakers are quite beside themselves about it. Well, it's said that a great multitude followed him to a desert place and he healed their sick. And when it was evening his disciples came to him, saying: "This is a desert place, and the time is now past; send the multitude away, that they may go into the villages, and buy themselves victuals." But he said to them: "They need not depart; give ye them to eat." And they said unto him: "We have here but five loaves, and two fishes." He said: "Bring them hither to me." And he commanded the multitude to sit down on the grass, and took the five loaves, and the two fishes, and looking up to heaven, he blessed, and brake, and gave the loaves to *his* disciples, and the disciples to the multitude. And they did all eat, and were filled: and they took up the fragments that remained twelve baskets full. And they that had eaten were about five thousand men, besides women and children.

You know, neighbor, no baker can put up with that; how could he? If it became the custom for anyone who liked to feed five thousand people with five loaves and two small fishes, what would become of bakers, tell me that? It doesn't matter so much about the fishes; they grow of themselves in the water and anyone who likes can catch them. But a baker must buy flour and firewood at a high price, he must employ an assistant and pay him wages; he must keep a shop, he must pay taxes, and this and that, and by the time he's finished he's glad if he has a few cents left over for himself so that he needn't go begging. And he— he just looks up to heaven and has enough bread for five or I don't know how many thousand people; the flour doesn't cost him anything, he doesn't have to have wood carted long distances, no expenses, no work — well, of course he can give the people bread for nothing! And he never thinks how he's depriving the bakers in the neighborhood of their hard-earned profits! I tell you, it's unfair competition and he ought to be prevented from doing it. Let him pay taxes like us if he wants to run a bakery! People come to us and say, what! you want an extortionate price like that for a wretched little loaf? You ought to give it for nothing, like him; and what bread it is too, so folk say: white and light, and fragrant, so that you can go on and on at it. We've had to bring down our prices as it is; I give you my word, we're selling below cost simply to avoid having to shut up shop. If it goes on like this, it'll be the end of the bakery business. I heard that in another place he fed four thousand men, besides women and children, with seven loaves and a few fishes, but that time they only took up four baskets of fragments, so perhaps his business isn't going so well; but he's finished us bakers for good. And I tell you here and now, he only does it from enmity to bakers. The fishmongers are crying out against him too, but you know they ask outrageous prices for their fish; theirs is not nearly such an honest trade as ours.

Look here, neighbor: I'm only an old fellow and I'm alone in the world; I've neither wife nor children, so what do I need? I told my assistant he could take on my bakery and run it by himself. I don't care about getting on; I tell you I'd really like to give away the modest little bit of property I've got and follow him and cultivate love to my neighbor and all the things he preaches. But when I see the stand he is taking against bakers I say to myself: No you don't! As a baker, I see that it is not the redemption of the world but absolute disaster for our business. I'm sorry, but I can't let him get away with it. It won't do.

Of course we lodged a complaint against him with Ananias and with the Governor for interference with trade and for incitement to rebellion, but you know how long it takes to get the authorities to move. You know me, neighbor, I'm a peaceable man and I don't seek a quarrel with anyone; but if he comes to Jerusalem I shall stand in the street and shout: Crucify him! Crucify him!

Translated by Dora Round; revised by the editor. Originally published in *Apocryphal Stories,* 1949. From the Czech "O Peti chlebích," 1937.

# Part IV
# THE MEASURE OF MAN

From the Life of the Insects—Act II
On Literature
Soil and the Gardener
Legs and the Gardener
The English Park
Traffic
The Fairbanks Smile
Goodwill

Karel Čapek repeatedly extolled the beauty and nobility of ordinary life. His wife, Olga Schein-pflugová, wrote in her biography: 'He was a champion of the everyday, because he considered the everyday festive.' On account of his attachment to the humbler side of life, Čapek was frequently accused of promoting a cult of the small. And it is certainly true that he disliked everything extreme, exaggerated, overblown, from supermen to superlatives.

Čapek attacked both the realist and expressionist schools of literature for concentrating unduly on the exceptional at the expense of common human qualities. 'The greatness and "human-ness" of a literary work are synonymous,' Čapek wrote early in his career.

His ultimate criterion of measure was the human scale. Metaphorically, this is expressed by the garden, a creation in which nature is given proportions consonant with human purposes, equally removed from the primal desert or the traffic-clogged jungle of the modern metropolis. Čapek was an avid gardener; he read widely on the subject and became an authority on certain plants. His villa in Prague was known for its exotic specimens, but these were not allowed to upset the overall balance and scale of the garden. According to Čapek's wife, he was never as happy as when his hands were plunged into the soil and his rear end pointed at the sky, or when visitors asked the author, perspiring and dressed in grimy overalls, whether Doctor Čapek was at home.

But in the early play *From the Life of the Insects* (1921), written with his brother Josef, Čapek presents a different view of the garden, in particular of its insects. Although a travesty of human qualities, it is so free of dogmatism and tendentious conclusions that the overall effect is comic; this expressionist revue shows a conflict of idealisms rather than a compendium of vices.

# FROM THE LIFE OF THE INSECTS

## ACT II — THE PREDATORS

By Josef and Karel Čapek

Translated by Tatiana Firkušný and Robert T. Jones

### CHARACTERS

CHRYSALIS
TRAMP
ICHNEUMON FLY
MR. DUNG BEETLE
MRS. DUNG BEETLE
FOREIGN DUNG BEETLE
LARVA
MR. CRICKET
MRS. CRICKET
PARASITE

*(A sandy hillock, sparsely overgrown with grass stems as thick as tree trunks. In the hillock's left side is the entrance to the* ICHNEUMON FLY's *tunnel; in its right side is a deserted cricket hole. In the foreground the* TRAMP *is sleeping. The* CHRYSALIS *is attached to one of the grass stems. Suddenly,* CHRYSALIS *is attacked by a band of insect robbers. From the left a small beetle comes running and detaches* CHRYSALIS *from her stem. From the right, another beetle comes running, drives away*

*the first one and tries to drag* CHRYSALIS *off. A third beetle jumps out of the prompter's booth, drives away the second one and begins to pull* CHRYSALIS *away.)*

CHRYSALIS: I. . . I. . . I!

*(The third beetle throws himself headlong into the prompter's booth. The first and second beetles run out from opposite sides and scuffle over* CHRYSALIS. *The third one darts out of the booth and drives them both away, then begins dragging* CHRYSALIS *himself.)*

CHRYSALIS: The entire earth is bursting! I am being born!

TRAMP *(raises his head)*: What's going on?

CHRYSALIS: Something great is about to happen!

TRAMP: That's good. *(He puts his head down.)*

PAUSE

VOICE - HE *(offstage):* You can't tumble it around like that!

VOICE - SHE *(offstage):* Who, me?

VOICE - HE: You!

VOICE - SHE: Me??

VOICE - HE: You!

VOICE - SHE: Me???

VOICE - HE: You! You oaf!

VOICE - SHE: Clod!

VOICE - HE: Idiot!

VOICE - SHE: Blockhead!

VOICE - HE: Tramp! Slut!

VOICE - SHE: Shit beetle!

VOICE - HE: Careful with the ball! Watch out!

VOICE - SHE: Easy now!

VOICE - HE: Care. . . care. . . careful!

*(An enormous ball of manure rolls onstage, pushed by a dung beetle couple.)*

MR. DUNG BEETLE: Nothing happened to it?

MRS. DUNG BEETLE: No! Nothing! Nothing! *(yammering)* Ye ye ye ye! Ah! The fright I had! You're all right, my sweet little ball, aren't you? You. . . you. . . you're our darling little ball!

MR. DUNG BEETLE: Haha! Our little capital! Our marvelous manure! Our golden sweetheart! Our everything!

MRS. DUNG BEETLE: You beautiful ball of turds! You treasure! You splendid little sphere! Our golden fortune!

MR. DUNG BEETLE: Our love! Our only joy! How we searched

297

and scrimped, piled up manure and saved up every stinking crumb. . . went to bed hungry. . .

MRS. DUNG BEETLE: . . .and . . . walked our feet down to our ankles, and all those piles of turds we rooted through, how we had to scratch till we got you so nicely molded and well-established. . .

MR. DUNG BEETLE: . . .and firmly rounded and neatly packed, our big darling sunshine!

MRS. DUNG BEETLE: Our jewel!

MR. DUNG BEETLE: Our life!

MRS. DUNG BEETLE: Our lifetime achievement!

MR. DUNG BEETLE: Just take a sniff, old girl! A beauty among beauties! Just try how heavy it is! And we've got so much of it!

MRS. DUNG BEETLE: So much of God's goodness!

MR. DUNG BEETLE: So much of God's blessings!

CHRYSALIS: The shackles of the world are breaking.
A new life is in the making.
I am being born!

TRAMP *(raises his head)*

MRS. DUNG BEETLE: Dung Beetle darling.

MR. DUNG BEETLE: What?

MRS. DUNG BEETLE *(giggles)*

MR. DUNG BEETLE *(giggles):* Wife!

MRS. DUNG BEETLE: What?

MR. DUNG BEETLE: Hahaha! It's wonderful to own things. To own a fortune. To own our dream.

MRS. DUNG BEETLE: Our own ball.

MR. DUNG BEETLE: The fruits of our labor.

MRS. DUNG BEETLE: Hahaha!

MR. DUNG BEETLE: I'll go crazy with joy. I. . . I. . . I'll go crazy with worry. Upon my soul, I'll go crazy.

MRS. DUNG BEETLE: Why?

MR. DUNG BEETLE: Because of worry! Now that we have our own ball. We were looking forward so much to having it, and now that we have it we've got to make a new one. So much drudgery!

MRS. DUNG BEETLE: Why a new one?!

MR. DUNG BEETLE: Stupid! So we'll have two.

MRS. DUNG BEETLE: Ah, two! Of course!

MR. DUNG BEETLE: Haha, just imagine! Two balls! At least two.

Better say three. You see, everybody who owns one has to start making another one.

MRS. DUNG BEETLE:  So he'll have two.

MR. DUNG BEETLE:  Or better still, three.

MRS. DUNG BEETLE:  Listen, Dung Beetle darling!

MR. DUNG BEETLE:  What?

MRS. DUNG BEETLE:  I have this terrible fear. That somebody might steal it!

MR. DUNG BEETLE:  What? Whom?

MRS. DUNG BEETLE:  Steal our ball! Our joy! Our everything!

MR. DUNG BEETLE:  Our b. . . ball? For God's sake, don't say that!

MRS. DUNG BEETLE:  Because. . . because. . . because, well, we can't keep rolling it along while we're piling up the second one.

MR. DUNG BEETLE:  We'll put it away, see? De-pos-it it somewhere. Hide it. Bury it nice and safe. Wait. . . somewhere in a pit, in a nice little pit, safe like. See? One has to deposit one's valuables.

MRS. DUNG BEETLE:  I just pray nobody finds it!

MR. DUNG BEETLE *(yammering):* Yi, yi, yi, yi! Be still! Anything but that! Anything but getting it stolen! Our ball! Our golden sweetheart! Our darling round capital!

MRS. DUNG BEETLE:  Our splendid shit ball! Our life! Our one and only!

MR. DUNG BEETLE:  Wait! Stay here and watch! Watch it! Guard it with care! *(He starts to run away.)*

MRS. DUNG BEETLE:  Where are you going?

MR. DUNG BEETLE:  To look for a pit. . . a little pit. . . a deep pit . . . to bury our ball. . . our darling. . . our golden sweetheart . . . safe like. . . *(He disappears.)* Watch care—fully. . .

MRS. DUNG BEETLE:  Dung Beetle! Dung Beetle darling! Come here! Wait! Over there! There is. . . Dung Beetle! He can't hear me anymore. And over there, there is such a good pit! Dung Beetle! He's gone. And over there, there is such a wonderful pit! That dunce! Oaf! Idiot! If I could at least go and look at it. No, I'm not going anywhere, sweet little ball. If I could just . . . one look. . . Little ball, darling little ball, wait just one second. I'll. . . I'll be right back, just one look and I'll be back. . . *(She runs toward the back and turns*

299

*around.)* Darling little ball, stay right there, be good. Right away, right away, I'll. . . *(She descends into the* ICHNEUMON FLY's *tunnel.)*

CHRYSALIS: To be born! Born! A new world!

TRAMP *(gets up)*

FOREIGN DUNG BEETLE *(runs in from the wings where he has been lying in wait):* They're gone. This is my chance. *(He begins rolling the ball away.)*

TRAMP: Hey, hey, don't knock me down.

FOREIGN DUNG BEETLE: Out of my way!

TRAMP: What's that thing you're rolling?

FOREIGN DUNG BEETLE: Hahaha! A ball! Gold! Capital!

TRAMP *(backing off):* It stinks, that gold of yours.

FOREIGN DUNG BEETLE: Gold doesn't stink. Gidyap, ball! Keep rolling! Capital, keep turning over! Having it means keeping it! Hahaha, that's the truth!

TRAMP: What is?

FOREIGN DUNG BEETLE: Well, I say, it's nice to own things. *(He rolls the ball to the left.)* My treasure! My beautiful little fortune! My jewel! My everything! *(disappearing)* To have my own! To put away a little something! To bury nice and safe like! Care. . . care. . . careful! *(gone)*

TRAMP: To own things? Why not? Everybody wants to have his own little ball.

MRS. DUNG BEETLE *(coming out of the* ICHNEUMON FLY's *hole):* Oh. . . *(yammering)* Ye, ye, ye, ye! Somebody is living in there! An ichneumon fly! And its larva. No no, dear little ball, we won't put you in there! Where is the ball? Where, where, where is my ball? Where is our darling little ball?

TRAMP: Just a minute ago. . .

MRS. DUNG BEETLE *(whirls on him):* Thief! Thief! Where did you put my ball?

TRAMP: I'm telling you, a minute ago. . .

MRS. DUNG BEETLE: Murderer! Give it here! Give it back!

TRAMP: A minute ago some gentleman was rolling it along.

MRS. DUNG BEETLE: What gentleman? Who?

TRAMP: A fat one. A big pot-bellied one.

MRS. DUNG BEETLE: My husband!

TRAMP: A bow-legged little beast, a stuck-up bully!

MRS. DUNG BEETLE: That's my husband!

TRAMP: And he was saying how wonderful it is to own something. And bury it.

MRS. DUNG BEETLE: That's him! He must have found a pit! *(She calls out.)* Dung Beetle darling! Sweetheart! Where is that idiot?

TRAMP: He went rolling out that way.

MRS. DUNG BEETLE: That good-for-nothing! Couldn't he have called me? *(She turns to the left.)* Darling Dung Beetle! Darling hubby, wait! Dar—ling lit—tle ball! *(She disappears.)* Li. . . li. . . li. . . little ball!

TRAMP: These are something else, quite different specimen.
These bugs have qualities of real and solid men.
I had a bit to drink, and I apologize, for
I began to think they're all butterflies,
beautiful butterflies of slightly shabby fame,
the global upper crust of the eternal mating game.
Those interesting ladies and their elegant consorts
— Haha! insects searching for pleasure and comforts.
Forget those snobs! They only annoy and irk.
The others stink, at least, of honest human work.
They pine for property, not pleasure, it appears.
They're simple folk; they're not cavaliers.
With earthy wisdom they trust only what will last,
They build their humble fortune of dung without a smirk:
Manure will go on stinking when more fancy smells have
    passed.
Even a dung ball's an opus and an honest piece of work.
Wages, not work, smell good when money is your goal.
You love for selfish reasons; work benefits the whole.
Work's always done for others: when grabbing more
    than's due,
if it's for your own family, it passes for virtue.
All universal rights the Family outbids,
and if they catch you stealing, Damn it, you did it for the
    kids.
That's how it is, and how it goes. It's always understood:
That anything will do, if it perpetuates your brood.

CHRYSALIS *(shouting):*
    Prepare the world to make more room!
    Something colossal will happen soon!

TRAMP *(turns toward her):* And what will that be?

CHRYSALIS: I will be born!

TRAMP: Good for you. And what exactly will you be?

CHRYSALIS: I don't know! I don't know! Something great!

TRAMP: Aha! *(He lifts her up and props her against a stem.)*

CHRYSALIS: I will accomplish something wonderful!

TRAMP: And what will that be?

CHRYSALIS: I will be born.

TRAMP: Chrysalis, thumbs up for you!
That same fever drives all things on earth
And urges them towards their birth.
They want to be, to live, to last; whatever else, they have persistence
That gets them to their final goal, the terrible delight of pure Existence.

CHRYSALIS: Announce to all, both far and near
the wondrous moment is now here
when I. . . when I. . .

TRAMP: What?

CHRYSALIS: Nothing. I don't know yet. I want to accomplish something great.

TRAMP: Great? Something great? Good! Get drunk on it! But you had better not depend
On good dung-ball folk to comprehend.
Small and thick is a ball of dung, big and empty an aspiration.

CHRYSALIS: Something immense!

TRAMP: Still and all, Chrysalis, you've got my hearty admiration!
So let it be something great! But really great, make no mistake!
What will crawl out of you, Chrysalis? Why don't you at last awake?

CHRYSALIS: When I am born, the entire world will be astonished!

TRAMP: Go ahead. Take your time. I'll wait. *(He sits down.)*

ICHNEUMON FLY *(with long, silent strides emerges from the rear, dragging the dead body of a cricket into his tunnel)*: Peek-a-boo, baby Larva! Guess what goodies Daddy has for you! *(He descends into the entrance.)*

CHRYSALIS *(shouting)*:
The pain of birth! The universe
Is cracking and about to burst
To bring me forth!

TRAMP: Get born!

CHRYSALIS: Clear the path! Clear the path! Lest I sweep away all
in sight
On my flight
Into the world.

TRAMP: Get born.

ICHNEUMON FLY *(backing out of his hole):* No no, darling daughter, just eat your din-din. You mustn't come out, little Larva. . . no, no, no! There, there, baby. Daddy will be right back and he will bring you something . . . din-din, all right? What would you like, you finicky little thing?

LARVA *(in front of the entrance):* Daddy, I'm bored here.

ICHNEUMON FLY: Haha, isn't she cute. What? Let me give you a kiss, little Larva! Your Poppy will bring you something crispy. What? You'd like another cricket? Haha! You come up with such good ideas!

LARVA: I'd like. . . I don't know.

ICHNEUMON FLY: My God, you're such a smart little Larva! For that, you deserve to get something. Bye-bye, baby. Daddy has to go to work, got to take care of his darling, his beautiful little maggot. . . Go on now, go little doll. Eat a lot.

LARVA *(descends into the hole)*

ICHNEUMON FLY *(with long strides toward* TRAMP): Who are you?

TRAMP *(jumps up and starts backing off):* I am me.

ICHNEUMON FLY: Are you edible?

TRAMP: No. I don't think so.

ICHNEUMON FLY *(sniffs at him):* You're not fresh enough. Who are you?

TRAMP: A bum.

ICHNEUMON FLY *(bows lightly):* Ichneumon Fly. Do you have any children?

TRAMP: No. I don't think so.

ICHNEUMON FLY: Oh. Did you see her?

TRAMP: Who?

ICHNEUMON FLY: My little Larva. Isn't she cute? A smart child. And how she keeps growing! And the appetite she has! Haha! Children are a great joy. What?

TRAMP: That's what everybody says.

ICHNEUMON FLY: Don't they? At least, then, one knows whom one is working for. You have a child, take care of it, work, struggle — That's real life. What? A child wants to grow, to eat, to snack, to play, no? Isn't that right?

TRAMP: A child wants a lot of things.

ICHNEUMON FLY: Would you believe I bring her two, three crickets a day?

TRAMP: For who?

ICHNEUMON FLY: For my baby. Cute, isn't she? And so smart! Do you think she eats them all up? Oh no! Just the most tender morsels, and while they're still alive! Haha! A brilliant child. What?

TRAMP: Sure is.

ICHNEUMON FLY: I'm proud of her. Really proud. And the picture of her dad. What? My blood, sir! Haha! But here I am chattering instead of working. All this chasing! All this running around! But never mind, as long as we have somebody to do it for, right?

TRAMP: That's what they say.

ICHNEUMON FLY: It's a pity you're not edible. Real pity, don't you think? I have to bring her something, don't I? *(He feels* CHRYSALIS.*)* What's this?

CHRYSALIS: I proclaim the rebirth of the world!

ICHNEUMON FLY: Not quite ripe yet. Of no use. What?

CHRYSALIS: I will create something!

ICHNEUMON FLY: Yah, raising children is some worry. A great worry, right? A serious business, sir. To raise a family — just think of it. To feed those poor little tots. To bring them up by hand, to provide for their future, right? No trifling matter. What? I've got to run now. Good day. See you around. At your service, sir. *(He runs off.)* Bye-bye, darling daughter, I'll be back in a jiffy. *(He disappears.)*

TRAMP: To bring up by hand. To provide. To feed the hungry
      mouth that squeals.

    A family demands all that. Plus live crickets for their
      meals.

    But even a cricket wants to live, and tries to get along,
    And happily, in praise of life, he chirps his cricket song.
    I don't get it.

LARVA *(crawling out of the tunnel):* Daddy! Daddy!

TRAMP: So you're the little Larva? Let's have a look at you.

LARVA: You're mean.

TRAMP: Why?

LARVA: I don't know. Oh, I'm so bored. I wish I could. . . I wish I could. . .

TRAMP: Could what?

LARVA: I don't know. Tear up something, something alive. . . Oh, I would just squirm.

TRAMP: What's your problem?

LARVA: You're mean! Mean, mean! *(She crawls back inside.)*

TRAMP: Some way to feed a family. How is this possible? When you see insects doing it, it looks pretty horrible.

(MR. DUNG BEETLE *returns.)*

MR. DUNG BEETLE: Snap to, old girl, I've found a pit! Where are you? Where is my ball? Where is my wife?

TRAMP: Your wife? Is she that old sourpuss? That fat, ugly big-mouth. . .

MR. DUNG BEETLE: That's her! Where is my ball?

TRAMP: . . .that filthy, bad-tempered slut?

MR. DUNG BEETLE: Yes! Yes! That's her! She had my ball! Where did she put my precious ball?

TRAMP: Well, your better half went looking for you.

MR. DUNG BEETLE: And where is my ball?

TRAMP: That big stinking globe?

MR. DUNG BEETLE: Yes, yes, my golden sweetheart! My lovely fortune! My everything! Where is my beautiful darling? That's why I left my wife here with her.

TRAMP: She got pushed this way and that, got rolled away by some gentleman. He behaved just like he owned her.

MR. DUNG BEETLE: I don't care what he did with my wife! Where is my ball?

TRAMP: I'm trying to tell you. A gentleman rolled her away. Your wife wasn't here just then.

MR. DUNG BEETLE: Where was she? Where is she?

TRAMP: She went after him. She thought it was you. Shouted for you.

MR. DUNG BEETLE: My ball did?

TRAMP: No, your wife did.

MR. DUNG BEETLE: I'm not asking about her! Where is my ball? Answer me!

TRAMP: That gentleman rolled it away.

MR. DUNG BEETLE: What, rolled away? My ball? Good God! Catch him! Catch him! Thieves! Murderers! *(He hurls himself to the ground.)* My hard-earned fortune! They've killed me! I'd sooner give up my life than my golden ball of manure! *(He*

305

*jumps up.)* H-e-e-e-lp! Catch h-i-m! Mur-der-ers! *(He rushes off left.)*

TRAMP: Haha, a dung ball got stolen! Cry murderer! Cry thief! And you expect the sky to fall and share your awful grief!
And yet, my friend, cheer up and try to smile a bit:
The thief was one of your own. Who else would want a ball of shit? *(He sits down on one side.)*

MR. CRICKET *(offstage):* Careful, darling. Careful you don't stumble. Here we are, here we are, our little home! Our new little house! Oops, careful! Did you hurt yourself?

MRS. CRICKET: No, Cricket, don't be ridiculous.

MR. CRICKET: But darling, you must be careful. When you're expecting. . . *(Enter* MR. CRICKET *and pregnant* MRS. CRICKET.)

MR. CRICKET: Open your little eyes now. There! Do you like it?

MRS. CRICKET: Oh, Cricket, I'm so tired!

MR. CRICKET: Sit down, my little soul, sit down. Wait, nice and easy. There.

MRS. CRICKET *(sitting down):* Such a long distance! All that moving! Cricket, you must be out of your mind.

MR. CRICKET: Hihihi! Mother! Peek-a-boo! Mom! Mamma! Momsie!

MRS. CRICKET: Leave me alone. Don't be a pest.

MR. CRICKET: Hihi! I won't say another word. I was just joking around. Mrs. Cricket is not expecting babies, of course not! Shame on you, what do you take her for!

MRS. CRICKET *(tearfully):* You nasty thing, it's easy for you to make fun of it!

MR. CRICKET: But honey! I'm just so happy! Just think: all those little baby crickets, all the screaming, all the chirping, hihihi! My darling little wife, I'm going crazy with joy.

MRS. CRICKET: You. . . you silly thing! Peek-a-boo, Daddy, hihi!

MR. CRICKET: Hihihi! How do you like it here?

MRS. CRICKET: Nice. This is our new home?

MR. CRICKET: Our nest, our mansion, our dear family shop, our — hihihi! — place of residence.

MRS. CRICKET: Is it going to be dry? Who built it?

MR. CRICKET: Would you believe it? Another cricket used to live here.

MRS. CRICKET: Did he? Why did he move away?

MR. CRICKET: Hihihi! Yah, he sure moved away. He sure did! Bet you don't know where to! *(He begins a children's song.)* "Close your eyes and take a guess. . ."

MRS. CRICKET: I can't. Lord, it takes you forever to say things. Hurry up, Cricket!

MR. CRICKET: Well, then. Yesterday a shrike got him and stuck him on a thorn for his supper. I swear it, Honey, spiked him all through and through. Just imagine! He's up there wriggling his legs like this, see? Hihihi! He's still alive. And I thought right away, there's something in this for us! We'll move into his apartment. Bang! What luck! Hihi! What do you say?

MRS. CRICKET: And he's still alive? Ugh! What a horror!

MR. CRICKET: Isn't it? Oh, we're so lucky! *(He launches into song.)* Tralala. . . Wait, we'll put up our shingle right now. *(He pulls out a sign which reads "Mr. Cricket's Music Shop.")* Where shall I hang it? About here? More to the right? More to the left?

MRS. CRICKET: A bit higher. And you say he's still wriggling his legs?

MR. CRICKET *(hammering and demonstrating):* I tell you, like this.

MRS. CRICKET: Brrr. Where is he?

MR. CRICKET: Would you like to see him?

MRS. CRICKET: I would. No, I wouldn't. Is it horrible?

MR. CRICKET: Hihihi, you bet. Is this hanging straight?

MRS. CRICKET: Yes, it's fine. Cricket, I feel so strange. . .

MR. CRICKET *(runs toward her):* Oh dear, maybe . . . your hour is here. . .

MRS. CRICKET: Stop it! Ooooo, I'm scared!

MR. CRICKET: But Momsie, who would be scared? Hihihi! Any woman can do it!

MRS. CRICKET: How can you talk like that! *(She starts to cry.)* Cricket, will you always love me?

MR. CRICKET: Of course, my little soul! *(yammering)* Yiyi! Don't cry! Mommy!

MRS. CRICKET *(sobbing):* Show me how he jerks his legs.

MR. CRICKET: Like this.

MRS. CRICKET: Hihihi, that must be funny.

MR. CRICKET: There, there, there! You see? No more tears. *(He sits down beside her.)* Just wait, we'll make it all nice and cozy, and as soon as we're a bit better off, we'll put in. . .

MRS. CRICKET: Pretty curtains.

MR. CRICKET: That too. Hihihi! Curtains, of course! Oh, you are so wise. Give me a kiss!

MRS. CRICKET: You don't have any sense!

MR. CRICKET: Of course I don't! *(He jumps up.)* Guess what I bought.

MRS. CRICKET: Curtains!

MR. CRICKET: No, something smaller. *(He searches his pockets.)* Where did I. . .

MRS. CRICKET: Quick! Let me see! Let me see!

MR. CRICKET *(pulls two baby rattles out of his pockets and shakes them):* Crickety, crickety, crick.

MRS. CRICKET: Oh, aren't they darling! Cricket, give them to me!

MR. CRICKET *(shakes the rattles and sings):*
"A little cricket boy, boy, boy,
His mommy's and daddy's joy, joy, joy,
When at night he starts to cry,
We'll chirp him a lullaby." Hihihi!

MRS. CRICKET: Let me have them! Quick! Oh, Poppy, I can't wait!

MR. CRICKET: Now listen, Honeyface. . .

MRS. CRICKET *(rattles and sings):* "A little cricket boy, boy, boy."

MR. CRICKET: I have to make a few rounds now, you know? To announce my presence, to knock at a door here, a door there.

MRS. CRICKET *(rattles and sings):* "We'll chirp him a lullaby. . ."

MR. CRICKET: . . .to introduce myself a bit, make contacts, have a look around. . . Give me a rattle, I'll crickety-crick along the way.

MRS. CRICKET: Oh, and what about me? *(in tears)* You're going to leave me here?

MR. CRICKET: Do crickety-crick after I go. And . . . maybe a neighbor will drop by, see? You can talk a little, ask about the kids or something like that. See? And. . . and with that . . . this. . . that thing, you'll wait, won't you? Till I get home.

MRS. CRICKET: Bad!

MR. CRICKET: Hihihi! Bye, Hon, do be careful. I'll be right back, back in a jiffy. *(He runs off.)*

MRS. CRICKET *(rattles the rattle)*

MR. CRICKET *(responds from far away):* "A little cricket . . . boy."

MRS. CRICKET: I'm scared!

TRAMP *(gets up):* No need to be scared. Pettiness gets born easily.

MRS. CRICKET: Who is there? Ugh, a beetle. Do you bite?

TRAMP: No.

MRS. CRICKET: And how are your kiddies?

TRAMP: I have none. Have none. Family love hatched in the
wedded state did not turn out to be my fate.
Nor did having a roof as shield from snow and hail,
Nor did knowing the sweet pleasures of watching others
fail.

MRS. CRICKET: Yeye, you have no kiddies? What a pity. *(rattles)*
Cricket! Cricket! Oh, he doesn't answer anymore. And why
didn't you get married, Beetle?

TRAMP: Selfishness, dear Madam. A most disgraceful trait.
A loner's life is safe and calm . . . a family would spoil
the fun.
He never is obliged to love, and not obliged to hate,
Nor does he have to envy those with places in the sun.

MRS. CRICKET: Yes, yes, you men! *(rattles)* "A little cricket boy,
boy, boy. . ."

CHRYSALIS *(shouting):* I bring to you the future! I. . . I. . .

TRAMP *(goes to her):* Get born!

CHRYSALIS: I shall accomplish something glorious!

MRS. DUNG BEETLE *(runs in):* Is my husband here? Where is that
fool? Where is our ball?

MRS. CRICKET: Yeye, m'am, you play ball? Let me see!

MRS. DUNG BEETLE: It's not a playball, it's our future, our property, our everything! My husband, that oaf, went off with it.

MRS. CRICKET: Oh my God. I hope he hasn't left you.

MRS. DUNG BEETLE: And where is yours?

MRS. CRICKET: He's away on business. *(rattles)* Cricket! Cricket!

MRS. DUNG BEETLE: And he leaves you all alone like this! Aren't
you expecting, you poor thing?

MRS. CRICKET: Ooooooo!

MRS. DUNG BEETLE: So young! And tell me, don't you make balls?

MRS. CRICKET: What for?

MRS. DUNG BEETLE: A ball . . . that means family. That means
the future. That's what life is all about.

MRS. CRICKET: Oh no. Life is having one's own house, one's nest,
one's shop. And pretty curtains. And children. And one's own
Cricket. One's own household. And that's it.

MRS. DUNG BEETLE: But how on earth can you go on living
without a ball?

MRS. CRICKET: What would we do with a ball?

MRS. DUNG BEETLE:   You'd roll it along with you everywhere. I
tell you, dear lady, nothing ties down a husband like a ball.

MRS. CRICKET:   Oh no, a house will.

MRS. DUNG BEETLE:   A ball.

MRS. CRICKET:   A house.

MRS. DUNG BEETLE:   God, would I like to have a talk with you!
You're such a nice. . .

MRS. CRICKET:   And how are your kiddies?

MRS. DUNG BEETLE:   If only I had that ball! *(She goes away.)*
B-b-b-b-ball! B-b-b. . .

MRS. CRICKET:   Ugh, what a slut! And her husband ran away from
her, hihihi! *(rattles)* "We'll chirp him a lullaby. . ." I. . . I
feel so strange. . . *(She tidies up around the gate.)* Hihihi,
how the one stuck up there on the thorn must keep wriggling
his legs!

ICHNEUMON FLY *(runs out of the wings)*: Aha! *(With long, silent
strides he moves toward her, pulls a dagger out of his coattail
and, with a wide swipe, stabs* MRS. CRICKET *and drags her
toward his hole.)* Out of my way!

TRAMP *(retreating)*: Oh! Oh! Murder!

ICHNEUMON FLY *(at the entrance of his hole)*: Peek-a-boo, darling
daughter! Come quick and see what Daddy has brought you!

TRAMP:   He killed her! And I. . . I stood here like a stone! Oh
God, she didn't even make a sound! And no one cried out in
horror! No one raced to her rescue!

PARASITE *(coming out from the background)*: Bravo, my friend.
That's my opinion exactly!

TRAMP:   To perish like that! So defenselessly!

PARASITE:   That's what I say too. I've been watching for a while,
but I'd never do anything like that. No, I couldn't. Everybody
wants to live, right?

TRAMP:   Who are you?

PARASITE:   Me? Actually, nobody. A poor wretch. A little orphan.
They call me Parasite.

TRAMP:   Is this kind of killing to be tolerated?

PARASITE:   My words exactly. Do you think that ichneumon fly
needs it? Do you think he's hungry like me? Certainly not!
He only kills to stack up supplies. He's hoarding. A scandal,
right? Is this justice? Why should he have a stockpile and
someone else go hungry? Just because he's got a dagger and
I've only got these bare hands? Right?

TRAMP: I'll say.

PARASITE: That's what I say too. There's no equality. For example, I don't kill anybody. My mandibles are too soft for the job. What I mean is, my conscience is too soft. I don't have the necessary tools of production. All I have is hunger. And this is supposed to be right?

TRAMP: No. . . no. . . one should not kill.

PARASITE: My words, my friend. Or at least one shouldn't hoard. You stuff yourself and you've had enough. Hoarding is robbing those who don't know how to hoard. Stuff yourself and then stop. Then there would be enough of everything for everybody, isn't that right?

TRAMP: I don't know.

PARASITE: That's what I say too.

ICHNEUMON FLY *(coming out from his entrance):* Enjoy it, baby, enjoy it. Just pick out what you like. Don't you have a nice papa?

PARASITE: How do you do, sir.

ICHNEUMON FLY: Hi. Hi there. Edible? *(He sniffs him.)*

PARASITE: Heehee! The gentleman must be joking. Certainly not!

ICHNEUMON FLY: Beat it, scum! Piece of filth. What do you want here? Get out!

PARASITE: Heehee! That's what I say too, sir. *(He retreats.)*

ICHNEUMON FLY *(to* TRAMP): At your service. Wasn't that something? Did you see?

TRAMP: I did.

ICHNEUMON FLY: A beautiful job, wasn't it? Hahaha! Not everybody can do that. My dear fellow, for that you need— *(tapping his forehead.)* expertise. An enterprising spirit. I-N-I-T-I-A-T-I-V-E. And vision. And love for your work, I say.

PARASITE *(coming closer):* My words exactly.

ICHNEUMON FLY: What I say is, he who lives has to hustle. And a lot. There's the future. There's the family. And there's also somehow, you know, ambition. A strong person must have his own niche in life, isn't that right?

PARASITE: That's what I say too, sir.

ICHNEUMON FLY: Exactly, exactly. To do one's job properly, to raise new ichneumon flies, to use your talents, that's what I call a useful life. What?

PARASITE: Quite so, your highness.

ICHNEUMON FLY:  Shut up, scum. I'm not talking to you.

PARASITE:  That's what I say too, sir.

ICHNEUMON FLY:  And the warm feeling you get when you fulfill your calling, when you've done a good piece of work. When you feel your life is not in vain! That's edifying, isn't it? So, at your service. Now I have to be on my way again. *Servitore! (He runs away.)* Bye-bye, darling Larva, *do svidania! (He disappears.)*

PARASITE:  That old murderer! Believe me, I had a hard time keeping myself from jumping at his throat. Sure, I'd work too, if it had to be. But why should I have to work when someone else has more than he can gobble up? I also have initiative, haha, but it's here! *(He thumps his belly.)* It's hunger, see? Hunger! Is this social justice?

TRAMP:  All this just for a bit of meat!

PARASITE:  My words exactly. All this just for a bit of meat, and the poor creatures should have nothing. That's against nature. To everyone only what he can eat, isn't that right?

TRAMP *(picks up the rattle and shakes it sadly):* Poor cricket lady, poor thing!

PARASITE:  That's what I say too. Everybody wants to live.

*(Offstage a rattle answers.)*

MR. CRICKET *(runs in rattling):* Here I am, darling, here, here, here! Where are you, sweetheart? Guess what your hubby's found!

ICHNEUMON FLY *(appears behind him):* Aha!

TRAMP:  Watch out! Watch it!

PARASITE *(stops him):* Leave it alone, citizen! Don't get involved in it. What must be, must be.

MR. CRICKET:  Little Momsie?

ICHNEUMON FLY *(with a wide swipe, stabs him and begins carrying him toward his hole):* Baby daughter! Darling Larva! Guess what your nice Daddy has brought you again? *(He descends into the entrance.)*

TRAMP *(lifting his fists):* Oh Lord Creator! And you can watch this?

PARASITE:  My words exactly. That murderer, he's got his third cricket and me nothing! And we're supposed to take that?

ICHNEUMON FLY *(runs out of his entrance):* No, no, baby, I don't have time. Daddy must be off to work again. Eat, eat, eat! Be quiet, I'll be back in an hour. *(He runs off.)*

PARASITE: I'm boiling with rage. That old villain! *(He approaches the entrance.)* This is injustice! This is a disgrace! I. . . I'll show him! Just wait! Is he gone? Well, I'm going to have a look down there. *(He descends into the entrance.)*

TRAMP: Murder and more murder! Be still, my heart, be quiet,
All these were only beetles, only an insect riot,
a tiny little drama played out in a grassy maze.
That's all, just beetle fights; that's all, just insect ways,
for insects with their habits differ a lot from men.
Oh, to be back among humans! One looks around and
     then
one sees that men are better than insect reprobates.
A man isn't ruled by his belly, he builds and strives and
     creates,
and his life has a certain purpose, and he makes his little
     ball. . .
No, those were the dung beetles! How I confuse them all!
Leave dung balls to the beetles, and ideals to the human
     race.
A man who lives a peaceful life, he lives in a state of
     grace.
You don't need much to be happy: just your own little
     resting place.
Mind your business, hurt no one, and of course procreate.
Life needs only to be fully lived. It's sweet to stop and
     wait
and see how you live and how your neighbor. . . wriggles
     . . . his legs. . .
No, again that was the crickets! Look how my memory
     reneges
and mixes things up with beetles! That trivial, narrow
     life
of stupid cricket bliss won't satisfy man nor wife.
A man needs more than merely food to sate his appetite.
He can't chew happiness like a cow can sit and chew its
     cud.
Life needs strong men, wants heroes bold, for Life
     demands a fight.
And if you want to conquer Life, then grab it and hang
     on good.
If you want to be completely a man, use power and all
     your skill.

If you want to live, you have to rule; if you want to eat,
  you must . . . kill. . .
No, that's the ichneumon flies! Hush! Listen! Can't you
  all hear
the silent jaws everywhere working and chewing in
  feverish strife,
the bloody, satisfied crunching that penetrates the ear,
while their food is alive and still breathing. . . Life falls
  victim to Life!
CHRYSALIS *(threshing about):*
  I feel something great!
  Something great!
TRAMP:  What is great?
CHRYSALIS:  To be born! To live!
TRAMP:  Chrysalis, Chrysalis, let me stay with you forever!
PARASITE *(scrambles out of the entrance, enormously fat, hiccup-
  ping):* Hahaha, hahaha, HIC, hahaha-haha! WHOOP! This is
  . . . hahaha . . . WHOOP, that old miser, he really had supplies
  for that pa. . . WHOOP . . . pale girl of his! WHOOP,
  hahahaha, hahaha, WHOOP! I feel like throw. . . WHOOP!
  I'm going to burst! *(burps)* But this is. . . WHOOP! WHOOP!
  Damned hiccups! I say, now I'm really . . . somebody! Not
  everybody could. . . isn't that. . . WHOOP! gobble up all
  that, right?
TRAMP:  What about little Larva?
PARASITE:  Hahaha, hahaha, WHOOP! Yah! Hahahaha! I. . .
  WHOOP. . . Yah, I gulped her down too! Nature's table is
  set for all! WHOOP! WHOOP! WHOOP!

  CURTAIN

# On Literature

Forgive me if I start off with something quite other than literature, something from the days when I was a small boy. Your city boy is a kind of super-boy, a born skeptic, lord of the streets; and it is quite natural that he have a huge contempt for hayseeds, nincompoops, bumpkins, and clodhoppers, as he calls country boys. Your country boy looks down with immense and justified contempt on city boys, for he is lord of the fields and forests; he knows all about horses and is on friendly terms with the beasts of the field; he can crack a whip and he has under his dominion all the treasures of the earth, from willow-switches to ripe poppy-heads. And even your boy from a small country town is by no means the least among worldly princes, for he includes in his circle more than any other mortal creature: he can watch all human activities at close quarters.

When I was a boy in a small country town I saw at home how a doctor's business is run, and at my grandfather's I could inspect the business of a miller and baker, which is especially fine and amusing. And at my uncle's I saw what a farmer has to do; but if I started on that I would never stop telling you all the things I learned. Our nearest neighbor was the painter who stenciled designs on walls, and that is a tremendously interesting job. Sometimes he used to let me mix the colors in their pots, and once, almost bursting with pride, I was allowed to smear a stencil pattern with his brush; it came out crooked, but otherwise most successfully. I'll never forget how that painter used to stride up and down the planks whistling, gloriously splashed with all the colors of the rainbow; and he stenciled in such miraculously straight lines, sometimes even painting something freehand—perhaps an amazingly well-nourished rose the color of stale liver, on the ceiling. It was my first revelation of the painter's art, and I lost my heart to it then and have been in love with it ever since. And then I used to go every day and have a look at how the innkeeper does his job, to see how they roll casks down into the cellar and how they draw beer and blow off the froth, and hear the wise tales the old gossips tell as they wipe froth from their whiskers with the backs of their hands. Every day I would look in on neighbor cobbler and watch in silence how he cut leather and hammered it on his last and then put on the heel, and all manner of other things, for shoemaking is intricate and delicate work, and if you haven't seen leather in a cobbler's hands you know nothing about it at all, even if you do wear shoes of cordovan or even of celestial leather. Then there was neighbor hurdy-gurdy man, and I went to see him too, when he was at home, and was so surprised that he didn't play his hurdy-gurdy at home, but sat and stared at one corner of the room till I felt quite uncomfortable. There was the mournful stone-mason who carved crosses and strange, short, dumpy angels on gravestones; he'd tap away all day and never say a single word, and I'd stand watching for perhaps an hour while he chipped away at the unseeing eye of a weeping angel. And then, ha ha! yes! there was the wheelwright with his beautiful wood throwing off sparks and his yard full of hastening wheels, as Homer says; and a wheel, you know, is a wonder in itself. Then there was the smith in his black smithy: I burst with pride when I was allowed sometimes to work the bellows for him while, looking like a black Cyclops, he heated an iron bar red-hot and hammered it till it sent out a shower of sparks; and when he put a shoe on a horse it smelled of burnt horn, and the horse would turn his wise eyes on the smith as much as to say, "All right, go on, I won't make a fuss."

A little farther on lived Tonca, the prostitute; I didn't understand her business very well, and I used to pass her little house with an odd, dry feeling in my throat. Once I looked in through the window, but it was all empty—just striped feather-beds, and some consecrated pussy willows above the bed. I had a look at the mill owners' businesses, and watched them hurrying through their counting-houses, and collected foreign stamps out of their waste-paper baskets; and I watched the mill hands at the vats full of tow, and the weavers at the mysterious mechanical looms: I went into the red-hot hell of the jute-drying kilns and scorched myself beside the stokers at the boilers, wondering at their long shovels, which I could hardly lift. I would visit the butcher, eyeing him with interest to see if he would cut off a finger. I would have a look in at the shopkeeper as he weighed and measured; stop at the tinsmith's, and go into the carpenter's yard where everything was a-whirr and a-clatter. I went to the poorhouse to see what the poor do with themselves, and went with them to the fair in the city one Friday to learn how the business of begging was carried on.

Now I have a profession of my own, and I work at it the livelong day. But even if I were to sit on the porch with my work I don't think a single boy would come—standing on one bare foot and rubbing his calf with the other—and watch my fingers to see how a writer's business is done. I don't say that it is a bad or useless profession: but it isn't one of the superlatively fine and striking ones, and the material used is of a strange sort—you don't even see it. But I'd like all the things I used to see to be in it: the ringing hammer-strokes of the smith and the colors of the whistling house painter, the patience of the tailor and the careful chipping of the stone-mason, the bustling of the baker, the humility of the poor, and all the lusty strength and skill which men of towering stature put into their work before the astonished and fascinated eyes of a child.

Translated by Dora Round; revised by the editor. Originally published in *Intimate Things*, 1935.

# Soil and the Gardener

The gardener is not a man who smells a rose, but one who is persecuted by the idea that "the soil would like a little lime," or that it is heavy (as lead, the gardener puts it) and "would like a little more sand." Gardening has become a scientific affair. Today a girl wouldn't dare sing out, "Under our windows roses bloom!" Rather she would sing that under our windows there is a pile of saltpeter and beech ashes, carefully mixed with wood shavings. A rose in bloom is only for dilettantes; the gardener's pleasure is more deeply rooted, right in the womb of the soil. After death, the gardener does not become a butterfly, intoxicated by the perfume of flowers, but an earthworm tasting all the dark, nitrogenous, spicy delights of the soil.

In spring, gardeners are irresistibly drawn to their gardens. As soon as they lay down their knives and forks, they are out on their beds, presenting their rumps to the splendid azure sky. Here they crumble a warm clod between their fingers, there they push nearer the roots a weathered and precious piece of last year's manure; there they pull out a weed, and here they pick out a little stone; now they work the soil around the strawberries and, in a moment, they bend down over some young lettuce, nose close to the earth, fondly tickling a fragile tuft of roots. In this position they enjoy spring, while over their behinds the sun describes its glorious circuit, clouds swim, and heavenly birds mate; the cherry buds are already opening, young foliage is expanding with sweet tenderness, and blackbirds are singing like mad. Then the gardener straightens himself, stretches his back, and says thoughtfully: "In autumn I will manure it thoroughly, and I'll add some sand."

But there is a moment when the gardener rises and straightens himself up to his full height; this is the afternoon, when he administers the sacrament of water to his little garden. He stands, straight and almost noble, directing the jet of water from the mouth of the hose. The water rushes in a silver, melodious shower; out of the puffy soil a perfumed breath of moisture wafts, every little leaf is almost wildly green and sparkling with an appetizing joy, looking almost good enough to eat. "So. . . and now it's had its share," the gardener whispers blissfully; by "it" he doesn't mean the little cherry tree foaming with buds or the purple gooseberry; he is thinking of the brown soil.

And after the sun has set, he sighs with deep content: "Today I really worked."

Translated by M. and R. Weatherall; revised by the editor. Excerpted from *The Gardener's Year*, 1931.

# Legs and the Gardener

The gardener has certainly arisen by cultivation and not by natural selection. If he had developed naturally he would look different; he'd have legs like a beetle, so he wouldn't have to sit on his heels, and he'd have wings, first for their beauty, and second, so that he could float over his garden. Those who haven't experienced it can't imagine how much your legs are in the way when there's no place to stand; how stupidly long they are when you have to fold them underneath to poke your finger into the ground; how impossibly short they are when you have to reach the other side of the bed without treading on a clump of pansies or on columbine shoots. If we could only hang in a belt

and swim over the beds, or have at least four hands, and on each one a head and a cap, and nothing else; or have limbs that telescope like a tripod! But because the gardener is constructed as imperfectly as other people, all he can do is what he's capable of: balance on the toes of one foot, float in the air like a Russian ballerina, straddle four yards wide, step as lightly as a butterfly or a robin, squeeze into a square inch of ground, maintain equilibrium in violation of all the laws of gravity, reach everywhere and avoid everything, and still try to keep some sort of respectability so that people will not laugh at him.

Of course, at a passing glance, from a distance, you don't see anything of the gardener but his rump; everything else, the head, the arms, and the legs, is hidden underneath.

Translated by M. and R. Weatherall; revised by the editor. Excerpted from *The Gardener's Year*, 1931.

# THE ENGLISH PARK

The most beautiful things in England are, perhaps, its trees. Of course, the meadows and the policemen too, but most of all the trees, the splendidly broad-shouldered, ancient, generous, free, vast, venerable trees. The trees at Hampton Court, Richmond Park, Windsor, and I don't know where else besides. It's possible that these trees have had a great influence on Toryism in England. I think they preserve the aristocratic instincts, the historical sense, Conservatism, tariffs, golf, the House of Lords, and other odd and antique things. I should probably be a rabid Radical if I lived in the Street of the Iron Balconies or in the Street of the Grey Bricks, but sitting under an ancient oak tree in the park at Hampton Court I was seriously tempted to acknowledge the value of old things, the high mission of old trees, the harmonious comprehensiveness of tradition, and the legitimacy of esteem for everything that is strong enough to preserve itself for ages.

It seems that in England there are many such ancient trees; in nearly everything here, in the clubs, in the literature, in the homes, you can somehow feel the timber and foliage of aged, venerable, and fearfully solid trees. As a matter of fact, here you see nothing conspicuously new—except the Tube, and maybe that's why it's so ugly. Old trees and old things contain imps, eccentric and jocular sprites, as do the English. They too are enormously solemn, solid, and venerable; suddenly there is a sort of rumbling within them, they make a grotesque remark, a fork of pixie-like humor flies out of them, and then once again they have the solemn appearance of an old leather armchair.

I don't know why, but this sober England strikes me as the most fairylike and romantic of all the countries I've seen. Perhaps it's on account of the old trees. Or no, perhaps it's due to the lawns. It's due to the fact that here you walk across fields instead of on footpaths. We Continental people won't dare walk except on roads and paved paths; this certainly has had a huge influence on the development of our minds. When I first saw a gentleman stroll across the lawn in the park at Hampton Court, I imagined that he was a creature from Fairyland, although he was wearing a top hat. I expected him to ride into Kingston on a stag or to begin dancing, or a gardener to come up and give him a good scolding. But nothing happened, and at last even I dared to make my way straight across the grass to an old oak. And nothing happened! Never have I had a feeling of such unrestricted liberty. It's very curious; here, evidently, man is not regarded as a obnoxious animal. Here, they don't subscribe to the dismal myth that grass won't grow beneath our hooves. Here, a man has the right to walk across the meadow as if he were a wood-nymph or a property owner. I think that this has had a considerable influence upon his character and view of the world. It opens up the marvelous possibility of walking elsewhere than along a road, without regarding oneself as a beast of prey, a highwayman, or an anarchist.

Translated by Paul Selver; revised by the publisher. Excerpted from *Letters from England,* 1925.

# TRAFFIC

As long as I live I shall never become reconciled to what is known here as "traffic," that is, the volume of vehicles in the streets. I recall with horror the day they first brought me to London. At the outset they conveyed me by train, then they rushed through some huge glass halls and thrust me into a barred cage which looks like a scale for weighing cattle; this is a "lift," and down it went through an ugly steel-plated well, whereupon they drew me out and led me through serpentine subterranean passages; it was like a nightmare. Then there was a sort of tunnel or channel with railway lines, and a snorting train flew in; they hurled me into it, and the train flew on. The atmosphere was oppressive with a mildewy closeness, evidently owing to the proximity of hell. Then they again took me out and rushed me through new catacombs to a moving staircase, which clatters like a mill and hastens upwards with people on it; I tell you, it's like a fever. Then more stairs and staircases and without end or interruption, in spite of my objections, they led me out into the street, where my heart sank. A fourfold belt of vehicles, buses, panting mastodons dashing along in droves with flocks of tiny mortals on their backs; purring automobiles, trucks, steam engines, cyclists, buses, buses, flying packs of automobiles, people rushing along, tractors, ambulances, people scrambling like squirrels onto the tops of buses, a new flock of motor elephants, and then it all comes to a standstill, a grunting and rattling flood, and it cannot move forward. I cannot move forward either; I recall the horror which was aroused in me by the idea that I must get to the other side of the street. I managed it with a certain amount of success, and since then I have crossed the London streets on countless occasions, but as long as I live I shall never become reconciled to it.

Then I went to my hotel room, crushed, despairing, overwhelmed in mind and body. For the first time in my life I had experienced a blind and furious repugnance to modern civilization. It seemed to me that there was something barbarous and disastrous in this dread accumulation of people; it is said that there are seven and a half million of them there, but I did not count them. I only know that my first impression of this huge assembly was almost a tragic one; I felt uneasy and I had a boundless yearning for Prague, as if I were a child who had lost its way in a forest. Yes, I may as well confess to you that I was afraid; I was afraid that I should get lost, that I should be run over by a bus, that something would

TRAFFIC

happen to me, that it was all up with me, that human life is worthless, that man is an enlarged bacillus swarming by the million on some moldy potato, that perhaps the whole thing was only a bad dream, that mankind would perish as the result of some dreadful catastrophe, that man is powerless, that for no reason whatever I should burst out crying, and that they would all laugh at me—the whole seven and a half million of them. Perhaps some time later on I'll realize what at first sight of it frightened me so much and filled me with endless uneasiness. But never mind now, today I have become a little more used to it. I walk, run, move out of the way, ride, climb to the tops of vehicles or rush through lifts and tubes just like anyone else, but only on one condition—that I do not think about it. As soon as I realize what is happening around me, I again have the tormenting feeling of something evil, ghastly and disastrous, for which I am no match. And then I am unbearably distressed.

Sometimes the whole lot comes to a standstill for half an hour, simply because there is too much of it. Sometimes at Charing Cross a knot is formed, and before they unravel it there is a - page of conveyances from the Bank to somewhere in Brompton Road, and in the meantime you in your vehicle can reflect on what it will be like in twenty years. As such congestion arises quite often, many people reflect about this. It has not yet been decided whether they are to walk on the roofs or under the earth; the only certainty is that it can no longer be done on the earth—which is a remarkable achievement of modern civilization. As regards myself, I give precedence to the earth, like the giant Antaeus. I have drawn you a picture, but the real thing is even worse, because it roars like a factory. On the other hand, the drivers do not sound their horns like mad and the people do not call each other names; they are such quiet people, after all.

In the meantime I have found out, among other things, that the wild cry "o-ei-o" in the street means potatoes; "oi" is oil, and "u-u" is a bottle of something mysterious. And sometimes in the most important streets a whole band takes up its position on the edge of the curb and plays, blowing trumpets, beating drums and collecting pennies, or an Italian tenor stands below the windows and sings "Rigoletto," "Trovatore," or a fervid song of yearning, just as in Naples. But I have met only a single person who whistles; it was on Cromwell Road, and he was black.

Translated by Paul Selver; revised by the editor. Excerpted from *Letters from England*, 1925.

# THE FAIRBANKS SMILE

I assume that at least once you've been to the movies and seen his forty-two teeth, or however many he has (he's certainly got more of them than other mortals, a whole bunch of them and so hard you can hear pebbles crunch in his mouth). You've seen him, the way you've seen the pathetically immobile face of Charlie Chaplin; you know him better than your childhood friends. He's the "man who laughs;" he's romantic as a Victor Hugo hero, but the romance of his smile is completely different. It isn't the bitter and frightening grimace of Hugo's fool nor the "carefree smile on his face but a heart heavy with grief;" of course not! Douglas Fairbanks has a simple, raucous laugh because he gets complete joy from life. He shows immense pleasure when he falls in love, he grins at you when he jumps out of a sixth-story window and lands without breaking a leg, he smiles at every obstacle to his heroic feats as if he, the wretch, were just playing; see, there he is laughing again. He can do everything and nothing; all he can do is laugh, and that really is everything; whether he's jumping up on a horse or climbing up a wall like a fly, he does it because he has a carefree and rejoicing heart. And when he tries something, he just naturally has to succeed, because he rushes into it with that sparkling and confident smile.

Douglas Fairbanks is no actor. He's a champ. No, he's something more: he's a type. To all the types of heroism created by mythology and poetry he adds the new and clean type of the born winner. He's a hero because his extraordinary joyfulness and high spirits must find an outlet. So what's he going to do? He gets restless, his legs start to dance and he smiles at you with his forty-two teeth. He's not after anything great; he doesn't want to vanquish the world or conquer the stars; this nice boy doesn't have a smidgin of the rebel in him. His moral paraphernalia include a knight's honor, love, fidelity, comradeship, and what else? He's tremendously primitive, this modern hero, don't expect him to tackle any of the world's problems; he's not even ambitious. Opportunity makes the crime, but opportunity also makes the hero. First of all, a Fairbanks has absolutely no agenda; he just goes along laughing without a thought in his head, and suddenly something comes up out of the blue and Fairbanks flies, jumps, shoots, climbs, tears along, climbs up walls, performs divine miracles, but if you were to cut him up, you'd discover nothing more than the unbridled joy it all gives him. And when he wins, he smiles all around; of course he does, he's happy.

I don't know if world literature has another example of such a naïve hero; anyway, I can't think of any. There are gloomy heroes, avengers and deliverers; there are ambitious titans, raised up to confront a superhuman task, with their hands stretched out to clasp the deity; there are Caesars and Brutuses, Phaetons and Spartacuses, rebels and conquerors, self-sacrificing heroes or born leaders. But all of this is Greek to Fairbanks. He performs heroic deeds like a boy climbs a tree, just for the joy of doing it, with boundless zest and a devil-may-care craziness. He's all of a piece, and there are no chinks in him where a speck of prudence might lodge. And when it's over he starts laughing at himself. The whole thing is just superhuman in its simplemindedness.

Fairbanks is the consummation of optimism; it makes him an almost mythical being. Everything works, everything is possible, a person can do anything if he has strong arms and legs and, most important, if he does it with gusto. What's there to be afraid of? An angel with wings will carry you safely across the abyss, things will obey you if you go at them with a smile and, well, with such playful finesse that we feel we could do it too if we had the chance. Look at that fellow: is it really possible, since we're not total clods, that our teeth can ache, that we can stumble, that we can fall off a streetcar? After all, everything's so simple and easy, it really is, just child's play, a bowl of cherries; from today on, everything's going to work out for sure, and everybody will be happy. And even if the worst should come and we've got twenty six-shooters aimed at our chests, haha, it's all just fun; we'll just wink and they'll drop the six-shooters, and we'll be standing there grinning with our forty-two teeth, because thirty-two aren't enough for a really optimistic smile.

Translated by Charles E. Townsend; © 1990 Charles E. Townsend. Originally published as "Fairbanksuv usmev," 1923. First English translation.

# Goodwill

Intellectual goodwill is not merely tolerance or bland complacence. It is an active effort to understand other people. If we listen to debates about culture, conflicts of opinion and clashes of points of view, we usually come away with the uncomfortable feeling that people care most about not being able to agree on things. It's as if everybody was shouting at each other in different languages and then each person went off with the smug feeling of really having given it to the other fellow. If it were a game, we would say it was a strange sport. But these debates can be serious, because they divide people into different camps. If you can't get through to people with words and arguments, then you may have to resort to tooth and nail. Still, in a debate about the truth it shouldn't matter *who* wins, but *what* wins. The subject of the debate gets lost if people talk at cross-purposes or if one person struggles *not* to pay attention to what the other says and means. Even the most passionate conflict of the most sophisticated views is a pointless farce if it's nothing more than verbal fencing against spurious opinions. And this isn't just a waste of time; it's a mortal sin against the spirit, since the task of the intellect is precisely to understand correctly. The task of the intellect is to organize a realm of reason, an authenticity of thinking, a sovereignty of truth researched and learned.

We could also say that intellectual goodwill is simply intellectual honesty. It is intellectually dishonest not to understand, not to want to understand. It is intellectually dishonest to classify truths and opinions according to who articulates them. We don't want to hear spiritual outpourings unless they're from our camp. We want *not* to know. We believe that plugging our own ears will keep other people silent. There's another name for this: intellectual cowardice. So let the concept "goodwill" be sufficient then, because goodwill which is neither courageous nor honest is neither good, nor is it will. And at the crossroads where we now find ourselves, between government by force and government by understanding, let there stand, first and foremost, goodwill.

Translated by Charles E. Townsend; © 1990 Charles E. Townsend. Originally published as "Dobrá vule," 1923. First English translation.

# Part V
# TOWARD THE RADICAL CENTER

Let's Be Revolutionary
Children of the Poor
The Mother
At the Crossroads of Europe


In the 1930's, as Čapek's reputation grew, so did the frequency and severity of hostile criticism, personal and literary. To a considerable extent, this was motivated by Čapek's stance of avoiding either extreme, thus antagonizing the left, which had long played a dominant role in Czech culture, as well as the right, which was rapidly gaining power and confidence. In addition, Čapek's closeness to President Masaryk made him a convenient target for people who wished to attack Masaryk but did not dare do so directly because of the immense personal prestige and popularity of the Republic's founding father.

With the rise of fascism, Čapek felt compelled to employ his skills in defense of democracy and his threatened homeland. He campaigned tirelessly in this cause, through essays, radio talks and speeches, in spite of the fact that he had always found an overt public role difficult and distasteful. The novel *War with the Newts* (1936) and the play *The White Plague* (1937) have strong political concerns. Čapek's play *The Mother* (1938) examines the conventional roles of the sexes, but it is above all a call to arms in defense of freedom. The idea of the play apparently arose from a news photo of a distraught mother during the Spanish Civil War.

Čapek's wife states that she originally wanted to write the play herself but that Karel persuaded her to leave the task to him. The play shows how difficult it was for the peace-loving, tolerant Čapek to adopt a single-minded, militaristic position. As usual in a Čapek work, many conflicting points of view are given a hearing, and it is only after much hesitation, at the very end of the play, that the heroine—and by implication, the author—makes a declaration of war.

'At the Crossroads of Europe' (1938) unhappily has a very contemporary ring to it. It was Čapek's last-minute *cri de coeur* to the Western democracies in which he had so fervently believed.

A persistent theme of left-wing critics was Čapek's supposed insensitivity to social ills and his reluctance to take an activist position on social issues, as Czech authors have traditionally been expected to do. There is some truth to this allegation. Only a small part of Čapek's vast output of essays and articles is directly concerned with poverty or other social problems. It is also true that when Čapek did address such issues he generally did so in the spirit of a compassionate witness rather than an impassioned reformer.

Yet nobody can doubt Čapek's deep empathy for human suffering and misery, explicit in such pieces as 'Children of the Poor' and implicit in just about everything he ever wrote. Above all, nobody can doubt Čapek's dedication to truth. As we have attempted to show in this Reader, he was a radical in a deep sense, a man who was never satisfied with surface appearance but always tried to get close to the root of things, to that elusive center.

# LET'S BE REVOLUTIONARY

Our forefathers, particularly our immediate spiritual forefathers, devoted themselves to a philosophy which was primarily evolutionary. For many reasons, they believed that everything in the world begins and continues through slow and gradual evolution. For example, over the course of many millions of years, a protozoan kept developing to a higher and higher state until it became a brewer's horse; over the ages an amoeba kept changing and refining itself until it became a big businessman or a university professor; and, perhaps in a few thousand years, through the same process, a bank president will develop into a superman. This theory of evolution has not yet been refuted, but it is getting just a little bit complicated, and the further we pursue it, the harder it gets for us to imagine how all this actually happened. Still, the concept of evolution has penetrated very deeply into our thoughts and habits; we say that things are evolving, that we have to wait for things to evolve further, that future evolution will bring us the answer, and so on. The word "evolution" has acquired the same status as the mysterious words "providence" and "divine ordinance." On the other hand, the words "upheaval" and "revolution" suggest something unnatural, destructive or violent, something which has no place in the natural order of things and is at odds with common sense.

All right, but in real life the word "evolution" seems, if I may say so, to imply very long periods of time, and amounts to procrastination. It may be true that a man must evolve from a child or an executive from a clerk, but this is only because the process takes so long. When a man wakes up in his bed in the morning, we don't say that he has evolved from a state of sleep to a state of wakefulness; it's a sudden change, and if you're hard to wake up, even a violent upheaval. A hungry man doesn't become a satiated man through a slow evolutionary process but as the result of a revolutionary act: eating his fill in a hurry. Sleep is not an evolutionary stage of wakefulness; going to sleep is almost like a jump into darkness. A young man who has fallen in love hasn't evolved through countless leisurely changes from an imperfect creature into a perfect fool; rather, he goes through a sudden, precipitous revolution which rocks his very being with passion. In most cases love doesn't evolve, it just breaks out. When even the most peaceful man lights up a peacepipe, he's playing with fire. A thought doesn't usually evolve slowly; it jumps up at you like a spry flea. From morning to night, life is more a series of small revolutions than a smooth evolution.

But what modern physics is doing to us is even worse. It turns out that all activity in matter is just a lot of small revolutions. Some electron suddenly hops like a crazy man into another orbit; all material processes are supposed to be internal, so to speak, communal revolutions in atoms. Everything that happens takes the form of a constant jumping back and forth from one state to another. Matter has neither gentle continuity nor smooth transitions, but only jumps; it's really quite terrifying. The ink from my pen dries by means of violent and precipitous events taking place in its black interior. A hundred thousand atoms carry out a homemade revolt so that one letter can dry. The ink itself, however, dries and blackens slowly; I would say that it evolves.

And precisely here we see the strange and profound thing about nature: electrons may prance about, but an inkwell isn't going to prance about a desk. The atom is terribly revolutionary, but the mass is basically peaceful. The last individual atom undergoes a violent transformation, but matter changes slowly. Human life during a day is a series of revolutions; during a year it is a small piece of evolution. But if we have to change the world, let's at least be revolutionary like atoms; let's each of us take a step forward by himself. The world won't take a step forward; the world is broad and peaceful, like matter. We need millions of individuals to accomplish revolutions in themselves, so that the people as a whole can evolve. We need every individual to do what he can do the best; then mankind will change a bit too, at its endless leisure, of course. The natural order of things dictates making not one revolution, but making a million revolutions. This is the only morality flowing from the revolutionary order of nature.

Translated by Charles E. Townsend; © 1990 Charles E. Townsend. Originally published as "Bud'me revolucní," 1925. First English translation.

# CHILDREN OF THE POOR

Once I had the opportunity to accompany a police patrol on a routine check of the Kosir slums: an abandoned brickyard, impoverished tenements, tiny houses and hovels. These remnants of a former village now swallowed up into the urban periphery bore eloquent testimony to the range of habitats—other than caves—in which twentieth-century man is capable of surviving.

"Open up, police!" A young man opens the door. A burrow two by four yards, nothing inside, not even a chair, not even a nail to hang oneself on. The flashlight beam runs over the walls, then probes a pile of rags in the corner. A young woman in the last stage of pregnancy gets to her feet. "Occupation?" The young man gulps. "Right now, unemployed." A fine future family!

Next door, another three-by-four hole, stifling air, two beds, eleven sleepers. Two families, seven children on the floor, fourteen eyes staring in rapture at the helmets and buttons of the policemen. What glory! The papers of one pair of parents don't seem to be in order, there is a lot of talk and severe scolding; in the meantime, fourteen young, wide-open eyes remain breathlessly fixed on three helmeted men.

The same kind of hole, on the floor the den of a woman and her brood of five, in the corner a bed with two tousled heads sticking out from under the blanket.

"Who is that in the bed?"

"That's my daughter and her friend," the mother says with indifference.

"Those are your children?"

"One is my sister's."

"Where is your husband?"

"Karlovo Square." That means under arrest.

Four hate-filled eyes burn from under the blanket.

"You have your papers?"

"Yes."

"Let's see, mother," says the young policeman gently. The police take their time shuffling through the dog-eared documents. In the meantime five children, boys and girls huddled under a single rag, stare at the gentlemen from the police.

Next door: eight children, three in bed with grandma, five on the floor, in the other bed their parents. "They are all yours?"

"All ours."

Somebody in the room must be sick, because the place has an awful smell. Let's get out, quick!

A grandmother and three children.

"They're yours?"

"My son's."

"Where is he?"

"Karlovo Square."

Another nest, a couple and three children on the floor.

"Who is that?"

"My sister's daughter."

"And the man?"

"Nobody, just a friend."

One of the youngsters on the floor is a fourteen-year-old girl. Lord, what a filthy blouse!

Another hole-in-the-wall, this one spotlessly clean, a thin woman with two pale, scrawny children.

"What do you do?"

"I work as a maid, sir."

"You have a husband?"

"No, sir."

Grandma and four children. A cage of misery, but not without a certain charm. Grandma looks for a pair of shoes which she wants to show off. "The boy got these in school, thank God, I only hope he won't wear them out!"

"She is a beggar," a policeman explains in a whisper. Well, that's already a tiny step toward the elite. Clean cups with a floral design, windows covered with something close to curtains. Grandma politely walks us to the door.

"May the Lord bless you for those shoes, gentlemen. . ."

And so it goes: twenty, thirty such places, with at least one hundred children; poverty is extremely fertile and multiplies enormously. Believe me, once you see for yourself you realize how poverty is born and bred. There is no helping it: for children who grow up like this there is no way out, no possible progress. They can never turn into anything but pitiful, declassed people who will propagate the terrible proto-humanity of poverty. Deprivation can still function as an impetus to action, but poverty is a state of malediction, something like a hereditary illness. If it is to be eliminated we must start with the children. Adults can be given some help, but children can still be transformed, they can be shown that *even for them* the world has something other than the lowest kind of misery. In our program of child welfare there must be special emphasis on saving children born into pauperism. It is not enough to feed and clothe them; they must be incorporated into society, brought out of the underworld, ferried from islands of misery to the other shore where there is still plenty of worry but not sheer hopelessness.

As long as such troglodytic misery exists among us, we cannot consider ourselves a civilized society; at best, a half-civilized society on the edge of a wilderness.

Translated by Peter Kussi; © 1990 Peter Kussi. Originally published as "Deti chudych," 1934. First English translation.

# THE MOTHER

## Translated by Norma Comrada

This play, suggested by the author's wife, the subject matter taken from the time in which we live, and the inspiration a picture of a widow kneeling on a contemporary battlefield, perhaps can manage without an introduction which would explain it more precisely. Only for the sake of realistic staging does the author beg that the dead in this play, who gather about the mother, be looked upon not as ghosts, but as living, dear, familiar people, moving about quite naturally in their own home, in the circle of their family. They are as they were when they were alive, for they live still in the imagination of the mother; they are dead only in that she cannot touch them—and in that they make a little less noise than do we, the living.

## CHARACTERS

THE MOTHER
THE FATHER
ANDREW
GEORGE
CORNEL
PETER
TONY
OLD MAN
MALE ANNOUNCER
FEMALE ANNOUNCER

# Act One

*The* FATHER's *room, with windows wide open. A portrait of
the* FATHER, *in officer's uniform, hangs in a prominent place;
on the walls are hung sabers, swords, pistols, rifles, chibouks,
and such mementos of colonial campaigns as spears and
shields, bows, arrows and scimitars, antlers, antelope skulls
and other hunting trophies. Also along the wall are bookcases
and carved wardrobes, a stand with a row of polished rifles,
oriental fabrics, maps and animal skins. In fact, the room is
cluttered with masculine knickknacks: a heavy desk with dic-
tionaries, a globe, pipes, a shrapnel paperweight, tobacco jars
and similar debris; a sofa with Turkish cushions, a frayed
armchair, tabourets, a small Arabian table with a chessboard,
another small table with a portable phonograph, military caps
and helmets on top of the wardrobes and, everywhere, exotic
figurines and African masks, brought back some twenty or
thirty years ago as souvenirs from travels and from the
colonies. Everything, however, is seen at a glance to be shabby and dated; it looks more like a family museum than a
living room.*

    TONY *sits on the sofa, his knees nearly to his chin; a
large book sits on his knees for support as he writes on a
sheet of paper. He reads to himself in a whisper what he has
just written and keeps time with his hand; he shakes his head,
crosses something out and again whispers while scanning the
page.*

PETER *(enters, whistling):*  Ah, Tony. What are you doing? *(He
walks aimlessly to the desk and spins the globe, whistling a
little tune.)*

TONY:  What?

PETER:  Are you writing poetry?

TONY:  Of course not. *(He hides the paper in the book.)* What do
you care, anyway?

PETER:  I don't. *(Hands in his pockets, he stares at* TONY *and
whistles to himself.)* Let me see it!

TONY *(pretending he is reading)*:  No. It's nothing.

PETER: Hm! *(He reaches over and tweaks* TONY's *hair.)* Have it your own way, you— *(He dawdles around the desk and fills a small pipe for himself from one of the tobacco jars.)* Don't you have anything better to do? *(He opens a desk drawer.)*

TONY: And what are you doing?

PETER: I'm loafing, Tony. *(He takes a small, tattered book from the drawer and flips through it.)* I'm loafing at top speed. My time hasn't come yet, you know. *(He goes to the little table with the chess set.)* Now I'm looking at the chess problem Dad once began to solve and — couldn't finish. I'd like to try it. *(He places a handful of black and white chessmen around the board and checks their positions with the little book, whistling softly to himself.)*

TONY *(hesitantly)*: There's something you don't know, Peter—

PETER *(absent-mindedly)*: What's that?

TONY: About our George.

PETER: What should I know?

TONY: Today he's going to try for — some kind of record.

PETER: What makes you think so?

TONY: He told me last night, "Tony, keep your fingers crossed for me, I'm going to try something." Around three o'clock, he said.

PETER: Around three? *(He looks at his watch.)* It's about that time now. He didn't say anything about it to the rest of us. *(He goes on placing the chessmen and whistling softly.)* Probably he didn't want Mother to know. She's always so worried when George is flying — Don't say anything about this in front of her, will you? *(He looks at the book and then at the chessboard.)* Q5. Q5. Dad marked Q5 as the first move here, but it looks to me like — I often think how bored he must have been in the colonies. That's why he worked these chess problems.

TONY: Are you bored, too?

PETER: Horribly. There's never been such a dull century. *(He turns around.)* Just skip all the ceremony, Tony, and show me your poem.

TONY: No! It's not ready yet!

PETER *(moves toward him)*: Don't make excuses!

TONY *(takes out the sheet of paper)*: It isn't any good! You'll just laugh at me!

PETER *(takes the paper from* TONY's *hand)*: I'm only going to see if there are any spelling mistakes. *(He reads the poem silently and attentively.)*

*(CORNEL enters, gun in hand.)*

CORNEL: You're both here? — *(He cocks the gun.)* I had to take the whole damn thing apart, but now it shoots like a dream. *(He puts the gun on a small stand.)* We'll have to try it out, Peter. — So what are you two youngsters up to? *(He takes out another gun and tests the hammer.)*

TONY *(looks nervously at PETER)*: Nothing.

PETER: Here in this line, Tony, you've got two syllables too many.

TONY: Which one? Show me.

PETER: The one that begins: But You, Beautiful Stranger, are coming—

CORNEL *(blowing on the gun's hammer)*: Ah, yes, poetry! The rhymes are off and running again with Tony? *(He places the gun on a table and takes gun oil and flax out of a drawer.)*

PETER: And who is it, this Beautiful Stranger?

TONY *(jumps up and tries to snatch the paper from him)*: Give it to me! I know I've got it all wrong. Give it back, I'll burn it.

PETER: No, I'm asking seriously. Don't be idiotic, Tony. It so happens your poems aren't as bad as you think.

TONY: You don't mean that?

PETER *(reads silently)*: I do. It doesn't sound at all bad, Apollo.

TONY: But surely you must know who she is . . . the Stranger.

PETER: You think — death? Is that it, Tony? *(He returns the poem.)*

TONY: Well, why do you ask if you already know?

PETER: I'm just surprised that you're writing about death. A mere boy like you!

CORNEL *(cleaning the gun on the desk)*: For the very reason that he *is* only a boy. Tony's so gloomy. Beautiful Stranger—forget it. I don't know what's so beautiful about death; unless—

PETER: —unless that death is *for* something, right?

CORNEL: Right. Golden words, Peter. For your precious Black rag on a stick, for instance. Death upon the barricades—our Peter wouldn't settle for anything less. Boom!

TONY *(almost tearfully)*: Stop it! You'll just start quarreling again!

PETER *(sitting down to the chessboard)*: But we won't, my child. I wouldn't think of quarreling with him. Who would listen to that decrepit, cranky, reactionary fossil, anyway? But there's nothing I can do about it, he was born half an hour before I was. There's a generation's difference between us, son. But you can't stop the wheels of progress; new generations are on the march—half-hour-younger generations— *(He moves a chessman.)* Q5. Q5. I don't think it will work the way Dad expected it to. *(He takes back his move.)*

CORNEL: Won't you show me your poem, Tony?

TONY: It needs more work first.

CORNEL *(wiping his fingers on the flax)*: Leave it alone. The more you work on it, the worse it will get.

TONY *(hands him the paper)*: But don't laugh at me, Cornel.

PETER *(over the chessboard)*: Impossible, Cornel never laughs. Cornel only wants to make sure there isn't some sort of sub-versive tendency there, free verse, for instance—

TONY: I'd never write free verse!

PETER: That's your good luck, Tony. Otherwise Cornel would declare you a traitor to the nation and a bolshevik. You mustn't be a destructive element, Tony. Leave that to me. I'm the black sheep in this family — How should I move this bishop? *(He shakes his head.)* No, that would leave me ex-posed, and white would strike a blow straight to my heart. Wait.— But You, Beautiful Stranger, are coming—

TONY: Let Cornel read!

PETER: Sorry, I'm thinking out loud. It's the oratorical talent in me coming out.

CORNEL *(putting the paper aside)*: Shocking!

TONY: Is it that bad?

CORNEL: It's terrible! Peter, the boy's going to be a poet! And such a respectable army officer's family, too — What do you think, should we spank him?

TONY *(immensely pleased)*: You really like it?

CORNEL *(ruffles* TONY's *hair fondly)*: No, you still have much to learn, Tony. And don't begin by concentrating on death, un-derstand? That's not for you, baby brother! One can also write about life—

TONY: Do you think I should go on with my writing?

CORNEL *(beginning to clean the gun again)*: Why, you know that in our family everybody does something different. Sort of a family curse, I think.

PETER: Did you know that our George is trying for a record today?

CORNEL *(stops cleaning)*: Who said so?

PETER: Tony. He says George told him to keep his fingers crossed.

TONY: Oh, no, I forgot! *(He quickly crosses his fingers.)*

CORNEL *(looks out the window)*:   The weather's good; with a bit of luck—

TONY:   What kind of record?

PETER:   Altitude.

CORNEL:   Altitude and weight. *(He bends over the gun again.)*

TONY:   It must be a wonderful sensation . . . to fly so high . . . to circle where nothing but blue surrounds you and sing to yourself:  Higher! Higher!

PETER:   What you'd do is freeze your tail, little man.

CORNEL:   You can bet Georgie will set that record some day. George takes after Dad.

TONY:   How?

PETER *(absorbed in the chess problem)*:   Bravado.

CORNEL *(over the gun)*:   Sense of duty, Peter.

TONY:   At least you knew Dad, but I— Was our Andrew like him, too?

CORNEL:   He was. That's why he went down there.

TONY:   And you?

CORNEL:   I try my best, Tony. I do what I can.

TONY:   And Peter?

CORNEL:   He tries desperately *not* to take after him.

PETER:   I? Listen, friend, I'm trying desperately to solve his chess problem.

CORNEL:   If not that, something else . . . that would surely surprise Father, poor man. A major in the cavalry, and here his own son wants to revolutionize the world. A ready-made family tragedy. — How is it that these guns of Dad's collect so much dust?

PETER:   Don't believe him, Tony. Dad was always in the forefront of everything. I inherited that from him. *(He moves a chessman.)* And so the black pawn proceeds to KB5. White resists.

CORNEL:   White resists? Show me! *(He goes to the chessboard.)*

PETER:   Black attacks. White loses ground.

CORNEL *(over the chessboard)*:   Wait, black sheep, that wouldn't be fair. Dad would have moved this knight to Q5.

PETER:   Possibly, but it's a different era now. Dad was a cavalryman, while my heart is on the side of the infantry. Infantrymen always move forward. An infantryman may fall, but he may never retreat. Pawns of the world, unite!

CORNEL:   But if the knight were on Q5—

PETER: Don't touch my move!

CORNEL: That's Dad's game. Look, with Q5 the white checkmates in three moves.

PETER: But that isn't what I want, dear brother. What I want is to annihilate the white. Therefore, the black pawn advances on the barricades and forces the white knight to retreat—

CORNEL: Damn it, there's a mistake here. The problem didn't anticipate that move.

PETER: Right. The problem allows for two solutions, your lordship.

CORNEL: The first is Father's.

PETER: And the other one is revolutionary. Oppressed pawns, forward! The white rook is exposed! Watch out!

CORNEL: Listen, Peter, put the black pawn back. You'll just spoil the whole game.

PETER: Which game?

CORNEL: Dad's. He would play on Q5.

PETER: Our Dad was a soldier. He'd say, "Black's a stout fellow, black doesn't give up." And he would plunge into battle against the white—

CORNEL: Come on, put the pawn back!

PETER: Why should I do that?

CORNEL: I'd like to see how Dad would have solved it.

PETER: But now we're playing a different version. It isn't Dad's. It's yours and mine. You kick in vain, white horse; nothing will stop the black pawn's advance. In the fourth move he'll become the all-powerful queen — but we call it something else.

CORNEL: What?

PETER *(suddenly serious)*: A new regime, dear brother. A Black regime. It's inevitable.

CORNEL: Not yet, Peter. One move remains.

PETER: Which one?

CORNEL: This one! *(He sweeps the chessmen from the board with his hands.)*

PETER: Aha. That's called the way of brute force. *(He rises.)* All right. Then we'll settle it a different way.

TONY *(who has been reading on the sofa, raises his head and cries out almost hysterically)*: Not your politics again, I can't stand it!

CORNEL: It's only a game, you softy. We're only going to do a little fencing, isn't that right, Peter?

TONY: It isn't just a game! I know what you're thinking!

PETER: True, Tony. It's a terribly serious matter. A fight between the old world and the new. But don't worry, I'll pin him to the wall like a bug! Down with tyrants! *(He claps a fierce-looking helmet on his head.)* Let the old world perish! *(He growls at* CORNEL.*)* Grr!

CORNEL *(has clamped on a hussar's helmet)*: I'm ready. *(He takes two swords from the wall.)* Your choice of weapons, sir enemy.

PETER *(bends one of the swords)*: Good. But a fight with equal weapons, friends, just isn't done these days. Dreadfully old-fashioned. *(They position themselves* en garde.*)* Give the signal, Tony!

TONY *(buries his face in the book and covers his ears)*: I don't want to!

CORNEL: Ready — go!
                    *(Both laugh while fencing.)*

PETER: La! La!

CORNEL: Ala!

PETER: Down with tyranny and all traitors! La! La!

CORNEL: La!

PETER: First hit!

CORNEL: Shoulder. A light blow. The struggle continues with a shift in power.

PETER: And then we shall rule!

CORNEL: Don't wait around for it! Touché!

PETER: A mere scratch. La! La! Forward, black pawns!

CORNEL: Oho, we stand fast as a rock, sir! La! La!

PETER: The final battle flares — Toccato!

CORNEL: What do you think? Now you get it — *(He pauses.)* Wait, didn't that hurt, Peter?

PETER: It's nothing. En garde!
                    *(Small tables and tabourets are knocked over.)*

PETER: La!

CORNEL: Ala!

PETER: Stop! That would have sliced your throat, Cornel. You're dead.

CORNEL: Wound me if you will, but I'll keep on fighting. To the last breath! Ala!

TONY *(crying out)*: Stop it!

PETER: In a minute, Tony. The pawn attacks. Ha! Ha! The old world totters—

CORNEL: Finito! That one went straight to the heart, Peter. *(He lowers his sword.)*

PETER *(saluting with his sword)*: I thank you, I am dead.

CORNEL *(also salutes)*: I am sorry.

PETER: But a thousand black pawns rise to take my place. Hurrah, comrades!

*(The* MOTHER *enters and stands in the doorway.)*

MOTHER: Boys, boys, now what are you up to?

PETER: Oh. Mom. *(He hurriedly hangs his sword on the wall.)* Cornel just killed me, Mom. With a thrust to the heart. *(He takes off his helmet.)*

CORNEL *(hanging up his sword)*: But Peter got me in the neck, Mom. Also a perfect thrust. *(He takes off his helmet.)*

MOTHER: You twins are forever brawling! And here you are, at it again, you scoundrels. And in your father's room, of all places!

PETER: We'll straighten it up again, Mom, don't worry. Come on, Cornel.

*(Both hastily restore order, picking up the overturned tables and stools.)*

MOTHER: Never mind, I know all about a man's idea of order. The more you try to fix things up, the worse they get.

CORNEL *(on all fours, straightening the rug)*: We'll do it right now. Let go, Peter!

PETER *(likewise on all fours, pushing him away)*: Let go yourself! *(Almost at once, they begin scuffling over a dagger and land in a pile on the floor.)* I'll pin you to the mat!

CORNEL *(panting)*: Just try it!

PETER: Just wait! *(They roll about the room.)*

MOTHER: That's enough! You'll just break everything else! You should be ashamed, such big— what will Tony think of you?

PETER *(letting go of* CORNEL*)*: Join in, Tony. I'll teach you the same lesson!

TONY: I don't want to!

MOTHER: Leave Tony out of this. And I don't want you in this room! Tony, why were they fighting?

TONY: Peter didn't want to move to Q5.

CORNEL *(picking up the chessmen from the floor)*: You see, Mom, that was Father's move. I was only defending family tradition.

PETER: That isn't true, Mom. The problem really has two solutions.

CORNEL *(placing the chessmen back on the board)*:  Well, why not play it the way Dad would have?

PETER:  And why not play it the other way? Maybe these days Dad would have had to play it the way I did.

MOTHER:  Shh! Stop your squabbling and clear out of here! Now I have to put everything back in order after your roughhousing.

CORNEL:  We'll help you, Mom.

MOTHER:  You'd be such a help! What do you know about order!

CORNEL:  Put things where they were.

PETER:  Put things where they should be.

MOTHER:  Oh, no. Put things where they're most at home; but you don't understand that. Out, twins, get away from me!

CORNEL:  Let's go out in the yard and practice with this gun, Peter!

PETER:  Good idea. Who can hit a bottle at a hundred paces, all right?

MOTHER:  You're always having to break something!

CORNEL:  Tony, aren't you coming? *(He takes from the rack the gun he had first brought in with him.)*

MOTHER:  No, Tony doesn't like your shooting, do you, Tony?

PETER:  I know. Tony's afraid.

MOTHER:  He isn't afraid. You don't understand him. He's different from the rest of you, that's all.

CORNEL:  Each of us is different, Mom.

MOTHER:  Less than you think. Now go, you big ruffians!

CORNEL *(kisses her on the cheek)*:  Are you angry?

PETER *(kisses her on the other cheek)*:  Impossible! She's used to it.

MOTHER:  Do you know where George is?

CORNEL:  No, where would he be? Do you know, Tony?

TONY:  I think. . . I think he's meeting someone.

MOTHER:  Meeting whom?

PETER:  You know, Mom. Probably some beautiful unknown stranger.

*(The two brothers shove each other out the door.)*

MOTHER:  And what were you doing here, Tony?

TONY:  Nothing. I was just . . . reading.

MOTHER:  Your father's books?

TONY:  Some travel diaries, Mom.

MOTHER:  Always those far-away lands. That's not for you, Tony. Surely you won't go traveling off like that, will you? *(She walks about the room and quietly puts things away.)*

TONY: I doubt it, but I can imagine what it must be like, you know—

MOTHER: For instance?

TONY: I don't know. Maybe the grass on the veldt, and suddenly a great herd of antelope — I don't understand how anyone can shoot living things.

MOTHER: Your Father shot them, but you'll be different, won't you? *(She turns her head toward him.)* I, at least, would like you always to be as you are now. Someone must stay at home, Tony. Otherwise, you see, there wouldn't be any homes in the world. *(She kisses him.)* And now you go, too. There's something I need to do here.

(TONY leaves.)

MOTHER *(silently putting things in order)*: Tony will be different. Tony must be different. *(She stops before the FATHER's portrait and stares at it, then shrugs her shoulders and goes to close the heavy curtains. Inside the room a twilight descends. The MOTHER comes back to the portrait and switches on a lamp standing in front of it.)* You see how you always draw them here! You know I don't like it. Even your Tony, whom you never knew, hides out here whenever he can. Please, why do you do this to me? I also want them for myself, Richard. I don't want them always drawn to you.

FATHER *(slowly materializes from a dim corner; he is wearing the same uniform as in the portrait)*: I don't draw them here, beloved. They do that themselves. You know that they've played with this rubbish since childhood. Don't wonder at them now.

MOTHER *(busies herself nearby without any evident surprise)*: You always say that, my dear. They're a bit old for these playthings of yours now, yet you still have them here.

FATHER: Reminders of their childhood, that's all. But you could have thrown out those knickknacks long ago, my dear. That's not my doing.

MOTHER: Throw them out? Remembrances of you? No, no, Richard, I have a right to these things, they're here because of me. These things *are* you. *(She sits in a chair.)* But when the boys come up here, something always remains in the air after they've gone. . . something, as if you yourself were here. You yourself.

348

FATHER *(seating himself astride a chair)*: That's only the tobacco, beloved.

MOTHER: Tobacco and life. You don't know what it's like for me afterwards. I need only close my eyes and I feel so strongly: Richard was here— Richard— This room is always filled with you, one almost breathes it. Don't say that these things are rubbish; they're you, they're you — You have too much influence on the boys, Richard.

FATHER: Don't believe that for a moment, Mother. Tell me, how could I possibly influence them? Once a man is— how many years has it been?

MOTHER: You ought to know that. Seventeen.

FATHER: Already? You can see, beloved, when a man has been dead for seventeen years, very little of him remains. Less and less of him all the time. I'm of no use to anyone now, dearest. All that's left of me is the dust you wipe from the junk that's here.

MOTHER: It doesn't matter. You intrigue them. That's why they're always in here. After all, there is quite a bit for the boys: a father who was soldier, a hero! I know how it fascinates them. It has always fascinated them.

FATHER: You shouldn't have told them about me, my girl. That was your error.

MOTHER: Shouldn't have! That's easy enough to say! Who else would have kept your memory alive, if not I? From the time of your death, Richard, I have not had many pleasures other than your memory and your children. I know what I owe to you, my darling. If all children could be so proud of their father — You have no idea what this has meant to our boys. Are you saying that I should have deprived them of that?

FATHER: You're exaggerating, beloved; forgive me, but you always did exaggerate this business. Some heroism! It was no great thing. A completely insignificant skirmish with some natives —and one we lost, at that.

MOTHER: I know, you always say that. But your general wrote me himself: Madam, you mourn a hero. Your husband himself requested the most dangerous of posts—

FATHER: That's only a figure of speech, my girl; perhaps they wanted to cover up the fact that. . . that they'd bungled it. Some hero! Someone had to go there. If I hadn't volunteered, someone else would have. That's all there is to it.

MOTHER: But perhaps someone else would not have been the father of five young children, Richard!

FATHER: No, true, but if someone has five children, he needn't therefore be a bad soldier, my love. Actually, I didn't do anything out of the ordinary . . . but you don't understand, my dear: in battle, a man's mind works in an entirely different way. It's hard to explain. Afterwards, what he did may seem to have been God-knows-what kind of daring deed. But when a man is in the midst of it—what else can he do? That's the whole point. Obviously, the flank had to be protected, my girl. Look, the front column was pushing forward here, and over there was a mountain pass, you see. And we had to occupy that pass with only a small detachment. That's all there was to it. Altogether, fifty-two died. It still doesn't make sense.

MOTHER: Fifty-two—out of how many?

FATHER: Well, out of fifty-two, dear heart; but we held fast for six whole days. The worst part of it was the thirst, I can tell you. We didn't have any water. The thirst was unbearable— and the anger. I was furious.

MOTHER: Why?

FATHER: Because, frankly, the whole thing was pointless. Our colonel had made a mistake, you see. The main column had to wait below, and at least two battalions had to be sent up to the pass. Plus a mountain artillery unit. I realized all this beforehand. I said as much to the colonel, and he said, It sounds to me, Major, as if you're afraid—

MOTHER: Richard! And so that's why you went — to your death?

FATHER: That's mostly why, dearest, mostly why. If only the colonel could have seen that I was right. What an idiot! To fall right into a trap that way!

MOTHER: And because of him— because of him—

FATHER: It seems silly to you, doesn't it? But in the regiment, my girl, it's called honor. That's how it is in the military.

MOTHER: Richard, you've never told me that! So you died only because this colonel gave a senseless order?

FATHER: That happens sometimes, dearest. But at least it turned out that I was right. It was worth it, too.

MOTHER: So that's what you were thinking about: proving that you were right! And you didn't think about us, did you? About the fact that I was pregnant with our fifth child, you didn't think about that, either!

FATHER: Indeed I did, dearest. How could I think about anything else? A man thinks about a lot of things in a situation like that, you have no idea. For example, he is riding along on horseback, and he thinks: In three months I can go home. The new baby will already be here. I'll very quietly set my sword down in the front hall and tiptoe. . . tiptoe. . . Why, here's our Andrew, who already shakes my hand like a man. Hello, Daddy, he says. —Hello, Andy; what are you up to in school? —Nothing, Daddy, —And Georgie, Georgie will show me some little machine: Look, Daddy! —And the twins will be rolling their eyes and scuffling over who will be the first to crawl into my lap. Here, you rascals, both of you come over here and stop your quarreling! —And my wife. . . I haven't seen her face for more than half a year. More than half a year. When I take her in my arms, she will yield and soften, as if she had no bones, and she will whisper: Richard—

MOTHER: Richard—

FATHER *(rising)*: Tell me, beloved, how have you been all this long time?

MOTHER *(with eyes closed)*: You know, my heart, how I've waited for you. I bore a fifth son for you — He's not strong, Richard, God knows why he is so frail. Perhaps it's because I wept so much for you.

FATHER: He'll grow out of that, Mother; he'll be a fine young man and a hero, you'll see.

MOTHER *(with sudden vehemence)*: No! I don't want that! I don't want Tony to be a hero! I've had enough of that, Richard, do you hear? I've paid too much for your heroism! Isn't it enough that you died? Do you know, does any of you know what it is to lose a husband? If you only knew how little was left for me, what that did to me, how could you have allowed yourself to be killed so needlessly?

FATHER: Beloved, it doesn't matter, when that ignorant colonel said that I was afraid — no, I had to go, didn't I? And he said it . . . in front of the other officers: It seems to me, Major, that you're afraid. If you had been there, dearest, I don't know what you would have said to me.

MOTHER *(quietly rising)*: I would have said: Go, Richard. You mustn't let him say a thing like that.

FATHER: You see, my love, you would have felt the same way.

MOTHER: Because I loved you, Richard, because I must always love you! But no, pay no attention to that; you don't know what it means to a woman, when she loves someone beyond all reason! I myself don't know what it is in us; I only know that I was so immediately drawn to you . . . you know, Richard, your soldiering, the clank of spurs, your boldness and dash, your sense of honor and your light-heartedness — I don't know why I so worshiped all that in you. Probably I was silly, I was infatuated, I was foolish; but even now. . . even now it would be unbearable if anyone humiliated you.

FATHER: Well, you see; and if I hadn't gone then. . .

MOTHER: No, no, Richard, forget what I just said. Perhaps . . . surely I would have accepted it, if you had not conducted yourself . . . like a soldier. You would have come back to me and the children . . . and left the army. I would have . . . become used to that. And I would have loved you, too. Perhaps . . . in a different way. I know that you would be terribly worried . . . without your soldierly honor, but we would have survived that . . . both of us; at least I would have you with me, Richard, and I would have been able to take care of you—

FATHER: —a worthless, tormented man. That would be enough for you, my love?

MOTHER: ——It would have to be enough for me. Don't think I haven't had to be content already . . . with very, very little.

FATHER: . . .I know, dearest. I'm terribly sorry. There was only a major's pension. . .

MOTHER: There were five children, Richard—and look at them. You don't know what that's like for a woman all on her own. No, no, you can't understand that. Forgive me, my love, I shouldn't talk about that, but you have no idea — Clothes, food, schools, and more clothes, food, schools — Always, always having to calculate, to stretch each rag, each penny, five times — how could you know what that's like! True, there's no heroism in it, but— that's how it had to be. Dearest, dearest, why are you staring at me that way? You know what I look like!

FATHER: You are beautiful, Mother. You are more beautiful than before.

MOTHER: Don't talk nonsense, Richard. We who are living change dreadfully. Not you, you haven't changed at all. I'm almost ashamed at how old I must seem compared to you. Don't look at me, please. I've had too many worries. It was difficult without you—

FATHER: I was of so little use to you!

MOTHER: At least, I wasn't alone! But most of all, most of all I needed you when the boys began to outgrow me. No, don't think that they weren't good boys. All of them—Andrew, George, the twins—they did everything to help me. But as they grew up, it was as if they began to speak another language. I don't understand them well enough, Richard. — Probably you would have understood them better.

FATHER: I don't know, my girl, I don't know. It seems to me that I don't understand them, either. What do I know about medicine or aviation or such foolishness as those twins have in their heads?

MOTHER: You mean politics?

FATHER: Yes. I don't have a head for those things, Mother. I was only a soldier.

MOTHER: No matter. They think more highly of you. I know, you wanted them to be soldiers, but when you fell. . . that's when I said to myself . . . no! You know I could have sent them . . . free of charge to the military academy; but I would rather. . . would rather have found a job so they could train for some other kind of work. I thought to myself, let it be medicine or engineering . . . anything, but not soldiering. Let them do something useful . . . something they won't have to die from. If you knew how I scrimped to send them to those schools — And just see how they've turned out!

FATHER: Indeed, dear heart, I think you can be very pleased with them, can't you?

MOTHER: I truly don't know. I feel like a hen who's hatched eagles, huddling next to the ground and clucking anxiously as one after the other they fly out of the nest. Sometimes I tell myself: Don't worry so much, don't be so faint-hearted, don't hinder them. — Richard, it's terrible what happens when one becomes a mother! I was such a complete fool then, yet Lord knows that I thought highly enough of myself — you know that, my love!

FATHER: I know, dearest.

MOTHER: After all, I left home to follow you; nothing else mattered to me, not even life itself. And now, I want to perch like a miser on top of what I have in this life and shout out to everyone: No more! I won't give any more! I've already given enough, Richard. You . . . and our Andrew. No more could be asked of me than that. The price of this so-called . . . heroism was too high for me. First you, and then Andrew—

FATHER: Let it be, Mother. Andrew had a beautiful death. Beautiful . . . and honorable.

MOTHER: Honorable, oh yes. You think it terribly honorable to die for something; but the fact that you are dead for me, you no longer think about that. Maybe you had to go to your death, Richard, you were a soldier. But Andrew didn't. He was a doctor and a scholar; he could have had his pick of hospitals — and he didn't have to catch that disease—

FATHER: That happens to doctors, my girl. One of the doctors in our regiment also died. He was a very dear man, I played chess with him. But you see, all of a sudden he came down with cholera—

MOTHER: But there was no need for our Andrew to go down there, to the colonies! That was your doing!

FATHER: But, Mother, I had already been dead for such a long time!

MOTHER: That makes no difference, you drew him here, to your room. You influenced him, my dear. This is where Andrew always studied, where he curled up with his books, where he paced the floor and smoked till all hours — And where he first told me, out of a clear blue sky: Mom, I'm going to go to the tropics so I can see a bit of the world. That he was going there to fight yellow fever. . . that he forgot to say. You always hide from me the fact that you're up to something. You tell me: Mom, it's only an outing; and then you stay there. Like a thief who's escaped!

*(From a dark corner, ANDREW approaches in a white doctor's gown.)*

ANDREW: But Mom, I've already explained that to you so many times — I didn't want you to worry. That's why I didn't say anything to you. That's the only reason.

MOTHER: Do you call that an explanation? You thought of that, I know; but the fact that you could become infected there or something, you didn't think about that. I for one would have thought about it, Andrew. Indeed I would.

ANDREW: But what good would that have done, Mom? I would have gone anyway.

MOTHER: You see, Andrew, you used to be such a serious and sensible boy! If you hadn't been, I don't know what I would have done. You were like a second father to the other boys— so serious and responsible — And suddenly, bang! you run off to the tropics and die of yellow fever. You didn't have to go there, Andrew, don't tell me that!

FATHER: You see, my dear, a doctor has his own sense of duty. That's simply a part of his job, isn't it, Andrew?

MOTHER: Whatever put it into your head to study this yellow fever? You could have cured people here at home — or helped bring children into the world—

ANDREW: Look, Mom: so many hundreds of thousands of people died of yellow fever each year — It would be shameful if nothing had been found to combat it. It is . . . simply an obligation, isn't it?

MOTHER: Your obligation?

ANDREW: The obligation of science. You see, Mom, it was a very cruel disease; and the people there—if you could have seen them die, you yourself would have said: Andrew, you mustn't leave them like that! It's a serious matter, Mother.

MOTHER: But it didn't have to be you, Andrew! Don't tell me that!

FATHER: And why not he? He has a good brain. In matters like this, my girl, only the best will do.

MOTHER: And the best must die?

FATHER: Of course. It doesn't happen any other way, dearest. The best will always be in the forefront, you know. Never mind, Andrew. You did well.

MOTHER: I know, you always side together against me, you men! You say he did well; but if you knew what it was like for me, when I received that telegram — I couldn't for the life of me believe it: Madam, your son fell like a hero on the battlefield of science—

FATHER: There you have it, Mother: Like a hero. Surely that's worth something, isn't it?

ANDREW: It's not, Dad. You know that wouldn't make any difference to me. To me, all that mattered was . . . to find out the cause of the fever. That's hardly heroism. If you become a scientist . . . then you must look for causes. And nothing else matters to you. What kind of heroism or honor is that? That's childishness, Dad. But a piece of knowledge—that's worthwhile.

MOTHER: And did you discover something?

ANDREW: Not I, Mom, but two others did. A Swede and an American.

FATHER: That's a pity. I don't like Americans.

MOTHER: So you think, Andrew, that it wasn't useless? It wasn't in vain?

ANDREW: It wasn't, Mother. You don't understand.

MOTHER: No, I don't understand! I never understand any of you. I hear it all the time . . . from George and the twins: Mom, you don't understand — I don't understand! I don't understand! My God, I no longer understand myself! Well, you are pieces of my body — you too, Richard; you are inside me, and you are my whole body, you are my whole soul. And I don't understand you? What do you have that's so different, what do you have that's so excessively your own, that I don't understand you?

ANDREW *(goes nearer to her)*: Please, Mom, don't upset yourself. You have a weak heart, this isn't good for you.

MOTHER: No, leave me alone! I understood you very well when you were small, do you remember, Andrew? Even from inside the house, I could tell when one of you scraped your knee, and I would already be running out to you — And when you were all sitting around the table, I could feel it so strongly — you were me. You were always me. Completely, physically, I felt it: You children, you are me! And now— Mom, you don't understand. Richard, what got into these children that is so strange and so . . . against me?

FATHER: You know that, dearest: they are grown now—and they have their own interests.

MOTHER: But their interests were always my own, don't you see? Now all of you follow your own ways, you have your own concerns, your own grand missions, I don't even understand them. But I, I followed only you. I had no mission other than you. I know, that wasn't very grand, merely to care for you and love you — But when I set food on the table before the five of you, it was like a holy sacrament for me. Andrew, Andrew, you don't know what an emptiness there was after you were gone!

ANDREW: I'm sorry, Mother.

MOTHER: It's true, I probably don't understand you. Your father, for example, fell because it was necessary to kill some savages. And you, Andrew, you died because you wanted to save their lives . . . I'm too stupid to understand that. Each of you does something just the opposite, and then afterwards you tell me: These are important matters, Mother; you couldn't possibly understand. One of you will build something, and two others will tear it down. And you say to me: These are tremendous things, Mom, we must do them even if it means an end to our lives. Life! You talk about life! To die oneself, that's easy enough to do; but to lose a husband or a son, if only you could know what that's like — If you could know—

ANDREW: In this instance. . . perhaps you're right, Mom.

MOTHER: And even if I weren't. . . I don't want to be right, I only want you, I want my children! You didn't have to die, Andy, you were such a good, earnest boy — And you were engaged, my son, you were going to be married — Perhaps I don't understand that, Andrew?

ANDREW: ——Yes, Mother.

MOTHER: So you see.

*(Two shots are heard from the garden.)*

FATHER *(raises his head)*: What's that?

MOTHER: Nothing. The boys are shooting at a target. Cornel — and Peter.

FATHER: That's good. Men who can't shoot aren't worth much.

MOTHER: Our Tony won't shoot, Richard. That isn't his nature. Andrew didn't like shooting either, did you, Andrew? You were interested in books, just like Tony—

ANDREW: But in Tony's case, it's like a drug, Mom. Dreaming with his eyes wide open. I think it's wrong.

MOTHER: But he's still only a child.

ANDREW: You will always think of him that way.

MOTHER: Because he isn't strong!

FATHER: You should encourage him to do something serious.

MOTHER: I don't want to! I don't want Tony getting ideas in his head right now! I try to keep him out of this room—

FATHER: Why?

MOTHER: Because you two would like to influence him! Because you would whisper into his ear: Be a man, Tony, be a man!

Do something! Go die for something: for glory, for honor, for truth — No, I don't want that, do you hear? Leave Tony alone!

FATHER: But surely, Mother, you don't want to turn Tony into a mama's boy?

MOTHER: I want to have him for myself. You have no right to him, Richard! Tony is a posthumous child! Tony is mine, only mine, do you understand? He cannot come in here again.

ANDREW: Mom evidently considers us bad company.

MOTHER: —Yes. Because you are dead.

*(Shots are heard from the garden.)*

ANDREW: Mom, are you afraid of us?

MOTHER: How could I be afraid of you, my son? Come closer, Andrew, look at me! If you knew how well that white gown suits you! I always thought that you would be near me until. . . until I finally say good-bye to my children—

ANDREW: Don't talk that way, Mom, you'll be here for a long time! You'll always be here, won't you?

FATHER: Your mother is stronger than she realizes. *(He goes toward the table with the chessboard.)* Who was playing here, dearest?

MOTHER: The twins. They said it was one of your problems.

FATHER: It is. I tried to solve it once — It was a nice problem.

MOTHER: The boys quarreled over it. Cornel wanted Peter to move to Q5.

FATHER: Correct. I would certainly move to Q5.

MOTHER: But Peter said there was a different solution. You know how those two are always at odds.

FATHER *(absently)*: A different solution? I'd like to know it —— Probably from a different school of chess. Unless the pawn were to move forward — Interesting! I see that Peter has a point.

*(GEORGE, in pilot's overalls, quietly enters the room.)*

GEORGE: Hello, Mom. Hello, Dad. Hi, Andrew.

FATHER *(turning around)*: Oh, here's George!

ANDREW: Hello.

MOTHER: Why so early, George — were you flying today?

GEORGE: I flew, Mom. Today I flew brilliantly.

MOTHER: And now you're home. Good. I don't like it when you fly; I'm always so afraid that— But you're home very early today.

GEORGE: You know, Mom, that I always come straight home first . . . to you.

FATHER: Right. That outfit looks good on you, my boy.

MOTHER *(rising in horror)*: Wait— George, you see . . . your father . . . and Andrew?

GEORGE: I see them, Mom. How could I not see them?

MOTHER: But they. . . they're dead, George! How can you see them . . . how can you speak to them — George!

GEORGE: Well, it's just that— You won't be angry with me? Something went wrong with the airplane, Mom. That's all.

MOTHER: George, something happened to you?

GEORGE: Nothing, Mom. Really, it doesn't even hurt. It's just that a wing broke away from the plane — and so—

MOTHER: George, tell me!

GEORGE: Don't be angry, Mom, but I was killed.

MOTHER: You. . . you. . .

GEORGE: Please, Mom, don't!

MOTHER: . . .you're dead, then, Georgie?

GEORGE: Yes, Mom, I am . . . as they say, dead.

MOTHER *(wailing)*: Jesus Christ! George! Georgie!

ANDREW: Hush, Mom, please. You must try to keep calm.

MOTHER: George, I've lost you!

FATHER: You must endure this bravely, dearest. You see, in fact, he died a hero. It was a beautiful death.

MOTHER *(as if turned to stone)*: A beautiful death. — There you have it, Richard. There you have it.

GEORGE: Mom, it's nobody's fault, truly it isn't. You see, I was testing something — and the motor failed. I myself don't really know how it happened.

MOTHER: My George— *(She sits in a chair and begins to weep.)*

ANDREW: Let her alone. It will make it easier for her. *(He stands over her.)*

FATHER *(leading GEORGE to one side)*: What were you doing, Georgie?

GEORGE; Trying for an altitude record, Dad. With weight. Fifteen hundred kilograms.

FATHER: And—it has some significance, this record?

GEORGE: Yes, Dad. In wartime, for example—to fly not only higher but with a heavier load of bombs, you see?

FATHER: True. There's something to that.

GEORGE: Or take aerial transport — That high in the air, you don't have the clouds or storms, see? That could have enormous significance.

FATHER: Yes, I see, and how high did you go?

GEORGE: Something like twelve thousand meters; but suddenly the motor began to sputter—

FATHER: Is that a record?

GEORGE: It is, Dad. In that category, it's the world record.

FATHER: That's very good. I'm delighted, young man.

GEORGE: Except that — when I landed, it was an awful mess, Dad. I think the altimeter was broken. Too bad.

FATHER: Why?

GEORGE: Because now it won't be in the record books that I ever flew that high.

FATHER: It doesn't matter, George. As long as you got there.

GEORGE: No one else will ever know about it!

FATHER: But it was done, that's the main thing. Who would have thought you could do it! You were always tinkering — I congratulate you, son.

MOTHER *(moaning)*: George — Georgie—

ANDREW: Be calm, Mother.

FATHER: Don't cry, dearest. It was worth it. So don't cry now. Look, we'd better start thinking about the funeral—

GEORGE: Mom, you mustn't look at me when they bring in my body, do you hear? What they're carrying, that's no longer me. I'm here now . . . just as I always was . . . and you're not to see me any other way.

MOTHER: Why didn't you tell me that you wanted to fly so high? I wouldn't have let you go—

GEORGE: That wouldn't have made any difference, Mom. I had to do it.

MOTHER: What made you do it, Georgie, what put it into your head! Why did you want to set that record!

GEORGE: When a man has such a good machine — It has to be, Mom, you don't understand. You see, a man is compelled to do it — the machine itself tells him to—

*(A knocking at the door.)*

FATHER *(turns off the lamp under his portrait; it is deep twilight)*: Don't grieve, beloved.

MOTHER: My George! Such a fine, strong boy! Why— Why—

GEORGE *(continuing to placate)*: You don't understand, Mom, you can't understand—

360

*(Knocking.)*

ANDREW *(whispering)*: You must be calm, Mother. You must be strong.

FATHER *(whispering)*: Farewell, dear heart.

*(Knocking.)*

MOTHER *(rising)*: Yes.

(CORNEL *stands in the doorway, silhouetted by the daylight.*)

CORNEL: Excuse me, Mom . . . I didn't mean to disturb you . . . but . . . I have something to tell you.

MOTHER: Yes.

CORNEL: We've just received . . . a message, you see . . . Our George . . . had some kind of accident with his plane. But you mustn't be frightened, Mom. It isn't so bad. . .

MOTHER: . . .Yes.

CORNEL: You see, George . . . Mother! You already know?

CURTAIN

# Act Two

*The same room, but a radio has been added.* TONY *kneels by the radio and turns the dial. The sound of a military parade is heard.* TONY, *with a grimace, turns the dial again. An announcer is heard.*

MALE ANNOUNCER: Attention! Attention!

TONY: You have a voice just like our Cornel's.

RADIO: We urge all citizens to maintain calm and order. We emphatically warn against any gathering in the streets; otherwise, police and military authorities will be forced to take the most severe measures. . .

TONY: Brrr! *(He turns the dial again; soft, distant music is heard.)*
(CORNEL *enters in a military-style uniform:*
*high boots, breeches and a coat with insignia.*)

CORNEL: Leave it alone, Tony. You know Mom doesn't like it when anyone fiddles with the radio. It was George's—

TONY: ——Listen, Cornel, it's beautiful!

CORNEL: Yes, but this isn't the time for beauty. Turn it off, Tony! I can't listen to it.

TONY *(switches off the radio and remains on his knees)*: Too bad. It was a foreign broadcast, but I don't know where it came from. I suppose it was . . . somewhere to the north. It sounded snowy—

CORNEL: You're always imagining something. *(He lights a cigarette and paces the room uneasily.)* It's silly, my having to be at home— *(He looks at his watch.)* Everyone's getting off work now. Anything could happen out there. Christ, if only I could be there! *(He stops near the window and listens.)*

TONY: ——Cornel?

CORNEL: What?

TONY: What's happened to Peter?

CORNEL: I don't know. He's locked up somewhere. He shouldn't have gotten mixed up in this.

TONY: You're mixed up in it too, Cornel.

CORNEL: Yes, but on the other side. There's a difference.

TONY: What kind of difference?

CORNEL: We stand for order — and the well-being of the nation. You don't understand it yet, Tony. Just be glad you don't.

TONY: Peter was for the well-being of the people, too, but you arrested him anyway.

CORNEL: Because his idea of well-being was something very different. He thought that a filthy mob could rule — that would be a fine thing! No thanks! They've already shown us what they'd do: looting and revenge— *(He crushes his cigarette).* That would have been the ruin of the country, Tony.

TONY: But Peter spoke out against all that!

CORNEL: So much the worse! Peter would like to have that gang become the government. But we can't allow that to happen.

TONY: Who's "we"?

CORNEL: Our side. We, the nation. If they were to rule over us with that utopia of theirs . . . with their pacifism and equality . . . that would be a free-for-all! What they want is nothing but a sell-out of the country! Dissolve the army — abolish authority — take over the factories — out of the question! That would be the end of our culture and everything else. No,

no, Peter, we don't want our country wrecked that way! —
High time, men, that we take care of those twaddlers and
traitors — But I won't go on lecturing you, Tony.

TONY *(rising)*: Cornel?

CORNEL: Yes?

TONY: What will happen to Peter?

CORNEL *(shrugs his shoulders)*: Nothing can be done. We'll just
have to wait. We arrested him and— now he's in custody.

TONY: As a criminal?

CORNEL: As a hostage — but don't worry, nothing will happen
to him there. But if that Black gang starts shooting in the
streets again, then— I don't know.

TONY: Then — you'll shoot Peter?

CORNEL: Not I, Tony; but you know that war is war. Nobody
forced Peter into this. You can imagine how horrible I would
feel if. . . if something happened to him. But that's no longer
in our power— The minute those villains put down their guns,
our Peter's free to go — and all the other hostages, too. That's
all there is to it.

TONY *(dumbfounded)*: Just imagine, Cornel. . . just imagine what
it must be like for Peter! Staring at the cell door and waiting,
just waiting . . . then it opens . . . Come with us! — Where?
— You'll find out. March.

CORNEL: Wait. *(He listens.)* It's quiet. Good thing there's no shooting going on. If a shot is fired anywhere, it'll be bad, Tony.
Then our side will go for him regardless — but I think that
riff-raff has gone into hiding. They're cowards. At least Peter
sees now what kind of people he's sided with! One look at
a machine gun and they scatter like chickens. — Do you hear
anything? It seems quiet out there. Probably they're negotiat-
ing. Although I don't see how anyone can negotiate with
gangsters.

TONY: Cornel, do they tie your hands?

CORNEL: Who? When?

TONY: When they take you away to be executed.

CORNEL: Of course. Of course your hands have to be tied. Why
do you ask?

TONY *(clasping his hands behind his back, as if they were tied)*:
You know, I can imagine it so clearly, exactly what it's like
. . . when a man stands there . . . facing the soldiers with
their guns. You know, how he stares at them . . . over their

heads, really . . . and he feels a cool breeze in his hair. Not yet . . . still a second more . . . Ready! Aim! — My God!

CORNEL: Stop it!

TONY *(shouting)*: You curs! Blood-thirsty curs!

CORNEL: Tony!

TONY: Fire! *(He staggers and falls to his knees.)*

CORNEL *(grabs him by the shoulders and shakes him)*: That's enough! Tony, that's sick, you have a sick imagination!

TONY *(covering his eyes and rising to his feet)*: Cornel, how can people hate each other so much?

CORNEL: You don't understand. You're too young to believe in something so deeply.

TONY: Believe in what?

CORNEL: In your own truth. Nobody would ever do on his own what he does for his cause. You shouldn't be so sensitive, Tony. Our mother's spoiled you.

TONY: How?

CORNEL: The way she's raising you. You'll never become someone who'll fight for something. Peace, love, compassion — I know, that's all very nice, but. . . there isn't time for that now, Tony. These times are too serious . . . and too important for that. Mom doesn't understand that. We have to be prepared for . . . anything. If something happens to Peter — Tony, Mom isn't to know what's happening to him. We must tell her only that he's been arrested, understand? And maybe they're already in retreat now; maybe that Black gang has surrendered, it's so . . . strangely quiet outside. —Don't go out, Tony.

TONY: But what about you?

CORNEL *(shrugs his shoulders)*: I should be out there, with our side. God, if only I were there in case something happens! It's so stupid, my being here at home with Mom. But you know, if anything happened here. . . She has such a weak heart — You never know with riff-raff like that. If they start looting — Somebody needs to stand guard over you here. *(With his back to TONY, he takes a revolver from a drawer and loads it; then he puts it back.)* I know where my place is. But Mom mustn't find out how serious things are, Tony. So I'll . . . stay here, at home. For her sake . . . and yours.

*(The MOTHER enters.)*

MOTHER: Cornel, where is Peter? Why isn't he home yet? You

said this morning that there was probably some kind of misunderstanding . . . that they would let him go soon . . :
Are you listening, Cornel?

CORNEL: Yes, Mom, but. . . those things take time. You know, they've probably jailed hundreds and hundreds of people, and then they have to investigate everything — It could go on for. . . maybe even a week.

MOTHER: A whole week? Cornel, could they do that to our Peter? No, no. I won't have it. I'll go talk to them—

CORNEL: You can't do that, Mom. They wouldn't even let you inside.

MOTHER: That would be something, not letting a mother in! I'm only going to take Peter some clean clothes and something to eat — surely they wouldn't keep a mother from doing that, young man. That's a mother's right.

CORNEL: You'll have to wait until later, Mom. Look, even the streets have been closed off by soldiers — no one is allowed to go into town—

MOTHER: But to keep a mother out— ! I'll tell them that I'm bringing something to my son — I must see Peter, Cornel. I have to know how he is. After all, Peter isn't some kind of criminal, to be put behind bars. I'll tell them, you can be sure of that. I'll tell them they have no right to hold my son in custody!

CORNEL: This is a serious matter, Mom. They do have the right.

MOTHER: Are you telling me that Peter really is some kind of criminal? That he did something terrible to someone?

CORNEL: He isn't . . . a criminal, Mom. No one is claiming that.

MOTHER: So you see! Then they have no right to arrest him for anything.

CORNEL: Mom, maybe you don't understand what this is all about—

MOTHER: I know. — Leave, Tony, go on out. This isn't for you. You shouldn't hear how simple-minded your mother is.

(TONY *leaves slowly and unwillingly.*)

MOTHER: I try hard to understand everything, Cornel. But obviously, I can't. How someone can imprison my son, who has never wronged anyone, I have great difficulty understanding that.

CORNEL: Forgive me, Mom. You just don't seem to realize that what's happening here is . . . civil war.

MOTHER: Oh? And we have to accept that?

CORNEL: We do. Because people are divided into two factions, and only one side can prevail, do you see? And this is the fight, Mom, that will decide which side rules.

MOTHER: And that's why you're shooting each other?

CORNEL: Yes. It can't be any other way.

MOTHER: Tell me, does it matter so terribly much which side wins? Don't both sides have families? They should be worrying about their families!

CORNEL: Families aren't everything.

MOTHER: They are, Cornel. They are to me. And don't tell me that Peter wants to rule over anyone. I know him; he couldn't even give orders to his dog — Maybe you, Cornel, but not Peter. Telling others what to do isn't his nature.

CORNEL: That doesn't matter, Mom; his side wants to take charge of everything; they want to change everything according to their own ideas — It would be a disaster for the whole country, do you understand? Why, they're nothing but a gang of criminals and traitors, Mom! They would take over and ruin everything—

MOTHER: That's not true, Cornel. Don't say that again! I know Peter . . . Peter wouldn't get mixed up with people like that. You wouldn't get mixed up with criminals and traitors either, Cornel.

CORNEL: Unfortunately, Peter has a blind faith in people—

MOTHER: Well, he's young! You were never young and outgoing that way, Cornel. You were never sociable with anyone, you were always a little standoffish — But our Peter would never associate with anyone who was evil.

CORNEL: Then I must be the one who associates with evil people, Mom. Either his side is right, or . . . we are. Damn it, one of us must be wrong!

MOTHER: Not you, Cornel. You're a bit arrogant and overbearing in your own way, but you'd never do anything low or . . . dishonorable.

CORNEL: Well, then, when I tell you truthfully that our Peter sided with a . . . dishonorable faction, and that that whole pack of his must be put out of the way if there's to be any kind of order in the world—

MOTHER: Wait, young man. We must lock up Peter for the sake of world order?

CORNEL:  ——We must, Mom. Once he got mixed up with that bunch of—

MOTHER:  It's shameful, Cornel! They were wrong to arrest our Peter!

CORNEL:  Mom, if it were the other way around, Peter would have let them . . . arrest me.

MOTHER:  Peter?

CORNEL:  His side, anyway. His party, do you see?

MOTHER:  Not unless they were crazy . . . and scoundrels, too! Surely you don't believe wrong things, Cornel! So they could arrest you, too? That would be just as wrong as arresting our Peter. They are evil people, Cornel. Evil, cruel, stupid people. My God, if I could hit them in the face with these fists—

CORNEL:  Mom, please!

MOTHER:  We mustn't leave him there, Cornel! Somehow you must help me — You said they'll keep him there a few days more?

CORNEL:  Maybe; but then they'll let him go free. It's already quiet outside; you'll see, it will all be over by tomorrow—

MOTHER:  And then you'll go with me for Peter?

CORNEL:  Yes, Mom.

MOTHER:  And I can't take him anything today?

CORNEL:  Not today, Mom.

*(Several shots in the distance. It grows dark.)*

MOTHER:  What is that?

CORNEL *(nervously)*:  Nothing. It's somewhere out in the street . . . Please, Mom, no one should go outside.

MOTHER:  But if Peter is still waiting—

CORNEL:  Always Peter! There's more at stake than just Peter, Mom.

MOTHER:  You think something could happen to Tony — or you?

CORNEL:  Mom, I'm thinking of our country.

*(Two distant shots.)*

MOTHER:  If only nothing happens to Peter!

CORNEL *(listening at the window)*:  If only nothing happens to our country, Mom. — Somewhere out there are troops, ready and waiting; if you only knew, Mom, what splendid young men they are — they're known as an elite corps. Crack shots, who'll be in the front line of battle. They're waiting for it to start, and they're asking each other: Where's Cornel? — I'm here, men. I can't join you. I . . . must stay at home. Someone has to be here, in case anything happens. Stand fast, boys; but I. . .

MOTHER: Cornel, what's the matter with you?

CORNEL: Nothing, Mom. Don't worry, I'll . . . stay here with you . . . and Tony. You know, when there's trouble in the streets all kinds of people come crawling out — But you mustn't worry about anything, Mom. I'll be here. *(He walks over to the gun rack.)*

MOTHER: What are you looking for?

CORNEL: Father's rifle, the one he had in Africa. It should be cleaned again. *(He takes a gun from the rack.)*

MOTHER: But I dust it every day!

CORNEL: You don't understand, Mom. A gun needs more than that. It needs to be fired from time to time, too. *(He places his hand on the* MOTHER'*s shoulder.)* No more worrying, Mom. Everything will soon be in order. You'll see.

MOTHER: And Peter will come back?

CORNEL: He'll come back, Mom. He'll come back.

*(He goes out with the gun. The light dims.)*

MOTHER: Dear God, what's happening to Peter? *(She sits in an armchair and clasps her hands.)* Great heavenly father, protect my Peter. Mary, merciful mother, have mercy on me and protect my children. Crucified Jesus, have mercy on my children.

*(*PETER *quietly appears at the door, wearing only trousers and an open shirt. It is now nearly dark.)*

PETER: Hello, Mom.

MOTHER *(rising instantly)*: Peter! They've released you?

PETER: Oh, yes! I won't have anything more to do with them, Mom.

MOTHER *(going to him)*: I was so afraid for you — Come here, Peter!

PETER *(avoiding her)*: No, Mom. Please stay there!

MOTHER *(reaching for him)*: What is it, son? Where is your jacket?

PETER *(still avoiding her)*: There. There. They'll probably send it to you, Mom. The jacket and everything. If nothing else, they're orderly—to a fault.

MOTHER: Who?

PETER: They. The Whites, you know. Don't turn on the light yet, Mom. I'm so sorry, but I have to tell you something. That's why I'm here. I thought it would be better if I told you myself.

MOTHER: Peter, what happened? *(She gropes her way towards him.)* Come here!

PETER *(moving away again)*: Don't be angry with me, but truly it wasn't my fault, Mom. It isn't Cornel's fault, either.

MOTHER: What are you talking about?

PETER: My God, Mom, you really are naïve! Everyone expected it to happen. Cornel expected it, too. And now it's over and done with.

MOTHER *(with growing anxiety)*: What's over and done with, Peter?

PETER: But it's so long ago, now. It was more than half an hour ago.

MOTHER: What was?

PETER: What else? They shot me, Mom!

MOTHER: Peter! *(She staggers and collapses on the floor.)*

PETER: Mom! Good Lord, what can I— Somebody come and help me! Andrew!

> (ANDREW, *in his white gown, appears
> instantly out of the darkness.)*

ANDREW: What happened?

PETER: Look — Mom—

ANDREW *(kneels by the* MOTHER *and takes her pulse)*: All right, let's see—

> *(The* FATHER, *in uniform, emerges from the shadows.)*

FATHER: What's happened to her?

PETER: I don't know, she suddenly fell to the floor—

FATHER: Why weren't you more careful! *(He kneels by the* MOTHER.*)* Dearest, are you all right?

> (GEORGE *now comes out of the darkness,
> wearing his pilot's overalls.)*

GEORGE: Hello, Peter. What's the matter with Mom? *(He turns on the light over the desk.)*

ANDREW *(on his knees)*: Heart. If you only knew how erratic her pulse is — poor Mother!

FATHER: If only we could send for someone!

ANDREW: What for? We're here, aren't we? She'll be unconscious for a little while. She's had a bad shock. It's best to let her rest quietly — get some pillows!

PETER *(hunting for pillows)*: There's some here.

GEORGE *(bringing an armful of pillows)*: Use these.

ANDREW: Raise her head, Dad. *(He places the pillows under her.)* There. Now lie quietly, Mom. *(He rises.)* Stand aside, give her some room.

FATHER (getting up): Why did you frighten her so, Peter? And tell me, what are you doing here, anyway?

ANDREW: Wait a moment, Dad. (He takes PETER under the light and inspects his forehead.) I see! One, and a second one. (He opens PETER's shirt and taps his chest.) One, two, three. This one went straight to your heart.

FATHER: Show me. Right on target! — Strange, that looks almost like— once we shot some Arabs — how did you get that, son?

PETER: Execution by firing squad, Dad.

FATHER: Son, son, soldiers executed you?

PETER: Soldiers, Dad.

FATHER: Peter, surely you didn't commit treason?

PETER: No, Dad. I stood for a fine — and honorable cause.

FATHER: Against the army? It doesn't sound that way to me, young man.

PETER: There is an army on our side, too, Dad.

FATHER: Soldiers on both sides?

PETER: Yes.

FATHER: Soldiers against soldiers?

PETER: Yes, Dad.

FATHER: I don't like that, Peter. Soldier against soldier — you must have it wrong, son. — Then you were a spy, Peter?

PETER: No, Dad. I only wrote for a newspaper.

FATHER: Don't lie, Peter. The army wouldn't have shot you for that. We only executed spies or traitors.

GEORGE: These are different times, Dad.

FATHER: So it seems. And evidently there are some new rules, boys. (He turns back to the MOTHER.) Tell me, how is she?

ANDREW (seated, bending over her): Nothing yet, she's still unconscious; you could say that she's sleeping.

FATHER: Good. Otherwise, she could hear us—

ANDREW: —and speak to us. Mom has been the only one who could. She never lost contact with us.

PETER (spinning the globe on the desk): It was so painful when I had to tell her—

GEORGE: I know. You have such a horribly foolish feeling at a time like that, as if you were confessing to some silly prank. (He opens a desk drawer and rummages around in it.) Boys, do you know that Mom has our pipes stored away? She's quite a woman, our mother! When we were alive, she used to say: Outside with that! *(He puts an empty pipe to his lips with the automatic motion of a smoker.)* Mm. Mmm. All the same, a man still feels at home here.

*(Shots outside.)*

FATHER *(going to the window)*: Seems like there's shooting somewhere. Boom! Boom! Army guns. *(He listens.)*

PETER *(aimlessly shifting ashtrays and paperweights around)*: That's our side. We're doing the shooting.

GEORGE: And my notebooks are here, too! That mother of ours saves everything! *(He leafs through a notebook.)* Aha, I drew this myself — This is fun! And look, here's where I tried out a new wing profile.

PETER *(places on the desk an African sculpture which had been in the cupboard)*: With your permission!

GEORGE: Why are you moving things around?

PETER: Because— well, I really don't know. Only for something to do, I guess.

FATHER *(turns away from the window)*: Let him alone, Georgie! That's just the restlessness of the dead. They want to draw attention to themselves, to the fact that they were here. He'll get over it — Listen, Peter, at least you bore up . . . like a man?

PETER *(moving a tobacco jar around)*: I bore up, Dad. I didn't even blink.

FATHER: That's good. You mustn't shame our family, you know.

ANDREW *(seated by the MOTHER)*: ——It must be . . . a damned unpleasant sensation, your own execution.

PETER: Don't even ask me about it! Standing there with my hands tied, facing those six country-boy soldiers — I almost felt sorry for them. I could never execute anyone—

FATHER: You weren't blindfolded?

PETER: No, Dad. I didn't want to be.

FATHER: Good man. Who was in command?

PETER: This puny, bird-voiced little lieutenant, Dad! He was strutting around so that nobody would see how awful he felt about it. But he loaded a revolver anyway, right in front of me . . . as if he'd finish me off if the soldiers were bad shots.

ANDREW: Damn!

FATHER: He had to do that, Andrew. That's how it has to be.

PETER: Christ, he got on my nerves, that pompous ass! So I told him, Get out of here, you peabrain, I'll give the order myself—

FATHER: You shouldn't have, Peter. An execution . . . is a serious thing. Once I attended one where— well, why talk about it!

PETER: Dad, a man has to screw up courage somehow. It was such a lousy situation — The soldiers laughed, and I did, too. In a way, that made it easier for all of us, you see? And he got red in the face, and he took out his sword and shouted: Rifles ready! Aim! — I can tell you—

GEORGE: What?

PETER: It took everything I had not to fall on my knees or something. Suddenly, you have this awful feeling of weakness in your legs . . . and in your stomach . . . ugh! I crumpled like a rag when they fired. It's funny, though, I don't even remember that little fascist squealing Fire! All I felt was this cool breeze blowing through my hair.

ANDREW: That was fear.

PETER: Could be. *(Restlessly he begins rearranging things again.)* But I tell you . . . it's a horrible feeling. Horrible.

GEORGE *(looking up from his notebook)*: I ought to know.

PETER: No, you can't imagine what it's like, George. Nobody can.

GEORGE: I can, little brother. When I fell with my plane.

PETER So what? That was over in a second.

GEORGE: Don't believe it. With twelve thousand meters to fall, it took quite a while. You can't really estimate how long it's taking. You have the impression that it's an eternity. And the whole time, the whole time it seems as if the world is rushing up towards you.

ANDREW: What were you thinking all that time?

GEORGE: Nothing, as a matter of fact. There was only this terrible silence. So this is the end, or something like that. You think very calmly and clearly but foolishly, and you look around you to see where you'll probably crash. I wouldn't want to land there, in the trees; but over there in that field, maybe that would be better—

PETER: You still had it good, George.

GEORGE: Don't think that. The apathy, that's worse and . . . more sickening than any kind of pain. As if everything inside you, everything alive, had gone stiff and you're no longer able to move — Brr!

ANDREW: That wasn't apathy, George. More likely it was terror.

GEORGE: I don't know; but I wouldn't want to go through it again — Ugh! Horrifying sensation!

PAUSE

PETER: And . . . what was it like for you, Andrew?

ANDREW: I had plenty of time. For me it lasted . . . a couple of days and nights.

PETER: Dying?

ANDREW: Yes. For three days I knew . . . that the end was coming. That gives you a lot of time to think about things . . . and remember, oh yes! And all the while. . . all the while I kept on observing myself: well, now I am at such-and-such a stage. Your liver is gone, Andy. And so it went, on and on—

FATHER: ——Tell me, Andrew, how did you catch this yellow fever?

ANDREW: It was an experiment, Dad. We wanted to find out whether the Stegomyia, that wretched mosquito, also transmitted it from patients who had survived the first stage in infection. You see, it wasn't known with any certainty. So I let myself be bitten by mosquitoes, as an experiment—

FATHER: And you caught it.

ANDREW: Caught it, and hard. But it went counter to our expectations.

FATHER: Tell me, does an experiment like that have any value?

ANDREW (*shrugging his shoulders*): It does, at least for a scientist. We wanted to find out how the bacillus is produced in the mosquitoes. That's pretty important, Dad.

GEORGE: This disease, Andy, is it — a hard way to die?

ANDREW: Yes. Hard. You lie there like a leper, fever and jaundice and— well, a number of other things. An atrocious disease, dear brother. Ugh! I wouldn't wish it on anyone.

PETER: ——So only our dad, then, had a beautiful death.

FATHER: I did? Why do you think that?

PETER: Why, falling in battle, at least the end comes fast; and you have a chance to defend yourself—

FATHER: But I didn't fall in battle, son!

PETER: No? You didn't? But we always thought—

FATHER: —that I fell in the final attack, I know. That was for your mother's sake, boys. I couldn't tell her how it really was.

GEORGE: Then how—

FATHER: I didn't die in battle, not at all. I just lay there.

ANDREW:  Wounded?

FATHER:  Yes. And the natives found me there.

PETER:  And then— ?

FATHER:  Well, and then they tortured me. *(He gestures with his hand.)* And that's enough of that, right? — Andrew, how is Mother?

ANDREW:  Her pulse is better.

FATHER:  Boys, of course your mother is not to know, ever—

PAUSE

GEORGE *(over his notebook)*:  You know, people say . . . to die for something great:  for science, for country, for faith, to save people or whatever . . . but when you're actually dying—

ANDREW:  —it seems just the opposite, I know. If people could ever realize what it's like at that moment, then . . . perhaps . . . they wouldn't spout off so much about how beautiful it is . . . to die for something. Beautiful! I never found anything very beautiful in my own death.

PETER:  Nor I.

*(Two shots are heard outside, in the distance.)*

FATHER:  Well, people have always died for something, who knows what for; maybe it has to be that way. But sometimes I think . . . if I were a retired colonel or general now, and lived here with your mother—I'd write my memoirs and work in the garden . . . That wouldn't be too bad, boys. Never mind, life is life; at least a man can do something. I know, all of you laid down your lives for something great:  Andrew here for science and George for technical progress, and Peter — what is it, anyway, you died for, Pete?

PETER *(setting the chessmen on the board)*:  For freedom and equality, Dad.

FATHER:  Aha. And I for king, country and the honor of the flag. Or perhaps because some colonel gave a muddle-headed order, but no matter. All sorts of beautiful, important causes, only. . . you know, I've been dead longer than any of you, and I can tell you—it wouldn't have been any disgrace to have lived a bit longer. I liked being in this world, boys. I liked it very much. And when I look at you, I think to myself, maybe one of you lads could have done something actually worthwhile . . . even something great. And instead, we're only heroes. It's sad, boys. We could be living out our lives.

ANDREW *(rising and stretching)*:  It's boring, isn't it? Just looking on while others do things — We dead can only tag along behind. *(He crosses to the bookcase.)* You know, if I were alive now, I'd be working my head off. Sleeping sickness, that's what interests me!

GEORGE *(over his notebook)*: I must be crazy!

FATHER: What's the matter?

GEORGE: Here's a very constructive idea. It's entirely possible, Dad. Damn, why didn't I finish that sooner? Wait, it should have been done this way — *(He draws, seated at the desk).* There, that ought to do it.

ANDREW *(opening the bookcase)*: That mother of ours is astonishing!

PETER *(over the chessboard)*: Why?

ANDREW: She's kept up the subscriptions to my medical journals! Here's the new issue of the *Bulletin of Tropical Diseases* — I wrote an article for them once.

PETER: They had a very nice obituary on you, didn't they?

ANDREW *(removing the journal from the shelf)*: I should really take a look at this. *(He settles himself comfortably on the sofa and looks over the untouched magazine.)*

FATHER *(standing beside the MOTHER)*: You see, dearest, once again you have the place filled with your own. They are right at home here. We'll always be alive to you, won't we?

PETER *(over the chessboard)*: No, that wouldn't work. Damn, this is difficult!

GEORGE *(over his drawings)*: That ought to do it, but the center of gravity would have to be lower.

FATHER *(opening the portable phonograph)*: I hauled this phonograph everywhere with me, boys. Even in the army. *(He begins to wind it.)* This was my favorite record. Your mother keeps it here in memory of me— *(He lowers the phonograph arm. The phonograph plays softly. The FATHER listens. The others are absorbed in their own activities.)*

ANDREW *(over his journal)*: Look, they've found something to combat leprosy! Good news for a change.

*(Shots outside.)*

GEORGE *(over his drawings)*: They're still shooting out there.

PETER *(over the chessboard)*: Wait, it's only the beginning. Dad, this problem of yours is at a stalemate. It looks like neither side will win. Neither black nor white. Too bad.

*(The shooting intensifies. The record comes to an end.)*

FATHER: That was my favorite— *(He turns to the window.)* Do you hear that? Ratatattat. Those are machine guns, Peter.

PETER: So it's starting! *(He jumps up.)* Too bad. I'd like to have been there. Stick with it, comrades!

ANDREW *(rises, flinging down the journal)*: Once again we'll have heroes, will we? — I hate that sound.

PETER: Why, it's like music! Now our side is advancing. They're here, men. Now they're attacking. Now they're sweeping the streets ahead of them with machine guns and they're running, running forward — it's magnificent! Boys, I didn't die in vain, after all!

*(The shots become louder and heavier.)*

FATHER: Those are anti-aircraft guns. Bam — bam — bam — bam. Distance, three kilometers, direction — over there.

GEORGE *(rises)*: The city center, Dad!

PETER *(feverishly)*: Those are our guns! And we're winning!

FATHER: Don't startle your mother.

ANDREW: She's not aware of anything. *(Mechanically he rolls and unrolls in his hand a strip of bandaging taken from his pocket.)* Fools, shooting in the streets! It'll be a massacre!

PETER: Let it! It's the only way to make room for the new world. Andrew, George, it's worth it! Even if thousands and thousands of lives are— Do you hear those shots? It's beautiful! If only I could be there, men—

FATHER: Now they're shooting over there, and there — I don't like it. It's not a skirmish anymore, boys. It sounds like a slaughter.

PETER: Who cares! That's how it has to be. Once people have settled their accounts with the traitors — let them get shot, those White bandits! Do you hear how it's spreading? We'll never give in! The infantry's with us. The navy's with us. The people are with us. The Whites only have the officers. They have the air force and the artillery, but they won't be able to use them in the city. They wouldn't destroy their own city, would they, Dad?

FATHER: I don't know, Peter. You have different rules now.

GEORGE *(by the radio)*: And who's in control of the radio station?

PETER: You can bet that we are. Turn it on, George, and we'll find out—

GEORGE: Fair enough. *(He turns on the radio.)* Let's listen.

MALE ANNOUNCER *(suggestive of* CORNEL'*s voice)*: Attention, this is the White headquarters.

PETER *(dumbfounded)*: That's not possible!

MALE ANNOUNCER: Attention! The commander of the White army demands for the last time that the Black mob stop the killing in the city streets. Lay down your guns! If this is not done within five minutes, the commander will order the artillery to fire on the city.

PETER *(shouting)*: But they can't do that! Dad, Andrew, can they do that? Those thugs have gone mad!

MALE ANNOUNCER: Attention! Attention! The commander of the White army orders all citizens to take shelter immediately. If the Blacks do not abandon their positions within four minutes, cannon fire will be launched against the city center. If necessary this will be reinforced by airpower.

PETER: Barbarians! Barbarians! You won't really do that! You're only trying to scare us, you White beasts!

MALE ANNOUNCER: Attention! Responsibility for the destruction of the city and the lives of its people lies with the leaders of the Blacks. They were given fair warning. We have negotiated up to this very moment, while the Blacks were treacherously murdering their hostages, our officers and citizens—

PETER: That's a lie! You began it, you dogs, you bloody dogs! *(He bares his chest.)* What do you call this?

MALE ANNOUNCER: We refuse to negotiate further. Anyone caught with a weapon in hand will be shot on sight. Anyone siding with the Blacks will be brought before a military tribunal. Attention! Attention! In two minutes the shelling of the city will begin. For the last time we ask the Blacks to surrender. Only by surrendering can you save our city from unprecedented destruction.

PETER: No, no, no, don't listen to that! Comrades out there, don't give up! Let the city be destroyed! Let it happen, it doesn't matter!

ANDREW: Let your death have been for something, is that it? Turn it off, George.

(GEORGE *turns off the radio.)*

PETER: Yes, let it be for something! Blacks, to war! For our freedom! For our victory! For a new world! Comrades, comrades, don't give in! Let the city fall, let the nation go under, let the whole world crack open: if only our cause is victorious! Better for everyone to be slaughtered than have those White dogs come out on top—

(*In the distance, cannon salvos.*)

FATHER: There go the cannon. Six-inch guns. You see, boys, they kept their word.

GEORGE: You know, now I'm almost glad—

FATHER: —that you're dead, right? I believe you. Bam! Those were eight-inch guns, boys.

PETER: Murderers! Dirty murderers!

ANDREW: Wait — Be quiet. Mother's coming around.

GEORGE: Poor Mom, at the very time—

FATHER: Lights out!

(*Darkness. Rumble of artillery and the sound of rifles.*)

ANDREW'S VOICE: Goodbye then, Mom.

FATHER'S VOICE: Don't worry, beloved. We're always with you.

GEORGE'S VOICE: It's only a thunderstorm passing over, Mom.

PETER'S VOICE: Murderers! Murderers!

(*Rumble of cannon and more gunfire. The reddish glow from the window becomes more fiery.*)

MOTHER (*raising herself*): Peter! — Cornel! — Tony! — Cornel, what's happening? Where's Peter? — Tony, where is Cornel? — Cornel, can you hear me?

(TONY *appears in the doorway.*)

TONY: Mom, Mother, you're here? (*He turns on the light.*) I was looking for you—

MOTHER (*covering her eyes*): Tony, where is Peter? Hasn't he come back yet?

TONY: No, Mom. Please—

MOTHER: What's happening out there, Tony?

TONY: There's been shooting, Mom, but it's very far away. You mustn't be afraid. I'll be right here with you. (*He opens a desk drawer and is about to remove the revolver* CORNEL *loaded.*) There's nothing to be afraid of!

MOTHER: What are you doing, Tony? — Leave the gun there! Don't touch it, that's not for you!

TONY: Mom . . . I only thought that if something . . . Cornel said. . .

MOTHER: Where is Cornel? Call Cornel!

TONY: Don't be angry, Mom—

MOTHER: Tony, where is our Cornel?

TONY: He went out, Mom. He took a rifle and said: Tony . . .

tell Mom she's not to be angry that I had to leave her . . .
but I must go!

*(Curtain falls as cannon rumble.)*

# Act Three

*The same room, but the weapons on the wall and in the rack
have been cleared away.*

MOTHER *(removes the last pair of pistols from the wall, locks them
in a drawer, and pockets the key)*: There. I don't want Tony
catching sight of any guns. *(She looks around.)* I don't want
it. *(She goes to the window and closes the shutters.)* And he's
not to look outside, either. *(She turns on the light switch by
the door.)* Now, is there anything else?— *(She goes to the
radio.)* And you, you keep quiet. Tony mustn't know what's
going on out there. *(She lingers by the radio.)* And I— I don't
want to hear anything. Nothing makes that much difference
to me now. *(She hesitates.)* So you see, you'd better be quiet.
But you'd like to talk, wouldn't you? You want to twist
Tony's thoughts again, don't you? No, no, you aren't going
to shout at us. Talk all you like—but not here. I'm here. So
there'll be no persuading my Tony. — Now, what do you say
to that? *(She turns on the radio.)* What about that, you— ?

FEMALE ANNOUNCER *(impassioned, imploring)*: It is a crime. A
crime has been committed against all laws, all treaties have
been violated, the most brutal force has been used against us.
Listen: without declaration of war, without cause, without
notification, a foreign army has crossed the borders of our
land. Without one word of warning, without cause, without
declaration of war, foreign artillery and aircraft have begun
to bombard our cities. Our enemies have taken advantage of
a time when our country was mortally weakened by a disastrous civil war, and they have invaded our territory under
the pretext of restoring order. Who gave them this right? What
is the reason for this intervention? They have no reason, they

have no right. We cry out to the whole world: hear us, this is an outrage, it is an unspeakable crime! Nous appelons toute l'humanité: voyez, quel crime! Wir rufen die ganze Welt: es wurde ein schreckliches Verbrechen begangen! Voláme z amplionu cely svet: slyšte, stal se zlocin, stal se nevyslovny zlocin! Our country, our exhausted, hapless country, is being butchered like an animal!

MOTHER *(turning off the radio)*: Why call to me? I don't want to hear you! Crime! Crime! Wasn't it a crime when they shot my Peter? And wasn't it a crime that my Cornel had to die? My Cornel! My Peter! You talk to me about crime! I, I know what crime is, I, a mother; worse crimes have been committed against me. It's true, you didn't know my boys; but if you could have seen how they filled this house — Go on, cry out to the world; I cried out, too, and do you think anyone answered me? *(She turns the radio on.)*

FEMALE ANNOUNCER: —We must help ourselves. We must defend ourselves to the last breath. We must build a bulwark of our hearts and bodies. Our regiments, thrown up against the enemy, are fighting with desperate courage; but they cannot hold their ground without reinforcements. We call on all men of this land: you must relieve them. Hear us: we call on each and every man. We call to you, our nation's men: report for armed duty! We call to you, our nation's women: step in to take the place of your husbands and sons who follow the flag—

MOTHER *(turns the radio off)*: No, no. There's no use calling to me. I can't send you anyone, I no longer have anyone to send. Tony can't go, Tony is still a child. You can't order children to be soldiers. That's nonsense. What right do you have, sending husbands and sons to war? They aren't yours, so stop talking! Do you have a son? Tell me that! *(She turns the radio back on.)*

FEMALE ANNOUNCER: —Not a human voice, but the voice of the nation itself calls you. I, the motherland, I call to all men. I, your mother country, beg my sons: protect me, protect all my children—

MOTHER *(turns the radio off again)*: No, you're not a mother! I am a mother, I, I, do you understand? What right do you have to my children? If you were a mother, you couldn't send your sons to war. You would hide them away, as I do, you would lock them up and shout: Enough! I won't give any more!

But I no longer have anyone to give, you see. There's no one here. Only I am here, an old, mad woman. I've already given all my sons. I have no more, no more—

(TONY *stands in the doorway.*)

TONY: Mom—

MOTHER *(turning around)*: What are you doing here? *(She cries out in horror.)* Tony, you too— ? *(She rushes toward him and grasps him.)* Oh, thank God, it's you, it's you! You're alive, aren't you? How you scared me! — What are you looking for here, Tony? You know I don't like you to. . . to listen to . . . that woman. I won't have it, Tony!

TONY: But Mom, she has such a beautiful and . . . frightening voice! You know, I can see her so vividly: she is tall and pale . . . and she has such large eyes—

MOTHER: Pay no attention to her.

TONY: She's calling to me!

MOTHER: That's no concern of yours, Tony. Let her say what she likes. And stay away from here, young man. I'm locking this room.

TONY: Why?

MOTHER *(sitting down)*: Never mind, I'm locking it. Do you know, I've stored up provisions for us. Since there's a war on now, I have to have something to feed you, son. We don't need this room anymore. — Thank God I remembered the supplies! You'll see, the two of us can live downstairs, in the cellar. If no one discovers us. This will look like a deserted house.

TONY: But Mom—

MOTHER: Wait, Tony. Don't be afraid. I'll hide you well. No one will know you're here at home. Don't leave the house, just wait it out — we'll wait out everything, until we outlast what's going on outside. You won't even know there's a war on. That isn't for you, do you hear? You're too young for that. We'll hide in the cellar like mice, and you, you'll read your books — and remember how the sun shines outside. Tell me, that won't be so bad for us, will it?

TONY: Mom, please — please, Mom, let me go!

MOTHER: But, child, what are you saying? Give that up, son.

TONY: Please, Mom, let me go, let me go so that I can sign up as a volunteer! Mom, I can't stay here—

MOTHER: You're crazy, Tony! Of course you can't go! You aren't even eighteen yet—

TONY:  It doesn't matter, Mom! Don't you see, everyone's going, our whole class is going to enlist, Mom, please, Mom, you must let me go!

MOTHER:  That's nonsense. You're being childish. What would they do with you?

TONY:  Don't think that, Mom! I'll be as good a soldier as anyone else in our class! I've already given my word. . .

MOTHER:  To whom?

TONY:  To my friends at school, Mom.

MOTHER:  I think, Tony, that this is more a matter for your mother than for your friends.

TONY:  Forgive me, Mom, but when they all go off—

MOTHER:  —You won't be going with them, young man. You'll stay at home.

TONY:  Just why can't I go?

MOTHER:  Because that isn't your nature, Tony. Because you haven't the strength for soldiering. And because I don't want you to, son. Will that do?

TONY:  Don't be angry, Mom, but — look, this truly has to do with everything . . . the country and . . . the nation. . .

MOTHER:  And you will save the nation? Without you it can't be done, is that it? I don't think, young man, you're that indispensable.

TONY:  If all mothers talked like that —

MOTHER:  I've wondered about them, my dear. Do you think they can reconcile themselves to all this, having someone take away their children, one after another? They wouldn't be mothers, my child, if they felt that way!

TONY:  But when it's such a terrible war, Mom—

MOTHER:  I'm not the cause of it, Tony. No mother caused it. We mothers, my son, have never started wars; we only pay for them with our children. But I'm not so foolish as to give up the last of what I have. Let others do it if they wish, but not I. I'm giving up nothing. I'm not giving you up, Tony.

TONY:  Don't be angry, Mom, but — I must. It's simply . . . an order. All men must report. . .

MOTHER:  You aren't a man, Tony. You are my child. I only need to close my eyes, and do you know what I see? I see a little child, sitting on the floor, chattering away and sticking toys in his mouth. No, no, Tony! Take that out of your mouth!

TONY:  I'm no longer a child, Mom.

MOTHER: No? Come here and let me look at you! So you want to be a soldier? I truly had . . . a fine son, Tony, but I expected . . . something other than this, do you remember? I had a son that I taught . . . to hate war, isn't that so? Who said, Mom, when we're big, then there won't be any more war; we won't go to war, we won't kill, we won't go around murdering people, Mom, how could anybody use a gun against somebody else? — true, Tony?

TONY: Yes, but — this is a very different matter, Mom. We're defending ourselves, don't you see that?

MOTHER: I wonder — could you kill another human being?

TONY: Yes, Mom. That is, I think . . . if I had to—

MOTHER: And you would be . . . glad?

TONY: . . .appallingly glad, Mom.

MOTHER: ——So you see, Tony. So you see. Now you, too, have slipped from my hands, my dear. I will no longer understand you, either. How you've changed, my young son!

TONY: Mom, are you crying? You. . . you'll let me go, then?

MOTHER: No, Tony. I am an old . . . and stubborn woman. I won't give up my son . . . for anything. I swore it. Your wars come too dear for me, son. You won't go. I won't let you.

TONY: Mom, you can't do this! You'll see, I'll. . . I'll leave you! I'll escape! I'll escape!

MOTHER (rising): No, wait. Look at me, Tony! Look at me!

TONY: Mom, I'm begging you—

MOTHER: Would you leave me here? Aren't you thinking about what would happen to me? How could I live if you left me? You can't do that to me, Tony. You're all I have.

TONY: But nothing will happen to me, Mom, don't worry! On my honor, I can feel it, I know it — I can't believe that anything could possibly happen to me.

MOTHER: No, you can't believe it, Tony, but I can. All, all of you went off, as if for a stroll, with only a Don't worry, Mom, you'll have us back again soon — I know you, young men. Don't try to tell me otherwise.

TONY: No, Mom, I'd never want to deceive you. I know that. . . that I could very well be killed. You know, I can imagine just exactly how it would be — From the moment I made up my mind to go, I've died so many times . . . I know, it's only been in my imagination, but it was so lifelike — Or else I see the boys from our class lying there—as if they had all fallen, too. Such a pile of them lying there, and they still have ink on their fingers — But you see, it doesn't make any difference to me. I'm not afraid of that. What it means, you see, is that I must go. I can't imagine not going . . . We talked about it, about this being nothing more or less than . . . our duty.

MOTHER:  Do you know what your duty is, Tony? To stay with me. You have an obligation to me . . . for your father . . . and for your brothers. You owe me something, all of you. Surely I, too, have . . . some rights, children!

TONY:  I know, Mom, but this is a greater obligation—

MOTHER:  Greater, greater — I realize, son, that I don't matter to you now. In the end I was . . . of secondary importance to all of you. I recognized your grand, masculine obligations long ago — but please don't expect me to take them as seriously as you do, nobody can ask that of me, Tony. I'm too old for that. Thousands and thousands of years too old, children.

TONY:  Mom, if you don't let me go, then— then—

MOTHER:  Then what? Then you won't like me? You'll hate me, is that it? You'll despise me and yourself as well, you'll jerk yourself free like breaking from a chain — I know it, Tony. Hate me, then, but I will have you here! And when the war is over, you yourself will say, You were right, Mom, men are needed for living, too. *(She places her hand on his shoulder.)* What do you say, Tony?

TONY *(moving away from her)*:  Please, Mom, let me go—

MOTHER:  All right. Hate me, son. I'm strong enough . . . even for that. Eventually, even love is hard and cruel, my dear. I feel like a she-wolf. Nothing in the world is as intense as motherhood — If you want to go then, Tony, go, but you will kill me. Well, why don't you go?

TONY:  Please, Mom, don't be angry; I don't know how to say this, but . . . let our country speak for itself, and you'll see . . . you yourself will see that I must go like the others. . .

MOTHER:  I don't see anything, Tony. Can't you see that I'm blind from weeping? What would I have to look at, I, an old mother! I saw only you, children, you, little children in rompers — Maybe I'm not accustomed even now to the fact that you're grown! Show me, child, come here! How tall you've become! You know, Tony, that now you must conduct yourself . . . like a grown man?

TONY:  Yes, Mom, I must.

MOTHER:  So you see. Then you mustn't leave your old, mad, grief-stricken mother, who would worry herself to death. You don't know what I might do; go out on the streets and scream that I curse this war, that I curse those who send you to fight it—

TONY:  Mom!

MOTHER:  You can't do this to me, Tony. You must be your mother's support . . . and shield. I have only you now. I know that this is a sacrifice for you . . . but you must bear that sacrifice like a man, Tony.

TONY *(biting his lips to overcome tears)*:  Mom, I . . . you know that when you need me . . . then I . . . I really don't know. . .

MOTHER *(kisses him on the forehead)*:  So you see. I knew that I could count on you. You are a wise . . . and brave young man. Your father would be pleased with you. Come, Tony, we must prepare ourselves . . . for the war. *(She leans against his shoulder and leads him out, turning off the light switch by the door. Darkness.)*

*(Sound of the door being locked
and the key being removed.)*

ANDREW'S VOICE *(in the dark)*:  —Poor Mother!

FATHER'S VOICE:  Poor Tony.

CORNEL'S VOICE:  It must be terrible for that boy.

*(A pause. Outside can be heard the sound
of drums and soldiers marching.)*

PETER'S VOICE:  Do you hear that? Soldiers.

GEORGE'S VOICE:  They're going to the front.

FATHER'S VOICE:  They're going well. One, two! One, two!

CORNEL'S VOICE:  I'd go with them right now.

*(A pause. The sound of drums dies away.)*

FATHER'S VOICE:  George, maybe you could find some news on the radio . . . We should find out what's happening.

GEORGE'S VOICE:  All right, Dad. *(He turns on the radio.)*

MALE ANNOUNCER *(muffled)*:  . . .Our eastern army is falling farther back from the heavy fighting; the right flank has positioned itself around the ridge of mountains and is boldly resisting the enemy forces.

FATHER'S VOICE:  If only they don't outflank us!

MALE ANNOUNCER:  In aerial fighting, seventeen enemy aircraft were shot down. Nine of our pilots did not return.

GEORGE'S VOICE:  Nine to seventeen, that's not bad.

MALE ANNOUNCER: The bombardment of our open cities continues. The number of slaughtered civilians is estimated at eight thousand. As of now we have no further details on what is happening in the city of Villamedia, which was attacked by enemy aircraft—

FATHER'S VOICE: Turn it off, George. Somebody's coming. *(The dial clicks.)*

*(Silence. The sound of a key turning a lock is heard, and the* MOTHER *enters the darkened room.)*

MOTHER *(locking the door, taking a few steps into the room, and then standing perfectly still)*: I know you're here. You collect here like cockroaches around beer. — What do you want from me?

FATHER'S VOICE: We only came for your sake, dearest.

MOTHER: Not for my sake, Richard *(She turns on the lamp over the desk and looks about her. Here and there about the room, sitting or standing, are the* OLD MAN, *the* FATHER, ANDREW, GEORGE, CORNEL, *and* PETER.)

CORNEL: Hello, Mom.

MOTHER: Well! You're all here!

FATHER: My dear, you didn't notice — Grandfather came with us.

OLD MAN *(seated in an armchair in an old-fashioned black suit, with medals on his chest)*: Good evening, daughter.

MOTHER: Grandfather is here too? Papa, it's been so long since I've seen you!

OLD MAN: You see me now, lass. Have I changed so much, do you think?

MOTHER: Not at all. But why, please— *(She looks from one to the other.)* Why have you all come here? Is this to be a family council?

ANDREW: Oh, no, Mother. We just wanted to be with you, since these are such difficult times.

MOTHER: Are you telling the truth, Andrew? It doesn't seem to me that you have been very much with me. — What have you been talking about here?

GEORGE: Nothing, Mom. We were only listening to the news.

MOTHER: Oh, come now. It's hard to believe you'd still find the news very interesting.

PETER: Because we're dead? It's extremely interesting, Mom. More than you would imagine.

MOTHER: I only meant that now, thank God, you can't be mixed up in it.

FATHER: But we are, dearest. More than you know. More than those of you living realize. In wartime, we dead arise—

CORNEL: That is, we're not quite as dead as you think, Mom.

PETER: You see, whatever happens is still our destiny, too. And our business.

MOTHER: Your business, I know. If that's your business, you shouldn't brag about it.

FATHER: But dearest, the war isn't over yet! It can still be won, beautifully! Just send in reinforcements — I'm worried about the left flank. Where did you put my staff maps, beloved?

MOTHER *(unlocking the desk)*: They're here. Tell me, what do you want with them?

FATHER: Only to look at something. Thank you. *(He places the maps around the table.)*

CORNEL: ——the worst of it is, Dad, that the cadres are broken. And there are very few officers. So many of them got killed off in the civil war, it was horrible. — Now we know what a disaster that was!

PETER: And that disaster was the fault of your side, Cornel.

CORNEL: Not us, Peter. This lies on your conscience. You Blacks with your anarchism, your mob rule, your suicidal pacificism—

PETER: And your side with your cannons. You were worse.

CORNEL: Don't believe it. We were supposed to look on quietly, perhaps, while you split the country apart? Thanks very much, that would have made a mess of things! Thank God we saved the best of the troops, at least, before you ruined everything!

PETER: And we, thank God, at least we taught the people how to fight. Some day you'll be glad they know how to die!

CORNEL: But not how to obey.

PETER: No, probably they won't listen to you now. You'll see, after the war!

CORNEL: You'll see, after the war nobody will have time for your ridiculous utopia!

PETER: They will! Oh, yes, they will! Once you give the people guns, friend — we'll see then what this war was good for!

CORNEL: Peter, if anyone comes out of this war victorious, it will be the nation. A strong, well-disciplined, self-reliant nation. I bless this war for that. For the fact that it will put an end to all that silly babble about new and better ways to rule the world—

MOTHER: Children, children, don't you ever stop quarreling? You should be ashamed, you twins: both of you died because of that. Haven't you had enough? What will your grandfather think!

OLD MAN: I don't understand it, lass; it must be their young blood!

PETER: Excuse me, Mom, but as long as we're still able to think — as long as what we fought for hasn't been resolved— That hardly leaves a man peaceful even in death.

ANDREW: We all go on fighting our battles, Mom. For truth, for the nation, for the people—for something or other. We always want our cause to win. And still we can lose everything — even after death.

FATHER *(bending over the maps)*: This line could be defended. Boys, it would be a classic maneuver: a firmly-anchored center, and a breakthrough on the flank — and then we'd drive those wretches clean to the sea!

CORNEL: I don't know, Dad; we'd have to bring in remarkable strength for a breakthrough.

FATHER: We'd have to, young man, we'd have to. But we'd all give it our best, wouldn't we?

MOTHER: All who, Richard?

FATHER: Well, everyone, my dear. We, too. We, too.

MOTHER: You'd be a great help!

ANDREW: More than you'd think, Mother. A nation can never be without its dead.

MOTHER: Is that why you arranged for so many of them?

PETER: You know, Mom, we're what the war is all about this time; if this war is lost—

CORNEL: —then we will have died for nothing, all of us; then nothing would remain . . . not even our memory, Mom.

MOTHER: Richard, children, you. . . you really want to go— ?

GEORGE: We must, Mom, it's our duty. You know they're calling us, don't you? Dad will go with his old regiment—

PETER: I'll go with the volunteers.

GEORGE: And I — well, I'll probably stick with my flying.

FATHER: If only Tony were in my regiment!

MOTHER: Richard!

FATHER: It was an excellent regiment, beloved. A famous regiment. It's always had the most casualties.

MOTHER:  So that's why you came here, isn't it? I thought so!
—But I'm not giving up Tony, do you hear? Tony cannot go!
He can't!

FATHER:  That would be a great pity, my dear. I would feel very
sorry for that young man.

ANDREW:  You've got to understand, Mom. It would be terribly
humiliating for Tony if he had to stay at home. Tony is so
sensitive — For him, it's a matter of conscience.

GEORGE:  And yet . . . he's the son of a major. His father fell in
battle . . . as a hero. What would it be like, I ask you, if our
boy didn't enlist? It's a question of honor, isn't it?

CORNEL:  This is a battle for our homeland, Mom. It has to be.
It's Tony's duty.

PETER:  Mom, I'm begging you, too. You know I was always. . .
I am opposed to war; but we must defend ourselves against
an outrage like this. It's a matter of conviction.

MOTHER *(looking about her as if at bay)*:  You want him to be
killed too, is that it? You did come for something, didn't you?
So you're all against me! You're all against me!

FATHER:  But, beloved, this isn't against you!

MOTHER:  It is! And see what you've lined up against me! Honor!
Conscience! Conviction! Duty! And is that everything? Isn't
there something else?

ANDREW:  What do you mean, Mother?

MOTHER:  You forgot to tell me:  You don't understand, Mother.
This is a matter for men.

FATHER:  You're right, Dolores; it is a matter for men.

MOTHER:  So you see. And I've made it . . . a matter for women.
A mother's concern. We probably . . . won't understand each
other, Richard. And you, children . . . I'm through talking
with you as well. I don't think I can say . . . anything more.

GEORGE:  But Mom—

MOTHER:  Leave me alone! And go away! I. . . I don't want to
look at you. *(She turns away.)*

*(A pause. The dead look at one another perplexedly.)*

ANDREW:  Our mother doesn't believe—

MOTHER:  I have reason enough, Andrew.

ANDREW:  We're a . . . bad example for Tony, aren't we? But if
Grandpa could talk to her—

OLD MAN:  What, me?

*(All turn to face the OLD MAN.)*

OLD MAN: Good Lord, it's such a difficult thing, children. After all, I'm no soldier, or a hero either — and I haven't any wars to remember.

MOTHER: Papa, would you send your last son to war?

OLD MAN: My girl, we were such an old world — You're different now. You're used to war and such things. One death, a thousand, a hundred thousand, what is it to you? But for us! For us, war was like a fable from long ago, like something that could never really happen to us.

MOTHER: But if it had, Papa, if it had— ?

OLD MAN: Wait a minute, we didn't tend to things in such a rush. You see, we only read about war instead; and we learned that it is honorable to die for your country. We old people believe that, my girl; true, in those days they didn't die in such great numbers as they do now—that was very rare, you know. But probably I couldn't do otherwise. To die for the homeland— I would go, lass. I would go.

MOTHER: I believe you, Papa. But would you send your own child to war?

OLD MAN: Wait, that's a different question. Don't confuse me. I'm only saying that if I were Tony, I would go. I'm an old man, children, and— well, I never made much fuss about heroism in my time. But I accomplished something too, didn't I? A wonderful career, I thought: such a high office and medals and titles — Wait, what was I going to say?

MOTHER: Papa, would you send your children to their death?

OLD MAN: Aha, now I know. Look, I lived my years to the fullest: I drank it all to the last drop . . . and I wanted to leave good memories behind. It was a happy life. And yet I sometimes think—was that all?— Well, you see, daughter, that's how it is.

MOTHER: What are you saying? What does that have to do with Tony?

OLD MAN: Nothing, dear girl, nothing; I only wanted you to understand about life. You know, when you were born . . . life could have ended for your mama. I knelt by her and. . . well, I felt very much ashamed, you see. I said to myself . . . here is a woman who has risked everything so that a child might be born — and what have I risked?— Well, then, that's the price of life: that it's paid for . . . sometimes even with life itself. That is also . . . a matter for women, my girl. And it's that way with everything, do you see? If our homeland had not been paid for with life . . . if honor or truth or freedom had not been paid for with life, they wouldn't have this huge, this fearful value, you see. Let him go, this young son of yours. That is . . . how it should be.

MOTHER: Papa, don't you have anything more to say to me?

OLD MAN: I don't know any more, daughter. I would like, you see, to have been of some value in this war. If I could at least send one grandson . . . at least one . . . I wouldn't be so completely dead, so completely worthless! You see, an old, dead man such as I cannot give much—

MOTHER: Papa, you've never even seen Tony! How can you talk this way?

OLD MAN: True, I haven't seen him, but he is my family. He would represent our family. Such a fine, old family—

MOTHER: Papa, Tony is not going!

OLD MAN: It's up to you, my girl. It's too bad. We were such a fine family—

PAUSE

FATHER: Look, beloved. Let the boy go!

MOTHER: Richard, you don't even know Tony! You never held him in your arms, never cradled him in your lap — if you knew how small and frail he was when he was born, if you had seen his tiny hands — You can't feel that way about him, you couldn't talk this way if you knew him! Tony cannot go. Tony hasn't the strength to be a soldier. You know him, Andrew; you were a doctor, so tell him— tell him now how Tony was always a sickly child! You yourself prescribed medicine for him, do you remember? Andrew, you took the place of your father: so you say, please, say now that Tony cannot go!

(ANDREW *shrugs his shoulders in silence.*)

MOTHER: Don't you want to speak? — Then you speak, George; you were the most active of the children — You teased Tony because he didn't know how to play and didn't want to! You always said, Tony's no good, Tony's a girl, Tony's a sissy — Just remember how you laughed at him! Say it, Georgie, say so yourself: how could such a timid boy go off to war? Can you imagine such a thing?

(GEORGE *also shrugs his shoulders in silence.*)

MOTHER: You don't want to talk either, is that it? Then you talk, Cornel, and you, Peter: after all, you know how Tony is . . .

pathologically sensitive! Always white as a sheet when the two of you began brawling, and he would almost cry — Remember the time he saw the horse being tormented? He nearly had convulsions . . . and for weeks afterward, he cried out in his sleep . . . Please, Cornel, what kind of a soldier would he be? For God's sake, Peter, at least you could speak — You two knew him best!

CORNEL: —It's so difficult, Mom. We must all go.

MOTHER: ——You don't like Tony! None of you!

FATHER: But dearest, we love him very much, only. . . the boy will worry himself to death if he has to stay at home. It's for his sake. . .

MOTHER: Then let him worry! If he's so. . . if it is such a sacrifice for him to remain with his mother. . . Certainly Tony no longer loves me!

ANDREW: He does, Mom. He loves you immensely. We all love you.

MOTHER: Don't, Andrew, don't talk to me! You have no idea what it is to love! You have always had something else, God knows what, but it was greater than love; not I, though. I know nothing greater, Richard. I can't imagine anything greater. If you knew what it is to have such a child— Richard, if you had seen Tony when he was born! He was so utterly helpless and sweet — If you had seen his funny hair— How can you people possibly think that Tony could go to war!

GEORGE: Mom, Tony is grown now.

MOTHER: So it seems to you, but not to me. I can see you don't understand anything! Tony is still the child who was crying when he was born, the child at my breast, a child who always had his whole hand in his mouth — dear Christ, you people have gone completely out of your minds! How could I give up a child like that to anyone?

CORNEL: You had to . . . let us go, too, Mom.

MOTHER: That isn't true! I didn't let you go! But you, you always had some other world of your own, where I wasn't allowed; you had your own world, where you played at being grown-ups . . . What makes you think that you ever seemed great and grown-up to me? You? Do you think that I ever saw heroes in you? No, boys; in you I saw only dead cubs, foolish children struck by disaster — and you, Richard! Do you know what you were to me? The husband who sleeps by my side with his mouth wide open; I hear him breathe and with my entire body, with utter joy I'm aware that he is mine. And suddenly this man is killed by someone somewhere far away! Don't any of you grasp how senseless it all is? How could this happen to me, what did your stupid, alien Africa mean to me? And yet I, I had to give up, for Africa, a man who was my—

FATHER: That is such a long time ago now, dear heart!

MOTHER: It isn't, Richard. Not for me. For me, everything is in the present. Or you, Andrew: to me you're still the serious, frowning boy who wanted so to be thought of as wise beyond his years; I walk with you in the garden, my hand on your shoulder, as if I could lean on you — Or you, Georgie: whose trousers I mended time and again. You were forever climbing trees — Do you remember how every evening I painted iodine on your eternal cuts and scratches? It doesn't hurt, Mom, you said, it's nothing . . . Or you, Cornel—

CORNEL: What's the point, Mom? These are little things. . .

MOTHER: What's the point? No, you really don't understand. Even now, each little thing seems a thousand times more important to me than all your crusades and wars. And do you know why? Because I, your mother, had only those little things from you. I could help you only in those little things. That was my world. The moment you set your minds on something bigger you slipped out of my hands — You couldn't even look me in the eyes, just as if your consciences were guilty. You don't understand, Mom! Now you have those evasive eyes again, all of you. I know you're up to something again, something all your own, something grand and—

ANDREW: Don't be angry, Mother, but this time, truly, it is something so serious—

MOTHER: I don't want to hear it, Andrew. If it's about Tony, I don't want to hear any of it. You have your reasons, but I have mine, too. I know, you have your work and obligations, your honor, your glory, your country and I don't know what all—

FATHER: Our duty, Mother.

MOTHER: Yes, your duty. I also had my glory, and that was you. I had my home, and that was you. I had my duty, and that was you, you, you — Please explain to me why it is I, why it is always I— why in the whole history of the world I, and only I, I a mother, I a wife —who must pay so horribly for your grand doings!

OLD MAN: Don't be so angry with them, lass.

MOTHER: I'm not angry with them, Papa. I'm angry with the world. It's always sending my children off to die for something splendid, for some sort of glory or salvation or whatever — And tell me, Papa, is this world the better for it? Was it worth something after all?

OLD MAN: It was, my girl. It was. There must be a great past, too, you know.

FATHER: I know, beloved, it was hard for you, but— but when I look at you—

MOTHER: Don't look at me, Richard, don't look at me, children! I look dreadful when I'm angry.

FATHER: You're so intense, aren't you? You would have gone to meet your death too, dearest, if it had to be.

MOTHER: But only for you! For all of you and nothing else! For my husband, for my family, for my children — What else could matter to me as a woman! No, no, no, I'm not giving you Tony!

PAUSE

ANDREW: You know, Dad, in a way she's right. Tony is genuinely . . . physically weak. He's such a frail, undeveloped boy—

GEORGE: You mean weak in character, Andrew. Excitable but at the same time timid. I've never known a boy with so little spirit or determination.

CORNEL: That's not his fault, George, it's his nerves. Tony is gifted, but he's impossibly nervous. I don't know what will become of that boy.

PETER: It's too bad. He'll never amount to anything that way.

MOTHER: No, you mustn't say that! You're not being fair to him! Richard, don't listen to them, they've always underestimated him! Tony is just . . . overly sensitive; but otherwise he's come a long way, I think . . . you would be so pleased if you knew how healthy and strong he is now! You didn't know this, but he actually wanted to enlist! All on his own he came and begged me—but it wasn't Tony's fault. I wouldn't let him go. I won't let him go.

FATHER: And why, Dolores?

MOTHER: . . .Because I don't want to be alone. Perhaps it is selfish of me —— but Tony is all I have now, Richard! Please, children, please, Papa, let him stay with me! If he goes, then how would I manage, who would need me, I would have nothing — Don't I have any right to this life I bore? After a thousand years of caring for you, do I deserve nothing now? Please, children, grant me one wish, the foolish desire of a weary mother, and tell me that I don't have to lose Tony — well, tell me! Can't you hear me?

PAUSE

OLD MAN: Dear God, dear God! These are difficult things. You mustn't upset yourself so, lass. Maybe they won't get to the boy after all. Maybe it's too late anyway and we've already lost—

FATHER *(bending over the maps)*: Not yet, Grandpa. This line here could be defended. If all available troops were placed—

PETER: I'm counting on our people, Dad. The people are armed . . . and they'll fight in the streets. You'll see, even the children will go; they'll be there with toy guns, right behind their dads.

CORNEL *(looking around the room)*: Mom, where have you put the weapons?

MOTHER: What did you say, dear?

CORNEL: Where have you put Dad's weapons?

MOTHER: I hid them. From Tony.

CORNEL: Too bad. That one rifle needs to be oiled.

GEORGE *(opening a desk drawer, takes out his old notebook and leafs through it)*: Too bad I never finished this design of mine. It would have been good. *(He sits down with the notebook.)*

FATHER *(over the maps)*: This position here, I'd like to defend it myself, boys. It's a nice little pass—

CORNEL: Please, Mom, where did you put that rifle?

MOTHER: You're pestering me! *(She unlocks the oak cabinet.)* Take it.

CORNEL: Thanks. *(He takes out the rifle and examines it.)* That'll do. *(He begins to clean it at the table with flax and oil.)*

PAUSE

OLD MAN: Well, dear girl, you have almost your whole family together here.

PETER: ——Do you hear that?

GEORGE: What?

PETER: Silence.

ANDREW:  As if someone were going to say something.

PETER:  Who— ? *(He looks from one to the other and then at the radio.)* Oh. I know.

FATHER *(raising his head)*:  What is it? *(He turns his head toward the radio.)*

GEORGE *(raising his head)*:  What is it? *(He looks expectantly at the radio.)*

*(All turn toward the radio. A pause.)*

MOTHER:  If that's what you want— You're not interested in anything else. Only the war. *(She turns the radio on.)*

CORNEL:  When there's war, Mom, that's all there is.

MALE ANNOUNCER:  ——The advance guard is approaching the river. Volunteer troops have blown up the bridge and are prepared to defend the bridgehead to the last man. The enemy must be held off at any cost. The volunteers send you the following message:  We may fall, but we will never yield.

FEMALE ANNOUNCER:  Attention! Attention! We call all men to arms. We call all men. What happens to us no longer matters. We are no longer fighting for ourselves, but for the land of our fathers and our children. In the name of the dead and of those to come, we call the whole nation to arms!

MOTHER:  No. Tony is not going. I'm not giving him to you!

MALE ANNOUNCER:  We interrupt to tell you that the northern army headquarters reports retreat under heavy fire. They are fighting over every inch of soil, every plot of land, every homestead. The people refuse to abandon their homes and are defending them with weapons in hand. The enemy has been forced to battle for each individual village, for every isolated farmhouse in the land. The loss of life has been extraordinarily severe.

ANDREW:  Those poor people—

FATHER:  Not at all, in fact it's good. It simply slows down the enemy's advance.

FEMALE ANNOUNCER:  Attention! We have just picked up a message from the ship *Gorgon.* — Please stand by, I can't make it out. Our ship *Gorgon* . . . Oh, God! *(Her voice breaks.)* I'm sorry, my son is there! *(Pause.)* — Attention! Our training ship *Gorgon* . . . with four hundred naval cadets on board . . . tried to break through the enemy blockade in an attempt to return to port. At seven minutes past five . . . the ship was struck by an enemy torpedo. The ship . . . is going down. *(A gasp.)* The cadets on board the *Gorgon* send . . . a final message home. They ask that . . . our national anthem be played for them . . . for the last time. — My son! My little boy!

MOTHER: What did you say? So you have a son, do you? You have children, too?

MALE ANNOUNCER: Attention! We are interrupting this broadcast — Attention! We are calling the training ship *Gorgon*! We are calling the *Gorgon*! — Hello! — Hello, can you hear us? — Cadets on board the *Gorgon*, attention! Cadets of the *Gorgon*, your country sends a final salute.

*(The national anthem is heard. Without a word*
*the dead all rise and stand at attention.)*

MOTHER: ——Four hundred young men! How can this be permitted, the killing of such young boys!

PETER: Please, Mom, don't talk now!

*(All stand as though turned to stone.*
*The music fades away.)*

MALE ANNOUNCER: Hello! Hello! The training ship *Gorgon* no longer answers.

CORNEL: Farewell, cadets. *(He hangs the rifle back on the wall.)*

FEMALE ANNOUNCER: Hear us! Hear us! Hear us! We are calling all men. We call the entire nation to war. The country calls its children to arms! To arms!

MOTHER: What? You're still shouting? You still haven't had enough, Mother? You'd send still more?

MALE ANNOUNCER: Attention! The western army headquarters reports: We are fighting on all fronts against superior odds. The fighting on both sides continues with unprecedented ferocity. Aircraft report the approach of new enemy divisions—

*(The sound of hammering on the door.)*

TONY'S VOICE: Mom! Mother!

MOTHER *(turning off the radio)*: Quiet!

*(More knocking.)*

TONY'S VOICE: Mom, are you there?

MOTHER: Yes, little one. *(Signals for someone to turn out the lights.)* I'm coming.

*(Darkness. A pause.)*

MOTHER *(unlocking the door)*: What do you want, Tony?

TONY: You're here in the dark?

MOTHER: Turn on the light.

TONY *(Turns the light switch by the door. The room is empty. Only the scattered maps remain on the table)*: Mom, were you talking with someone?

MOTHER: No, no one, child.

TONY: But I heard voices here—

MOTHER: It was only . . . this, son. *(She turns on the radio.)*

MALE ANNOUNCER: Attention! Central headquarters reports that at dawn this morning an enemy air raid destroyed the city of Villamedia. Some eight hundred civilians lost their lives, most of them women and children. The ancient castle, our beloved national monument, was reduced to ashes.

TONY: Do you hear that, Mom?

MALE ANNOUNCER: Another bomb fell on the hospital, killing sixty patients. The city of Villamedia is in flames.

TONY: Mom, I beg you—

FEMALE ANNOUNCER: Hear us! Hear us! Hear us! We call to the whole world! We call on all people everywhere! Enemy aircraft this morning attacked the village of Borgo and bombed the elementary school. Those children who escaped were machine-gunned. Eighty children were wounded. Nineteen children were killed by gunfire. Thirty-five children caught in the explosion were . . . dismembered.

MOTHER: What are you saying? Children? Why would anyone kill children?

TONY *(looking at the map)*: Where is it. . . where is it. . .

MOTHER *(standing as if turned to stone)*: Children! Little, runny-nosed children! *(Silence. She works the rifle free from the wall and places it in* TONY's *hands with a powerful gesture):* Go!

## CURTAIN

# At the Crossroads

# of Europe

If you were to look for Czecho-slovakia on a map, it would suffice to place your finger precisely in the middle of Europe; it's right there. Just halfway between North and South, between West and East, just in the middle between the four seas whose shores outline the complicated contour of Europe. To be anchored in the very heart of Europe is not merely a geographical location; it means the very fate of the land and of the nation that inhabits it.

This specific fate began long enough ago—in the days of our continent's geological history. None of the tectonic or climatic forces that gave rise to the soil of Europe missed this small country; all the geological periods joined in forming it, all the upheavals of the earth's crust that worked at the birth of Europe met within the frontiers of this small land. Primeval mountains gave this land its basic form, and the sediment of the seas settled here; here volcanoes burst forth and the convulsions that kept altering the contour of Europe wrinkled this country's surface. Equiseta and araucaria from tropical forests were deposited here, and the land was scoured by Nordic glaciers; at the dawn of humanity the impenetrable Hercynian Forest and Pontic steppes ran through here. To this very day you can enter forests that nearly two thousand years ago blocked the northward path of the Roman legions. This is the heart of Europe from the viewpoint of climate and nature, too; here the frontier of the Southern vine, maize and tobacco runs along the margin of the Nordic forest. Here is the watershed of three seas, the natural division between the North and South of Europe; here the mild oceanic climate of the West meets the rude continental climate of Russia and Siberia. Still more expressive, however, though more modest and monotonous to the eye, is the last of the geological forces—a thousand years of human toil modeled this land. You will find few lands that are so patiently smothered by the plough, so intensively tilled to the last inch, as the soil here.

Over hill and dale the endless chessboard of small peasant fields stretches uninterrupted to the frontier forests where the world still remains as it came from the hand of the Creator—inviolate and great.

It stands to reason that a land thus located in the geographical center of Europe was from times immemorial the crossroads of European humanity and its history. There are few places in the world where beneath the surface of the soil lie buried so many memorials of the earliest ages of man as here; beginning with cave dwellers and whole towns of mammoth hunters, here lie one over the other the cultural layers of all periods of the 50,000 years of European evolution, and the bones of every European race. This spot of earth was successively overrun by the Celts, the Thracians, the Germanic tribes and the Slavs. Here the oldest European trade routes crossed one another. Here ran the Northern limits of the ancient Roman Empire; here in the northernmost arch, the cultures of Rome and Byzantium met, and today, as a thousand years ago, the boundary between the Eastern and Western Churches runs through this land. The incursions of oriental invaders—Huns and Avars, Tartars and Turks—were held up at the mountains along the borders. Here in the Middle Ages was the most Eastern outwork of Romanesque culture, the seat of the oldest university north of the Alps, and for a time the political and intellectual center of the Holy Roman Empire. Here, in the heart of Europe, arose the first attempt at a great religious reformation, and on this soil the struggle between Southern Catholicism and Northern Protestantism broke out—a struggle which practically exterminated the Czech nation and destroyed its national culture for centuries to come.

To be thus exactly in the center of Europe means being of necessity at the very heart of every melee through which Europe has passed, and indeed this country has not been spared any one of the clashes of the races, of cultures and ideas, and has paid with her blood for all that the rest of Europe did. Yet here, for twenty centuries, the small and vigorous nation of the westernmost Slavs has held its ground; held it against neighbors far more powerful than itself, against whom, for the greater part of its often bloody history, it had to defend itself. A mere glance at the map will show you that this was no light task. The frontiers you see today are densely studded with the battlefields of twenty centuries; sometimes those frontiers moved up to the Baltic or down to the Adriatic, in order to give the nation breathing space after the pressure to which it had been subjected. Two equally strong motives mark its whole history. First, to defend at all costs, weapon in hand, its frontiers; and second, by alliances and treaties to emerge from its geographical isolation and pursue what is today called a policy of European cooperation. You will find in Czech history great and pathetic proofs of that old policy of defense and of peace: the Hussite Wars when this nation, armed with peasants' flails and the world's first artillery, defended its land and its liberty against the Crusader armies sent to crush it from the four corners of the earth, and then a few decades later the ideas of King George of Podiebrad, the national hero who as early as the fifteenth century—prematurely it is true—drew up the scheme of an alliance of Christian rulers, a scheme anticipating even in its details the institution which today we call the League of Nations. At that time—somewhat prematurely too—the idea of religious tolerance here received legal sanction for the first time in the history of Europe.

Czechoslovakia, as you will see from the map, is reckoned among the minor states, and rightly so to a certain extent, for from North to South it is no bigger than Belgium or Holland; but on the other hand, from West to East it is as long as Great Britain from the Orkneys to Plymouth, as France from Calais to the Pyrenees, as Germany from the Rhine to the Gulf of Danzig, or as Italy from the Alps to the Gulf of Taranto. It ranks thirteenth among the countries of Europe as regards area, and its fifteen million inhabitants give it ninth place in terms of population.

But this long line from West to East has far greater significance; it is a distance in civilization as would be represented by a line drawn from Birmingham or Lille to the Caucasus. In the West of the Republic you will find features typical of Western Europe—extensive and highly specialized industry, intensive and completely rationalized agriculture, life wholly urbanized, a life that displays the latest technical development and progress in every sphere of culture. As you pass along the West to East line, the regions and the life within them become more and more rustic, picturesque and even, of course, more primitive, until finally in the extreme East you can wander for days through the depths of primeval forest, armed with your gun, and not meet a soul beyond some honest bear or a semi-nomadic herdsman tending his flocks on the mountain slopes. In the West there are overpopulated places reminiscent of Manchester, Charleroi, Essen or Pittsburgh; in the East you will find areas where nature and people, costumes and customs have been preserved through the centuries, with a dignity and beauty unique in Old Europe. These eight or nine hundred kilometers represent a greater disparity in civilization than you would find in any other country of Europe. This is not then a small country, it is Europe in miniature; it is the European West and the European East, so to speak, in the palm of one hand.

This elongated contour of Czechoslovakia is certainly somewhat striking. There are, it is true, other countries whose fate has given them a no less drawn-out form, such as Chile, Italy and Norway. But their situation is different. Their length is due to seashore or mountains. Czechoslovakia, though Shakespeare gave Bohemia a shore, neither lies on the sea nor has the support everywhere of a continuous mountain range. It is not, however, only mountain ranges or seashores that are geographically long. Routes are also long. Narrow and long are the bridges that connect two river banks. Czechoslovakia is long by virtue of her position and by her mission to link up West and East.

You will notice that other European nations and states run roughly parallel with the meridian, that is, from North to South, while Switzerland, until recently Austria, and Czechoslovakia represent a West to East geographical orientation. Imagine Czechoslovakia removed from the map of Europe and there at once emerges something like a North to South barrier which crosses Europe and divides it both geographically and culturally into West and East. Let us not look at Europe in terms of temporary regimes. Points of contact rather than of division will be essential for the future of mankind in Europe. In the spiritual and political economy of the world, Czechoslovakia will find the historical mission along the West to East line. She is called to this by her very position, her appurtenance to the culture of Western Europe and her kinship with the Slavonic East of our continent.

Czechoslovakia is reckoned among the new states. This is partly correct, for in 1938 she is celebrating only the first twenty years of her independent existence. Yet nine years ago it was possible to commemorate the millenary of the old sovereign Czech State. It is a state older than the kingdom of William the Conqueror, older than the Empire of the Capets, older than the Holy Roman Empire of the German nation. It is nearly six hundred years ago that Prague University, the oldest university in Central Europe, was founded; three hundred years ago a Czech, Comenius, Teacher of the Nations, reformed the world's system of education; and yet a hundred years ago there was not a single Czech or Slovak higher school in this country. Stitny, Huss, Chelcicky and Comenius bear witness to the high level of the culture of the Czech nation on the threshold of the Modern Age; about the year 1400, the Czech literary tongue was already a settled institution, but it is only about a century ago that this nation was once again compelled to create its literary language and its literature. Think of a nation from whose cultural evolution the whole of the seventeenth and eighteenth centuries is blotted out! At the time when Voltaire, Lessing and Swift were writing their immortal works, this nation in the heart of Europe did not possess even spelling books for its children; the schools were German, the towns Germanized; only the villages preserved the national tongue, but the villages themselves were villages of serfs. It was only a hundred odd years ago that it occurred to a handful of romantic spirits, under the stimulus of the great French Revolution for freedom, to issue Czech or Slovak books and newspapers for the poor, for artisans, servants and peasants—books written in a rugged language. where literary cultivation had been lacking for two hundred years. Miracles sometimes happen in the life of nations: Dobrovsky, the first grammarian of this reborn tongue; Palacky, its first historian; Macha, its first genuine poet; Havlicek, its first political journalist, were geniuses of such caliber that at one stroke, as it were, they created the highest cultural tradition—precisely for the reason that they were able to pass over the two preceding centuries and link up with the previous thousand-year-old tradition.

Eighty years ago, Prague did not possess a single Czech theater; our first theater was built out of the proceeds of collections from village to village, penny by penny. Sixty years ago, the ancient Czech University was recalled to life. It was only after the independent Czechoslovak State had arisen that it was possible to found a university in Slovakia. I do not know where in the history of civilization it would be possible to find a finer example of indestructibility of spirit than that presented by this small, energetic nation in its cultural advance.

Look once more at the map. At no point does Czechoslovakia touch the sea; its population is largely one of workers and peasants, that is, of people bound to the land and to the sources of production. In substance, Czechoslovakia is a nation of stay-at-homes, not favored by nature with adequate opportunities to go forth as adventurers and conquerors. And yet was it not these stay-at-homes, these mild and sedentary people, who fought in the Great War for the freedom of their country on the battlefields of Serbia and the Dobrudja, in Lombardy and in the Argonnes, in the Urals, and in Siberia as far as Vladivostok? Was it not they who waged war for their native Czechoslovakia in the French, Italian, Serbian, and Russian armies? Was it not they who, when taken prisoner, asked for arms to fight against the Habsburg Empire—men condemned in advance to die as rebels on the scaffold if the Allies should not win a decisive victory? Seventy thousand ill-armed volunteer soldiers had to cut their way through the Siberian tundra in order once again to reach the battlefields of Europe, and although throughout all this more than 8,000 kilometer journey they had to make their way through an alien and hostile land with their weapons in their hands, as they went along they founded their own printing press, they printed books and newspapers, they established a bank of their own and a theater, wrote down from memory the plays and musical compositions of their faraway homeland, arranged sports and athletics, used the old linoleum which covered the floors of the cars of the Trans-Siberian Railway to make blocks for the illustrations in their comic paper, carried their workshops with them, hunted up their forage in Turkestan, in Mongolia, in China; maintained communications, order and public services over a line thousands of kilometers in length; and after two years of this self-conducted adventurous journey from West to East round the world, returned on board Japanese ships to their native country as disciplined regiments, capable of taking the field again the very next day. Those of you who know something of the War from your own experiences can judge the moral and physical achievement of these seventy thousand young men and aging fathers led by thirty-year-old generals. Will you still say it is a little country?

For three hundred years the Habsburg dynasty ruled over this country, and ruled it badly; it destroyed religious freedom, drove the elite of the nation's church and nobility into exile, distributed offices and estates to an alien nobility, made an ill-administered province out of the old state, and turned the nation into an impotent minority. Finally, it attempted even to suppress its language. Offices of state, the schools, the big landed estates, industry, property and education were in German or Hungarian hands. It is easy to denationalize the poor and persons who are socially dependent upon others. Throughout the whole of the nineteenth century, the Czech and Slovak nation struggled to preserve its language, its schools, its economic equality; for a hundred years that conscious, determined and bitter struggle on the part of the whole nation endured against an alien and hostile regime. I mention this to show that there never was a more justified revolution than that which in the course of the Great War was conducted by Czechs and Slovaks against the Habsburg Monarchy. That revolution took the form of a movement abroad led by Masaryk, of fighting on the Allied fronts, and of revolt at home.

It is worthwhile to note with what means and methods this nation shook off the hated alien dominion. A handful of our people headed by T.G. Masaryk, the aged philosopher and great humanist, with lofty ideals but scarcely a farthing in their pockets, succeeded in getting out of the country. They journeyed during the War through Europe and America, striving to convince the conscience of the world not merely that it was necessary to liberate the Czechs and Slovaks, but also that it was essential to free the Poles, the Ruthenians, the Rumanians, the Yugoslavs, the Italians of southern Austria from an alien yoke. They did not go forth into the world with a map of their own country but with a map of Europe, a Europe better and more just to all nations. Four years later the aged Platonist returned home as the first President of the new State; his young collaborator, Eduard Benes, savant and sociologist, conducted the nation's foreign affairs from the day of its liberation, while the third conspirator, the young Slovak astronomer Milan R. Stefanik, returned home from Rome as a general of the French Army, and over the frontiers of his native land crashed with the airplane he was piloting himself in his desire to get home quickly, and perished. As you see, it was a revolution made by professors, and thus romantic in a way that few events in contemporary history have been.

In the meantime, the nation at home had on the 28th of October 1918 proclaimed itself independent of the Austrian Monarchy. It was a revolution in which not a drop of blood was spilled, in which not even a window was broken. The nation took no revenge upon those who had oppressed it for three centuries; it took no revenge even for the executions and the imprisonments with which it had been terrorized during the War. The first law passed by the revolutionary committee declared that "All existing laws remain in force." Two or three days after the declaration of independence, the Government offered the leaders of the German minority seats on the revolutionary committee. A nation which carried out its revolution in this manner was certainly ripe for the restoration of its ancient sovereignty.

In one respect, the Habsburg regime had a most profound influence, without intending it, upon the character and the lot of our nation. By depriving it after the Thirty Years War of its nobility and its bourgeoisie, and by placing all public offices, all property, all dignities, all privileges and all economic power in alien hands, it made our people a democratic nation to the very core. For three hundred years it was a nation of peasants and of people who lived by the sweat of their brow. Its democracy is hereditary and inborn as the democracy of the American nation; it lacked only liberty in order to be able to express its democracy in laws, institutions and political life.

From the very outset of her independent existence, Czechoslovakia has based her whole life on democratic principles. Alone among the states which surrounded her, she has never for a moment swerved from the great European tradition of spiritual and intellectual liberty, of civic equality and of social rights. Equally remote from communism as from authoritarian ideas, without internal convulsions, violence or revolution, she has restored the national soil to the peasant and farmer, she has carried through a system of modern social legislation, she has undertaken great economic, technical and organizational tasks the weight of which falls increasingly upon the state, and last but not least she endeavors, in the spirit of democratic freedom and justice, to regulate her life in common with that of the ethnic minorities. From the foundation of the Republic, the Government of this country has been in the hands of a coalition in which representatives of the Conservative farmers, the Catholics and the Socialists have never been missing. From the moment when the German parties themselves decided to take this step—now more than ten years ago—the German minority was directly represented in the Cabinet by its own elected Ministers. It would take too long to recount all that has been accomplished in the first twenty years of independence, and what has been made out of a once neglected Austrian province. It is worthy of note, however, how little was written about Czechoslovakia, during those twenty years, outside its own frontiers. Peace and quiet and good order do not make good topics for writing upon.

This democratic spirit, this love of liberty and of peace is part and parcel of the very character of the Czechoslovak nation. Over and above that, however, T. G. Masaryk, the Liberator and first President of our Republic, made those things the moral and political program of our people. For him, who for eighteen years and to such a ripe old age guided our State, politics represented a realization of love of our fellow men; in his eyes democracy and liberty were based on respect for man, for every man; they issued from recognition of his immortal soul and the infinite value of human life; for Masaryk the ultimate goal of all honest politics and all true statesmanship was to bring about the Kingdom of God on earth. It is of profound significance that the instructive Slavonic humanism of our nation at such a fruitful moment should have been crossed on the one hand with Anglo-Saxon humanism based upon religion and morals, as represented by T. G. Masaryk, and on the other hand with the enlightened, rationalistic, humanitarian idealism of the French and Latin type, which found its representative in Eduard Benes. As you see, at this moment just as in all its history, this land is the spiritual and intellectual crossroads of Europe; and it will always be a question for all Europe who will guard this crossroads, and in what manner and for what ends he will guard it.

Thus in these few contradictions, Czechoslovakia is most easily characterized for you: it is a country old and yet new, great yet small, rich yet humble, highly cultivated and yet very primitive. Nature and history have imposed upon it the fate of being the heart of Europe, of being a crossroads and a link between nations and cultures. This implies the historical necessity of defending itself with all its powers, and preserving itself as a free and independent nation, coupled with a second necessity—that of seeking with other nations the path of understanding, peaceful cooperation and European solidarity. A thousand years of tradition suffice for a nation to learn once and for always these two things: to defend its existence, and with all its heart and all its strength to stand on the side of peace, liberty, and European and world solidarity.

This is the nation's will, and the fair destiny Fate has bestowed upon it.

This selection was the introduction to a book entitled *At the Cross-Roads of Europe: A Historical Outline of the Democratic Idea in Czechoslovakia*, published by the PEN Club of Prague in 1938, just prior to the German invasion of Czechoslovakia. The volume does not give the name of the editor of the collection or of the translator of this selection. The translation has been revised by the publisher.

# ENGLISH-LANGUAGE TRANSLATIONS

*The Absolute at Large,* tr. Thomas Mark, Macmillan/Macmillan, 1927; Hyperion, 1974; Garland, 1975.

*Adam the Creator,* tr. Dora Round, Allen & Unwin/Smith, 1929.

*Apocryphal Stories,* tr. Dora Round, Allen & Unwin, 1949; Harmondsworth/Penguin, 1975.

*The Cheat,* tr. M. & R. Weatherall, Allen & Unwin, 1941.

*Dashenka; or, The Life of a Puppy,* tr. M. & R. Weatherall, Allen & Unwin/Holt, 1933, A&U 1949.

*Fairy Tales,* tr. M. & R. Weatherall, Allen & Unwin/Holt, 1933.

*The First Rescue Party,* tr. M. & R. Weatherall, Allen & Unwin/Macmillan, 1939.

*\*The Gardener's Year,* tr. M. & R. Weatherall, Allen & Unwin/Putnam, 1931; A & U, 1943, 1946, 1951, 1966; Dover, 1963; Wisconsin Univ., 1984.

*Hordubal,* tr. M. & R. Weatherall, Allen & Unwin, 1934.

*How a Play Is Produced,* tr. P. Beaumont Wadsworth, G. Blés, 1928.

*How They Do It,* tr. M. & R. Weatherall, Allen & Unwin, 1945.

*I Had a Dog and a Cat,* tr. M. & R. Weatherall, Allen & Unwin/Macmillan, 1940, 1944, 1950.

*In Praise of Newspapers,* tr. M. & R. Weatherall, G. Allen/Arts, 1951.

*\*The Insect Play, or And So Ad Infinitum,* tr. Paul Selver, adapted by Nigel Playfair and Clifford Bax, Oxford Univ., 1923. In same volume with *R.U.R.* However, the translation is an incomplete adaptation; see *The World We Live In* for a superior translation.

*Intimate Things,* tr. Dora Round, Allen & Unwin/Putnam, 1935; Books for Libraries, 1968.

*Krakatit,* tr. Lawrence Hyde, G. Blés/Macmillan, 1925; as *An Atomic Phantasy,* Allen & Unwin, 1948; Arts, 1951; Arno, 1975.

*Letters from England,* tr. Paul Selver, G. Blés/Doubleday, Page, 1925, Allen & Unwin, 1957.

*Letters from Holland,* tr. Paul Selver, Faber and Faber/Putnam, 1933, 1935, 1944, 1950.

*Letters from Italy,* tr. Francis P. Marchant, Besant, 1929.

*Letters from Spain,* tr. Paul Selver, G. Blés/Putnam, 1931.

*The Makropoulos Secret,* tr. Paul Selver, adapted by Randal C. Burrell, Luce, 1925; Holden, 1927; International Pocket Library, 1965.

*Masaryk on Thought and Life*, tr. M. & R. Weatherall, Allen & Unwin, 1938; Books for Libraries Press and Arno, 1971.

*Meteor*, tr. M. & R. Weatherall, Allen & Unwin/Putnam, 1935.

*Money and Other Stories*, tr. Francis P. Marchant, Dora Round, F. P. Casey, and O. Vocadlo, Hutchison/Brentano, 1930; Books for Libraries Press, 1970.

*The Mother*, tr. Paul Selver, Allen & Unwin, 1939.

*An Ordinary Life*, tr. M. & R. Weatherall, Allen & Unwin, 1936.

*Power and Glory*, tr. Paul Selver and Ralph Neale, Allen & Unwin, 1938. This adaptation is seriously flawed; see *The White Plague* for a correct and complete translation.

*President Masaryk Tells His Story*, tr. M & R. Weatherall, Allen & Unwin/Putnam, 1934; Arno, 1971.

*\*R.U.R. (Rossum's Universal Robots)*, tr. Paul Selver, Oxford/Doubleday, 1923. In same volume with *The Insect Play*, Oxford. However, this translation is of an incomplete adaptation.

*Tales from Two Pockets*, tr. Paul Selver, Faber & Faber, 1932; Allen & Unwin/Macmillan, 1943; Folio, 1962.

*\*Three Novels: Hordubal, Meteor, An Ordinary Life*, tr. M. & R. Weatherall, Allen & Unwin/Wyn, 1948; Catbird, 1990.

*Travels in the North*, tr. M. & R. Weatherall, Allen & Unwin/Macmillan, 1939.

*\*War with the Newts*, tr. M. & R. Weatherall, Allen & Unwin/Putnam, 1937; Bantam, 1955, 1959; Berkeley, 1967; Gregg, 1975; AMS, 1978; Northwestern Univ., 1985. Published in a new translation by Ewald Osers, Unwin Hyman, 1985/Catbird, 1990.

*\*The White Plague*, tr. Michael Henry Heim, Theatre Communications/Plays in Process, 1988; also in *Crosscurrents: A Yearbook of Central European Culture* 7, Univ. of Michigan Slavic Dept., 1988.

*The World We Live In*, tr. Paul Selver, adapted by Owen Davis, French, 1933. Of the two published adaptations, this one is superior, although still incomplete.

Harkins, William E., *Karel Čapek*, Columbia Univ., 1962.

Matuška, Alexander, *Karel Čapek*, tr. from the Czech by Cathryn Alan, Artia, 1964.

> Note: This list includes only book-length works in English. For a more complete bibliography, see George J. Kovtun, *Czech and Slovak Literature in English: A Bibliography*, European Division, Library of Congress, 1984, for which we give much thanks. Books that are still in print have an asterisk before their names; however, certain of these translations are incomplete adaptations. Certain books are available in library editions, but since these are not generally available to the public, they have not been given an asterisk.

**Karel Čapek** (1890-1938) is generally considered the greatest Czech author of the first half of this century, and he was one of the first modern Czech writers to achieve world renown. His first two plays—*R.U.R. (Rossum's Universal Robots)* and *From the Life of the Insects*—were hits on Broadway and in London soon after the end of World War I, and his novels, stories, columns, travel books, and other works were quickly translated into English and other European languages. Karel Čapek was also his nation's leading literary voice in favor of preserving democracy in the midst of fascist governments and threats, and he wrote an excellent biography of Czechoslovakia's president, Tomáš Garrigue Masaryk. In addition to this Reader, Catbird Press is publishing Čapek's two greatest fictional achievements — *Three Novels* and *War with the Newts*—to celebrate the centennial of his birth.

**Peter Kussi** has translated and introduced to an English-speaking audience works by a number of prominent Czech authors, including Milan Kundera, Josef Škvorecký, Jiří Gruša, and T. G. Masaryk. Along with Antonin Liehm, he edited *The Writing on the Wall: An Anthology of Contemporary Czech Literature*. He teaches at Columbia University.

**Arthur Miller** is the author of such modern classics as *Death of a Salesman, All My Sons,* and *The Crucible*. His most recent work is an autobiography, *Timebends: A Life*.

**Garrigue Books** is the imprint for Catbird's translations from the Czech and Slovak languages. The name Garrigue is meant to honor the American who became most deeply involved with Czechoslovakia: Charlotte Garrigue. Born and raised in a French Huguenot family in Brooklyn, New York, Charlotte Garrigue married Tomáš Masaryk, a young Moravian whom she met while studying in Germany (Moravia, now the central section of Czechoslovakia, was then part of the Austro-Hungarian Empire). Tomáš Masaryk took Garrigue as his middle name, something at least as unusual in nineteenth-century Austria as it would be in the U.S. today.

During the First World War, the imprisonment of Charlotte Garrigue Masaryk and her daughter Alice by the Austrian government led to mass protests by women's groups in the United States. When, in 1918, Tomáš Garrigue Masaryk founded and became the first president of Czechoslovakia, Charlotte became the nation's first first lady.

Other books published under the Garrigue imprint include Vladimír Páral's novel *Catapult,* translated by William Harkins, and two fictional works by Karel Čapek, *Three Novels* and *War with the Newts.*